Natural Law and the Origin of Political Economy

Samuel Pufendorf's work on natural law and political economy was extensive and has been cited by several important figures in the history of economic thought. Yet his name is rarely mentioned in textbooks on the history of economic thought, the history of political science or the history of philosophy. In this unprecedented study, Arild Sæther sheds new light both on Pufendorf's own life and work, as well as his influence on his contemporaries and on later scholars.

This book explores Pufendorf's doctrines of political economy and his work on natural law, which was translated into several major European languages. *Natural Law and the Origin of Political Economy* considers the influence he had on the writings on political economy of John Locke, Charles Montesquieu, Jean-Jacques Rousseau, Francis Hutcheson and Adam Smith, amongst others. If Smith can be called the father of modern economics, this book claims that Pufendorf can be called the grandfather.

This volume is of great importance to those who study Pufendorf's extensive works, as well as those interested in history of economic thought, political economy and political philosophy.

Arild Sæther is Professor Emeritus. He retired from University of Agder, Kristiansand Norway in 2011 and is now affiliated with Agder Academy of Sciences and Letters. Recently he received his Doctor of Philosophy (Dr. Philos) from the Norwegian School of Economics, Bergen. Previously he worked for two and a half years as a Professor of European Economic Integration in Maastricht, the Netherlands, and three years as Director of EuroFaculty Tartu-Riga-Vilnius. Sæther has published books on economic theory and a number of journal articles. For over twenty years his main area of research has been the history of economic thought.

Routledge Studies in the History of Economics

For a full list of titles in this series, please visit www.routledge.com/series/SE0341

186 The Origins of Neoliberalism
Insights from Economics and Philosophy
Giandomenica Becchio and Giovanni Leghissa

187 The Political Economy of Latin American Independence
Edited by Alexandre Mendes Cunha and Carlos Eduardo Suprinyak

188 Jean-Baptiste Say and Political Economy
Jean-Baptiste Say
Gilles Jacoud

189 Economists and War
A Heterodox Perspective
Edited by Fabrizio Bientinesi and Rosario Patalano

190 Great Economic Thinkers from the Classicals to the Moderns
Translations from the Series *Klassiker der Nationalökonomie*
Bertram Schefold

191 Business Cycles in Economic Thought
A History
Edited by Alain Alcouffe, Monika Poettinger and Bertram Schefold

192 Economics, Ethics, and Ancient Thought
Towards a Virtuous Public Policy
Donald G. Richards

193 Ricardo on Money
A Reappraisal
Ghislain Deleplace

194 Natural Law and the Origin of Political Economy
Samuel Pufendorf and the History of Economics
Arild Saether

Natural Law and the Origin of Political Economy

Samuel Pufendorf and the History of Economics

Arild Sæther

Routledge
Taylor & Francis Group
LONDON AND NEW YORK

First published 2017
by Routledge
2 Park Square, Milton Park, Abingdon, Oxon OX14 4RN

and by Routledge
605 Third Avenue, New York, NY 10017

Routledge is an imprint of the Taylor & Francis Group, an informa business

British Library Cataloguing in Publication Data
A catalogue record for this book is available from the British Library

Library of Congress Cataloging in Publication Data
Names: Saether, Arild, author.
Title: Natural law and the origin of political economy : Samuel Pufendorf and the history of economics / Arild Saether.
Description: Abingdon, Oxon ; New York, NY : Routledge, 2017. | Includes bibliographical references and index.
Identifiers: LCCN 2016052474| ISBN 9781138670907 (hardback) | ISBN 9781315617350 (ebook)
Subjects: LCSH: Pufendorf, Samuel, Freiherr von, 1632-1694. | Natural law. | Economics–Political aspects–History. | Law–Political aspects.
Classification: LCC K457.P82 S25 2017 | DDC 330.15–dc23
LC record available at https://lccn.loc.gov/2016052474

ISBN: 978-1-138-67090-7 (hbk)
ISBN: 978-1-315-61735-0 (ebk)

Typeset in Times New Roman
by Taylor & Francis Books

Figure 0.1 Samuel Pufendorf

Contents

Preface ix
Acknowledgements xi

Introduction 1

PART I
Childhood and Education **9**

1 Childhood: Turbulent Times 11
2 University Education in Leipzig and Jena 14
3 A Creative Imprisonment in Copenhagen 20

PART II
A True European **25**

4 Academic Career 27
5 A Champion of the Enlightenment 37

PART III
Doctrines of Political Economy **51**

6 Method of Analysis 53
7 Theory of Human Behaviour 60
8 Private Property and the Four-Stages Theory 75
9 Theories of Value, Money and Trade 87

10 The Foundation of States and Councils 107

11 Division of State Powers and Principles of Taxation 119

PART IV
Diffusion of Pufendorf's Economic Ideas **135**

12 A Great Popularizer 137

13 John Locke: An Admirer of Pufendorf 148

PART V
Early French Philosophers and Pufendorf **167**

14 The First French Followers 169

15 Charles Montesquieu: A Great Philosopher 182

16 Jean-Jaques Rousseau: A Political Thinker 191

17 The First Economic Model Builders 201

PART VI
Scottish followers of Pufendorf **209**

18 Gershom Carmichael brought Pufendorf to Scotland 211

19 Francis Hutcheson a User of Pufendorf 215

20 Pufendorf as a Predecessor of Adam Smith 228

PART VII
How Could Pufendorf Be Overlooked? **253**

21 The Bedevilled Historians 255

22 Have Economists Overlooked Pufendorf? 261

23 Pufendorf the Grandfather of Political Economy 268

References 271
Index 294

Preface

This study has been in the making for many years. My discovery of the natural law writings of Samuel Pufendorf in general and his writings on political economy in particular, goes back more than thirty years.

In the 1980s I explored the sources of the Dano-Norwegian history of economic thought before 1814. To my great surprise I discovered that Ludvig Holberg (1684–1754), professor of history at the University of Copenhagen, a writer of comedies, and a great representative of the Nordic Enlightenment and a founder of Dano-Norwegian literature, also had a keen interest in political economy. His second book *Moralsk Kierne* or *Kunskab om Natur og Folkeretten* (Moral Source or Knowledge of Natural and International Law) that was published in 1716, contains several parts where he discusses topics of political economy. On the front page it says; 'drawn from the works of the most distinguished jurists, in particular Grotius, Pufendorf and Thomasius'. A closer inspection reveals that Holberg had organized his account chapter by chapter as the natural law philosopher Samuel Pufendorf (1632–1694) did in his *De Officio Hominis et Civis* (The duty of man and citizen). A further inquiry reveals that he has also recapitulated parts of Pufendorf's major work *De Jure Naturae et Gentium* (On the law of nature and nations). Some of Holberg's sections, in particular those that discuss matters of political economy, are essentially copied from Pufendorf.

I had not heard the name Pufendorf before, nor had any of my closest colleagues. Furthermore, I could not find his name in any of the textbooks in the history of economic thought that were readily available to me. My curiosity was aroused, and it led me to ask who this Pufendorf was. What topics of political economy had he discussed and what kind of influence had he had in seventeenth- and eighteenth-century Europe?

These questions and the lack of satisfactory answers led me to this investigation. First, an exploration into his doctrines of political economy. Second, an inquiry into the diffusion of his doctrines through the translations of his natural law works into the major European languages. Third, the diffusion of natural law, or moral philosophy as it was transformed into, as a subject at almost all Protestant universities across Europe and North America. Fourth, the influence Pufendorf had on the writings on political economy by John

Locke, Charles-Louis Montesquieu, Jean-Jacques Rousseau, Francis Hutcheson, and last but not least Adam Smith, just to mention a few. The result of these investigations is presented in this treatise.

When studying Pufendorf's extensive writings on political economy I became more and more puzzled. Some new questions arose. To what extent had his writings on political economy been recognized by economists in the twentieth and twenty-first century? Why is it that his name hardly can be found in textbooks on the history of philosophy, political science or the history of economic thought? Why had most authors of such textbooks no account of his contribution? Why do we rarely find any discussions on his possible influence on his successors' writings on political economy? Had Adam Smith studied the works of Pufendorf and if so did it influence his writings on political economy.

All these questions and the lack of satisfactory answers in existing literature has been the starting point for this inquiry. The objective has been to remove the veil of oblivion that surrounds Pufendorf's name, to shed some light on and find the answers to as many of these questions as possible.

It is my hope that some economists, who are interested in the history of economic thought in the seventeenth and the eighteenth century will read at least part of this study and that the reading will be an appetizer for going back to Pufendorf's original texts. If they do, and peruse in Pufendorf's natural law works that include political economy, I am convinced that they in such an inquiry will find much 'food for thought' and make new exciting discoveries. Discoveries that I surely have overlooked in this work.

Acknowledgements

This treatise has been in the making for many years: the list of people and institutions I want to thank is correspondingly long. What there is of merit in this project is due largely to the generous support I have received over many years.

First, to acknowledge my gratitude for the inspiration, encouragement and support given me over many years by my close colleagues at the University of Agder in Kristiansand, Norway. While I was carrying out research on Samuel Pufendorf's contributions to political economy we had numerous discussions on various topics. I have benefited greatly from these exchanges of opinions.

Second, financial support is necessary. Thanks are therefore due to the university for general support through many years and particularly for granting me research leave for the academic year 2009/10. This enabled me to concentrate full time on my project. Furthermore, thanks to Deutsche Akademische Austauschdienst (DAAD) in Bonn and Ruhrgas Scholarship Programme, administered by the Norwegian Research Council, for financial support. This enabled me to do research at Christian-Albrechts Universität Kiel, Friedrich-Schiller Universität Jena, Universität Leipzig, Freie Universität Berlin, Ruprecht-Karls Universität Heidelberg, Leiden University and the University of Lund. At all these universities, I met friendly colleagues who took an interest in my work. Thanks also to the Wilhelm Keilhau Memorial Fund for financial support. It made it possible for me to attend international conferences, where I could present my research.

Third, financial support is important but the assistance I have received from numerous people has been invaluable. I am especially grateful to the librarians of the above-mentioned universities and in addition to the Library of the University of Glasgow, Bibliothèque Nationale de France in Paris and La Bibliothèque Diderot de Lyon, and the library system of University of Minnesota. They have all been very friendly, sorted out all my requests, and helped me to find answers to a great number of peculiar questions. Without their assistance and encouragement, I would not have been able to find the literature that has enabled me to carry out this study.

To provide full acknowledgements for the help I have received in the writing of this manuscript is not possible. It is, however, right to single out the following people as having a special role in the creation of this book.

Dr. Gerald Lee Allen, my friend from Graduate School at the University of Minnesota, has been of great service as both a commentator and 'language washer'. His learned and penetrating comments on different stages of my manuscripts and his encouragement and support have urged me forward when I was on the point of giving up.

I am also indebted to Paul Schneebeli whose bibliographic scholarship is matched only by his intuitive grasp of the research requirements of an economist who tried to sort out the connection and influence of Pufendorf in the French-speaking parts of Europe.

Finally, I would like to express my sincere thanks to three anonymous referees of an early manuscript for their encouragements, valuable comments and corrections.

My depth of gratitude to my wife Ellen is overwhelming. I thank her for her patience, love, continuous encouragement, support and insightful comments on major and seemingly minor points and for pushing me on with my research. She has read, questioned and corrected many drafts of what has become the present book. I dedicate this work to her.

For all the omissions and inaccuracies that remain in this work, I am fully responsible.

Introduction

The idea of an objective moral and judicial order based on human nature and right reason is as old as philosophy. In the Western world, it therefore goes back to the early Greek philosophers, the most important being Plato (427–347) and Aristotle (384–322).[1] Formulated as a doctrine and called natural law it relates to Stoic and Roman jurists before the sixth century, with the Schoolmen, particularly from Thomas Aquinas (1225–1274) to Francisco Suarez (1548–1617) in the Middle Ages, and with the sixteenth- and seventeenth-century natural law theorists, Hugo Grotius (1583–1645), Thomas Hobbes (1588–1679) and Samuel Pufendorf (1632–1694).

Terence Hutchison in his book, *Before Adam Smith: The Emergence of Political Economy 1662–1776* from 1988 claimed that throughout the seventeenth and much of the eighteenth century there were at least two distinct streams of economic thought and literature, which flowed mainly independently of one another. One was the mercantilist literature, which was mostly found in pamphlet form. However, there was another stream of ideas 'which eventually was to prove, arguably, of greater significance for the theoretical foundations of political economy'. These were the ideas of the natural law philosophers, the two most important being Grotius and Pufendorf (Hutchison, 1988: 5). True, a few elements of political economy can be found in the works of Grotius. However, it is with Pufendorf that political economy developed into a substantial part of natural law. Furthermore, it is with him, and the influence he had on his successors, that political economy started its advancement as a science.

Neither Pufendorf, nor his direct descendants were to any great extent influenced by the mercantilist literature. There were very few interactions between the mercantilist and the natural law tradition or stream of economic thought. The mercantilists were mainly concerned with current practical problems. The natural law tradition had its centre of gravity at academic institutions and was mainly concerned with the underlying economic principles. It is the natural law stream of ideas that will be explored in this investigation.

This book will probe Pufendorf's life and career, his writings on political economy and how his ideas were dispersed and used by his followers, the most important being Adam Smith. It tries to answer how it is possible that most historians of economic thought have overlooked him when they developed their theories. It ends with his influence on Adam Smith

Childhood and Education

Samuel Pufendorf was born in Saxony in 1632, and grew up during the violence and devastation of the Thirty Years War. The insecurity of the times sets an imprint on his life and authorship. As a student at the universities of Leipzig and Jena he was introduced to the works of Hugo Grotius, Thomas Hobbes and the methods of René Descartes (1596–1650). On completion of his studies, he was not able to find work close to home. However, he secured a post as a tutor for the children of the Swedish envoy to the Court in Copenhagen. His arrival in the summer of 1658 could not have been at a more inconvenient time. The Swedish army had besieged the city. He was immediately arrested, accused of being a spy, and thrown into prison. During eight months of imprisonment, under harsh and miserable conditions, he reflected on his previous learnings and produced a manuscript on natural law.

A True European

After his release he travelled with the envoy's sons to the Netherlands where they matriculated at the University of Leiden. His manuscript *Elementorum Jurisprudentiae Universalis* (Elements of Universal Jurisprudence) was published in 1660. It became an immediate success and earned him a position as professor of natural law at the University of Heidelberg. Here he stayed until 1668, when he with his family moved to Lund in Sweden, where he became Professor Primarius at the newly founded university. In 1672 he published his major natural law work *De Jure Naturae et Gentium* (On the law of nature and nations) and the year after an abridged version *De Officio Hominis et Civis* (The duty of man and citizen). In 1677, he accepted an offer of a position as historian and counsellor at the Court in Stockholm. Here he produced more than thirty history books on the Swedish kings and an essay on religion. In 1688 he moved again, this time to Berlin, where he got a similar position at the Court of Brandenburg-Prussia. There he continued his historical writings and produced numerous books. A new essay on religion was also published. He died in 1694, after strenuous return journey from a visit to Stockholm, as a true European.

Pufendorf became a champion of the Enlightenment, through his efforts to better life not only for himself and his family but for all people. The means to make this vision true were his academic writings, his teaching of students, his tutoring of prospective civil servants and future rulers, and his work as a counsellor to three important enlightened Protestant rulers. He became the most read scholar in Europe in the last quarter of the seventeenth century and the first three quarters of the eighteenth century.

Doctrines of Political Economy

Pufendorf presents his doctrines of political economy, but develops first his method of work. In his *Elementorum Jurisprudentiae Universalis* he used the reformed Euclidean Aristotelian geometrical method, with twenty-one definitions, two axioms and five observations, to develop his natural law. In his main work *De Jure Naturae et Gentium* he abandoned this method and substantiated his opinions, his arguments, and the truths he claims to have discovered by numerous quotations. His index lists 400 authors. These authors he frequently quotes to support his views.

He develops a comprehensive theory of human behaviour. Man is a moral being with a 'the distinctive light of intelligence'. This intelligence can be used to understand things more accurately. The reason why it is inappropriate that man should be endowed with a lawless liberty is drawn from his revolutionary principle of the natural condition of human nature, the dignity of Man's nature. Man has an internal director or mediator to assist him in making the right decision. Man's ability to distinguish between right and wrong is not innate, but can be found in the condition of man, together with two driving forces that decides human action. Self-interest is the strongest driving force. But he also has another; he must be sociable.

He uses his theory of human behaviour, and in particular the human attributes of self-interest and sociability to develop his theory of property and the four stages. Private property developed from a stage where everything was held in common. The establishment of private property assumes an act of man and an agreement among men, whether this agreement is just tacitly understood, or clearly expressed. Private property was progressively introduced, when growing populations and depleted natural resources forced human kind to move from one stage of economic development to the next; gathering or hunting, herding, agriculture and finally a commercial society. A commercial society involves trade, growth of markets, creation of prices, introduction of money and the advances of civilization. Such a society where all individuals attempt to satisfy their own needs and thereby satisfy the need of others is a cornerstone of his doctrines.

Pufendorf advances a comprehensive theory of value, money and trade. In a commercial society, with private ownership, goods must be exchanged. Such a society gives rise to prices, the introduction of money and the growth of civilization. The market price is determined by the interactions between scarcity and vent, supply and demand. Human motives that determine demand are discussed in some detail. A distinction is made between the legal price, the natural price and the market price. He discusses changes in price when shifts in demand and supply occur. The origin of money, money and commerce, and the question of whether governments can change the value of money are discussed. Money is linked to the development of domestic commerce and international trade. Debasement of money is clearly against natural law.

His foundation of states and how council decisions are carried out is based on the claim that man enters into a state by his free will to avoid greater evils.

States are therefore established to gain security and protection from the evil or wickedness of men. The union of individuals that form a state must be regulated by two pacts, one of association and one of subjection, and one decree. He discusses the advantages and disadvantages of aristocracy, democracy and monarchy. If the power of the state is expressed through a council, there has to be an agreement about how to reach decisions. He discusses veto rights, unanimity versus simple majority, weighted voting, qualified majorities, equality of votes and the paradox of voting. He is fully aware of the possibility that voting agendas can be manipulated.

Finally, his theory of the division of state powers and his principles of taxation are outlined. He claims that a state is understood to have one will. Since it is not possible to combine the individual wills of many people into one will, a unified will in a state can only be produced by having all the persons in the state submitting their will to that of one man, or of a council, in whom the supreme sovereignty has been vested. It is the duty of the supreme sovereign, the one man or the council, to make clear and prescribe for the citizens what can be done and what should be avoided. He discusses the division of the highest power of the state, the legislative power, the punitive power, the judicial power, the power to wage war and declare peace and to accept or reject treaties, that is, the constituent power, and finally the power to levy taxes. His emphasis is on his discussion of the three regular forms of states: democracy, aristocracy and monarchy. He discusses the comparative advantages of these forms of states.

The business of a state cannot be carried out without expense. The duties of the sovereign with respect to the levy of taxes and his economic responsibilities are emphasized.

Pufendorf stresses budget discipline and he gives considerable attention to how taxes or other burdens are levied and collected on the citizens.

Diffusion of Pufendorf's Economic Ideas

The story of how Pufendorf's natural law, including political economy, spread across Europe and North America due to his popularization and fame is sketched. *De Officio* became an international 'best seller' that was translated into nine European languages and published in more than 150 editions. Natural law became a compulsory subject at almost all Protestant universities. His writings on natural law contributed to the beginning of the Enlightenment, characterized by a belief in progress. The first scholar of any importance to use his natural law works was John Locke (1632–1704). He was an admirer and a user of Pufendorf's natural law works, but listed very few of his sources. It is therefore difficult to establish exactly whose ideas Locke used when he put his own thoughts into writing. However, this investigation determines that he had in his possession Pufendorf's natural law works and that he used these extensively as an important point of departure when he developed his own doctrines. This is particularly the case when he discusses topics of political economy.

Early French Philosophers and Pufendorf

An investigation is carried out into the early French philosopher's use of Pufendorf's natural law works. Pufendorf's self-interest and sociability is found in the works of Pierre Nicole (1625–1714), Jean Domat (1625–1696) and Pierre Le Peasant de Boisguilbert (1646–1714). Pufendorf's French translator, Jean Barbeyrac (1694–1748), had an important role in the diffusion of natural law including political economy across Europe. A similar role had Jean-Jacques Burlamaqui (1694–1748), and the editor of the *Encyclopédie* Denis Diderot (1713–1784).

The great philosopher of the Enlightenment, Charles-Louis Montesquieu (1689–1755), used Pufendorf's works when he wrote his discourses and his *De l'Esprit des lois*. Pufendorf's claims that there are no innate ideas and his human attributes, self-interest and sociability, are found. He summarizes Pufendorf's four stages theory and he is clearly inspired by Pufendorf, when he outlines a theory of money, and warns against debasement of coinage. Montesquieu does not claim that pacts are necessary to establish a state, but a state of war among individuals and nations leads to human laws and government. The allusions to Pufendorf's pacts of association and subjections are strong. Like Pufendorf, he discusses democracy, aristocracy and monarchy and the legislative power, the executive power and the judicial power. On political liberty Montesquieu's superiority over his predecessors is clear. Like Pufendorf, he warns against corruption. He discusses different forms of taxes in different countries and under different governments. Like Pufendorf, he claimed that taxes should be posted, easy to collect and they should not be abused by the tax collectors.

Jean-Jaques Rousseau (1712–1778), gives only a few direct references in his works to the natural law philosophers. But there can be no doubt that he used Pufendorf's works extensively when he developed his own ideas. Obvious and not so obvious allusions to Pufendorf are particular strong when he discusses topics of political economy. His treatment of human behaviour has elements of Pufendorf's self-interest and sociability. He, like Pufendorf, did not believe in innate ideas. With strong allusions to Pufendorf, he explains how the idea of property developed in man's mind. He does not develop either a theory of value or a theory of money or trade. He sees the introduction of money, at best, as unavoidable. However, his social contract is close to Pufendorf's pact of association and his discussion of the relationship between government and sovereign corresponds roughly with Pufendorf's contract of subjection. Furthermore, like Pufendorf, he claims that there is only one law, which by its nature requires unanimous consent. That law is the social pact. Rousseau has an extensive discussion of decision rules and, like Pufendorf, he discusses three major forms of government: democracy, aristocracy and monarchy. His principles of taxation are very close to Pufendorf's principles.

A group of French intellectuals, at first named *Économistes*, but later Physiocrats, spoke out against the deplorable economic conditions in France. Their leader was François Quesnay (1694–1774) and his close collaborators were Victor Marquis de Mirabeau (1715–1789), Paul-Pierre Mercier de la Rivière (1720–1793) and Pierre Samuel du Pont de Nemours (1739–1817). Du Pont asserts that, for all the Physiocrats, political economy was the science of natural law applied, as it should be, to civilized societies, and of enlightened justice in all social relations – internal and external. It is therefore reasonable to claim that Pufendorf, who was a well-known philosopher of natural law, have been appreciated and used in the milieu of the Physiocrats.

The Physiocrats, like most other writers in the eighteenth century, did not overwhelm us with quotations. There are scarcely any references to the sources of their ideas in the articles and books that comprise what can be termed the Physiocratic library.

Scottish Followers of Pufendorf

Gershom Carmichael (1672–1729) was the first to introduce natural law and political economy into Scotland. He used Pufendorf's *De Officio* as the textbook in his moral philosophy class at the University of Glasgow at the end of 1690s. In 1718 he published a new edition, in Latin, with his commentaries. In Scotland, natural law was transformed into moral philosophy.

When Carmichael resigned in 1729, one of his former students Francis Hutcheson (1694–1746) was asked to take over the chair. He continued the practice of his predecessor and used Carmichael's edition of *De Officio* as a textbook. In 1747 he published *A Short Introduction to Moral Philosophy*. In 1734–1735 he began writing a manuscript, which was not published until after his death in 1755 as *A System of Moral Philosophy*. His two books were built, as Hutcheson admits, very closely on Pufendorf's works.

Like Carmichael, Hutcheson could not accept Pufendorf's emphasis on self-interest; he points to man's passion towards altruism and cooperation. He also believed that man's conception of right and wrong is innate. In his theory of property, he departed from Pufendorf and built on Locke's labour theory of property. Hutcheson's theory of value, money and trade, his theory of the foundation of states and councils, and his theory of the division of state powers and principles of taxation are mostly a copy of Pufendorf.

Adam Smith (1723–1790) was introduced to Pufendorf's natural law works when he matriculated at the University of Glasgow and became a student in Hutcheson's moral philosophy class in 1737. Important facts about Smith's study of Pufendorf's natural law works, including political economy, are revealed. Smith studied these works further as a student in Glasgow and at Balliol College, Oxford. He used these works when he prepared his freelance lectures in Edinburgh at the end of the 1740s and his ordinary lectures at the University of Glasgow in the beginning of the 1750s and in the 1760s. In spite of these facts no one points to Pufendorf as a major source for Smith. Smith does not overwhelm his readers with references or quotations.

In his *The Theory of Moral Sentiments* he, like Pufendorf and contrary to Hutcheson, claims that self-interest is the primary drive in all human beings. Furthermore, self-interest is not incompatible with sympathy or benevolence. The allusions to Pufendorf's sociability are strong. Furthermore, man's conception of right and wrong is not innate. Smith does not in his *Lectures on Jurisprudence* directly use Pufendorf's tacit pact as a foundation for his theory of property, but there are clues indicating that he comes close. His four-stage theory is close to Pufendorf's.

From Smith's theory of value, money and trade, which he discusses in his *Lectures on Jurisprudence* and in *The Wealth of Nations*, it is clear that he used Pufendorf's natural law works. In his discussions of the need for cooperation in a commercial society, the determination of price, the paradox of value, the origin of money, the question of debasement of money and many other issues, there are clear clues to his use of Pufendorf.

Smith, like Pufendorf, contended that states were established to gain security and protection from the evil wickedness of men. The origin of government did not arise from consent or agreement. He explained the development of government using the same historical account of the four stages theory that he had inherited from Pufendorf. In his discussion of voting rules, he used both Hutcheson and Pufendorf. The allusions to Pufendorf are everywhere to be found, when Smith discusses the division of responsibilities in government. That is also the case when he discusses taxation both in his *Lectures* and in *The Wealth of Nations*. From this exposition, it is clear that Pufendorf was Smith's major source.

How could Pufendorf be Overlooked?

Immanuel Kant had a tremendous effect on the development of philosophy. He had no respect or uses for philosophers that he believed were eclectics. Therefore, Pufendorf and his followers were eliminated from the history of philosophy. During recent years, it looks as though a new breed of philosophers has rediscovered the natural law writers. Hopefully this will be reflected in future history of philosophy textbooks.

An investigation of forty-five textbooks on the history of economic thought is referred to. Only seven of these have attached some importance to Pufendorf. Of the seven, there is only one, Terrence Hutchison from 1988, who attaches an important role to Pufendorf, and contends that he deserves a significant place in the history of economic thought. Furthermore, an investigation of some books and articles where the authors have explored the sources of Adam Smith has been carried out. The facts are clear; none of the books and only three of the 225 articles in the so-called Wood collection seriously discuss Pufendorf's influence on Smith. There is no thorough discussion in any of these articles of how Smith in his writings used Pufendorf's ideas.

Pufendorf the Grandfather of Political Economy

This concludes the story and briefly recapitulates Samuel Pufendorf's remarkable career, his writings on political economy, the diffusion of his contributions to political economy in general and his influence on Adam Smith in particular. This author argues that if Adam Smith deserves to be called the Father of Modern Political Economy, then Pufendorf is worthy of being called the Grandfather.

Note

1 See for example Barry Gordon (1975), *Economic Analysis before Adam Smith: Hesiod to Lessius.*

Part I
Childhood and Education

Events in childhood and experiences in schools and universities might have a significant imprint on the development of a person's character and career. It is therefore of interest to give an account on Samuel Pufendorf's childhood, his schooling, his university education and his life as a student to uncover the influence it had on his later career decisions and writings.

1 Childhood

Turbulent Times

Samuel Pufendorf was born on 8 January 1632 in the middle of the devastating Thirty Years War, 1618–1648. Coincidentally, Pufendorf shared his year of birth with the well-known philosophers John Locke (1632–1704) and Benedict de (Baruch) Spinoza (1632–1677). At the time of his birth, Pufendorf's family lived in a small hamlet, Dorfchemnitz, southwest of Chemnitz in the rural region of old Saxony, where his father was a minister in the evangelical Lutheran church. A year after Samuel's birth his family moved to the village of Flöha in the Saxon Erzgebirge, where his father secured a better position.

Saxony had up to this time escaped the direct effects of the pervasive violence and destruction of the war, but this would soon change. The Elector of Saxony, Johann Georg I (1585–1656), had, at the time, worked to establish good relations with the emperor of the Holy Roman-German Empire Ferdinand II (1578–1637),[1] the reason being that he wanted to increase his power base and secure for himself the secularized properties of the Catholic Church. He also wanted to firmly establish his supremacy within the Evangelic Union and his control over the territory of Lausitz, which he had acquired in 1623.[2]

However, in 1629 the emperor had issued the so-called Restitution Edict. Consequently, all secularized properties were to be handed back to the Catholic Church. The armies of the Catholic League under their chief commanders, Tilly and Wallenstein, were given the task of carrying this out.[3] Their predatory armies moved into Thüringen and Saxony, plundering and murdering even more thoroughly than usual in order to force the Saxons to make peace. The Elector Johann Georg at once made an alliance with King Gustav II Adolf (1594–1632) of Sweden. Gustav Adolf had intervened on the Lutheran side the year before, when Wallenstein had laid siege to Stralsund, at that time a Swedish port. Tilly's army captured Leipzig, but was defeated by the Swedes at Breitenfeld outside the city in September 1631. Furthermore, Wallenstein and his army were also defeated in the battle of Lützen in November the year after.[4] In this battle, Gustav Adolf fell, but the Swedes continued their involvement under Lord High Chancellor Axel Oxenstierna (1583–1654).[5] For the next 14 years, until the Peace in Westphalia in 1648, German and foreign armies reduced the German Empire to a state of misery beyond description.

All this brought war, death and devastation close to Pufendorf's home.[6] Flöha had a central position on the main road between the cities of Chemnitz and Freiberg. Therefore, troops of all categories marched through, bringing with them all kinds of horrors: plundering, rape, hunger and death. Although Samuel and his family were lucky and escaped direct violence, they saw and heard of horrors almost every day. The family were also forced to leave their home for a short time.

The Peace of Westphalia, which ended the war, was signed in Münster and Osnabrück in 1648. In this year Pufendorf was approaching maturity and was close to entering the University of Leipzig. He therefore belonged to the generation that knew the horrors and chaos of war, a war that lasted for thirty years.[7] There is no question that his childhood experience of violence and turmoil made an imprint on all his works. His emphasis on international peace and order, and his reluctance to support demonstrations and revolts, even against rulers who did not protect their own people, should always be seen against this background.

Like his brothers, Pufendorf was home-schooled until he was 13. In 1645, his mastery of Latin and the fact that he came from a rather poor family qualified him, as his two older brothers before him, for admission to the subsidized humanistic Prince's School of St Augustin, in the neighbouring town of Grimma. This school was a Protestant secondary grammar school for the sons of the nobility and other gifted boys. He studied grammar, logic, rhetoric, the Bible, Lutheran theology, and the Greek and Latin classics. All these subjects were to give the students access to the classical texts seen as necessary for their intellectual development. In his small Pufendorf biography, Paul Meyer (1894: 11) recounts that the school also offered some time for free studies, which Pufendorf used to further his study of Greek and Roman classical texts. His particular relish for the latter laid the foundations for a broad philological competence evident in and formative of his natural law writings. Pufendorf spent his years at Grimma as a diligent and hard-working pupil, and obtained a classical education that prepared him well for university studies. Indeed, shortly before leaving Grimma, he was chosen to compose a Latin poem celebrating the 100th anniversary of the school. However, it should be mentioned that the effects of the war were also felt at the school. For some years it was partly used for billeting wounded soldiers (ibid.: 9). After five mostly happy years, Pufendorf graduated at the top of his class in the autumn of 1650 (ibid.: 12).

Following the wishes of his father, who had passed away two years earlier, Pufendorf, now 18 years old, moved to Leipzig. Like his older brother Esaias (1628–1689), he matriculated at the university with the intention of studying theology.[8] Pufendorf's brother had in fact, as was customary at the time, matriculated at the university when he was 13 years old. His father had managed to pay a fee of 12 Groschen, a little more than the minimum requirement, which shows that he was not among the poorest students. The cost of sending his sons to the university was, however, a burden and a strain on the financial situation of the family.

Notes

1 In a decree following the 1512 Diet of Cologne, the name was designated as the Holy Roman Empire of the German Nation. In short it is mostly called the Roman-German Empire. It lasted from 962 until 1806.
2 The Evangelic Union was a Protestant defensive alliance of princes and cities, established to secure the Protestants right to worship freely within the Empire.
3 Johann Tserclaes Count of Tilly (1559–1632) and Albrecht von Wallenstein (1583–1634).
4 Wallenstein was murdered two years after by his own lieutenants, with the full sanction of the Emperor, because of allegations that he planned a *coup d'état*.
5 Gustav Adolf's only surviving child, Kristina (1625–1689), who then became Queen, was only six years old when her father was killed. Oxenstierna as one of her guardians ruled on her behalf.
6 For the social and economic effects of the Thirty Years War see, for example Friedrich Lütge (1960: 287–298).
7 See also Klaus-Peter Schroeder (2001).
8 Esaias Pufendorf had also been a pupil at the Princes School in Grimma. Thereafter he matriculated at the University of Leipzig, where he received a Magister degree in 1648. He taught for some time at the university before he went into Swedish Diplomatic service in 1657. Here he served as an envoy in Denmark, Holland, England, Prussia, Austria and Saxony. Then he became Chancellor in Bremen and Verden. In his last years he joined the Danish service as an envoy to Regensburg.

2 University Education in Leipzig and Jena

Pufendorf abided by his father's wishes and started at the University of Leipzig with the intention of embarking on the study of theology. His intent was to enter the pastorate on the completion of his studies. It is not quite clear whether he spent twelve or fourteen semesters at the university, since it looks like he moved back and forth a few times between Leipzig and the University of Jena. It is clear that he left Leipzig in 1658 when he was 26 years old.

The university archive does not give any information about what courses were taught or what studies the students were engaged in at this time. Pufendorf himself has not given us much information either. His later writings and letters make only sporadic references to his student days, and then mainly to counter the accusations made against him by former students of the university.

The descriptions of the economic situation in Leipzig and Saxony, and the intellectual environment at the university during Pufendorf's student years, have generally not been very positive. Although the city and its hinterland had not suffered significantly during the first years of war, this changed dramatically when Tilly's army occupied the city before the first battle of Breitenfeld in 1631. The next decade brought considerable unrest and economic decline.

At the second battle of Breitenfeld in 1642, the Swedish army won a decisive victory over the Imperial Army. The Protestant victory in this battle brought an end to the fighting in Saxony, and ensured that the German states would not be forcibly reconverted to Roman Catholicism. After the battle Swedish troops occupied Leipzig. In spite of the fact that the Swedish troops had been a defender of the Lutheran cause they were, as the years went by, still seen as an occupying force by the local population and they were certainly an economic burden for the city, which had to pay for their maintenance. The Thirty Years War formally ended in 1648, but the Swedes did not leave the city until the summer of 1650.

The withdrawal of the Swedish army was celebrated with festivities and theatre plays. Pufendorf must have taken part in some of these events since he arrived shortly before it all started. His first experience of Leipzig could therefore not have been depressing. In addition, there were other celebrations he might have participated in including a major one, the hundredth anniversary of the Peace of Augsburg in 1655. This treaty between the Emperor Charles V

(1500–1558) and an alliance of Lutheran princes allowed German princes to select either Lutheranism or Catholicism.

However, the fact that Pufendorf as well as Gottfried Wilhelm Leibniz (1646–1716) left Leipzig and that Christian Thomasius (1655–1728) was banished in 1690 has been taken as proof of the sterility of the learning conditions at the university and a sign of its parting from the intellectual life of the nation at that time. Detlef Döring (1994: 14) in his booklet *Samuel Pufendorf als Student* claimed that the university was never considered more negatively than in the century between 1600 and 1700.

Examples of the slide in quality of the university are numerous. Meyer (1894: 12) in his Pufendorf biography mentions that the Faculty of Theology during the last decades before Pufendorf arrived had degenerated into a dogmatic place. He went on to tell us that the student environment was rather rough and that the professors turned out to be 'fossilized and quarrelsome slaves to authority'. Heinrich Treitschke (1929: 318) in his Pufendorf biography also paints a very black picture of Leipzig University by the end of the Thirty Years War. 'The academics of Leipzig University were never as hostile towards the living forces of the time as during this time.' A 'famished Lutheranism' held the university in a firm grasp in order to keep control and secure the financial support of the church. The academic environment in the faculty has been described as degenerated Lutheranism. Treitschke believed that Pufendorf could 'not have learned [scientific thought] at Leibzig, this happened instead after he moved to Jena and learned it from Professor Erhard Weigel'.[1]

Even the university historian Konrad Krause (2003: 71–73), who describes Leipzig and Jena as two centres of the German Enlightenment, points to the fact that the Faculty of Theology in Leipzig prohibited Pufendorf's works soon after they were published. In addition, the university reacted strongly against Thomasius when he held his first lecture in the German language in 1687. It has been said that Thomasius was the first to lecture in German. However, Lewis Beck (1969) in his *Early German Philosophy*, claims that this is not true. What was revolutionary in Thomasius' act was that he announced that he would lecture in the vernacular. He held the view that the backwardness of Germany was in part due to the use of Latin.

Kasper Eskildsen (2008: 323) in his book about Thomasius claims that three years later Thomasius, partly because he had lectured on Pufendorf, was ordered by a Saxon court not to publish, give lectures or dispute any further. He was therefore forced into exile in Brandenburg-Prussia, and remained there for the rest of his life, as professor at the newly established University of Halle.

Döring (1994: 7) in his booklet re-examines some of these descriptions and concludes: It is true that the economic situation after the warfare, destruction and population decline caused by thirty years of war was not good. The university also suffered from the horrors, destruction, and general uncertainty of war. The number of new students sank to below 100 at the end of the war, the lowest since 1529. Later Döring (2004), in his article about the learned Leipzig, re-examines some of these descriptions and claims that the University of Leipzig was far more cultivated and diverse than acknowledged by nineteenth-century authors like Treitschke (1897). In any event, it remained a centre of Lutheran orthodoxy, anti-Calvinist and anti-Catholic, and generally devoted to metaphysical scholasticism and Aristotelianism, closely tied to theology. Furthermore, Döring suggests that the time Pufendorf spent in Leipzig may overall have had a positive and important influence on his later development. He also points to the fact that the economic situation improved substantially during the years when Pufendorf was a student.

To fulfil the wishes and request of his father, Pufendorf had chosen the study of theology. Unfortunately, his brother Esaias' warnings turned out to be true. Already in his first semester, he realized that theology, as taught by the Leipzig professors, was dogmatic. Therefore Pufendorf soon developed an aversion to this pedantic orthodoxy. Although, as Meyer (1894: 13) wrote, Pufendorf stayed a true Lutheran through his whole life, his experience from Leipzig shaped his theological views. He always stressed that in dealing with questions of theology one should keep far away from slander and damnation and always practise Christian brotherly love in discussions.

Disenchanted with theology, Pufendorf changed direction and turned first to law. However, his older brother Esaias, who remained close to him through his whole life, advised his younger brother to get a broader education than the dry juristic propositions. Klaus-Peter Schroeder (2008: 74) reports in his book about the Thirty Years War, without giving any source, that Pufendorf, who was eager to learn, attended lectures in law, natural philosophy, cameral sciences and even medicine. During 1652 or 1653 he probably also followed the lectures in mathematics and philosophy by a young lecturer, Erhard Weigel (1625–1699), who drew large audiences to his classes.

Pufendorf was probably not a very efficient student in Leipzig, but he was an active student. He founded a scholarly society called Collegium Anthologicum, where students met for discussions and entertainment. Here, as pointed out by Döring (1995), he gave lectures and took part in the discussions and disputes about theology, philology, history and political philosophy.[2]

Döring discusses why Pufendorf spent almost seven years in Leipzig, which is rather a long time since students in that century often spent time at different universities. One reason for this long-lasting stay can be found in his financial situation. It was hard for his father to raise eight children during the difficult times of the Thirty Years War, and it was not easy to keep his sons at their studies. When Samuel still was at school in Grimma, in the spring of 1648, his father died from a stroke. The oldest son, Jeremias, could take over his father's ministry, Esaias studied in Leipzig, Samuel and Johannes were still in school and of the four sisters only one was married at that time. We do not know if Samuel received any of the few stipends available in Leipzig, but Esaias had a *Kurfürstliches Stipendium* when his father was still alive, so it is possible that the younger brother could also hope for such support. However, Pufendorf's name is not to be found in any catalogue of recipients. A remark from his brother Esaias in December 1657 that Samuel 'unfortunately has lost a prominent patron', suggests that he had received financial support from a private source. Mainly he would have been covering the expenses of his own studies by tutoring other well-off students. At the time, this was a widespread method to finance one's studies. Döring (1994: 32) refers to Peter Dahlmann's Pufendorf's biography from 1710, which explains that Pufendorf early on in his studies could instruct others 'from his own ability to learn and his prudence' but 'this on the other hand still failed to pile profit in his lap'.[3] It is known that when he studied in Jena in 1657 he was responsible for a few 'to him trusted professor-sons from Leipzig'. This reference gives an idea of Pufendorf's living conditions in Leipzig. A student in the seventeenth century normally lived in the house of one of the citizens of the town. Often the professors provided room and board as well as extra tutoring for their students. The university preferred this to the students renting rooms with a citizen in town. The students not only depended on the support of the professors or other established scholars for the possibility to have a small income and a place to live, but also on the use of their books. The university library was not easily available for students, and it lacked much of the required literature.

It was not until Esaias entered the diplomatic corps of the Swedish Crown in 1656 that the financial situation of the Pufendorf family improved. The transfer of 50 talern (dollars) to Samuel by the end of 1657 suggests this. Thirty talern was for him, and the rest he should transfer 'to our beloved mother'.

We hardly know anything about the development and progress of Pufendorf's studies. However, Döring (1994) explains that he probably would have started with the *studium generale* at the Faculty of Liberal Arts, which normally lasted for two years. Often, but not always, the degree of Magister was obtained after the successful end of this study. It is extraordinary that Pufendorf, despite the long period of time he studied in Leipzig, did not obtain this degree and not even the degree of Baccalaureus. Esaias, on the other hand, had obtained both degrees. After only three and a half years of study, he had become Magister. Their father was at that time still alive and could take part in the celebration.

Döring (1994: 43) refers again to Dahlmann's biography and mentions that it was Pufendorf's intention to make his reputation in the world without obtaining the academic honour and dignity of a degree, but only through his high scholarly standards.[4] Nevertheless, it is uncertain whether this was his real reason. In fact, Pufendorf passed the Magister examination in Jena. It was quite unusual at that time to pass an exam in a different university from where the actual study took place. He did this in a very short period. He left Leipzig at the end of July 1656, entered the University of Jena on 14 August, received his Magister degree five days later, and at the latest on 30 August he was back in Leipzig for a short time (ibid.: 43). It is not known what he was doing there, since he returned to Jena for the whole year of 1657, but it is known that the university was opposed to 'foreign Magisters'. Herman Schüling (1970) claims that it was the unconventional mathematician-philosopher Professor Eberhard Weigel, whom Pufendorf had first met in Leipzig, who had urged and prudently persuaded him to earn the Master's degree, since this would be essential for a university career. Pufendorf's disdain for academic ranks and titles had inspired him to refuse a doctorate.

It is, however, remarkable that there is no trace of a dissertation from Pufendorf's degree, while there still are such written works from his brother Esaias. According to his own account, Pufendorf spent the year 1657 in Jena. The reasons for this change are clear: the Magister degree he received from Jena, and the move from Leipzig to Jena of several young scholars close to him, such as Weigel and the historian Johann Andreas Bose (1626–1674). There was also the example of Esaias, who had continued his studies in Jena.[5] Finally, but yet importantly, there was the offer that he could continue tutoring 'Leipziger professor sons'. In Jena Pufendorf became a protégé of Professor Weigel and had room and board with him. He embarked on the study of mathematics, philosophy and natural law. Weigel, who guided him and had a tremendous influence on his spiritual development, taught these subjects simultaneously. Here he also learned about the method and philosophy of René Descartes.[6] Descartes claimed that genuine knowledge should be marked by clarity and distinctness, and he therefore attempted to use Euclidean geometry to demonstrate philosophical propositions. All basic concepts should be defined and certain principles should be formulated as self-evident axioms and postulates. From these, propositions or conclusions may be deduced by rigorous inference. Weigel taught how this Cartesian demonstrative geometrical method could be used to understand and explain human society. He convinced his students of the value of the Cartesian, scientific method in the realm of moral and political philosophy. Under his supervision his students in general, and Pufendorf in particular, were given a thorough introduction to the natural law writings and theories of Grotius and Hobbes, and he emphasized their theories of society. He also stressed the importance of natural science and the philosophical knowledge of Galileo Galilei (1564–1662). Throughout his life, Pufendorf remained gratefully devoted to his eminent teacher and friend. It was in his studies in Jena that he discovered natural law as the unifying principle for his scientific endeavours. Occasional references to Weigel can be found in all of Pufendorf's writings. Under his influence, Pufendorf soon broke with the Lutheran Scholasticism. Although he never became a Cartesian, he saw that it was useful to learn mathematics to be able to grasp and learn science.

After having completed his studies in Jena Pufendorf returned to Leipzig before Christmas of 1657. Here he tried to seek employment, probably with the intent of making an academic career at the university. However, this turned out to be very difficult. With no money and his unwillingness to compromise, the university seemed to be closed to him. Albert Weppler (1928: 4) claims in his Pufendorf study that he tried to get a position but to no avail.

'As an enemy of the established academic learning, too poor and too proud, to beg for favors from the academic rulers he was soon in a great crisis.' He also declined, as reported by Erik Wolf (1963: 317) in his Pufendorf study, an unacceptable offer from University of Halle, since it included an undesirable marriage. Thirty years later he tells that he was offered 'a position and wife' there: 'Because both did not appeal to me I asked my brother for the love of God, to find other possibilities for me.' Consequently, his brother Esaias came to his rescue and urged him to leave his home country since the opportunities were too few for his ability and qualifications. Esaias who had joined the Swedish Foreign Service was able to offer his brother a position as house tutor for the children of the Swedish envoy to Copenhagen. He urged him to accept this position, with the argument that it would open possibilities for a better future career. Pufendorf accepted the offer.

Notes

1 Heinrich Treitschke, 'Samuel Pufendorf', in *ders.: Aufsätze, Reden und Briefe*, Band 1, Meeresburg, 1929. The quotation is from Döring (1994: 7).

2 Detlef Döring (ed.), (1995) contains some of Pufendorf's early writings at the Collegium, and other short writings on philosophy, history and religion.

3 This degree was at most German universities disappearing during the seventeenth century, but not in Leipzig where it was frequently used well into the eighteenth century.

4 Döring (1994) p. 32, note 31: P.H. Adlemansthal, 'Vita, Fama et Fatal Literaria Pufendorfiana' (ed. Peter Dahlmann), in Samuels Freyhrn, *Von Puffendorf Gründlicher Bericht von Zustande des H. R. Reichs Teutscher Nation*, Leipzig, 1710.

5 Pufendorf recounted, in the prefatory dedication of his *Dissertationes academicae sectiores* (Sections of academic dissertations) to his brother Esaias, that he had interested him in ethics and politics, 'where he now had discovered natural law as the unifying principle for his polymathic endeavours'.

6 John Cottingham in *The Penguin Dictionary of Philosophy* (1999) contends that Descartes is universally acknowledged as one of the chief architects of the modern age.

3 A Creative Imprisonment in Copenhagen

At the end of April 1658 Pufendorf said farewell to Leipzig and embarked on his journey to Copenhagen, where he was going to join the family of Peter Julius Coyet (1618–1667), who was one of the two Swedish envoys to the court of Denmark-Norway.[1]

However, when he arrived by ship in Copenhagen in the summer of 1658 the timing could not have been worse. The capital was under siege from the Swedish army, which prepared its assaults. The king and citizens of Copenhagen, on the other hand, prepared its defences. They mobilized their population and fortified the city. The capital was naturally a hotbed and Pufendorf, as a young and innocent man, became entangled in the troubled times between the Nordic rivals.[2] Disregarding diplomatic privileges, the Danes tried to arrest the Swedish envoys. They claimed that the Swedes had broken the peace without a declaration of war, and therefore did not have the right to protection. They did not succeed in arresting Coyet, who managed to bring himself to safety while leaving his family and their tutor behind.

Failing to arrest Coyet the Danes seized the minister's entire retinue, included the house tutor, who had just started his work. The reason given for the arrests was that the Swedish envoys had taken active part in the negotiation of important issues concerning a peace agreement that had been signed earlier that year. The Danes therefore accused them of treason and claimed that they had no duty to guarantee immunity. The house tutor, Pufendorf, was accused of espionage, and thrown into jail. He sat as a carefully guarded prisoner under very bad conditions at the Kastelle fortress.[3] During his imprisonment, he contracted typhus. Throughout more than eight months of harsh captivity, Pufendorf had been deprived of learned books and the possibility of normal contact and conversation with other people. However, in spite of his solitude, he managed to put his incarceration to good use. He reflected and meditated on his studies of natural law and especially upon what he had read in the works of Descartes, Grotius and Hobbes and not least the teaching of his acclaimed professor Weigel. As Herman Schüling (1970) in his Weigel study writes, Pufendorf, whenever his health condition permitted it, began composing for his own diversion, an already planned system of ethics, jurisprudence, government and political economy that inaugurated the rest of his career.

Maybe he also was inspired by the fact that Grotius had used the time when he was imprisoned to write his work on Dutch law. In his own work, Pufendorf attempted to make a synthesis of the philosophies of Grotius and Hobbes, and to construct a system of natural law based on evident and indubitable principles.

After eight months, Coyet managed to convince the Danes that they should release his family and that Pufendorf actually was his house tutor and not a spy and that he should also be released. This happened in April 1659.[4] After his release Pufendorf spent some months recovering from his illness and dreary experience. This recovery took place on Zeeland, first in Helsingör, where Coyet was carrying out negotiation with envoys from England, and thereafter in Roskilde and Sorö.[5] In the old Academy of Knights at Sorö, he had access to a library with a substantial number of books. Coyet also received many important books as his part of a library at Ringsted monastery, which was taken as spoils of war by the Swedes.[6] After his recovery, Pufendorf travelled with Coyet, who had now become Swedish envoy to Holland, and his two sons to Leiden in the Netherlands. Here they according to Jacobus Th. de Smidt (1986: 94), matriculated at the university in March 1660.[7] It should be emphasized that the Netherlands, in the seventeenth century, in many ways was the melting pot of Europe and widely considered the most progressive and culturally diverse society. Its policy of tolerance made it a haven for many people who feared persecution at home.

The University of Leiden was at the time, Russell Shorto (2005: 133), the premier academic institution in the Netherlands and a major European centre of learning. It had ties to the early days of the Dutch rebellion against Spain. Leiden had withstood a Spanish onslaught in 1574, and as a reward for bravery, it was chosen as the site of a university, something that the Dutch provinces needed to become a nation. In a remarkably short time, the university achieved a status equalling that of Bologna or Oxford and became a breeding ground for the new nation's top scientists, politicians, lawyers and religious figures. The Dutch spirit of tolerance pervaded the town. Scientists and scholars from all over Europe came there to study, to teach or to have their books published. Descartes, for example, enrolled at the university in 1630, and Grotius dominated the way law was taught, with his natural law books.

Although there is not much information about Pufendorf's stay or studies at the University of Leiden, it appears that he pursued studies in classical philology, which at this time was the speciality of the university. Here he made the acquaintance of the great German classical scholar and critic, Johann Friedrich Gronovius (1611–1671).[8] He became more familiar with the Stoic philosophers, edited, and annotated two studies in this field.[9] Bo Lindberg in his study of natural law in Uppsala from 1976 claims that Pufendorf's familiarity with the Stoics would play an important role in his mature system of natural law. During Pufendorf's stay in Leiden, he also met Spinoza. Unfortunately, they disliked each other both as philosophers and as persons, an antipathy that would prevail throughout their lives.[10] However, his acquaintance with Peter Grotius (1610–1680), the son of Hugo Grotius, who was the representative in Holland of the Prince Elector of the Rhineland-Palatinate Karl Ludwig (1617–1680), was perhaps more important for his future career.[11]

Pufendorf apparently did not intend to publish the manuscript, which he had started during his captivity in Copenhagen, but he showed what he had written to his teachers and friends. They all strongly urged him to publish it. He followed their advice and his first natural law work *Elementorum Jurisprudentiae Universalis* (Elements of universal jurisprudence) (EJU), in two books was published in The Hague in 1660.[12] However, as argued in the *Introduction to Pufendorf* by Hans Wehberg (1922: xi), Pufendorf must have consulted the principal work of Grotius before the manuscript was sent to the publisher. Weber also adds that all "the original ideas of Pufendorf" are found in it. Thomas Behme (2009: ix) in his *Introduction* to a new edition claims that Pufendorf with this work inaugurated the modern natural law movement in the German-speaking world. It certainly established Pufendorf as a major figure in natural law and made the foundation for his later works that were to sweep across Europe and North America.

This natural law work, which included jurisprudence, ethics, society and political economy, attracted great attention, as well as earning Pufendorf an enviable reputation in greater parts of the European academic community. However, it was also criticized and some Catholic fundamentalists wanted it banned. Here it should be mentioned that Descartes' books, in spite of Leiden's reputation for tolerance, had been put on the Index Librorum Prohibitorum (List of Prohibited Books) in 1648 and a few years later it was extended to the whole country. This meant that they were deemed heretical, anti-clerical or lascivious and therefore not considered appropriate reading by the Church.

Following a suggestion by Peter Grotius, Pufendorf had strategically dedicated the book to Prince Elector Karl Ludwig of the Rhineland-Palatinate 1617–1680 of the Palatinate. The prince was an alumnus of the University of Leiden. Furthermore, he was at that time known as one of the most tolerant and enlightened Calvinist rulers in the Roman-German Empire. Leonard Krieger (1965: 18) in his *Politics of Discretion* claims that 'it was, for Pufendorf, a shrewd selection'. In return for a flattering dedication, the prince, on recommendation of Peter Grotius, whom he had a great affinity towards, invited Pufendorf in 1661 to the University of Heidelberg.[13]

Notes

1 Jacobson (1931 B9: 23–33).

2 In short, the situation can be explained in the following way. Frederick III (1609–1670) became king of Denmark-Norway and the duchies of Schleswig-Holstein in 1648. Early in his reign, he made the promise that he would reconquer the territories that his father, King Christian IV (1577–1648), had lost in his wars with Sweden. He saw an opportunity, when King Karl X Gustav (1622–1660) of Sweden became engaged in a war with Poland, and declared war on Sweden in the autumn of 1657. Karl X Gustav who was a nephew of Gustav Adolf, became king in 1655 when

Queen Kristina, daughter of Gustav Adolf, converted to Catholicism and abdicated from the Swedish throne. He stood up to the new challenge and made an unexpected and fast move. First, he untangled himself from his affairs in Poland. Thereafter he marched his battle-trained army from Poland through Northern Germany and Schleswig-Holstein and into Southern Jutland, where he met very little resistance. In a risky operation that had not been attempted, either before or after, he moved his army across the frozen ice, first to the island of Fyn, and thereafter, across the ice to the islands of Langeland, Lolland, Falster, and onwards to Zeeland. All resistance was crushed, and in a short while, he threatened to take Copenhagen. King Frederick admitted defeat and, on 26 February 1658, signed a peace treaty in Roskilde. In this humiliating and devastating treaty, vast areas of Norway and Denmark were ceded to Sweden. Norway lost the county of Bohuslän, and more disastrous the counties of Trøndelag and Romsdal, which split the country in two. Denmark lost the island Bornholm and the counties of Halland, Scania (Skaane) and Blekinge, areas that today form the southernmost parts of Sweden. It was clear from the beginning that this peace was not sustainable. The relations between the contending parties degenerated fast and both kings planned and armed for a new war. Karl X Gustav, who now had lost his touch with reality, wanted to create a Nordic grand state with Malmö as its capital, took the initiative and moved first. In the beginning of August 1658, without any declaration of war, he restarted the war and again landed his forces on Zeeland. He took the Danes by surprise. Very soon, he defeated the forces that opposed him and laid siege to Copenhagen. This siege lasted one and a half years. Several times, he tried to take the city. The first assault was carried out on 8 February 1659, but the defenders had been warned and it failed. So did his later attempts.

3 Pufendorf's own description of his imprisonment can be found in his anonymous *Gundaeus Baubator Danicus*, Amsterdam 1659. Text in *Pufendorf Schriften*, pp. 125–155. Letter to Eberhard Weigel, Helsingör 17.04.1659, in Briefwechsel, pp. 14–15.

4 The powerful European states did not want one state in Northern Europe. In May 1659 representatives from the Netherlands, France and England had met in The Hague and decided that King Frederik III and King Karl X Gustav should be forced to make peace on the basis of the Treaty in Roskilde. The countries that had been engaged in war with Sweden therefore came to Fredrick's aid. The Dutch fleet landed troops in Copenhagen and troops from Brandenburg, Poland and the German Emperor moved into Schleswig-Holstein and Jutland. Karl Gustav's forces in Jutland surrendered in the summer and his forces on Fyn in November. Negotiations started in March 1660 and the peace was signed in Copenhagen on 26 May. Norway got back the two counties that had divided the country, Denmark got back the island of Bornholm, otherwise the boarders stayed as in the treaty of Roskilde.

5 In his *Epistola Ad Amicos fuos per Germaniam* (1672: 93) Pufendorf describes his sickness, and his travel to Helsingör, after his release.

6 Otto Walde (1920) points out that this library of 26,000 volumes belonged to the Danish government official Jörgen Seefeld (1594–1662).

7 Jacobus Th. de Smidt (1986), *Das Album Studiosorum 1875*, Sp. 479 erwähnt am 31. März 1660 'J.G. Coietus, Suecus; Petrus Trotsius, Martinus Trotsius, Samuel Pouffendorf Misnicus, Ephorus horum adoles- centium 26, J.'

8 Gronovius was a German classical scholar and critic. He wrote books, edited and annotated many works by Roman scholars and edited Grotius's *De jure belli et pacis* in 1660.

9 *J. Laurenberg's Graecia antiqua*, Amsterdam, 1660, and *J. Meursius' Miscellanea laconica*, Amsterdam, 1661.

10 They both criticized each other. Pufendorf expressed strong views against Spinoza's views on the state of nature in De Jure Naturae et Gentium Libri Octo (DJNG) II.2.3.

11 In the Holy Roman-German Empire the electoral princes formally had the function of electing the next Emperor. However, often they merely formalized what was in fact a dynastic succession. The electoral princes were quasi-independent rulers within their own domains.

12 References to this work, *Elementorum Jurisprudentiae Universalis* (EJU), is made to the Clarendon Press 1931 edition. For example: EJU:I.Def.I is understood as Book I. Definition I.

13 Peter Grotius's father, Hugo Grotius, had, when he was the Swedish ambassador to the court in Paris, negotiated the release of Prince Karl Ludwig from imprisonment in France.

Part II

A True European

Karl I Ludwig told Pufendorf that he would establish a new chair for him. However, when Pufendorf received an offer of a chair in Roman law he turned it down. He expressed a wish to be professor in politics at the faculty of law. However, the professors of the faculty did not accept this, probably because Pufendorf did not have a degree in law. His Magister degree was in philosophy. He then accepted an offer to become 'extraordinarius professor iuris gentium (international law) et philologiae' at the faculty of philosophy, hoping that he later could turn it into a real professorship in natural and international law. In October 1661, he was appointed to this position at the university and moved to Heidelberg.

4 Academic Career

Although Pufendorf was disappointed that he did not get an appointment at the faculty of law, he took up his position in the autumn of 1661. Because of the Thirty Years War the Rhineland-Palatinate was one of the most devastated and depopulated regions of the Roman-German Empire and the university had delayed reopening until 1652, four years after the war ended. Great challenges therefore awaited the new professor.

Pufendorf as Professor at the University of Heidelberg

The archive of the university does not have much concrete information about these years in general or about Pufendorf's stay in Heidelberg in particular. However, some evidence has been gathered. It is known that most of his time was taken up with lecturing, writings and consulting. He taught international law, natural law and philology using his own works and the writings of Grotius and the Roman historian Gaius Cornelius Tacitus (56–117). He developed and extended the ideas he had presented in his first book, particularly through a series of dissertations written by him, primarily for the use of his students. Finally, like the other university professors, he worked as a consultant and adviser to the Prince Elector. He wrote several opinions for him and was also entrusted with the education of his son.

Pufendorf's activities were not limited to teaching at the university and being an adviser to the prince. Through the exchange of letters with his brother Esaias and as a subordinate to the diplomat Coyet, he had learned and experienced the importance of having high-level contacts. In Heidelberg, he therefore took care of and worked as a patron for several students who attended his classes. Many of these students had important connections, among them several young Swedish noblemen. One of them, who lived in Pufendorf's house, was the son of the Swedish State Marshal Earl Gabriel Oxenstierna (1619–1673). He also became acquainted with Earl Erik Lindschöld (1634–1690), who was a friend King Karl X Gustav. These contacts turned out to be important for his later career.

According to Gerald Hartung (1997: viii), Pufendorf never succeeded in his attempts to get a position at the Faculty of Law. He made a new effort to join the law faculty in 1664, by vying for a vacant professorship in German constitutional law. Nevertheless, after being spurned once more by the juristic establishment, he had his existing position transformed into a chair in natural law and politics, but he was paid as a full professor of law. He filled his appointment with much credit and he drew large audiences of students to his lectures.

In spite of his conflicts with the law faculty, his seven years in Heidelberg were among the happiest of his life. An important and satisfying event took place in 1665 when Pufendorf married Katharina Elisabetha, born von Palthen (1629–1713), the widow of one of his deceased colleagues. She brought with her into the marriage her daughter Sophia. Together they had two daughters, Christina Magdalena, born 1666, and Emerencia Elisabeth, born 1668. His wife also had a comfortable house, which made it possible for them to take in students not only for room and board but also for tutoring.

From Pufendorf's dissertations and his books, it is clear that his almost eight years in Heidelberg turned out to be very productive. He supplemented his concrete political education as a chancellor at court by utilizing the excellent university library to further expand his already broad and diverse learning. He was able to buy new books for both the university and his own library as well. This became evident in his later work. In short, he read books that had not been available to him before, he researched and he wrote.

The 1648 Treaty of Westphalia, which ended the Thirty Years War, attempted to establish peace in Europe. This treaty had reduced the imperial power of the Roman-German Empire by reducing sovereign princes to territorial princes. The new system created considerable unrest and it caused outbreaks of warfare in the following decades. It was against this background and because he again had been passed over by the law faculty, that Pufendorf in 1667 published under the pseudonym Severinius de Monzambano, his historical and political work *De Statu Imperii Germanici* (On the constitution of the German Empire).[1] This book was an expansion of some themes he had written in two essays to demonstrate his qualification for the chair he unsuccessfully tried to get at the law faculty: *Dissertatio de obligatione erga patriam* (On the subject of patriotism) from 1663 and *Dissertatio the Philippo, Amyntae filio* (On the distinction between regular and irregular states) from 1664. Treitschke (1897: 221) claims that Pufendorf later admitted that he had written the book out of anger at being denied a professorship in law.

The book *De Statu Imperii* is a broadside and a merciless criticism of the disastrous condition of public law in the Roman-German Empire and the guild of constitutional jurists that defended it. It was completed at the end of 1664, but not published until 1667, at the request of Prince Elector Karl Ludwig, who had nonetheless approved its publication. It became an instant bestseller. Numerous editions were published. Although, the imperial censor banned it, it was translated into several languages and distributed across all of Europe. Michael Seidler (2007: xiii) claims that few works had seen so many editions, officials and pirated, and that a 1710 editor had estimated a total distribution of over 300,000 copies. 'Even if the figure is exaggerated, the book was clearly a seventeenth-century best-seller, achieving a notoriety that lasted for decades. Indeed, even its critics contributed to the book's success by sometimes republishing it with their own commentaries and refutations.'

Simone Zurbuchen (1998: 418) claims that it is well known that Pufendorf in his book termed the Roman-German Empire a 'monster' because sovereignty was divided between the emperor and the states. He considered it an 'irregular state', because it represented neither a monarchy nor a confederacy of states. However, he also points the way to its regeneration through a European commonwealth of sovereign states based on natural and international law. In this sense, he was the first to present a comprehensive theory of the existing European state system. James Tully (1991: xx) states that 'Pufendorf is the first philosopher of modern politics'. Furthermore, Walter Simons (1934: 14a) claims, that some of his 'ideas came to fruition' through the unification of numerous German states into a powerful German Empire by Bismarck.[2] Today it can be claimed that peace in Europe, through the construction of the European Union, is a better example. In 2012, the European Union got the Nobel Peace Prize 'for over six decades contributing to the advancement of peace and reconciliation, democracy and human rights in Europe'.

The book raised 'a hue and cry' throughout the Empire, and it was quickly banned from universities and condemned by the imperial censor and the Pope, the Empire's spiritual head. Nonetheless, since it expressed what many already thought, but did not dare to say, it soon became very popular among those content to let others risk their views for them.

With this book, Pufendorf's reputation was also extended to non-academic circles. He achieved both fame and criticism. At the university, however, conflicts arose between him and his colleagues.

His *Elementorum Jurisprudentia Universalis* has been called the first textbook of natural law. In it, Pufendorf had started his mission to construct an intellectual system of natural law, based on a set of universal principles. He wanted to develop a comprehensive political and moral philosophy, appropriate to the conditions of modern Europe. However, it follows from his correspondence that he was not satisfied with his work. At the end of his stay in Heidelberg, as noted by Günther Dickel (1961) in his study of the Heidelberg Faculty of Law, Pufendorf had designed and partly completed the manuscript of what became his masterpiece and major work in natural law.

Pufendorf as Professor at the University of Lund

His brother Esaias, who had risen to prominence and influence in the Swedish foreign service, again intervened on his behalf and effectuated contact between him and the court of King Karl XI (1655–1697) of Sweden. In 1666, a new university, Caroline Academy of the Goths (University of Lund), had been established in Scania, the former Danish province conquered by Sweden in 1658. The founders had ambitions to create a university with an international direction. Pufendorf, who now had become famous on a European scale, should make the new academy 'illustrious'. He was therefore offered a full professorship in natural and international law at the Faculty of Law. His own contacts with young Swedish nobles in his Heidelberg classes and his role as their tutor probably also played an important part in the negotiations. It might also have had some significance that he let it be known that he would dedicate his new book manuscript to the king. At the end of 1667, Pufendorf was offered a full professorship in Lund with a salary substantially higher than the other professors.

Prince Elector Karl Ludwig had supported Pufendorf's work and he did not want to lose his now internationally famous scholar. He even asked Pufendorf's brother to induce him to remain in Heidelberg. However, when Pufendorf decided to accept the offer from Sweden, he did not place any obstacles in his way. After some months of negotiations, and after seven years at University of Heidelberg, Pufendorf resigned his professorship in 1668 and accepted the offer to become Professor Primarius in Natural Law and to take part in the development of the new university in Lund. There has been some speculation about the reasons for his departure from Heidelberg. Had his conflicts with the professors of law escalated? Had his criticism of the conditions in the Roman-German Empire made it impossible for him to continue as a professor? This inquiry did not confirm any of these speculations. His decision to leave was apparently only a career move to improve his fortunes, but no doubt, the increased hostility of his colleagues at Heidelberg, especially after the publication of his *De Statu Imperii*, also played a role. His relationship with the Prince Elector was not a factor, as these had remained amicable. Pufendorf always spoke positively of his time in Heidelberg. This is also pointed out by Stig Jägerskiöld (1985: 57–70) in his article about Pufendorf in Sweden, he explicitly valued the 'freedom to philosophize' that he had enjoyed there. In the year 1668, the whole Pufendorf family moved to Lund in Sweden.

At the University Pufendorf did not put the expectations of his superiors to shame. They held him in high regard, as did his students. Many international students were drawn to Lund because of his reputation. Furthermore, he lectured on natural and international law, tutored many students, and a substantial number of them lived in his household. In the summer of 1670 he was elected pro-rector. Baron Niels Banér (1654–1684), being an aristocrat held the titular title of rector. Pufendorf's teaching assignments included natural law and international law at the Faculty of Law. In 1671, his professorship was also extended to '*ethica et polithica*', which was almost equivalent to practical philosophy, at the Faculty of Philosophy.

Pufendorf's time in Lund turned out to be a new productive period in his life, but also a troublesome one. Shortly upon his arrival, he published an anonymous defence of his *De Statue Imperii* entitled, *Dissertatio de republica irregulari* (A dissertation on irregular states).[3] His next task was to complete the large manuscript he had brought with him from Heidelberg. This was done in the autumn of 1669. He did not want it to be censored in Lund, because he had good reason to fear the result. Therefore, in the spring of 1670, he travelled to Stockholm, where he had important contacts among his former Heidelberg students, and delivered his manuscript personally to his majesty's government and applied for a printing permit. This was granted in the summer the same year. In 1672 his long-awaited masterpiece *De Jure Naturae et Gentium* (On the law of nature and nations) (DJNG), in eight books was published in Lund.[4] According to Carl Fehrman *et al.* (2004) in their study about the learning in Lund, it was the first academic book published in Lund that had a European dispersion.

This work was an important enlargement of his *Elementorum Jurisprudentiae Universalis* and the result of years of studies and research at Heidelberg. His friends as well as his enemies had eagerly awaited it. According to Will and Ariel Durant (1963) in their *Story of Civilization*, this work was Pufendorf's '*chef d'oevre*'. It was the first comprehensive exposition of the state of the art in natural law, which included jurisprudence, ethics, society and political economy.

Shortly after this work was published in 1672, strong reactions came from two prominent theologians in Lund, Professor Josua Schwartz (1632–1709) and the Bishop and Pro-chancellor Peder Winstrup (1605–1679). Their reaction proved that Pufendorf's fears had been real. The specific argument that was used against him was, he claimed, based on the Lutheran orthodoxy's limited understanding of natural law. They accused him of heresy and atheism and claimed that the book was a prescription for anarchy and godlessness. They also asserted that the author was an enemy of religion and government, and which was particularly offensive, a seducer of youths.

The reason for the controversy can be seen in Pufendorf's effort to build a natural law and a standard of morality capable of uniting a Europe divided by confessional differences. He did this by emphasizing that the study and practice of natural law should be distinguished from civil jurisprudence and the institutions of civil law on the one hand and from moral theology and divine law on the other. For Pufendorf, this was extremely important because he grew up in Saxony during the Thirty Years War, and had seen the destruction and violence a war partly based on religious disagreements brought to the people. He tried to achieve his aim by building an ethics of natural law that did not have any attachment to confessional differences.

The year after, in 1673, Pufendorf published, again in Lund, an abridged version of his main work called *De Officio Hominis et Civis Juxta Legem Naturalem* (The duty of man and citizen according to the natural law) (DOH), in two small books.[5] The first book treats the duties of the individual and the second book the duties that arise from membership in a community. A unifying theme in the two books is that man is not alone but is instead a social creature whose conduct should be governed by the necessity of community life. It is 'excerpted almost entirely' from his main natural law work, but it is more normative. Furthermore, it does not include the long and often tedious arguments that support his conclusions. In his major work, we are almost overwhelmed by quotations from Greek and Roman philosophers,

Roman laws, the Bible, the Koran and contemporary sources. This is not the case with his abridged version. Here it should be noted that Michael Seidler (1990: 56), who refers to Pierre Laurent (1982), found that *De Officio* is more than an abridged *De Jure Naturae*, 'He finds therein an important expansion of Pufendorf's natural theology as well as an effort to base his naturalistic ethics – in contrast to Kant – upon a theodicy.'

Following the publications of his two natural law works Pufendorf also wrote his essay *De statu hominum naturalis* (On the natural status of men), which was published in 1675.

The conflict in Lund developed, according to Bo Lindberg (1941), into a great international 'brouhaha' among academics when Pufendorf's colleague at the Faculty of Law, Professor Nicolas Beckman, anonymously published his *Index Noviatatum* (An index of certain novelties) in Giessen in 1673. This index was presented as a survey of dangerous asseverations. There was, in fact, no theological basis for his attack. He was, instead, trying to take advantage of the theologians' animosity to Pufendorf. Beckman simply had a grudge and a hope that he would get back a position he had lost at the university. In the beginning, it looked like Beckman, who used extremely harsh words, might realize his hopes when the authorities in Saxony decided to prohibit the sale of Pufendorf's major natural law work. This drew Pufendorf into bitter conflicts with professors there that lasted several years. In this context, it should be noted that it was not only the attackers that used harsh words. In a letter to Christian Thomasius at University of Halle Pufendorf stated (Carl Fehrman *et al.* 2004: 22): 'We are dealing with thick-skinned animals, and therefore we have to stick them with the dung-fork.'

The religious coloration of some of the accusations against Pufendorf made it for some time look as if the attacks would do serious damage to him. However, due to his long-standing connection in the higher circles of government, he had the support of the authorities. Since he had had *De Jure Naturae* investigated and approved in Stockholm a prohibition had been issued against any criticism of the work, and when Beckman was exposed as the man behind the attacks he lost his position and his honour. The *Index* was burned by the executioners at the marketplace in Lund. However, in the following years Pufendorf was attacked by a row of German theologians. By wit and arguments, he managed to vindicate both his doctrine and his character. He did it in a series of explanatory essays, and it was done so successfully that his numerous hordes of enemies were silenced and his public honour increased.

Pufendorf as Historiographer in Stockholm

In 1676, a new war broke out between Denmark-Norway and Sweden. The Danish army invaded Scania and seized Lund for a period. Even though King Karl XI defeated the invaders, the university remained closed for a few years. This event led the king to offer his displaced professor of natural law, who also had gained a reputation as a political scientist, the combined position as

Royal Swedish Historiographer and State Counsellor at the king's court in Stockholm. This offer probably came about through the intervention and arrangement of Pufendorf's benefactor Earl Erik Lindschöld. In 1677, the new court historian moved with his family, and settled in Stockholm. Here he continued to maintain close contacts with important people in the Swedish power elite, such as Chancellor Magnus Gabriel De la Gardie (1622–1686), and even with the abdicated Queen Kristina, who resided in Rome. Beginning in 1682, Pufendorf also functioned as privy councillor and private secretary to the dowager queen Hedwig Elenora (1636–1715), but he did not have anything to do with political affairs. The only exception was a small tract he wrote about the relations between Sweden and France.

At the University of Lund, Pufendorf had also lectured on history and politics. During his time in Stockholm, he concentrated his work on historical, political and theological studies. However, he did not totally abandon his work on natural law. He was not fully satisfied with his major work *De Jure Naturae et Gentium*. During the years since its first publication in 1672, he had continuously pondered how he could improve it. It led to enlarged and revised editions, one published in Frankfurt in 1684 and a second in Amsterdam 1688. The Amsterdam edition was enlarged by more than one-fourth compared to the first. According to Fiammetta Palladini (2008), in her article *Pufendorf Disciple of Hobbes*, the edition of 1688 had significant changes, which emphasized the similarities to the English natural law philosopher Richard Cumberland (1631–1718) and Stoicism, and perhaps made its problematic Hobbesian inheritance less obvious. There were further two editions in his lifetime, one in Lund in 1692 and one in Frankfurt in 1694.

In the following years Pufendorf published several works of importance. His encyclopaedic works in European history and comparative politics, *Einleitung zur Historie der Vornehmsten Reiche und Staaten so itziger Zeit in Europa sich befinden* (Introduction to the history of the principle realms and states of Europe to the present time) was published in 1682–1686. It was explicitly intended as a textbook for politically aspiring young aristocrats and it became a standard historical work across Europe. In 1686, he published *Commentariorum de rebus Suecicis libri 26 ab expeditione Gustavi Adolphi in Germaniam ad abdicationem usque Christiane* (History of Sweden from Gustav Adolf's campaign in Germany to the abdication of Kristina) in 26 books, based on public records. Here he introduced careful and objective empirical studies of archives and gave in this history of Sweden and Northern Europe an effective example of his new method of historical insight.[6] Today he is therefore regarded as a progenitor of nineteenth-century historicism. In the same year, he also collected and published a series of polemical essays called *Eris Scandica* (Scandinavian Quarrel), which he had written to refute the numerous attacks directed at his works. It includes his essay *De origine et progressu disciplinae juris naturalis* (On the origin and progress of the discipline of natural law). Simone De Angelis (2004) claims that this work not only reveals Pufendorf as a consummate polemicist but it is also valuable for the clarification of important points in his natural law treatises, and as an entry into the bitter debates (in Germany) between early modern natural lawyers and the conservative Lutheran scholastics, whom they challenged.

In 1687, he published *De habitu religionis christianae ad vitam civilem* (On the nature of Christian religion in relation to civil life) in response to the revocation of the Edict of Nantes in 1685 by King Louis XIV of France.[7] In this book, Pufendorf discussed the relationship between Church and state and he energetically advocated freedom of conscience and religion, toleration and the subordination of the Church to the state.

During a journey to Berlin in 1684, with the purpose of gathering archival materials, Pufendorf entered into negotiations with the Great Electoral Prince of Brandenburg and Duke of Prussia Friederich Wilhelm I (1620–1688). The Electoral Prince made him an offer to come and work for him in Berlin. The same year he was elevated to the Swedish aristocracy by King Karl XI, maybe to tempt him to stay in Stockholm. However, in the beginning of 1688, after almost three years of negotiation enough diplomatic tangles had been resolved to allow Pufendorf to accept the offer to become historiographer and judicial counsellor in Berlin. After an agreement was reached between Karl XI and Friederich Wilhelm I, he was formally on loan for two years, but with the understanding that he would not return permanently to Sweden. After 11 years in Stockholm he moved with his family to Berlin in the late summer of 1688.

Pufendorf as Historiographer in Berlin

It is not known for sure why Pufendorf decided to change employers. It might at the time, according to Seidler (1990), have been attractive for two reasons. First, he makes the observation that by this time Prussia's power was ascending while Sweden's was in decline, and he asserts that Pufendorf was eager to serve the strongest monarch. Brandenburg had, during the last decade, replaced Sweden as the main defender of an increasingly beleaguered Protestantism now squeezed between Catholic Austria and France. Second, he points to the fact that Sweden's internal affairs had also taken a sharp turn to the right, toward monarchical absolutism and religious conservatism. In addition, he also noted that Pufendorf could have been drawn to Prince Elector Friederich Wilhelm I by their common view on the revocation of the Edict of Nantes. The book Pufendorf had written on religion was also dedicated to him. As a leader of the Protestant opposition to this act of Catholic intolerance, Friedrich Wilhelm I with his Edict of Potsdam from 1685 opened Prussia to religious refugees from France. Pufendorf might therefore have thought that he, by moving to Berlin, could have some positive influence on the political and intellectual development in Germany.

It is also a fact that Pufendorf's working conditions in Stockholm had changed. Although he still had close relations with King Karl XI and the dowager queen Hedwig Elenora, some of his main supporters at court had died or been dismissed. His historical research and writings had also begun to approach his older contemporaries and as a consequence some tension appears to have risen between him, in his role as an autonomous historian, and some members of the Swedish aristocracy. In addition, his brother Esaias, whose pro-French stance was out of favour, left the Swedish foreign service and took up a position in Denmark in 1687.[8]

In the autumn of 1688 Pufendorf started in the position he had accepted, serving under Friedrich Wilhelm I. Shortly after his arrival Wilhelm died, so he continued serving under his son Friedrich III (1688–1713). Friedrich III also appointed Pufendorf court councillor. The same year he was ennobled into the Prussian aristocracy and in 1690, he was made baron in the Roman-German Empire. As court councillor he obtained considerable influence and worked closely with his friend Eberhard von Danckelman (1643–1722), who was de facto prime minister of Brandenburg-Prussia during the years 1692–1697.[9]

In Berlin he first completed *De rebus a Carolo Gustavo Sueciae rege gestis commentariorum* (The achievements of King Karl Gustav of Sweden based on public records), in seven books. This work was not published until two years after his death in 1696. He then began writing history books concerned with the reign of the two sovereigns mentioned, and continued his works on theological issues. *De rebus gestis Friederici Wilhemi Magni Electoris Brandenburgici commentariorum* (The achievements of Friedrich Wilhelm the Great, Elector of Brandenburg, based on public records) in nineteen books was completed in 1692, but not published until one year after his death in 1695. He had also started his work *De rebus gestis Friderici III, Electoris Brandenburgici, post primi Borussiae Regis* (The achievements of Friedrich III Elector of Brandenburg later Friedrich I of Prussia) in three books, but did not manage to finish it. This work was not published before 1734. During his historical work, he had access to and used with assurance the documents of the state archives. He did not hesitate to use even the most secret documents. This created, Kåre Foss (1934: 262) claims, 'a storm of embitterment' at foreign courts. There was some effort to confiscate and if possible to destroy all copies of these works.

In 1692, Pufendorf finished his second essay on religion *Jus feciale divinium cive de consensus et dissensu protestantium* (The law of covenants, or on the consensus and dissension among Protestants). This work was not published until after his death in 1694. In this work, a system of a new theology is in the forefront. Here he discussed the possibility of reconciliation and the development of a confessional union between the Lutheran and the Calvinist reformed churches. Since Pufendorf was strongly in favour of religious and political tolerance, he favoured such a union.

In the spring 1694, Pufendorf took upon himself to make a journey to Stockholm. He had two reasons for this venture. First, he wanted to retrieve a manuscript about the history of King Karl X, which the Swedes had held back when he left for Germany and, second, he wanted to follow the call of King Karl XI. Because of his outstanding work during his stay in Sweden, the king had decided to ennoble him as a baron. The manuscript was released when Pufendorf formally agreed not to alter the text. He then received royal permission to publish and was allowed to take a copy of the manuscript to Berlin. He also became a Swedish baron. However, his journey and success proved a pyrrhic victory. A stroke or aneurism while in Stockholm, which led to other medical complications, combined with a strenuous return journey, were too much for the ageing scholar. He succumbed shortly after his return to Berlin, on 26 October 1694. Pufendorf was inhumed in St Nikolaikirche.[10] On his tombstone, which today can be seen inside the church, is engraved '*fama per totum orbem*' ('his reputation is spread all over the world').

Notes

1 Klaus-Peter Schroeder (1999), 'The constitution of the Holy Roman Empire after 1648: Samuel Pufendorf's assessment in his Monzambano', *The Historical Journal* 42(4): 961–983. *De Statu Imperii Germanici* was published in The Hague, although Geneva was given as the fictive place of publication.

2 Otto von Bismarck (1815–1898) nicknamed 'The Iron Chancellor'.

3 This was later included in his *Dissertationes.*

4 References to this work are taken from the Clarendon Press 1934 edition. Translation from the third edition Amsterdam 1688. For example, I.i.1:3 is understood as Book I, chapter 1, section 1, and page 3.

5 References to this work are taken from the *Cambridge Texts in the History of Political Thought*, Cambridge University Press, 1991. Translation from the first edition. DOH.I.ii.3 is understood as Book I, chapter ii, section 3.

6 English translation: Samuel Pufendorf, *The Complete History of Sweden*, in 2 volumes (translated by Charles W. Brockwell), J. Brudenel, London, 1702. Reprinted Folcroft Library Editions, Folcroft, PA, 1977.

7 The Edict of Nantes issued on 13 April 1598, by Henry IV of France, granted the Calvinist Protestants, also known as Huguenots, substantial rights. King Henry aimed primarily to open a path for secularism and tolerance.

8 Esaias Pufendorf was in 1689 sentenced to death in absentia by a Swedish court, accused of having left his last Swedish post without permission.

9 Eberhard Christoph Baltasar Freiherr von Dankelman.

10 St Nikolaikirche was totally destroyed at the end of WWII. However, Pufendorf's tombstone was rescued from the ruins, and the church has been rebuilt.

5 A Champion of the Enlightenment

In retrospect, Pufendorf's life can be seen as a long, but rapid, journey where he worked diligently both to make life better for himself and his family, but also through his work to improve the conditions in Europe, and make it better to live in for all. Born in a time of turmoil and violence and seeing the consequences of unscrupulous wars, destructions and human sufferings around him, his main vision was to enlighten people about the right conditions for enduring peace. The means to make this vision true were his academic writings, his teaching of students, his tutoring of prospective civil servants, and his work as a political adviser to three important, and given the conditions of the time, enlightened Protestant statesmen.

Pufendorf's Writings

Pufendorf's writings can be divided into three groups.[1] The first group is his attempt to construct a comprehensive political and moral philosophy based on a set of universal principles or natural laws. It is developed primarily in his *Elementorum Jurisprudentiae Universalis* from 1660, *De Jure Naturae et Gentium* from 1672 and *De Officio Hominis et Civis* from 1673. However, this approach was somewhat moved aside when, the Danish army, in an attempt to reconquer lost territory, captured Lund in 1676. The university closed and Pufendorf moved to Stockholm and took up his work as a royal historiographer and councillor at the Swedish court. There he did not completely give up his natural law writings but he concentrated on historical analyses.

The second group is therefore Pufendorf's attempt to analyse the relations within and among contemporary European states. He did this by means of a comparative and historical analysis of their interest and relative powers with a view to predictions and recommendations to state builders in general and the rulers he served in particular. His main source for this analysis was the state archives. When he moved to Berlin in 1688, he continued these writings. His numerous books of historical writings belonged to this group. However, special attention should be drawn to his monumental introduction to the history of the principal state of Europe. This work Tully (1991: xv) asserts; 'with its rigorous concept of state interest and relative powers and its comprehensive design, was republished throughout the eighteenth century'. A number of other history writers across Europe adopted the method he used and to some extent just copied him. One of these was the Dano-Norwegian natural law philosopher and author Ludvig Holberg,[2]

The third group compromises Pufendorf's attempts to define the correct subordinate relations of religion to politics in Protestant states after the Peace of Augsburg, which recognized diversity within Christianity. He advocated toleration and the unification of the different Protestant creeds. His views on these issues is primarily expressed in his two essays: *De habitu religionis christianae ad vitam civilem* (On the nature of Christian religion in relation to civil life) published in 1687, and *Jus feciale divinium cive de consensus et dissensu protestantium* (The law of covenants, or on the consensus and dissension among Protestants) finished in 1692, and published posthumously in 1695. A short discussion of Pufendorf's religious views can be found in Zurbuchen's 'Introduction' to the Liberty Fund editions (2002) of these two religious essays. A more thorough representation of his views on theological issues is carried out by Horst Rabe (1958) in his *Naturrecht und Kirche beid Samuel von Pufendorf.*

The idea of an objective moral and judicial order based on human nature is as old as philosophy. Formulated as a doctrine and called natural law it is usually connected with Stoic and Roman jurists in the antiquity, with the Schoolmen, particularly from Thomas Aquinas (1225–1274) to François Suarez in the Middle Ages, and with the sixteenth- and seventeenth-century political theorists, in particular Grotius, Hobbes, Pufendorf and Locke. Some of the terms used have survived the development through the centuries, more or less unchanged: human reason, justice and the belief that society is created through some sort of agreements.

The idea of a natural moral order can, according to Bo Lindberg (1976), function in two ways: it can be seen in opposition to the present political order and will therefore have in it a revolutionary content or it can view the present order as reasonable and necessary and will therefore favour this order. The first interpretation can be found with the Greek Sophists (400 BC), who criticized slavery, and with the Monarchomachs,[3] and others who fought against the absolute power of the kings in the fifteenth and sixteenth centuries, and with revolutionaries in France and North America in the late seventeenth century. The second interpretation defended the existing order, dominated by the Catholic culture in the late Middle Ages, and in the Lutheran culture in the sixteenth and seventeenth centuries.

This could imply that the philosophers belonging to the last strand, such as Pufendorf, did not contribute to the political and social upheavals and progress that occurred in Europe and America in these centuries. However, nothing could be more wrong.

It is true that most seventeenth-century natural law philosophers defended the rulers they served and thereby the existing order. There were at least two reasons for this fact. First, this century was characterized by upheavals, wars, destruction, extreme violence and death. To advocate radical changes in state governance or revolutions against the present rulers would probably only create more havoc and devastation. Second, they had no choice. During these years, there were limited legal protection for most people, and freedom of expression did not exist in most European countries. Consequently, there were limits to what scholars could write without losing the support of their benefactors and thereby their livelihood, or even their heads. Considering these facts, it is astounding how they in their writings dared to discuss both improvements, and alternatives to the present order. Alternatively, they left so much ambiguity in their discussions that their writings could be used by their descendants to advocate political changes.

Pufendorf's writing was also open to interpretation. He can be characterized as an eclectic, who united authoritarian and liberal elements. This approach made it possible to break away parts of his doctrines and use them in new connections. He also developed his theories in connection with the political realities in existing states. He was not a radical, who wanted violent changes and he did not challenge the masters he served. Furthermore, he also needed his benefactors support in his controversies with his colleagues at the universities of Heidelberg and Lund, and most importantly in his struggle with the leaders of the Lutheran orthodoxy in many European countries. These struggles with his adversaries were fierce at the time and could have seriously threatened his position, without him having the support of his masters. However, these clashes also strengthened his position and made him a well-known scholar in the seventeenth century.

Knud Haakonssen (1996: 43), in his *Natural Law and Moral Philosophy*, claims for example that there are several ambiguities in Pufendorf's representation of his natural law, but that 'these ambiguities gave rise to a debate which lasted for a generation or more, and which was as fierce as any in the history of philosophy'. Furthermore, 'it also helped to secure to Pufendorf an influence that was European in scope and lasted well into the eighteenth century' (ibid.). Therefore, when Jonathan I. Israel (2001:802) in his *Radical Enlightenment* calls Pufendorf 'a German natural law theorist' he is positively wrong. Pufendorf was a true European scholar.

Michael Seidler (1990) argues that there were two kinds of streams of natural law during the seventeenth century. One stream draws heavily on medieval and Renaissance scholasticism and attempted consciously to integrate its own doctrine with Christian revelation. As a consequence, it had a theological character. The German philosopher Gottfried Leibniz represented this stream. The other stream owed more to antiquity and its humanist revival in the Renaissance as well as to modern science, while deliberately trying to conflict with Christian doctrine. Religion was 'natural' instead of revealed. Grotius, Hobbes and Pufendorf, to mention the most important, represented this stream.

Grotius and his Followers Selden, Hobbes and Cumberland

Pufendorf outlines in his *De Jure Naturae et Gentium* an historical account of the development of modern natural law.[4] The founder is Hugo Grotius and his important followers were the English jurist John Selden (1584–1654), Thomas Hobbes and Richard Cumberland. To understand Pufendorf it is helpful to know something about these scholars. Their basic ideas will therefore be briefly outlined.

Hugo Grotius was born in Delft in Holland. Arthur Eyffinger (1982), in his *Inventory of the Poetry of Hugo Grotius*, contends that his Latin verses,[5] which he wrote before he was nine years old, gave early proof of his genius. He was admitted into the University of Leiden in 1595 when he was only twelve years old. Here he studied several disciplines, among them theology, jurisprudence, mathematics and philology. In 1598, he accompanied the Dutch ambassador to France. The same year he became Doctor of Jurisprudence at the University of Orleans. His treatise *Mare Liberum* (On the freedom of the seas), which was published in 1609, became a famous manifesto advocating free navigation and free trade. In Holland it earned him such a reputation, that he was entrusted to lead a delegation to Great Britain to settle a dispute concerning fishing rights in the North Sea.

Unfortunately, Grotius got involved in a theologically and politically infected dispute. Although he had a sincere belief in tolerance and tried to prevent religious conflicts, he was brought to trial. In 1619 he received a sentence of life imprisonment in the fortress of Lowenstein. Here he was allowed free time, and he used it to study and to write. Among his writings was the treatise *Bewijs van den waren Godsdienst* (On the truth of the Christian religion), written entirely in didactic verse. It has been claimed to be the first textbook in Christian apologetics. William Enfield (1837: 624f.) in his *The History of Philosophy from the Earliest Periods*, has pointed out that this essay was translated into eleven languages, among them Arabic, Persian, Indian and Chinese. Another important publication was his *Institutionen des Holländischen Rects* (Institutions of Dutch law). It saw more than thirty editions.

After two years of confinement, Grotius, with the help of his wife, managed a dramatic escape, first to Brabant and later to Antwerp and Paris, where he got a small pension from the French government.[6] During his time in exile he completed his great natural law work *De Jure Belli ac Pacis* (On the law of war and peace) in three volumes. It was published in Paris in 1625. When Cardinal Richelieu (1585–1642)[7] deprived Grotius of his pension, he left Paris in 1631 and returned to Holland. However, the authorities found his stay unacceptable, and when an order for his arrest was issued six months later, Grotius continued to Hamburg. In 1634 he accepted an offer from Queen Kristina of Sweden to become her ambassador to the French court. He had been strongly recommended for this position by the Swedish Chancellor Axel Oxenstierna. Returning to Paris, he worked for almost ten years diligently, in very difficult negotiations, to create peace in a war-torn Europe. When the

French King Louis XIII (1601–1643) called back his ambassador in Stockholm, Queen Kristina reciprocated and called Grotius back to Stockholm.[8] To his disappointment, she now wanted to include him in a group of eminent scholars at her court. He declined and resigned from his position as ambassador. On his voyage back to Holland, his ship wrecked, he fell ill and died in Rostock in 1645.

Grotius's fame rests primarily on the content and diffusion of his treatise *De Jure Belli ac Pacis.*[9] Here his main objective is to describe the rules that should exist in peace and in war primarily between independent states. He hoped that this would bring an end to unscrupulous wars and human sufferings. Here it is, however, appropriate to point out that Richard Tuck (1993: xxi), claims that Grotius 'was in fact much more of an apologist for aggression and violence than many of his more genuinely pacific contemporaries'.

Today Grotius is considered by most to be one of the fathers of *modern* natural and international law. However, it should be stressed that some, like Michael Zuckert (1994: xvii), in his *Natural Rights and the New Republicanism*, are satisfied by saying that 'he introduces major changes into the existing doctrines'. Using the term 'modern' emphasizes the fact that natural law, as mentioned, played an important role among Greek and Roman philosophers of law. The Scholastic theologians and jurists of the Reformation later adopted their views. All of them used the term *jus naturae.* Grotius bypassed and broke free from the Schoolmen and the late sixteenth and early seventeenth-century jurists of the Church. He rediscovered the Greek and Roman philosophers, like Aristotle (384–322) and the Roman philosopher and orator Marcus Tellius Cicero (106–43), and found the source of what is right and wrong in human nature. He did mention that natural law also had its source in God, but states daringly:

> What we have been saying would have a degree of validity even if we should concede that which cannot be conceded without the utmost wickedness, that there is no God, or that the affairs of men are of no concern to Him.[10]

Pufendorf's thesis is that Grotius succeeded in secularizing natural law. His natural law had only to do with our living together in this world, and had nothing to do with our relation with God and salvation. God had, strictly speaking, no importance for natural law. It is developed from reason and human nature, and these rules would exist even if God did not exist. It was therefore not until Grotius, that the principles of natural law were seen as independent of divine sanctions. Torsten Gihl (1932: 42) in his article on Pufendorf and natural law, supports this view and claims that Grotius carried out 'what one could call the de-Christianization or secularization of natural law'.[11] Michael Nutkiewcez (1992) in an article on Pufendorf, claims that; 'Scholars have not noticed that his bold assertion has its model in the philosophy of the Spanish Scholastic Francisco Suarez.' In his discussion of *Roman*

Law in International Law, Randall Lesaffer (2005: 46) argues that only from Grotius onwards did natural law depart from bordering 'with Christian morality and the Thomistic tradition and came to be perceived as truly universal'. Nevertheless, this departure did not go without a long struggle. Tanya Kevorkian (2007: 115), in her book about *Baroque Piety*, writes; 'While the Christian natural law tradition became obscure after 1700, it was common currency throughout the 17th century; its proponents included Veit Ludwig von Seckendorff and Gottfried Wilhelm Leibniz.'[12] She adds that their natural law was connected to the Lutheran Aristotelian tradition with emphasis on the Ten Commandments. This view is in marked opposition to the natural law of Grotius and his secularist German followers: Pufendorf and Thomasius.

The foundation of Grotius' theory can be summarized as follows: law and right are human constructions with their origins in human nature. We therefore have to understand human nature. Grotius starts out by first describing the sceptical view, represented by the Greek philosopher Carneades (214–129 BC), that humans in their actions are led by nothing other than their own interests and that those who try to act just are simple beings and therefore will lose. Against this, Grotius contends that in human nature there exists a *societatis appetitus*, a quest for a quiet and peaceful coexistence with other people. This implies that people not only look after their own interests but also the interests of their fellow beings. Reason will tell us the rules that will be in accordance with the demands of society (fellowship). The comprehensive principle of natural law and its source is the need to preserve peaceful coexistence (*societatis custiodia*) among men. What is special for humans is not their care for their own preservation, since man has this in common with all living creatures. What is special for humans is their 'sociableness'.[13]

Human reason will inform us how this desire and craving for intercourse with other humans can be satisfied; reason is man's means to decide what is right and what is wrong. Right is what is good for the preservation of peaceful coexistence, and wrong is what hurts this. From these premises, Grotius deduced a system of natural and international law, which included what today would be termed jurisprudence, social sciences and political economy.

A natural law developed from reason sounded very attractive in that age, where a rationalistic, geometrical axiomatic ideal of science was in the process of breaking through. Natural law was a *dictatum reactae rationis* (dictate of right reason) and its basic foundation had the character of mathematical axioms. It gave natural law a scientific *imprimatur* and great power. The new discipline appealed, as argued by Seidler (2013), to concrete observations, 'attempting thereby to create a shared outlook possessing both systematic coherence and empirical plausibility'.

Another important element in the doctrine of Grotius was his theory of agreements, the idea that society and its various constructions are based on agreements between people placed on equal footing, and who originally had equal rights. This was not a new thought either. It can be found in Roman law, and the German jurist Johannes Althusius (1557–1638) had made it a central element in his theory of society.[14] With Grotius it became part of natural law, and, as will be clear later, was taken over by Pufendorf.

John Selden was born in Sussex, England in 1584. In 1600 he was admitted to Hart Hall College, Oxford. Already in 1612 he was called to the bar. He is known as both a scholar of England's ancient laws and constitution, and a scholar of Jewish law. In 1623 Selden became a Member of Parliament, and he served in several parliaments until 1649. All through these years he continued to be a staunch supporter of parliamentary rights, and a steady opponent of the crown's prerogative. In 1618 he wrote *Mare Clausum* (The closed sea). But this work, which was a reply to Grotius's *Mare Librum*, was not published until 1635. His main work, *De Jure Naturali et Gentium Juxta Disciplinam Ebraeoram* (The law of nature and nations according to the method of Abraham) was published in 1640. Here he tries to find the source of natural law in the Old Testament. Selden is by many considered 'the father of English legal history'.

Thomas Hobbes was born in Wiltshire, England in 1588. He entered Magdalen Hall, Oxford in 1603, where he studied Scholastic philosophy with little enthusiasm but did well in Logic. He received a bachelor degree in 1608. His first book, *Elementorum Philosophiae Sectio Tertia De Cive* (The citizen), was published in 1642. The English text appeared in 1651 as *Philosophical Rudiments Concerning Government and Society.* This book was the third part of a planned trilogy on body, man and citizen. The outbreak of civil war in England persuaded him to write the third part first. His philosophical starting point can be found on one of the first pages: 'We must therefore resolve that the origin of all great and lasting societies consisted not in the mutual good will men had towards each other, but in the mutual fear they had for each other.' The year 1651 also saw the publication of Hobbes's most famous work, *Leviathan, or, The Matter, Form, and Power of a Commonwealth Ecclesiastical and Civil.* In 1655, he published *De Corpore* (The body), and in 1656, *Questions Concerning Liberty, Necessity and Chance.* The second part of his treatise, *De Homine* (The Man) came in 1658. Several works were published posthumously.

In both *The Citizen* and in *Leviathan* Hobbes, according to Perez Zagorin (2009: 12) in his *Hobbes and the Law of Nature*, 'regarded moral philosophy and natural law as one and the same …'. Like Grotius, Hobbes saw the source of what is right and wrong in human nature. However, in *The Citizen*, he claims that the craving for intercourse between people is not the driving force but fear and pure egoism: 'the disposition of men are naturally such that, except they be restrained through fear and some coercive power, every man will dread and distrust each other'. If men seek intercourse, it occurs out of fear or because they believe that profit could be made from it. In the natural state, everyone has the same equal and unlimited right to everything. But this will result in 'a war all against all' and will consequently lead to self-destruction.[15] Concern for self-preservation makes it therefore necessary for men to seek an agreement of cooperation or commonwealth with each other.

This commonwealth must, however, be based on a covenant where each gives up a part of one's unrestricted right. From this it follows that, with the opposite starting point, Hobbes had reached a similar result as Grotius.

With his thorough, acute and well-formulated analysis Hobbes became one of the most famous thinkers of his time. His writings were widely read not only in England but also on the Continent, where his work was admired. This was particularly the case in France. However, his materialism, that denied the existence of minds, spirits and divine beings, aroused strong attacks from theologians, philosophers and politicians across Europe and North America. He exerted a powerful influence also on his critics, and they were many. In particular, it was his probing and confident writings, expressing hard deterministic and materialistic views that made him both famous and infamous and brought upon him a hoard of angry, hostile attackers. In his *The Hunting of Leviathan* Samuel Mintz (1962) claims that *Leviathan* was censured in Parliament for promoting atheism, profaneness, and blasphemy and his ideas were denounced from the pulpits. He was also accused of heresy and atheism by his clerical opponents and in these circles his name became a swear word. It was in particular his views on human behaviour that were hard to swallow both for the theologians and non-professionals of the Church. They could not accept that self-interest and 'a war of all men against all men' were the foundation of human nature. Such a view was found in serious conflict with the words of the scripture. To develop natural law and political theory on such a foundation was considered unacceptable not only by the Church establishment and their laymen, but also by many university academics. In 1683 the University of Oxford condemned a number of Hobbes' works to the flames. Nevertheless, Hobbes's writings enjoyed a significant influence on the evolution of British moral philosophy and Continental political philosophy.

Richard Cumberland was born in Aldersgate, England in 1632. In 1649 he entered Magdalen College, Cambridge, where he had obtained a fellowship. He took a bachelor degree in 1653 and a master in 1656. His master degree was the following year accepted at University of Oxford, where he for some time studied medicine. In 1663 he became Bachelor of Divinity and Doctor of Divinity in 1680. In 1691, he became Bishop of Peterborough. Cumberland published his major natural law treatise, entitled *De Legibus Naturae* (On natural laws) in 1672, the same year as Pufendorf published his main work. Pufendorf found this treatise recommendable and commended it in subsequent editions of his own work. Cumberland propounded utilitarianism and opposed in his treatise the egoistic ethics of Hobbes.

Stephen Darwall (1995: 81) in his book *The British Moralists* claimed that Cumberland's treatise 'was regarded as one of the three great work of the modern natural law tradition', the others being Grotius's *De Jure Belli ac Pacis* and Pufendorf's *De Jure Naturae et Gentium*. They all had one thing in common. The Swiss Protestant eighteenth-century natural law theorist Jean Barbeyrac (1674–1744) translated their works into French with detailed annotations. He managed with his translations and extensive commentaries to place the ideas of modern natural law before as wide a public as possible. His editions of Grotius and Pufendorf in particular led to new translations into many languages and new editions in many countries.

Pufendorf's System of Natural Law

Pufendorf's representation in his main work *De Jure Naturae et Gentium*, is a systematic integration of moral, legal, societal and political economy relations under the general rubric of natural law. He makes it clear in the preface that God has created men as social beings. The basis of natural law is therefore the social life of man: 'I have found no other principle, which all men could be brought to admit, without violation of their natural condition, and with due respect to whatever belief they might hold on matters of religion' (Preface: ix). Pufendorf's system of natural law was consequently valid for all human beings, regardless of their religious beliefs. At the time, such a view was revolutionary and could possibly, be dangerous for the author. However, it had an immediate and wide impact on the intellectual debate in Europe and North America. This impact was magnified by the publication of his *De Officio Hominis* in 1673, which was a much shorter epitome of his main work. It was successful beyond expectations and it became the standard textbook on natural law in Protestant Europe.

In the introduction to his first natural law work *Elementorum Jurisprudentiae Universalis* (EJU), Pufendorf makes it clear that his main sources were Grotius and Hobbes. He has 'drawn much from that marvelous work, *De jure belli ac pacis*, by the incomparable Hugo Grotius'. Grotius was very important to him since he had succeeded in secularizing natural law. Pufendorf therefore introduced this book as required reading in his natural law classes at University of Heidelberg. He also points out that he owes no small debt to Thomas Hobbes, 'whose basic conception in his book, *De cive*, although it savors somewhat of the profane, is nevertheless for the most part extremely acute and sound' (EJU: xxx).

Like Grotius and Hobbes, Pufendorf took over and adopted the philosophical and fundamental (basic) position of the science of his time. He can therefore not be placed within any certain philosophical school. His writings can rather be seen as an eclectic combination of elements from different schools.[16] As in all new philosophical schools from the late seventeenth century, a common basic tendency was to doubt and criticize established authority and to strive for truth that would make it possible to build a new science on secure ground.

Pufendorf's natural law theory can be described as a Stoic moral philosophy and Roman law modernized with the assistance of the method of natural sciences. The philosophy of the antiquity played a great role for him and it should be noted that he also got a deeper insight into classical philology and the Stoic philosophers during his time in Leiden, which was after he had learned about the modern scientific method in Jena. He stressed that his doctrines were interdependent of Stoic philosophy and also in the tradition of the philologist and humanist Justius Lipsius (1547–1606),[17] and Grotius.

Pufendorf's work is also important for its critical discussion of the arguments of previous natural law thinkers. As an eclectic, he also used the arguments of his predecessors to develop his own theories. His theoretical foundation points forward to the liberal state, where the state can be seen as a union of individuals and is there to protect the natural rights of the individuals. He united authoritarian and libertarian views on liberty. However, in its actual content his doctrine is authoritarian and built on order, discipline, sense of duty, individual subordination to the state and the common interest. In this way Pufendorf fulfilled the Lipsonian and New Stoic traditional demand for a strong state and the ordination of the religion and Church to the state.

Pufendorf wanted to remove natural law from both civil law and moral theology. He distinguishes between three sciences:

1. Natural law, which is common to all men and derived from reason alone.
2. Civil law, which is valid only in the individual state.
3. Moral theology, the dictates of which God has given to Christians in the Holy Scripture.

The greatest difference between natural law and moral theology consists in the fact that natural law, rooted only in this life, will make man a worthy member of human society only for his life, while moral theology trains the citizen for the heavenly city (DOH: 17–18).

The fundamental task of Pufendorf's natural law, Ian Hunter (2001:162) in his *Rival Enlightenments* argues, was to remove metaphysical moral philosophy from academic ethics and politics and to replace it 'with a civil philosophy suited to the moral comportment of the subject of the deconfessionalised state'. He attempts to construct his theory of natural law on the basis of the dignity of man, human reason, and man's free choice. The dignity and equality of man is the basis of his whole system of natural law and it makes a clear break with Roman law.

Pufendorf's doctrine of the dignity and equality of humans became the foundation of the American constitution. Fritjof Haft (1997: 81) in his *Introduction to the Study of Law*, argues that Pufendorf can be considered 'the spiritual father of the American revolution'. The title of the 1906 French translation of his *De Officio* by Jean Barbeyrac is *Les devoirs de l'homme et du citoyen*. Walter Simons (1934: 14a) argues that this title is indicative of the often truly revolutionary ideas of Pufendorf. We meet this title, with one term changed, in the heading of the French National Assembly's famous declaration of human rights from 1789. It has the title *Déclaration sur les droits de l'homme et du citoyen*. In an article entitled *Untastbar* (Inviolable) in the German national weekly newspaper *Die Zeit* from 2008, legal historian Professor Uwe Wesel (1933–) claims that Pufendorf's greatest deed was that his concept of human dignity became on 10 December 1948, the foundation of the United Nations Declaration of Human Rights.[18] The preamble reads: 'Whereas recognition of the inherent dignity and of the equal and inalienable rights of all members of the human family is the foundation of freedom, justice and peace in the world.' In 1949, this principle also came into the German constitution and later into the constitutions of other European countries. Wesel also notes that the US president, Calvin Coolidge (1872–1933), in 1926 during the 150-year celebration of the Declaration of Independence, praised Pufendorf and said that his writings 'had shown the Americans the road to liberty'.

The natural law of the Enlightenment had its great creator in Pufendorf. It was his work through the medium of Christian Thomasius that prepared the ground for the eighteenth-century system of jurisprudence. The connection between theology and law was, according to Leonard Krieger (1957) in his *The German Idea of Freedom*, weakened in Germany by Pufendorf and was finally broken by Thomasius.

Pufendorf sought to mediate between Grotius and Hobbes. He wanted to unify Hobbes' natural law doctrine of self-interest with Grotius' natural law doctrine of 'man's inclination for society' and to integrate these ideas with the Cartesian and Scholastic methods of the sixteenth-century thinkers. He sought to bridge the apparent antagonism between man's self-interest and man's existence as a social being.[19] The duties of man and citizen will converge in a state where a superior has been granted the right to govern others in exchange for the security and protection that he can offer them. His writings on natural law include ethics, jurisprudence, government, and political economy. These elements are seen as integral parts of a totality.

In his law of nations (international law), Pufendorf claimed that there does not exist any acute positive law that arises from custom or from treaties among nations. One reason for this is that there cannot be found an authority above the states that can bind them.[20] For him the source of the law of nations was natural because reason defines it. According to Andreas Aure (2010: 133) in his article about Pufendorf's rejection of customs and treatises as sources for international laws, Pufendorf's views may be contrasted with the views of his contemporary, the natural law philosopher Samuel Rachel (1628–1691). He held the opinion that the law of nations in particular is about customs and practice.[21] Rachel and Pufendorf discussed these questions during the 1670s–1680s. Rachel refuted Pufendorf's argument in his *De Jure Naturae et Gentium Dissertations* (Dissertations on the law of nature and nations) from 1676. Pufendorf, on the other hand, added comments to Rachel's refutations in his later editions of his main work.

Pufendorf became the founder of the purely natural law conception of the law of nations. His theory is therefore considered auspicious for the development of the law of nations. The history of international law is largely characterized by whether one thinks it can be deduced from natural law or if it wholly can be seen as resulting from customs and treatises, the positivistic science of law. In his *Introduction* to the English translation of *Elementorum Jurisprudentiae*

Universalis, Hans Wehberg (1922: xiv) claimed that Grotius and Pufendorf were 'champions of the great thought that in international life one should stand for all and all for one in repelling every injustice'. Pufendorf's idea of a system of universal jurisprudence valid for all nations was 'a daring one' (ibid.: xxii). Aure (2010: 135) argues that there is a growing understanding among jurists of international law that the law of nations needs a stronger philosophical basis and that for this reason it would be helpful to refresh our knowledge of Pufendorf and his theories of law. With his integrated theory of natural and international law Pufendorf became famous all over Europe and in the New World. A first approach to a discussion about the place of Pufendorf's natural law works in the history of natural law can be found in Simone Zurbuchen (1998: 413–428). She claims that it depends to a large extent on the perspective of interpretation. 'Whereas historians of ideas who consider him as an ancestor of the moral philosophy of the Enlightenment focus on the "modern" elements of his thought, contextualist historians such as Döring accentuate his indebtedness to the past.'

Horst Dreitzel, (1995) discusses tolerance and the freedom of opinion and expression in the German Empire between the Peace of Augsburg in 1555 and the beginning of the Enlightenment a century and a half later. Here he describes Pufendorf's position within the context of the crisis of the confessionals' theory of the state at the end of the seventeenth century. An overview of theories of toleration and freedom of conscience leads him to the conclusion that Pufendorf's theory marks the transition to the Enlightenment. According to Dreitzel, he belongs to the founders of a modern tolerant state, because he separated the political function of religion from revealed religion.

The authors of a history of Lund University, Carl Fehrman, Håkan Westling and Gøran Blomquist (2004), also discuss his influence and conclude: 'Through his secularized view on society and the judicial system Pufendorfs achievements points forward towards the Enlightenment in the 18th century'.

Samuel Pufendorf's academic career, his research and literary production, his teaching of natural law, and his service to three enlightened courts, made him not only a champion of the Enlightenment but a true European.

Notes

1 See also James Tully (1991: xiv–xv) in an article called *Locke* in J.H. Burns (ed.) (1991).

2 Ludvig Holberg's first book, *Introduksjon Til de fornemste Europæiske Rigers Historier* (An introduction to the illustrious European nations' history) was published in Copenhagen in 1711.

3 The Monarchomachs were originally French Huguenots who opposed absolute monarchy at the end of the sixteenth century. Later meaning 'those who fight against monarchs'.

4 Seidler (2013) argues that Pufendorf's account is disputed.

5 *Poemata Collects* published in Leyden 1610 and reprinted many times.

6 Grotius hid in an empty basket, which his wife had used to bring him books, and was carried out.

7 First Chief Minister to the French King Louis XIII.
8 Conelia Ridderikhoff (1995: 169).
9 *De Jure Belli ac Pacis* has been translated into many languages, among them Dutch, English, French, Italian and Russian, and published in numerous editions, which can be found in private and public libraries all around the world.
10 Prolegomena to his *De Jure Belli ac Pacis.*
11 Seidler (1990: 17–18) mentions some authors who question this statement but he himself supports it.
12 Veit Ludwig von Seckendorff (1626–1692), German statesman and scholar, and Gottfried Wilhelm Leibniz.
13 Prolegomena, pp. 6–8. The term 'sociableness' is taken from the Stoic, Prolegomena, p. 6.
14 *Politica Methodice Digesta, Atque Exemplis Sacris et Profanis Illustrata* (Politics methodically digested, set forth and illustrated with sacred and profane examples), edited by Frederick Smith Carney, Liberty Fund, Indianapolis, 1995.
15 *Philosophical Rudiments Concerning Government and Society* ch. I, sec. 12.
16 An eclectic here means a person who selectively adopts ideas from different sources and uses them in his development of new theories. The pejorative ring the term has had in philosophy since the German philosopher Georg Wilhelm Friedrich Hegel, suggesting a lack of originality and inability to integrate the selected elements into a coherent whole, does not apply here.
17 Justitus Lipsius lived in the Spanish-ruled Southern Netherlands (Belgium). He was the archetype of a political Humanist. With philology as an aid he tried, based on Stoic philology and ancient writings of history, to collect cleverness and an ideal of statesmanship that could be used in his time. For him the time of the Roman emperors, with their organizational skills, fighting power, statesmanship, and military leadership was the closest to his ideal. Many of his contributions were to create and to consolidate ideals. Roman and Stoic virtues can be summarized under two main groups: virtues and prudence. These he wanted to teach the princes and statesman of his time.
18 Uwe Wesel, professor of civil law and history of law at The Free University Berlin. *Die Zeit*, no. 49, 27 November 2008.
19 New research into the connection and relation between Grotius, Hobbes and Pufendorf has lately put more emphasis on Pufendorf's dependence on Hobbes. See for example Fiammetta Palladini, *Samuel Pufendorf – Discepolo di Hobbes. Per una Reinter-pretazione del giusnaturalismo moderno*, Il Mulino, Bologna, 1990. A review of this book can be found in Klaus Luig, *Zeitschrift für Historische Forschung*, Heft 3, Duncker & Humbolt, Berlin, 1993. Kari Saastamiinen (1995:79) examines in some detail the relation between Pufendorf and Grotius and Hobbes. Furthermore, he claims that there is a crucial difference between the social inclination on which Grotius founded his theory and the one Pufendorf speaks of in his *Elementorum Jurisprudentiae Universalis.* The author also tries to vindicate the opinion that Pufendorf's natural law is intimately connected to his Lutheran background.
20 *Elementorum Jurisprudentiae Universalis.* Definition XIII § 24. *De Jure Naturae et Gentium* II.3.23.
21 Samuel Rachel was professor of natural law at the University of Kiel. His *On the Law of Nature and Nations* from 1676 is an early imitation of Pufendorf. He is considered to be one of the most important predecessors of the idea of a positive law of nations. See Curt Rühland (1925), 'Samuel Rachel, der Bahnbrecher des völkerrechtlichen Positivismus', *Niemeyers Zeitschrift für Internationales Recht* 34.

Part III

Doctrines of Political Economy

Only a few elements of political economy can be found in Hugo Grotius' great natural law work *De Jure Belli ac Pacis*. Samuel Pufendorf radically expanded these elements in his three important natural law works. These natural law works encompass what today is understood as ethics, jurisprudence, society, and political economy. Although these subjects are integrated into a totality, we find his doctrines of political economy in distinct parts of his works. When appraising Pufendorf's contribution to political economy we should keep in mind that he was an eclectic who collected, evaluated, expanded and amalgamated the contributions of his predecessors, from the Greek and Romans until the present day's writers, into a comprehensive state of the art. In the next chapters, using mainly the 1688 edition of his main work, his doctrines will be treated in this order: method of analysis, theory of human behaviour, private property and the four-stage theory, theories of value and money, foundation of states and councils, and finally division of state powers and principles of taxation.

6 Method of Analysis

During Pufendorf's time, it was important for authors of philosophical texts to clarify the method that would be used in the analysis. In his book about Pufendorf's natural law Hans Welzel (1958: 13–14) points out, there were two main directions running side by side, soon intimately intertwined in achievements and successes of the ingenious scientists, Galileo Galilei, Sir Isaac Newton (1643–1726) and René Descartes.

One branch or direction was the empirical: it started from experience and tried to gain through induction new knowledge. This branch had at its disposal the right to watch and to do experiments. The other branch was the rationalistic: it wanted to build on fundamental, direct, and evident principles, and from these deduce the exceptional features of the object. This branch used strict mathematical deduction. Welzel notes that both branches are united in Galileo's resolutive and compositive method and in Descartes's analysis and synthesis. In his *The Political Theory of Possessive Individualism* Crawford B. MacPherson (1962: 30) claims that:

> the resolutive-compositive method which he [Hobbes] so admired in Galileo and which he took over, was to resolve existing society into its simplest elements and then recompose those elements into a logical whole. The resolving, therefore, was of existing society into existing individuals, and then in turn into the primary elements of their motion. Hobbes does not take us through the resolutive part of his thought, but starts us with the result of that and takes us through only the compositive part.

Furthermore, this dualism is also revealed in Pufendorf. He knew two types of principles: rational and experience-based. The first he called axioms, the second observations. Truth, certainty and necessity flow from axioms out of reason itself, without perceptions from particular appearances, or through spiritual display. The certainty from observations produces itself from comparisons, and the perception steadies itself in accordance with appearances. In harmony with the support of Descartes, Welzel (1958) claims that the features of science could be found solely from fundamental principles.

Pufendorf had ambitions to create a scientific theory of morality and society. He would therefore also like to find for natural law an important proposition, from which all features of knowledge and all natural regulations could be produced clearly and plainly. He had a powerful will to undertake a systematic analysis and create the whole natural law in clear logic from a sole principle. This fundamental principle of natural law is, according to Pufendorf, not an immediate reasonable axiom or a presupposed observation from experience and surveillance. The doctrine of natural law as a method, therefore does not proceed from deductive mathematics, but rather in the first instance from the experience-based natural science. Pufendorf clearly tied it to Galileo's analytic-synthetic method (from appearances to causes of those effects and from causes to appearances) and from him to the highly respected Descartes.

The Method used in *Elementorum Jurisprudentiae Universalis*

The methodology Pufendorf claims to use in his *Elementorum Jurisprudentiae Universalis* is the reformed Euclidean Aristotelian geometrical method, taught to him by Professor Eberhard Weigel in Jena. He claimed that this method was universally applicable and should not only be used in the theoretical disciplines of mathematics, physics and metaphysics. This method could also be serviceable in formulating ethical standards for human actions.

Based on reason, a man, who is about to set forth some body of doctrine at the outset must explain precisely what is meant by the subject matter, then he must search for fixed principles from which necessarily true declarations concerning the subject matter may be deduced, and finally every body of doctrine ought to be complete in three parts.

The first is taken up with a theoretical analysis concerning human behaviour, followed by a series of definitions derived from the analysis of human behaviour. Twenty-one definitions in all are found in the first book. In the second part, the definitions from part one is used to identify issues whose resolution can be used to form a foundation for principles of morality. He sets forth two principles or axioms. The first determines which human actions can be approved and which cannot. The second ascertains how a party in possession of power can bind those subjected to it. In the third, he derives from these principles or axioms (at least that is what he claims) five observations. These observations or conclusions are about the nature of morality and political life. The axioms and observations are contained in the second book. If it appears necessary, a fourth part can be added. It will then include the topics in which certainty does not clearly appear.

However, it is not clear how his exposition uses the geometric method. His definitions included a presentation of theories, and it is hard to see how these observations are deduced from his definitions and axioms. It can therefore be questioned how suited this method is for the treatment of these subjects. Pufendorf himself seems to be aware of this dilemma since he abandons this approach in his later works.

The Method used in *De Jure Naturae et Gentium*

Upon the publication of his *Elementorum*, supporters as well as sceptics and adversaries, urged Pufendorf to expand on the topics he had presented and the arguments he so eminently had expounded. In response, he started on such an undertaking, when he took up his position in Heidelberg in 1661.

During his work with the revision and extension of his first natural law work he rejected the reformed geometrical approach that he had previously used. In his article 'Pufendorf's Moral and Political Philosophy', Michael Seidler (2013) claims that Pufendorf did this initially in reaction to criticism by two professors: Hermann Conring (1601–1681), who was Professor of History of Law and Public Law at the University of Helmstedt, and Johann Heinrich Boecler (1611–1672), who was Professor of History and Constitutional Law at the University of Strasbourg. They both urged him to include a consideration of other writers, particularly the ancients. In his work Pufendorf now employed an 'eclectic' method, in which he defended man's ability to understand reality and draw conclusions based on observations from the reality of life. This method still involved rational analysis and argumentation. His objective remained the same and his analysis was based on systematic understanding and demonstrative certainty of his subjects, which he also developed from his study of history and contemporary events.

He therefore in what became his major natural law work *De Jure Naturae et Gentium* substantiated his opinions, his arguments, and the truths he claims to have discovered by numerous quotations, just as Grotius and others of his predecessors had done. These important quotations he found in the Bible, the Koran, the Roman *Corpus Juris Canonici*, and not least in the writings of the ancient Greek and Roman philosophers and jurists. He has a few quotations from the philosophers of the Middle Ages but numerous quotations from philosophers, jurists and historians of the fifteenth and sixteenth centuries. In the *Index of Authors Cited*, in the 1688 edition, 400 names are found. These Pufendorf frequently quotes. When he discusses particular issues, or argues for a certain opinion he uses the views of famous scholars in support of and to give weight to his own views. The quasi-mathematical format used in his first work therefore disappeared, Stephen Buckle (1991: 55). However, Leonard Krieger (1965: 55) in his *Policy of Discretion* claims that Pufendorf at this stage does not totally reject the geometric method he used before, but that his approach now is 'less explicit and less intrusive'.

In his preface, Pufendorf draws our particular attention to three contemporary authors, whom he thinks had contributed most to natural law: Grotius, Hobbes and Selden. First, he starts praising Grotius, who was the first to call his generation to the study of natural law. He was also so grounded in its theories that in a large part of the field he has left others 'nothing further than the task of gleaning after him' (Preface vi). However, although Pufendorf cherished the fame of Grotius, he states that it must be acknowledged that even Grotius 'has entirely omitted not a few matters, some he has accorded but a passing touch, and introduced some other matters, which prove that after all even he was only a man'. Second, in the same manner, he emphasized that Hobbes in his work on civil government produced a great deal of the highest value, 'and no one who understands such matters would deny that he has so thoroughly explored the structure of human and civil society, that few before his time can in this field be compared to him' (Preface: vi). Moreover, even where he goes astray, he still causes a reader to think about matters, which in all probability would otherwise never have occurred to him. Third, he contends that Selden might have held a position, second to none, if he had applied his law of nature to all mankind and not just to the Hebrews. It should be stressed that Grotius and Hobbes are fundamental to Pufendorf's natural law work. He uses their work extensively to build his own natural law theories of jurisprudence, ethics, government and political economy.

However, it should be stressed that they were not his only sources. In support of his views, he admits that he prefers to cite the authors of antiquity, in particular the Greeks and the Romans to witness his theses. 'To add to them by calling in a cloud of more recent writers seemed superfluous' (Preface: vii). Half of the 400 authors cited belong to this era. Nevertheless, he also quotes the moderns. There are more than 180 authors from the fourteenth, fifteenth and sixteenth centuries. Although there was a general attitude, of the time that Protestant authors should not cite Catholic authors and vice versa, this is not the case for Pufendorf. The *Index* encompasses 43 French, 30 Italian, 10 Spanish and 5 Portuguese authors, all from Catholic countries. Of the predominantly Protestant countries, the *Index* contains 33 German, 24 Dutch and 14 English authors.

Pufendorf says that he has excluded from his work followers of 'the Roman sect', that is, authors closely linked to the Catholic clergy. The reason being that to know one of them 'is to know them all – so they all devote futile labour to utter trifles – with the result, however, that there is scarcely any question on which they do not break up into factions' (Preface: viii).

He goes on to explain that the hidden reason for this condition is that these men are not directed by reason but by the authority of priests, that is their adherence to the Scholastic method and juristic clericalism. Furthermore, they did not recognize the principle of human sociability as a sufficient basis for natural law. He used strong words and called them representatives of the kingdom of darkness. 'Nay, he makes poor use of his time, yokes foxes to the plough and milks he goats, who put himself out to list their views on one side or the other and reconcile them with sound reason' (Preface: ix). Despite these strong statements, it is apparent from Pufendorf's writings that he was familiar with the works of writers of the Dominican and Jesuit orders who held academic positions. He even quotes a few of these writers. For example, Professor Francisco Vitoria (1483–1546),[1] Professor François Suarez and Professor Diego de Covarruvias (1512–1577), all three from the School of Salamanca.[2]

Given these considerations Pufendorf claims that he has arranged all his material in an order, which appeared most suitable, and he has tried to establish all his contentions with strong and clear reasons, in so far as this was possible. Furthermore, he tried to avoid those errors that writers of repute before his time had made. In this context, he tells us that we all should bear in mind the words of the Roman rhetorician Quintilian (AD 35–100):

> If men had been inclined to think that no one could surpass the man who had hitherto been the best, those who are now accounted best would never have distinguished themselves. And although there is no hope of excelling, it is yet a great honour to follow closely behind.
>
> (Preface: vii)

In his exposition Pufendorf has incorporated references from almost every field of literature. The translators into English of Pufendorf's 1688 edition, Charles H. Oldfather and William A. Oldfather (1931: 63a), made the observation that Pufendorf often took considerable liberties with the text of the authors he referred to in his many quotations. He did this by omitting words and phrases at will and sometimes whole sentences as well as changing the word order. However, they added that he apparently was 'most scrupulous in not modifying the actual views expressed by his authorities'.

The Social Life of Man

Pufendorf stresses that he has made the social life of man the foundation for his work on natural law, the reason being that he has found no other principle, which all men could accept, without violation of their natural condition. Furthermore, he claims that it is also obvious, that since the Creator made man a social being, the nature of man is the norm and foundation of that law, which must be followed in any society. This is so whether it is universal or particular. His system of natural law is valid for all human beings, with due respect to whatever belief men might hold on the matters of religion (Preface: ix).

He starts by pointing out that the task of prime philosophy is to give the most comprehensive definition of things and to divide them appropriately into distinct classes. In addition, it should give the general nature and condition of every kind of thing. Furthermore, he argues that his predecessors have treated the classification of natural things sufficiently, but they have not been as much concerned with moral entities 'as the dignity of these requires'. It is, however, very important that the nature of things should be known by man, since man has been given the power to produce them and since man's life is 'deeply penetrated by their influence' (I.i.1: 3).

Thereafter he presents the assumptions and method that his system builds on, including a systematic explanation of numerous legal conceptions applying to moral beings: their conditions, qualities and actions. Furthermore, he claims to prove that by starting from the divine destiny of man as a spiritual and social being and following the route of strictly logical deduction, we may arrive at results as safe as those in the natural sciences physics and chemistry. Man has been given the distinctive light of intelligence, which he can use to understand things more accurately. He can compare them with one another, judge the unknown with the known and he can decide how things relate to each other. So man is free from confining his actions to one mode. He can even exert, suspend or moderate his actions. Furthermore, man 'has been granted the power to invent or apply certain aids to each faculty, whereby it is signally assisted and directed in its functioning' (I.i.2: 4).

The Certainty of Moral Science

Pufendorf then goes on to investigate the degree of certainty of the moral sciences as contradistinguished from that of mathematical sciences. Following his teacher Professor Weigel, he attempts to prove this by starting from the divine destiny of man as a spiritual and social being and then following the route of strictly logical deduction. He contends that for long most scholars have held that moral science, that is natural law, which included ethics, law, society and political economy, lacks the certainty, which characterize other knowledge based sciences, and especially mathematics. The reason being that moral science, according to these scholars, had no place for demonstration, which is the act of proving by reasoning or display of evidence. From such a demonstration alone is derived knowledge that is pure and free from fear of error. This knowledge rests on probability alone.

Pufendorf argues that this has created an immense injury to the noblest of sciences and to the life of man. It has caused scholars to investigate with mistrust shallowness in sciences that they believed rested 'on so slippery foundation'. Others that neglected the moral sciences were given the plausible excuse that they were not founded on supporting evidence and therefore could only be treated in 'a rough and ready fashion'. Pufendorf claims that this error to a large extent was 'fostered by the authority of Aristotle' (I.ii.1: 22).

From this fact, he goes on to discuss the nature of demonstration. Demonstration is to deduce by a syllogism, which can be understood by an argument in which a conclusion follows from several premises. Science is that 'certain and pure knowledge', which we seek by means of demonstration, that is, 'a knowledge, in every way and at all times constant and free of error' (I.ii.3:23). Moral science manifests this certainty because:

> that knowledge, which considers what is upright and what base in human actions … rests entirely upon grounds so secure, that from it can be deduced genuine demonstrations which are capable of producing solid science. So certainly can its conclusions be derived from distinct principles that no further ground is left for doubt.
>
> (I.ii.4: 25)

Notes

1 Pufendorf argues against what he claims is Vitoria's view in his *Relectiones de Indies*, which was published in Lyons in 1577, that: 'The law of nations allows every man to carry on trade in the provinces of others, by importing merchandise which they lack and exporting gold and silver, as well as other merchandise, in which they abound' (III.iii.12: 370). According to Pufendorf, no one could force trade on another country. Marten van Gelderen (1994) claims that natural law had convinced Vitoria that there existed a human society where Christians, Muslims and also Indians were equal members. Vitoria was, according to Van Gelderen, in strong opposition to the donation (partitioning of America) by Pope Alexander VI in 1493, when he in his *Political writings* from 1534 wrote; 'no business shocks me or embarrasses me more than the corrupt profits and affairs of the Indies. Their very mention freezes the blood in my veins' (Gelderen 1994: 17).

2 The name was introduced by Marjorie Grice-Hutchinson (1952) in her book *The School of Salamanca*. Pufendorf must have been introduced to the Salamanca School during his stay at the University of Leiden.

7 Theory of Human Behaviour

The foundation of Pufendorf's treatment of all his natural law themes, including political economy, is his theory of human behaviour that is the character of man and what motivates human activity. An account of his fundamental doctrines concerning human behaviour is found in all his natural law books. In *De Jure Naturae et Gentium* it is treated in the first two books.

Man's Distinctive Light of Intelligence

Pufendorf starts by pointing out that the task of prime philosophy is to give the most comprehensive definition of things, and to divide them appropriately into distinct classes. In addition, it should give the general nature and condition of every kind of thing. Furthermore, he argues that while his predecessors have treated the classification of natural things sufficiently, they have not been as much concerned with moral entities 'as the dignity of these requires'. It is, however, very important that the nature of things should be known by man, since man has been given the power to understand them and since man's life is 'deeply penetrated by their influence' (I.i.1: 3).

Man is a moral being, who has been given not 'merely beauty and adaptability of body, but also the distinctive light of intelligence' by the Great and Good Creator. This intelligence can be used by man to understand things more accurately. He can compare these things with one another, judge the unknown with the known and decide how things relate to each other. So man's actions are not confined to one mode. He can even exert, suspend, or moderate his actions. Furthermore, man has also been granted the power to invent certain aids, or to apply certain aids to each faculty he has, whereby they will be improved. It is for us to observe how a specific kind of attribute has been given to things, and their natural motions, from which certain priority in the actions of man has arisen. These attributes Pufendorf calls moral entities, because by them the morals and actions of men are judged and tempered 'so they may attain a character and appearance different from the rude simplicity of dumb animals' (I.i.2: 5).

Therefore, humans seem able to define moral ideas and to direct or temper their freedom and voluntary acts and thereby 'secure a certain orderliness and decorum in civilized life'. Furthermore, Pufendorf stresses that since man has been endowed with intellect he is able 'by means of reflection and comparison of one thing with another, to form concepts, which are suitable to be the guides of a consistent faculty' (I.i.3: 5).

Since moral beings have been instituted to bring order into the lives of men, they should also adopt a set standard in their relations toward one another in determining their actions (I.i.5: 6).

The very being of man is a state from which certain obligations and certain rights arise. Pufendorf contends that it will not be amiss at this point to consider when that state begins in individual men. He claims that the fulfilment of obligations 'requires of man a knowledge of himself and of that which he is doing'. From this it follows that man must know how to regulate his actions to some norm and how to distinguish these norms from one another (I.i.7: 8).

The Understanding of Man

Pufendorf claims that man's chief task is:

> concerned with the demonstration of the right or the wrong, the good or the evil, the just or the unjust in human actions, all the principles and the affections of these actions will first have to be considered, and then why they are understood to be connected morally by imputation with man.
>
> (I.iii.1: 38)

The dignity of man outshines that of beasts, since he has been endowed with a most exalted soul, and with it a highly developed understanding.

This understanding, which the soul of man carries like a light, gives man the ability to examine and judge things and actions and therefore to embrace or reject them. It has two qualities which man uses in his voluntary actions. By the first quality an object is displaced to the will, as if in a mirror, and it can be seen, at first glance, to be agreeable or not, good or ill. By the other the reasons for good or ill should be weighted and compared before a judgement is finally passed, as well as what should be done, why it should be done and when it should be done. Pufendorf underlines that the initiative for any voluntary action, without exception, proceeds from man's understanding. He also points out that there is no desire for an unknown object, but that the knowledge preceding a voluntary act is not always distinct, since even a confused knowledge can be sufficient to make the will act. Therefore, a desire often arises in man to try out something unknown.

It is within man's power to give his undivided attention to the object he considers and by careful thought to balance well 'the reasons for good and ill' and indeed not stop with a mere superficial examination, but to penetrate 'into the very innermost being of the matter' (I.iii.2: 39).

An Internal Director – Freedom of the Will

Pufendorf contends that the wise Creator wished to make man an animal to be governed by law. He therefore in his soul implanted a will. This will act as an *internal director* of his actions (I.iv.52).[1] Therefore, when objects were proposed and understood the internal director made it possible for a man to move himself to them by an inherent principle. He would then be able to choose what seems to him the most fitting, 'as well as turn from those which did not seem agreeable to him'. This will work in human actions through two capacities. Through one, it works spontaneously, and through the other, it works freely. To spontaneity, man attributes certain acts or motions. Some of these are internal and some are external. The internal are those which are produced immediately by the will and are received back by the will. Acts are termed *external* if they are turned over for execution by other human faculties, as these are moved by the will.

Pufendorf claims that man calls *freedom* a faculty of the will. With this freedom, a man is able to choose one, or some, and to reject the rest if he has many objects to choose from. If only one object is presented to him, he can admit or not admit it, or do or not do it. He also claims that liberty is supposed to add to spontaneity. 'Liberty also adds a free determination, so that the will by an internal impulse may choose here and now either of its acts, this is, to will or refuse' (I.iv.2: 53).

However, there are many factors that will influence man's decisions, and Pufendorf discusses many of these. He makes it clear that it belongs to the nature of the will always to seek what is inherently good and to avoid what is inherently evil. Nevertheless, lack of information might, for example, sometimes lead men 'to reject what should have been desired, while they desire what should have been shunned' (I.iv.4: 57). Decisions made by the will might also be:

> affected by the temperature of the humours of the body, arising from the race to which a man belongs, his age, food, health, manner of life and other causes, by the form of the organs which the mind uses in performing its functions, and similar considerations.
>
> (I.iv.5: 58)

The will is also in no slight degree impelled to certain action by those motions of the mind, which are called passions and these might 'greatly becloud the judgement of the mind' (I.iv.7:60). Moreover, the will might be powerfully enticed to irrational behaviour 'by drunkenness, caused usually from a drink, or fumes of different kinds, or also by opium' (I.iv.8:61). It should also be observed 'that sometimes in the face of most grave ills, and such as are held to exceed the ordinary strength of man's mind, the will is under so strong a compulsion that it agrees to undertake something from which it would shrink in perfect horror were it not under such necessity' (I.iv.9: 63). Referring to

Aristotle, Pufendorf contends that fair-minded men accept such actions of this nature, which would have merited reproval, without such a cause, if they are undertaken under the pressure of such a necessity, and the man who executed such a deed is adjudged innocent.

Man Should Be Governed by Law

Pufendorf sets forth to discuss the contradiction which seems to exist between man's freedom of will and his being bound by right and law. He contends that it does not suit the nature of man to live without laws and he brings up the question 'whether it would accord with man to pass his life without any law'. From the answer to this question, it will be clear why the great Creator did not grant man liberty to do everything entirely as he pleases without 'any restraint of right, rule, or necessity' (II.i.1: 145). In answering this question, it seems best to show 'first of all, that an unlimited liberty would be disadvantageous and prejudicial to the nature of man, and that, therefore, it is conducive to his welfare for him to be, as he is, constrained by laws' (II.i.2: 145). At the same time, it will also be clear how far man should be free from the curb of constraint.

The Dignity of Man's Nature

The reason why the Creator was unwilling to endow man with a lawless liberty, and why such a liberty would be utterly inappropriate to him is drawn from what became Pufendorf's revolutionary principle of the natural condition of human nature, the Dignity of Man's Nature:

> The dignity of man's nature, and that excellence of his in which he surpasses other creatures, required that his actions should be made to conform to a definite rule, without which there can be no recognition of order, seemliness, or beauty. And so man has that supreme dignity, the possession of an immortal soul, furnished with the light of intellect and the faculty of judgement and choice, and most highly endowed for many an art.
>
> (II.i.5: 148)

For this reason, Pufendorf calls man a 'creature above all others precious and endowed with lofty reason fitted to rule over the lower animals'. He also quotes the third-century Roman grammarian and compiler, Gaius Julius Solinus, who calls man an animal 'which the nature of things has set over all other animals by virtue of his passing judgement upon sense perceptions and his capacity for reason' (ibid.).

The Power of Man's Soul

Man's soul is chiefly concerned with things relating to the service of God, and to social and civil life. It has the power to proceed from known to unknown principles, and to decide what is suitable, and what is not. Furthermore, it can form universal ideas through induction; it can devise signs by which the ideas of the mind can be imparted to others. It can understand numbers, weights and measures, and it can compare them. It can also understand and observe their order and meaning, to excite, repress, or allay affections. Man's soul can also remember a multitude of things, recall them, as it were, for the eye to gaze upon, to turn its sight upon itself and to recollect its own dictates and compare them with its actions, from which recollection and comparison and the force of conscience come. Pufendorf concludes that there would be little or no use for all such faculties in a lawless, brutal and unsociable life. In support of this view, he refers to the Bishop Richard Cumberland, and the first-century Roman astronomer Marcus Manilius (ibid.: 149).

However, there is also another reason why man should not be allowed so great a licence as the beast. 'That was his greater proneness to evil' (II.i.6: 149). Pufendorf points out that no one will be surprised by this if he has probed to the depths of nature and pursuits of men. Beasts are excited by their appetite and lust. The latter stirs them only at certain seasons and only for the procreation of their kind. The same is true with animal's hunger; when it is satisfied 'no further cares disturb them' (II.i.6: 150). In addition, no animal has a need for covering itself. Man's desire, on the other hand, is not stirred only in certain seasons and 'man has made the tenderness of his body an occasion to parade his vanity and pride'. He also has a great many affections and desires which are unknown to beasts. 'A craving for luxuries, ambitions, honours, and the desire to surpass others, envy, jealousy, rivalries of wit, superstition, anxiety about the future, curiosity, all these continually trouble his mind, none of which touch the senses of brutes' (ibid.). If we therefore consider the nature of the contentions and wars that are waged continually among men, we will realize that most of them are undertaken because of wants that are unknown to beasts. Pufendorf asks what would have been the future of man had no right been established to compose them. He answers:

> You would see a pack of wolves, lions, or dogs fighting among one another to death. Every man, indeed, would have been a lion, a wolf, or a dog to his neighbour and something even worse than these, for there is no animal that can and does more injure man than man himself.
>
> (Ibid.)

He concludes with a question: 'And since men cause so many injuries to each other even now, when law and punishment hang over them, what would future hold, if there were no control over anything, if no direction from within curbed the desires of man?' (ibid.). The weakness of man made it necessary that he should not live without law. Only a few days after birth an animal will be sufficiently developed enough to take care of its own maintenance. A human being, on the other hand, is at birth unfit to take care of himself and this weakness will last for a long time after his birth.

It is therefore clear that human beings owe it to the intercourse and relations with other men that they do not have an existence more miserable than other living beings. The saying 'It is not good for man to be alone' is applicable to all men in general. Then again a society of men cannot be constituted nor maintained in a peaceful and firm state without law. 'And so if man was to be prevented from being the most degraded and miserable of all creatures, it was not fitting that he should live without law' (ibid.: 152–153).

Consequently, Pufendorf concludes that it is apparent that the term, 'the natural liberty of man' is not perceived merely as an abstract idea. It 'should under all circumstances be understood as something conditioned by certain restraint of sound reason and natural law' (ibid.: 153).

The Natural State of Man

Pufendorf claims that the natural state of man is that condition for which man is understood to be constituted by the mere fact of his birth. This condition is understood to include not only the different forms and general culture of the life of man, but especially civil societies at the formation of which a suitable order was introduced into humankind's existence (I.ii.1: 154). He continues:

> To get a more distinct idea of this state we will consider it in itself, especially as to what advantages and rights accompany it; that is, what would have been the condition of individual men had mankind discovered no civilization and introduced no arts or commonwealths; and second in relation to other men, whether it bears a resemblance to peace or to war; that is whether men who live in a state of mutual natural liberty, wherein no man is subject to another, and they have no common master, should be considered foes or friends.
>
> (Ibid.)

For us to form some conception of this natural state we must imagine man as dropped from somewhere into this world and left entirely to his own resources with no help from his fellows after birth nor aided by any special attention from God. Pufendorf claims that such a condition must be regarded as miserable. To support this claim he quotes several Greek and Roman writers who give a 'a wretched picture of the primitive state of man' (ibid.).

Now the right attendant in this natural state of man can be easily imagined. First, men will use every means to preserve their body and life and to avert everything that would destroy them. Men in a natural state may use and enjoy everything that is open to them, and may secure and do everything that will lead to their preservation if no injury is done to the right of others. Second, from this fact those who enjoy this state are subject to no man's orders. They may use their own judgement and occasion, provided of course that it is framed on natural law, just as they use their own strength, to serve their own defence and preservation.

The state of nature has therefore been described as a natural liberty, since every man is understood to be under his own right and power and not subject to the power of any other man. So every individual is considered equal to every other individual, since neither is the subject of the other (I.ii.3: 158).

A purely natural state is the condition of man, when all things that have been added by human institutions have been separated from it. However, nature never intended man to spend his days in such a state (I.ii.4: 164).

The Natural State of Man is Peace

Pufendorf brings up for discussion a question of great importance. Does a natural state, as it concerns other men, bear the character of war or peace? Or what amounts to the same thing: Should those who live in a natural state, that is, those who have no common master and neither obey or command one another, be considered mutual enemies or peaceable people and friends? In this connection, he considers and discusses Hobbes opinion, 'where he calls a purely natural state one of war, not a single war, but one of all men against all other men' (I.ii.5: 165).

Pufendorf observes that when we discuss the state of man we are not discussing the state of some animal, which is directed only by its senses, but rather 'one whose chief adornment and master of the other faculties is reason' (II.ii.9: 172). This reason, in a state of nature, has a common and abiding uniform standard of judgement. This standard offers a free and distinct service in pointing out general rules for living and the law of nature. Furthermore, if any man is to adequately define a state of nature, he should include the proper use of that reason and should use it in the operation of his other faculties. The use of that reason will show man that Hobbes's view of a war of all men against all others is wrong. Pufendorf uses:

> a twofold principle, of which one side is wholly concerned with present considerations, while the other centers upon future and not present concerns, when by craving of the former he sees himself driven into dangers, perplexities, and disgrace, but led by the latter into safety and respect, surely it is not difficult for him to conclude that his Creator's wish is for him to accept the guidance of the latter and not the former.
>
> (Ibid.)

The natural state of men is not one of war, but of peace. It is a peace founded on the following laws:

> A man shall not harm one who is not injuring him; he shall allow everyone to enjoy his own possessions; he shall faithfully perform whatever has been agreed upon; and he shall willingly advance the interest of other, so far as he is not bound by more pressing obligations.
>
> (Ibid.)

Pufendorf claims that since a natural state assumes the use of reason, any obligation, which reason points out, cannot and must not be separated from it, since every man is able to appreciate that it is to his own advantage to conduct himself in such a way that he can profit from a friendly attitude of men rather than to incur their anger. Finally, he claims that man can easily judge, from the similarity of nature, that other men feel the same. To those who are not entirely convinced by what he has written, Pufendorf advises them to read Richard Cumberland's *De Legibus* Naturae (II.ii.9: 173).

The True Basis for the Law of Nature

Pufendorf contends that most men agree on the point that the law of nature should be deduced from reason by man himself, and should flow from that source. To make his point he quotes the first-century Greek rhetorician Dio Chrysostom. 'Since you have a mind, you may know of yourself what you should do and how' (II.iii.13: 201). However, from this he does not maintain that the general principles of the law of nature came into and are imprinted upon the minds of men at their birth 'as distinct and clear rules which can be formulated by man without further investigation or thought as soon as he acquires the power of speech' (ibid.). Anyone who undertakes an examination of the different steps of children as they gradually advance from the ignorance of infancy would recognize that this is a mere fancy. 'Nor should it be considered unimportant that the Sacred Scriptures regularly describe infancy as a state of ignorance of right and wrong' (ibid.: 202).

According to Pufendorf, children and the uneducated distinguish right from wrong with ease. However, this ease comes from experience that goes back to their earliest days. As soon as they show some use of reason they have seen good deeds approved and rewarded and evil ones reproved and punished. The law of nature is therefore not innate.

Most men do not know or understand the method, 'whereby the commands of the law of nature are demonstrated'. Most learn this law, and observe it, by training or by following the examples of others in society. Daily we can see workmen do many things by imitation or with tools, whose method of use they cannot demonstrate. Such operations can, nevertheless, be based on good reason. 'From this it is clear how the fitness of the reason to work out the law of nature may be measured, and on what basis it can be seceded whether some command proceeds from a sound or a depraved reason' (ibid.: 203).

The dictates of sound reason, Pufendorf claims, are therefore a true principle that is in accordance with the properly observed and examined nature of things. Furthermore, it is deduced by logical sequence from prime and true principles.

To show how easy it is to know what the law of nature commands, Pufendorf quotes several authors, among them Hobbes, who recommended the following rule: 'When anyone questions whether what he plans to do to another will be done in accordance with the law of nature or not, let him imagine himself in the other man's place' (ibid.: 204).

Self-Interest – Man's First Human Attribute

Pufendorf discusses how the true basis for the law of nature is found in the conditions of man. A society cannot exist unless its members have a common feeling, basis or ideology about the proper way to conduct its affairs. This ideology he finds in the fact that man has been endowed with a free will together with the driving forces behind human actions.

The pursuit of self-love or self-interest is man's first human attribute, inclination or driving force.

> In the first place man has this in common with all beings which are conscious of their own existence, that he has the greatest love for himself, tries to protect himself by every possible means, and tries to secure what he thinks will benefit him, and to avoid what may in his opinion injure him.
>
> (II.iii.14: 205)

However, pursuit of self-interest is not only the first human attribute, it is also the strongest. 'And this love of each one for himself is always so strong that any inclination towards any other man yields to it' (ibid.: 205–206). It is true that there are instances when some men seem to cherish others more highly than they do. They rejoice more in their success and they grieve more in their misfortunes than in their own. Here he draws attention to Descartes and his *Les Passions* from 1649, in which the love that good parents bear toward their children is so pure that the parents wish to get nothing from them, they strive for their advantage and they are not fearing even their own lives if they can save them. However, Pufendorf claims that, when for example parents are so greatly affected by the successes of their children, it is principally because they think that it constitutes credit for them to have brought them into the world. This attribute or force of self-interest is so strong that any attachment or devotion to other human beings has to submit to it. Furthermore, Pufendorf rejects the possibility that people can act altruistically.

Pufendorf also refers to the French Huguenot Francis Caron (1600–1673), who in his *Descriptio Japoniae*, published in Amsterdam in 1648, writes that human sacrifices are the present custom among the Japanese.[2] Furthermore, he refers to the Greek historian Diodorus who in the first century BC describes similar customs among the Ethiopians. Nevertheless, to Pufendorf the truth is that such people hold the boasting of friendship and love and the glory they derived from it above all other things, and therefore they feel that 'they are well purchased even at the cost of life itself'. He concludes that without doubt 'in whatever a man does for another, he never forgets himself'.

Self-interest is the strongest human attribute 'because man is so framed that he thinks of his own advantage before the welfare of others for the reason that it is his nature to think of his own life before the life of others. Another reason is that it is no one's business so much as my own to look out for myself' (ibid.: 207).

Sociability – Man's Second Human Attribute

In addition to this self-interest and self-love, and man's desire to preserve himself by any and all means, Pufendorf contends that it can be observed in the character of man 'the greatest weakness and native helplessness' (ibid.: 207). If one could have imagined a man deprived of any assistance from other men in the world he would think of the life given to him as a punishment. 'It is also evident that no greater help and comfort, after that granted man by God, comes to him than that from his fellow-creatures' (ibid.). On the one hand, individuals need the assistance of the united efforts of other men to live well and comfortable because their own strength and time would fail to give them many useful and necessary things. On the other hand, individuals can contribute many things to others, of which they have no need or use themselves. It is therefore clear that men are born to cooperate with other men. To support this view Pufendorf quotes the Roman philosopher Seneca the Younger: 'Man was born for mutual assistance' and the Roman Emperor Marcus Aurelius (121–180): 'For we have come into being for co-operation' (ibid.).

Pufendorf states that it is easy to find the basis of natural law because man has an attribute, inclination or driving force other' than self-interest that distinguishes him from other animals. It is quite clear that man is unable to exist 'without the help of his fellow-creatures.' Man is also fitted to contribute to the common good. But yet at all times he is 'malicious, petulant, and easily irritated, as well as quick and powerful to do injury'. For such a man to live and enjoy the good things, it is necessary for man to be sociable (II.iii.15: 207). Consequently, it will therefore be a fundamental law of nature that: 'Every man, as so far as in him lies, should cultivate and preserve towards others a sociable attitude, which is peaceful and agreeable at all times to the nature and end of the human race' (ibid.). To drive home this point he quotes the Roman Cicero and the Greek Iamblichus.

It is important to make it clear that Pufendorf does not say that 'man is naturally sociable' but rather that 'man must be sociable'. This is emphasized by John Chipman (2012), who in his article about the existence and optimality of political equilibrium in natural law quotes Fiammetta Palladini (1990): 'being sociable is the ideal to which men must tend, not the natural data from which one starts out', and Norberto Bobbio (1980) who remarked:

> Man's need to live together with others does not derive, in contrast to Grotius, from a natural tendency towards society, but rather … from two objective conditions, self-love and weakness, which cause men to desire to live in society. So explained, life in society appears more as the product of a rational calculation, of an interest, than as an instinct or

appetite, for which Pufendorf must once more be held to be more a follower of Hobbes than of Grotius.[3]

A Social Attitude should be Cultivated

Pufendorf emphasizes that every man should by his life promote and cultivate a social attitude 'so far as in him lies'. He makes it clear that it is not in our power to make all others conduct themselves towards us as they should. However, we have done our duty if we have done what is within our power to move them to be sociable towards us. From this it follows logically that 'since whoever obligates a man to an end obligates him as well to the means without which the end cannot be obtained' (II.iii.208). Pufendorf claims that all things promoting that sociable attitude are understood to be commanded by natural law. All that disturb or destroy this attitude is forbidden by natural law. Furthermore, it is obvious that this way of presenting the law of nature is not only the clearest 'but the majority of scholars recognize that it is also the most fitting and proper' (ibid.). Although he contends that there is no need of piling up a mass of testimony, he still quotes Seneca the Younger, the Roman Plinius Secundus, Marcus Aurelius, and the Greek rhetorician Libanius the Sophist (314–390). The last emphasizes that: 'Nature has appointed man to be a helper to his fellow man and a partner in his life' (II.iii.15: 209).

Pufendorf also adds what he calls other less important reasons for man to be sociable. An example is the fact that nothing is sadder for man than continued solitude. He quotes Cicero who says: 'no one would like to pass his life in solitude even if surrounded with an infinite abundance of pleasures'. Therefore, 'it is easily perceived that we are born for communion and fellowship with man, and for natural association' (ibid.).

Referring again to Bishop Cumberland, Pufendorf emphasizes that when he says that man is a social animal he does not intimate that man should hold his own advantage distinct from others. He should hold the advantage of others as well, and he should not seek his own advancement to the neglect of others, nor should a man 'hope for happiness if he disregards and injures others' (ibid.: 210).

From the social nature of man and from the fact that he was born not for himself alone but for the human race, Pufendorf points out that the English philosopher Francis Bacon (1561–1626) has drawn some excellent corollaries; for example:

> That the active life is to be preferred to the contemplative; that the happiness of man is to be sought in virtue, not in pleasure; that we should not withdraw from active life or separate ourselves from contact with others because of unforeseen events; finally, that we should not retire from public life because of timidity or disinclination to conciliate men.
>
> (Ibid.)

For man to be able to attend his needs, it is necessary to be sociable. Man's needs are radically different from animals and they are insatiable. Man, harbours desires beyond the usual craving for the material needs he has in common with animals: 'man is filled through and through with a great conglomeration of affections and desires unknown to beasts', for example love, lust, honours and powers (II.i.6: 150). Man seeks society with his fellow man for the fulfilment of his own needs and desires. Pufendorf therefore gives an individualistic explanation of how man socializes in society. In his article *The Language of Sociability and Commerce* Istvan Hont (1987: 267), claims that what Pufendorf had in mind was 'precisely what Kant was later to christen man's "unsocial sociability"'.

Man's Duties towards Himself

Pufendorf argues that nature has not commanded us to be sociable to the extent that we neglect ourselves. The sociable attitude is cultivated by men in mutual exchange among many 'of assistance and property'. This cultivation enables men to take care of their own concerns to a greater advantage.

> And even though a man, when he joins himself to any special society, holds before his eyes, first of all, his own advantage, and after that the advantage of comrades since his own cannot be secured without that of all, yet this does not prevent his being obligated so to cultivate his own advantage, that the good of the society be not injured, or harm offered its different members; or at times to hold his own advantage in abeyance and work for the welfare of the society.
>
> (II.iii.18: 214)

Although man has his interest in self-preservation in common with other animals, this interest should be far more refined and of a higher type than those beasts observe. The reason is that he has received far more endowment than they have, and that the duties to which he is bound cannot be fittingly observed, 'unless he quickens his native endowment by education, and renders it fitted to worthy conduct' (II.iv.1: 231). So, as man studies to fulfil the laws of that sociableness he should properly give his first attention to himself. Pufendorf claims that he would then fulfil his duties towards other more satisfactorily.

Nevertheless, this regard for oneself is as difficult as it is necessary and 'not only because men come into the world entirely ignorant of all things'. It is also because man's innate evil desires draw him away from the dictates of right reason. Unless these evil desires are restrained, they will throughout his life produce a flood of evil actions.

All men are constrained to undertake the cultivation of the mind since this is necessary to the complete fulfilment of the duty of man. This cultivation should be done in the following way: First, that his conclusions on matters, concerning his duty should be rightly reached. Second, that his judgement and opinion in matters, which commonly arouses his appetite should be properly formed. Third, the impulses of his mind should be regulated and governed by the rule of right reason (II.iv.2: 232).

The Importance of Education

Pufendorf then presents a knowledgeable discussion of man's duties in the cultivation and development of his mind. Man, should be instructed in a non-dogmatic Christian religion, he should be acquainted with himself, his nature, and his duties and he should know his strength and limitation and how far he could strive for fame, riches and pleasure. It is also the duty of man to govern his passions by reason (II.iv.2–12: 231–248).

Education is necessary for the cultivation of the mind; therefore, this should be of special concern to those 'who have laid upon them the education of others'. The absence of this cultivation or attitude is contrary 'to the duty of man'. Pufendorf argues that not everything, which passes under the title of letters, is of the same nature and should not be considered of the same value. He calls some learning useful, some elegant and curious, and some idle. He divides useful learning into three classes: moral, medical and mathematical sciences.

Moral science is concerned with the cultivation of the mind and the promotion of social life. Medical science is concerned with the health of the body. Mathematical science, which has manifest utility, is concerned with the various arts that contribute very great advantage to the life of man.

Elegant and curious learning is worthy of a free man since it either leads one more deeply into the study of the works of nature, or witnesses to the excellency and ingenuity of the human mind, or preserves the memory of the human race and its accomplishments. To this class belongs the acquaintance with several languages, the higher departments of mathematics, all fields of history, criticism, poetry, oratory and the like. By idle learning is meant not only that which is concerned with false and erroneous matters, but that which troubles itself with the opinions of smooth-speaking or idle men, whereby the mind is perplexed and prevented from aspiring to the substantial knowledge of things. 'A man has the greater disdain for this idle learning the better acquainted he becomes with sound learning. Finally, the evil of pedantic learning and addled pedagogues is not to be laid at the door of letters' (II.iv.13: 250–251). Furthermore, it is the duty of man to take care of his own body and life.

Man's Duties Toward Other Men

After having discussed what duties the law of nature instructs upon man toward himself and how much freedom it allows him in the preservation of his person, Pufendorf turns to those restrictions, which concern the duties to be observed towards other men. He divides these duties into *absolute* and *hypothetical*. Under *absolute* duties, he articulates two admonitions: that no one should hurt another and that if someone has caused another a loss, he should make it good. This duty is of all duties the most important. 'Nay, this duty is of the greatest necessity, since without it the social life of men could in no way exist' (III.i.1: 313).

Pufendorf emphasized that if any damage or loss has been caused, it should be made good. The reason being that men are so depraved that 'they will never refrain from hurting each other, unless they are forced to make restitution, nor will it be easy for a man who has suffered some loss to make up his mind to live at peace with another, so long as he has not received proper restitution' (III.i.2: 314).

The word damage should be viewed broadly to include every injury against a man's body, reputation, and virtue.

> So it signifies any hurt, destruction, diminution, or seizure of something which we now possess, or the interception of something which we should have had by perfect right – whether it was given us by nature, or allowed us by the agency or law of man – or, finally, the avoidance or refusal of some act which a person was under perfect obligation to perform for us.
>
> (Ibid.)

Externalities

As an illustration of the latter, Pufendorf quotes the Roman rhetorician Quintilian (35–100), from his *Declamations*, where it is revealed that a man who covered the flowers in his garden with poison, from which his neighbour's bees died, had been the cause of his neighbour's loss. The argument that carried the case was that:

> Since all men agree that bees are roving animals, which cannot possibly be trained to get their food in any one place, therefore, wherever it is right to keep them, the neighbours of such a place are understood to be under a kind of liability of easement, whereby the bees are allowed to wander here and there without any one preventing them.
>
> (III.i.3: 315)

Discounted Value of Damage

In determining the amount of damage Pufendorf claimed that one should not only take into account merely the thing belonging to us or owned by us, which is damaged, destroyed or frustrated:

> but the fruits as well which come from it, whether they have already been received – in which case they may already be estimated as separate

> items – or are only hoped for, provided the owner might have received them; although the expenses, necessary to secure such fruits or profits, should be deducted, lest we become more rich at another's cost.
>
> (Ibid.: 316)

Then, something about discounting future gains is added. 'But the estimate of expected fruits is raised or lowered, according as they are nearer to or farther from the time of their uncertain harvest. Thus a crop lost in the blade must be estimated at a lower figure than one that is yellow in the full head' (ibid.).[4] A similar economic argument is forwarded if someone burns another man's house. In such a case, he should not merely rebuild it. He should also make good the rent, which the owner might have collected from it before it is rebuilt.

All Men Are Equal

Every man cherishes his life, his person, and his possessions. In addition, according to Pufendorf, there can be observed, deep-seated in his soul, a most sensitive self-esteem. If someone undertakes to impair this self-esteem, he is rarely less and often more disturbed than if someone tries to injure his person and property. The prime source of this self-esteem is human nature.

Since human nature belongs equally to all men, and since no one can live a social life with a person by whom he is not rated as at least a fellow man, it follows as a precept of natural law, that 'Every man should esteem and treat another man as his equal by nature, or as much a man as he is himself' (III.ii.1: 330).

From this equality flow other precepts that will have the greatest influence in preserving peace and friendly relations among men. If a man wishes to benefit from the assistance of other men, he must in turn lend his own talent to their accommodation. Surely a man will offend others if he considers them his inferiors, for example, if he demands that they labour for him, while he himself never gives something in return. Such behaviour gives occasion to a breach of peace.

Every man knows his own nature best, but he understands the general inclination of the nature of other men as well. From this it follows that a man, who decides one way in another man's right, and another way in a similar right of his own, is guilty of a contradiction in the very plainest matter. Pufendorf contends that this is evidence of a seriously disordered mind. 'No sufficient proof, indeed, can be advanced why something that I feel to be proper for myself, I should feel to be improper for others who are my equals, other things being equal' (III.ii.4: 336). A man is best fitted for a social life if he is willing to allow the same things to others as to himself.

Notes

1 In *Elementorum Jurisprudentiae* Universalis (II. Oii.1) he uses the term 'internal mediator'.

2 Caron served in the Duch East India Company for thirty years and became its Director-General. Later he held a similar position in the French East Indies Company.
3 Fiammetta Palladini, *Samuel Pufendorf-Discepolo di Hobbes. Per una reinterrpretazione del giusnaturalismo modern*, Il Mulino, Bologna, 1990, pp. 96–97; and Norberto Bobbio, 'Il giusnaturalismo', in Luigi Firpo (ed.), *Storiadella idee politiche, enonomiche e sociale*, vol. 4, Part I, Unione Tipografico-Editirce Torinese, Turin, 1980, pp. 491–558.
4 This has also been noted by Gaertner (2005).

8 Private Property and the Four-Stages Theory

Pufendorf uses his theory of human behaviour, in general and his theory of the social man, with its dictates of reason as the basis to build his theory of property or what he calls dominion. A theory of property is found in all his natural law work. In Book IV of the *De Jure Naturae et Gentium* a comprehensive treatment of this theory is carried out.

The Right and the Power of Men

Pufendorf's starting point is that the constitution of man's body is such that it cannot live from its own substance, 'but has need and substance gathered from outside, by which it is nourished and fortified against those things which would destroy its structure. Nay, nearly all nature serves man to the further end that he may live his life more advantageously and easily' (IV.iii.1: 524). God gave man the power, not merely over plants, but also over animate things produced in heaven, earth or sea. This granted concession does not have the force of a command. It is a privilege that a person can use as far as he pleases. He is by no means bound to use it on every occasion. Consequently, men have the right and the power to harvest the fruits of the earth, its animal and vegetable kingdom. The fruits of the earth include animals, birds and fishes. Furthermore, God's gift embraces the use of the labour performed by animals in cultivation and transport, and food and produce that come from animals such as milk, eggs, wool and the like. However, he stresses that this power cannot be interpreted as a right to the abuse of either animals or nature.

Sustainable Harvest

Pufendorf advocates a sustainable harvest and use of the earth's fruits. He supports this view by referring to the Chinese Confucian philosopher Mencius (372–289 BC), as we are told in a report from China, by the Jesuit missionary Martinus Martini (1614–1661).

> The king should not permit the use of fine mesh nets in fishing, in order that only the large fish should be caught, while the smaller fish allowed in

this way to escape might increase in size in the course of years, and thus always be sufficient for everyone.

(IV.iii.6: 531)

This also agrees with a statement of the sixth-century BC Greek poet Phocylides: 'And let no man take all the birds at once from the nest, but leave the mother bird, that you may have chicks from her again' (ibid.).

The important question is then whether man's harvesting and use of the fruits of the earth implies private property? In Pufendorf's opinion, it does not. This harvesting and use, could also be carried out in common.

The Origin of Property

However, when this power of men over things began to take root in relation to other men, he contends that private property arose from an unclear right, where one thing belongs to one man and not to another. Before he continues he makes it clear that private property and community (owned in common) are moral qualities, which have no physical effect upon things themselves, but only produce a moral effect in relation to other men, and that they own their birth to imposition among men.

It is therefore idle to raise the question whether private ownership in things is due 'to nature or to institution'. His answer is that 'it is clear that it arises from the impositions of men' since 'there is no change in the physical substance of things, whether proprietorship is added or taken away from them' (IV.iv.1: 532).

Next we must carefully consider and weigh the question of what common property is and what private property is. The term common property can be taken either negatively or positively. In the former negative case things are said to be common property as they are before any human act that has made them belong to this man rather than to that man. Things are said to be nobody's, 'more in a negative than a positive sense', meaning that they are not yet assigned to a person, not that they cannot be assigned to a person. Furthermore, they are called 'things that lie open to any and every person'. In the second positive case things differ from things privately owned in the respect that the latter belong to one person while the former to several persons. Moreover, private property is a right whereby the substance of something belongs to one person in such a way that 'it does not belong in its entirety to another person in the same manner' (IV. iv.2: 533).

Again, this does not imply private property. Property is developed from a stage where everything was held in common, things were 'not yet assigned to a particular person' (IV.iv.2: 532). Pufendorf also discusses how things can be held in common and why there are different kinds of property and how property can be restricted by civil law.

Private Property Assumes an Agreement

When Adam was the only man, 'things to him were neither common nor proper' (IV.iv.3: 536). Common property implies that there is someone to share with, and private property brings in the barring of another's right to the same thing, therefore there has to be more than one person. However, when the number of people grew, it did not imply that private property was introduced. Neither is the fact that God allowed men to use the product of the earth an immediate cause of private property. Private property assumes, Pufendorf contends, an act of man and an agreement among men, whether this agreement is just tacitly understood, or clearly expressed (IV.iv.4: 536).

Property is looked upon as a human institution, and not as an order sanctified by God. It is true that God allowed men the use of the products of the earth to their own good. He gave men an indefinite right to them, but the extent of this power and how it should be organized 'were left to the judgement and disposition of men' (ibid.).

Pufendorf argues against those writers who claim that private property is based on natural law. Such a view was, for example, expressed by the German Johann Boecler: 'Let there be property and distinction among things; let each man keep his own and not covet what is another's.' Therefore, although natural law did not in itself introduce private property it clearly 'advised that men should by convention introduce an assignment of such things to individuals, according as it might be of advantage to human society' (IV.iv.5: 537).

Furthermore, it is understood that the law of nature approves all convention that has been introduced by man, 'provided they involve no contradiction or do not overturn society' (ibid.). From this discussion Pufendorf concludes: 'it is clear that before any conventions of men existed there was a community of all things … that all things lay open to all men, and belonged no more to one than to another' (ibid.). Since things are of no use unless someone can annex their fruits, and since this is not possible if others can take the same fruits, it follows that the first convention, agreement or pact between men was about this important matter.

The Limitation of Private Property

Pufendorf discusses what right the preservation of our own property allow us over the property of others. In his exposition he first presents the view of Grotius, who believed that man in extreme necessity had a perfect right to the property of others (II.vi.6: 303).

This view he could not accept. He claimed that 'a man of means is bound to come to the aid of one, who is in innocent want, by an imperfect obligation'. This obligation can give the same result as a perfect right, that is 'a special appeal may be made to a magistrate, or, when time does not allow anything of the sort, the immediate necessity may be met by taking the thing through force or stealth' (ibid.: 304–305).

Most natural law theorists found, according to Hont and Ignatieff (1983: 30–31), Grotius' view dangerous; 'if the need claims of the poor were given priority over property society could be reduced to a state of anarchy even in times of relative plenty'. The shift between Grotius and Pufendorf was decisive. 'In one, the focus was upon the rights of the poor, while in the other, it was upon the voluntary obligations' of the rich.'

An Historical Process

Pufendorf's theory of property is genuinely historical in the sense that it describes a process in time. He makes it clear that it was not so that the whole earth or all things at once were divided among all men, and that everything at once passed into private ownership. It came about as society developed under pressure of a growing population and depleted natural resources. In his treatment, he stresses repeatedly that the development occurs successively as 'the state of things, or the nature and number of men seemed to require' (IV. iv.6: 539). He refers to the third-century Roman historian Marcus Junianus Justinus who tells us that the Scythians used to allow property in flocks and household goods, but their fields were held in original community.

The first concern of the law of nature is the maintenance of peace and tranquillity of mankind. Therefore, the law of nature made no uncertain suggestion as to what might be the most productive arrangement by men in establishing dominion. For after the human race had multiplied and 'acquired a cultured mode of life, the peace of men did not suffer so that there should remain for every man an equal power over all things, that is, that all things should lie open to all for the promiscuous use of every man' (ibid.: 539).

Pufendorf asks why things fall into private ownership. His answer is that in the beginning immobile things produced by nature, without use of labour, such as fields, existed in abundance, considering the small number of people. Every man who wished was then free to take whatever he wanted. The rest was left for everyone that in the future wanted to take it. In such a situation, there was no need for private ownership.

However, when mankind grew more numerous the situations gradually changed. Most things that had been necessary for men's nourishment and their immediate use were no longer produced by nature itself, in sufficient abundance for men to help themselves. There would no longer be enough for everyone to fulfil their needs. Consequently, if two or more find that they want the same thing or if some individuals try to appropriate for themselves the same thing, and there is not enough for all, an occasion for quarrels and wars lay ready at hand.

The Use of Labour

Moreover, most things require cultivation, that is the use of labour, to make it fit for human use. In such cases it would be improper that those who contribute little or no labour, should have the same rights to the things that were produced, equal to those who by their labour and industry had made the final products possible (ibid.: 540).

Private ownership would also contribute to the avoidance of war and to secure peace among men. To support this view, he refers to the Greek philosopher Aristotle, who undertook to refute the Platonic common property. He also refers to the Greek fifth- and fourth-centuries' poet Aristophanes who claimed that if all men should labour in common, lay up their earnings in common, and should be maintained from a common store, quarrels would arise because of the inequality of their toils and its product. 'There is always a difficulty in men living together and having things in common' (IV.iv.7: 541). The introduction of private property does away with such quarrels and every man takes greater interest in his own things. At the same time, man who has private ownership over things, is given the opportunity to sell liberally out of his own stores, to others who are not as fortunate. He also quotes the Roman satirist Decimus Juvenal (40–125), who points to another positive effect of private property: 'There is the greatest pleasure in doing a kindness or service to friends or guests or companions which can only be rendered when a man has private property' (ibid.).

Common Ownership

However, Pufendorf has to admit that all arguments in favour of private property have not prevented some from trying to introduce common ownership among men. He mentions the English philosopher Thomas More (1578–1635) in his *Utopia*, from 1515, and the Italian philosopher Tommaso Campanella (1568–1639) in his *City of the Sun*, from 1602, as examples. In their books everything was held in common. Pufendorf assumed that they believed man was perfect. However, 'perfect men are more easily imagined than found' and he adds: 'But this also shows the falsity of the old saying: "Mine and thine are the causes of wars".' Rather it is that 'mine and thine' were introduced to avoid wars. He adds that for this reason the Greek philosopher Plato (428–348) designated a boundary stone as 'the stone which is the sworn arbiter of friendship and hatred between neighbours' (ibid.).

Pufendorf then points out that other writers, both ancients and more recent, held a different view on the origin of property. He then discusses what force there is in the arguments of some of these authors.[1] He also points to Grotius, who claimed that if societies, who had common ownership were to continue to live without disturbance to the common peace they had to live in great simplicity, being satisfied to subsist on natural fruits while living in caves and clothing themselves with bark from trees and the skins of animals 'while if they wanted to live a more refined life, the advantages which had to be secured by industry, property in things was necessary' (IV.iv.9: 546: Grotius (1625), *De Jure Belli ac Pacis*, II.ii.2).

What things are of such a character that they fall under private ownership? Pufendorf claims that two conditions are required. First, that the thing is able to produce, by itself or together with other things, some use to men, today or in the future. Second, that the thing should be such that men can acquire it and keep it in their possession. For surely it will be idle and foolish to lay claim to things of no service. In addition, it will be stupid to claim the right of a thing when you cannot with any reason prevent others from using it against your will.

However, some things, although they are useful to men, are because of their extent inexhaustible, and lie open to the use of all. Moreover, the use by one person of such a thing will not make the use by another person worse off. To subject such things to proprietorship would, Pufendorf claims, 'be malicious and inhuman' (IV.v.2: 558). Men therefore exempt from proprietorship 'the light and the heat of the sun, the air and flowing water, and the like' (ibid.). In this group, we can also include those parts of the oceans, lying between the great continents, which are farthest away from land, since all can use these areas of the oceans. The use by one does not prevent others from using it.

The Role of an Agreement or Pact

Pufendorf claims that if one group of men get ownership of things, and thereby exclude all others, this dominion has to be confirmed at least by a tacit pact or agreement. This pact contains, at the same time, a tacit renunciation on the part of the rest. The reason being that when things have been assigned to one person, the rest of mankind do not care to advance any claim to them on the alleged ground that the earth, as the common home of men, has contributed their substance and nourishment to those same things. Hence, it was understood that a pact was agreed upon, formally or informally, that such fields should belong to those who by their labour cultivated them (IV.iv.6: 540).

Pufendorf emphasizes the role of an agreement or a pact in constituting property. He introduces a 'tacit convention' in the first stage.

> Now so long as the actual bodies of things were not yet assigned to certain individuals, there was a tacit convention that each man could appropriate for his own use, primarily of the fruits of things, what he wanted, and could consume what was consumable.
>
> (IV.iv.9: 546)

This universal use of proprietorship was then introduced, in the sense that what one man had taken in this way, another man could not take from him without doing him an injury. Here he refers first to the Roman Justinius, who describes the aborigines as people who held all in common living where the entire country belonged to a people and had not yet been divided into estates since those men 'were content with fruits that grew of themselves, which the expanse of forests and fields brought forth in profusion for a small population'. Pufendorf points out that this primitive state was not a positive but a negative community and refers again to Grotius, who maintained that if people in such communities were to continue without disturbing the peace, they had to live in great simplicity: 'while if they wanted a more refined kind of life, the advantages of which had to be secured by industry, property in things was necessary' (ibid.).

He further emphasizes that the initial appropriation of 'the fruits of things' established a right. In this respect it would be unjust to interfere with what another had seized. 'An oak-tree belonged to no man, but the acorns that fell to the ground were his who had gathered them' (IV.iv.13: 554). Nevertheless, although a tacit pact suffices at first, such a pact must give way to express agreements:

> Therefore, there was need of an external act or seizure, and for this to produce a moral effect, that is, an obligation on the part of others to refrain from a thing already seized by some one else, an antecedent pact was required and an express pact, indeed, when several men divided among themselves things open to all; but a tacit pact sufficed when the things occupied at that time had been left unpossessed by the first dividers of things.
>
> (IV.iv.9: 547)

It was then understood that these men agreed that those things, which at first had not been assigned to a definite individual, should pass to him, who was the first to take possession of them.

How Much Could an Individual Acquire of Property?

Pufendorf's answer is that consent set the limitation of what each could acquire of property. The generosity of God toward men was such that 'He supplied them abundantly with what serves their needs' (IV.v.9: 567). Reason prescribed the bounds of possession to men. This should leave them content with acquiring what would likely meet both their own and their dependents' needs. They should also take care of their future needs, provided their envy and craving for more than they needed does not prevent others from providing for their own necessities. Should someone gather to much wealth by the oppression of others he could be brought in line. 'If any person ranges too far afield and heaps up superfluous wealth by the oppression of others, the rest will not be blamed if, when opportunity affords, they undertake promptly to bring him into line' (ibid.).

The Four-Stages Theory

How does Pufendorf explain the order and process in which private property developed? As mentioned, his theory is genuinely historical in the sense that it describes a process in time. He makes it clear that it was not so that the whole earth or all things at once were divided among all men, and that everything at once passed into private ownership. It came about when man wanted a more refined kind of life, the advantages of which had to be served by industry, private property was progressively introduced.

Gathering and Hunting

In the state of nature there was no need for distinct ownership; there was enough of the fruits of the earth for everyone, and as mentioned, all things 'lay open to all'. Every man was then free to take whatever he wanted. The rest was left for everyone that in the future wanted to take it. In these first small communities, there were few people and no rivalry among them and therefore very little need for private property.

But when men had to gather food by hunting and fishing, which required some labour and tools, ownership of implements and some rude furniture and sheds were introduced. When such societies grew, rivalry came into existence as well as 'the consideration that each one's industry might be his own gain and his idleness his own burden' (IV.iv.11: 550).

It should not be understood 'that all things once and for all passed under proprietorship'. In the beginning, it was satisfactory that those things should be made private property 'which are either immediately and indivisibly of use to several persons, such as clothing, habitations, and fruits gathered for food, or which required some labour and care, such as implements, household furnishing, herds and fields' (ibid.: 551). Little by little what remained came under private ownership, 'according as the inclination of men or their increasing numbers directed' (ibid.). It is of interest to note that Pufendorf claims that things, which require labour and care, should first be made private property.[2] Gradually all what remained came under private property, as mankind multiplied or their need and wishes changed. Therefore, in this stage only a tacit agreement was required.

Shepherding

Pufendorf emphasizes that not all passed into private ownership at one time but successively 'as considerations of concord seemed to require'. As society developed people started to hold domestic animals, but in the beginning there were few. Pastures were then in abundance in proportion to the small number of people. Every man who wished was then free to take whatever he wanted. The rest was left for everyone that wanted to take it in the future. 'Thus for a long time pasture lands remained in primitive community, until as herds multiplied and quarrels arose, it was to the interest of peace that they also be divided' (IV.iv.11: 551). Again full dominion was not required at this stage and only tacit agreements were necessary.

Agricultural Production

The next development was the discovery of the use of grain, which led to the cultivation of land and to an agricultural society. Pufendorf refers to the fourth- and fifth-century Roman grammarian Marius Servius Honoratus, who also claimed that before the discovery of the use of grains, mankind had been controlled by few laws. However, after laws had arisen from the division of fields, Pufendorf claims that private property at this stage was firmly established and that there was now a need for 'a more complicated legal apparatus' (IV.iv.13–555).

The general impression Pufendorf gives is that the first things that is likely to be taken into proprietorship would be the sheds and 'rude furniture' of the hunters and fishers; that flocks and herds would probably follow; and that the land itself would be the last thing to come under private ownership. In the eighteenth century this view, was to become associated with the notion that an original mode of subsistence based on hunting and fishing gave way to one based on pasturage, and this in turn to one based on the cultivation of land.

Full dominion was not required in the shepherding and agricultural stages as long as pasture and land remained in abundance. But when land became scarce relative to population and living conveniences were increased by industry the necessity of preserving social life led to the introduction of private property.

Commercial Society

In his treatment of the theory of value and money Pufendorf also develops the fourth stage. It is need that holds all things together; it is not only the sole foundation of price but of exchange and commerce. 'For if men had need of nothing, or of another thing no more than what they have, there would be no commerce and no exchange, since each man would keep what was his own and enjoy that' (V.i.4: 677). To support this view, he quotes Aristotle, who wrote in his Politics 'The art of exchange extends to all (possessions) and it arises at first in a natural manner from the circumstance that some have too little, others too much. For they were forced to use exchange until they had enough' (ibid).

As men give up their primitive existence and commerce increased, the next step will be the introduction of money. 'Now after most nations have given up their primitive simplicity they easily appreciated the fact that the old ordinary price no longer sufficed to carry on the business and commerce of men as these increased from day to day' (V.i.11: 689–690). For commerce used to consist only in the exchange of goods, and the work of others could be paid for, only in the work or in kind. When a society grows to a sufficient size, individuals are no longer satisfied with what they could produce at home using their own time and resources. They feel a need for goods and services produced by others if they are to live comfortably. On the other hand, individuals can also contribute many things to the use of others of which they themselves do not feel the need. However, this will come to nothing if these individuals could not exchange and barter their different goods and services.

When a society based on private property by agreements grew, it therefore brought with it commerce, that is, trade, and the growth of markets, the creation of prices and the introduction of money. 'It is perfectly plain that those nations which are unacquainted with the use of currency have no part in the advances of civilization' (ibid.: 690).

Pufendorf was fully aware of the fact that in a commercial society citizens were divided into different classes with increasing inequality as a result. With commerce and the use of money avarice increased and the urge for more wealth with it. 'For as long as wealth lay only in stores of grain, herds and the like the desire for unlimited gain was ultimately quenched by the work involved in such things, the difficulty of handling and keeping them, and the further fact that they were easily destroyed' (V.i.14: 695). But, when gold and silver money was introduced, 'it is easy for avarice to amass even millions' (ibid.). It was clear that with commerce and the introduction of money, it brought with it luxury, avarice restlessness and inequality.

The foundation of a theory of a commercial society with the use of money in which all individuals attempt to satisfy their own needs and thereby satisfy the need of others is therefore a cornerstone in Pufendorf's natural law theory.

Did Pufendorf Develop a Stadial Theory?

There has been some claim that Pufendorf did not adopt a theory of stages since he wrote on the authority of the Genesis, that these modes of subsistence, which characterize the different stages had in fact coexisted in society from very early times. Ronald L. Meek (1976: 19) contends that Pufendorf firmly believed this. 'We know that primitive man by the aid of God learned very early the most necessary arts (see Genesis, iii.21,23; iv.2,17,22) to which the sagacity of men added a considerable number of others' (II.ii.2: 157). However, before such a rather hasty conclusion is drawn one should recall that Pufendorf had to be very careful not to offend the Church. It should also be noted that Simone De Angelis (2004), in her study about Pufendorf and the Cartesianism, claims that Pufendorf during his months in the Netherlands had taken over the so called 'accommodation theory' from Christopher Wittich (1625–1687). Wittich defended a non-literal interpretation of biblical texts, because the Bible used the language of its time and words change their meaning over time. This interpretation made it possible to defend new discoveries in natural sciences without coming into conflict with the teaching of the Church.

Notes

1 The Roman historian Cicero, the Greek historian Dionysius (70–7), the Roman Justinus, the third-century Roman apologist Lactantius, the Assyrian rhetorician

and satirist Lucian (125–180), the Roman poet Ovid (AD 43–17), the Roman Pliny the Elder, the Roman Seneca the Younger, the Greek Diodorus, the Roman historian Sallust (86–34), the Roman epic poet Virgil (70–19) and the French essayist Michel Montaigne (1533–1592).

2 John Locke's ideas regarding the labour theory of value and his use of this theory to explain the introduction of property could have been inspired by Pufendorf. This will be discussed in Chapter 13.

9 Theories of Value, Money and Trade

Pufendorf has a comprehensive treatment of the theory of value and of money in his treatment of contracts law. His starting point is the price as the standard for the value of the things to which the contracts refers. He gives a comprehensive account of the state of the art of the theory as it has developed from the Greeks, the Romans,[1] the Scholastics and the moderns: Grotius, Giovanni Vittorio Rossi[2] (1577–1647), John Nieuhoff (1618–1672), and Selden, to mention some of the ones he builds on and quotes. There are particularly many quotations from Aristotle's *Nicomachean Ethics.* He is also here very careful in advising us of his sources.

What is Price?

Pufendorf's starting point is that when private ownership was introduced, and as society grew, some people had things or goods and services (actions) they did not need, and at the same time they sought after and wanted to acquire goods that were in other people's possession. Goods and services therefore had to be exchanged for each other.

By agreement of men, some measures therefore had to be set for the goods and services that changed hands, 'according to which measure things of different nature could be compared to and made equal with each other' (V.i.1: 675). In exchange goods and services are compared and made equal on the basis of quantities and the common measure. Goods and services can be valued according to their physical substance but also according to what is called a moral quantity, that is a subjective evaluation, 'it follows that in addition to a physical quantity there is also a moral quantity, by which, of course, things are valued morally' (ibid.: 675–676). Services are valued in the same way.

Price[3] is then the common measure or standard for the value of the goods and services to which the agreement or contract refers to: 'This quantity of things and actions is called price, which is a moral quantity or value of things and actions, as they enter into exchange, according to which they are usually compared with each other' (ibid.: 676). It is clear from the outset that for Pufendorf this price is the worth, or value, of a good or service in terms of its capacity to satisfy human wants by being exchanged for another good or service.

Pufendorf makes it clear that here he only investigates the value or price of goods and services that 'serve some purpose in common life' and 'may be able to serve the ends of commerce' (ibid.). It is therefore commerce that gives rise to prices.

The Market Price and the Monetary Price

Price can be divided into *ordinary*[4] (*pretium vulgare*) and *eminent* (*pretium eminence*). The former is the exchange or what today can be called the market price for goods and services. It 'is found in things and actions [services] or labours, which enters into exchange, in so far as they afford service and pleasure for man'. The latter is found in money or whatever serves in its place such as nobler metals, gold, silver or bronze. It is 'understood virtually to contain the prices of all things and labours, and to furnish a common standard for their measurement' (V.i.3: 676).

In his detailed analysis, Pufendorf first discusses the factors that determine the exchange or market price of a commodity or service, and then what causes it to change. Thereafter he discusses the origin of money as a common measure of value, and what causes the value of money to change. To be able to get a correct understanding of 'the nature of ordinary price', that is the exchange or market price, Pufendorf claims that it will help to first consider 'its foundation' and second to study why the price 'rises and falls' (V.i.4: 676).[5]

What is the Foundation of the Market Price?

The foundation for the exchange or market price is, according to Pufendorf, first of all 'the aptitude' of a good or service, by which it, now or later, contributes something to the necessity of human life, or to making it more advantageous and pleasant. To emphasize what he means, he has some critical remarks on a statement by Grotius (Bk. II. xii.14): 'The most natural measure of the value of things is the need for it' (ibid.: 676). Following Pufendorf this statement does not hold true universally, if Grotius means that the foundation of price is want, or that men merely value a thing because it is needed.[6] Should this be true, goods that serve idle pleasure will have no price, and this, of course, is not so. However, if the 'need of a thing' is not defined merely from the circumstances that it helps to preserve or to make our existence pleasurable, but that it in some people's view, also contributes some delight or satisfaction than its true. Pufendorf did not use the word 'utility' but his term 'aptitude' has clearly the same meaning. Furthermore, he maintains that the cause of economic activity comes from the demand side.[7] It is men's need, their mutual utility of goods and services that creates exchange and commerce and as a consequence prices. It is therefore the demand side that binds the economy of a society together.

Why do costs of production or other factors that determine supply not enter into the picture and influence the price? The answer is that Pufendorf, at this stage, considers an exchange situation where supply (he uses the word scarcity), is fixed. It is therefore clear that his starting point is a subjective theory of value where the focus is on the demand side. This was also the view that was forwarded by some of the Scholastic writers. However, he later returned to the supply side where the factors of production and their prices are discussed.

Why do some Goods or Services Lack a Price?

The art of exchange extends to most possessions, but there are some very useful goods and services for which it is understood that no price is set, because:

1 They are and should be exempted from private ownership.
2 They are removed from man's use in commerce.
3 In business relations, they are considered as nothing more than an accessory to something else.

Pufendorf first claims that the upper reaches of the air, the sky, celestial bodies and the open ocean are removed from human ownership. No one can therefore properly put a price upon them, although they serve the greatest use for the life of man. No one has a property right to the air; it is held in common for all, and therefore it has no price. Second, Roman law has excluded hallowed and sacred places from commerce and thereby deprived them of any price, although many of them otherwise would have had a price since they then would come under human ownership. Third, no price can be set upon:

> the warm light of the sun, pure and wholesome air, a beautiful landscape in so far as it only delights the eye, or upon wind, shade, and similar things in themselves or considered apart, since men cannot enjoy them without the use of the land; yet everyone realizes how important such things are in influencing the price of district farms, and estates.
>
> (V.i.5: 678)

The reason that these accessories have no price is that they cannot be separated from the land. A property with a lot of sun and a nice view will therefore gain a higher price than a property with no sun and no view.

Finally, whatever actions, laws of God or of men, ordained to be performed freely, or forbidden entirely from exchange, cannot be owned and therefore will have no price. Examples given are priestly absolution of sins, public offices, and justice. Furthermore, the Italian scholar Giovanni Vittorio Rossi claims that it is surely a disgrace to the calling of letters, that in some places men sell doctor degrees for money (ibid.: 679).

Why do the Market Price Rise or Fall?

There are, 'various reasons why the price of one and the same thing rises or falls, and why, therefore, one thing is preferred to another, although the latter apparently affords as much or greater service in the life of man' (V.i.6: 680).

The use people have for a good or service lays the foundation for the price, but it is nevertheless not the only factor that determines the price. The reason is that the need of an article does not always come first. In many such instances, the need will have little influence at all on the price. On the one hand, we observe that the things men are least able to do without are cheap. On the other hand, we observe that goods which people have a great desire for, but if necessary they can easily do without, are expensive.

The Paradox of Value

It is therefore clear that it is not only subjective valuations that determine the price. The chief factor for high price is therefore scarcity. This view is supported by a quote from Plato: 'Only what is rare is valuable, and water, which is the best of things … is also the cheapest' (V.i.6: 680). So nature has provided in great abundance the goods that we cannot be without and therefore these goods have no price or a low price. At the same time there is a great shortage of the goods, which we, if necessary can do without, and therefore these have a high price. Consequently, the chief factor in a high price is scarcity. Pufendorf therefore was fully aware of and had no problem with what later became the so called 'Paradox of Value' or 'Diamond-Water paradox', that certain goods that are very useful and valuable to man such as water, are very cheap to buy; while other less useful goods, such as diamonds, are expensive.

Creation of Scarcity

Pufendorf goes on to discuss why certain goods are scarce and therefore have a high price. One important reason is that business people themselves can create scarcity, by reducing output, and as a consequence they are able to raise the price and thereby increase their own revenue. In other words, they create a monopoly situation. This point is illustrated by quotes from the Greek geographer and historian Strabo (63 BC – AD 23).[8] Strabo, who undertook a journey up the Nile, wrote that the Egyptians did not permit the papyrus plant to grow in many places; they thus raised the price 'because of scarcity and increased their own revenue'. Furthermore, Pufendorf tells us how the Dutch in many sections of India destroyed the clove and nutmeg plants in order to prevent an over-supply of these species (V.i.6: 680).

Human Motives

However, human motives can also play an important role in determining the price. Attention is drawn to some inclinations or motives behind consumer behaviour, which deviates from right reason, and therefore affects the price of goods or services. These inclinations are ambition of men, perversion, bragging, mischievousness or envy and want of luxury. First, he observes what he calls *the ambition of men* since some men 'especially values what they have in common with but a few others, while on the other hand whatever is seen in almost any one's house, is of little worth in their eyes' (ibid.: 681). Second, men's perversion: 'Nay men are often so perverted that a thing is rated highly because its use has been forbidden, the mere proscription serving to whet their curiosity'. The Assyrian Lucian, rightfully ridicules those 'Who glut themselves with roses in mid-winter, loving their rarity and unreasonableness, and despising what is seasonable and natural because of its cheapness' (ibid.). Third, men are also governed by bragging or what today might be called conspicuous consumption: 'So also in general men scarcely ever consider a thing valuable, which does not yield to the holder some distinction and position above that held by the rest of men, and by reason of which they cannot vaunt themselves above others' (ibid.). Fourth and fifth, if men are not moved by boasting it might be that they delight in the mischiefs of others or is moved by envy of the ones that have more than themselves. 'Therefore, whoever prides himself on the fact that others lack the good things in which he abounds, appears in fact to delight in the ills of others, while whoever holds his goods of less value because others also enjoy them, is moved by envy of them' (ibid.: 682). The sixth point want of luxury consumption, is explained by the fact that 'as in many other things, so also in this, the general inclination of men deviates from right reason'. Because of their overweening luxury men has therefore 'set enormous value upon things which they could very easily do without' (V.i.6: 681). This fact is due to 'the depravity and corruption of human nature' that put value of these goods because they are scarce. The prices of such goods are set by the desire, which anyone have for them. This view is supported by a quotation from the Roman Cicero (106–43): 'The only limit to the valuation of such things is the desire which any one has for them, for it is difficult to set bounds to the price unless you first set bounds to the wish' (ibid.).

The price of luxury goods will fall sharply when such goods become abundant because people will not fancy them anymore. Pufendorf gives the price of tulips as an example. It is taken from the Italian Rossi, who explained that originally tulips grew high up in the Alps, without receiving any cultivation or attention. Then they were brought into the cities, and their price increased drastically, because of the desire for their novelty. But after they had become abundant their price fell so greatly that scarcely anything was considered cheaper.

People value highly commodities consumed by important people and they might pay a high price for certain goods because high prices gives them some distinction and position above that of others. To support this view, he quotes many Greek and Latin authors. For example, Pliny the Younger (61–113): 'Nay, the folly of men fancies that some great value lies in anything that has had a high value placed upon it' (ibid.). To underscore his point he also quotes several Roman sources. Here only two will be brought to light. The Roman biographer Lampridius, who wrote: 'He loved to hear the price of food served at his table exaggerated, asserting it was an appetizer for the banquet.' The satirist Juvenal who, in the first half of the second century, expressed it more clearly: 'Those please the more which are bought for more' (ibid.).

Furthermore, Pufendorf points out that it happens that certain commodities are highly valued not by the whole world but by certain individuals, because they see them valued by important individuals, whom they want to please. 'Thus the price of certain kind of food or clothing rises because the king fancies it' (V.i.7: 685). It is usually called the price of fancy.

From this discussion it is clear that Pufendorf, drawing on quotations from the Greek and the Roman philosophers, was aware of what today are called the snob and bandwagon effects and conspicuous consumption. These observations are also close to what Thorstein Veblen, more than 200 years later, described as conspicuous consumption and the eccentricities of 'the pecuniary culture'.[9]

The difference between our willingness to pay and what we actually pay, which is the basis for the concept of Alfred Marshall's consumer surplus, is also clear to Pufendorf. He quotes the Roman philosopher Lucius Annaeus Seneca the Younger who wrote: 'Some things are of greater value than the prices which we pay for them' (V.i.6: 684).

Elastic and Inelastic Demand

Pufendorf also seems to have a rudimentary understanding of what we today describe as elastic and inelastic demand. Luxury goods have an elastic demand, and the demand for necessities is inelastic. A decline in the supply will therefore raise the price of everyday goods much more than for luxury goods (ibid.: 683). This view is backed up by several quotes, for example the Roman Marcus Fabius Quintilianus (35–100), who wrote: 'In great want anything that can be bought is cheap.' Or Gaius Plinius Secudas (23–79), who wrote: 'At the siege of Casilinum by Hannibal, a mouse was sold for two hundred denarii, and the person who sold it perished with hunger, while the purchaser survived' (ibid.).

Cost of Production

The scarcity or supply of goods and services are also influenced by the cost of production. 'The price of manufactured articles is usually raised not only by their rareness but because of their workmanship' (ibid.: 683). Other factors that determine the cost of production are the difficulty of the work and the abundance or scarcity of workers. It is also made clear that the price of labour and services is determined in the same manner as the price of a commodity. That is, by the difficulty of the work, the qualifications required of the workers, how the labour force can be of benefit to the producer, how necessary the workers are for the production, how scarce the workers are, how well known they are, and finally how free are the labourers to take work which they choose (ibid.: 684).

What is the Legitimate Price?

Pufendorf claims that the deliberations mentioned in the previous sections will regularly raise the prices of goods as their opposite lowers them. However, when it comes to the determination 'on the spot' of the exchange or market prices, other factors should be considered.

His discussion starts with an observation: 'that among those who live in natural liberty each man is allowed to fix the price of an article of his own pleasure, since every man is the final arbiter of his possessions and actions' (V.i.8: 685). Any person who wants an article of mine may set another price by his own valuation. but it is within my power to accept or reject his offer. If a person set what others think is an outrageous price of an article of his, nobody can complain, since they can either accept or reject his price. On the other hand, if a person wants to force an article of his upon someone else he should accept whatever price a purchaser chooses to quote. He points out that:

> There can, therefore, be just cause of complain only when a man, through inhumanity or out of hatred or envy, either refuses to sell to one in need, things which he enjoys a superfluity, or else is willing to part with them only upon very hard terms.
>
> (Ibid.: 686)

He concludes that in a state of nature the prices of all goods and services will be determined by agreement between the parties concerned, 'and that man cannot be charged with a sin against the rules of commerce' (ibid.).

All the participants in the market will try to maximize their profit. This is a legitimate motive 'provided he shows no inhumanity towards the needed' (ibid.). Self-interest is balanced by sociability, which is our inclination to live in society with other people.

Legal Price and Natural Price

In organized states, prices are fixed in two ways. One way is by some decree or law of those in authority, the other by the general valuation and judgement of men, with the further consent of those who are the parties of the bargain. Pufendorf claims that some are accustomed to call the former legal, and the latter the common or the natural price (ibid.).

The legal price is regularly assumed to agree with justice and equity. However, Pufendorf forwards a clear warning and states that the opposite can be manifestly true. In fixing this legal price, gross ignorance may now and then intervene. Furthermore, those in authority, who decide the price, might show hatred or favour towards buyers or sellers, or there might exist some other form of corruption. In setting the legal price they might also have more regard for their own profit.

The legal price is generally fixed at 'a definite point' and admits no latitude. Any variation therefore constitutes an injustice. Pufendorf also discusses how the legal price can be set in favour of either the seller or the purchaser. If the price is set in favour of the seller, the buyer cannot rightfully try to persuade the seller to accept less. However, the latter may accept less if he chooses, since every man has the right to renounce what is to his advantage. If the price is set in favour of the purchaser the seller cannot demand more. Pufendorf gives an example of how 'in some places a more subtle procedure was adopted so that the prices of certain things may not become too high'. In the states of Greece there was a rule that fish vendors should not sit but stand; 'so that worn out by the monotony and strain of standing they would sell their fish while fresh and at a fair price' (ibid.: 686–687).

How is the Natural Price Determined?

The common or natural price is not fixed by law. It has some latitude within more or less can be demanded or supplied. Pufendorf claims that the Roman philosopher Seneca the Younger (d. AD 65) must refer to this price when he says:

> What does their real value matter, since the buyer and seller have settled the price between them? ... The price of everything varies according to circumstances; after you have well praised your wares, they are worth only the highest price at which you can sell them.
>
> (V.i.9: 687).

He also realized that when supply is given it is not individual evaluation but total evaluation or total demand, which determines the price. Again, a quote from Seneca: 'The prices of things are not fixed by fancy, nor by their utility to individuals, but by their common utility, that is, they are worth as much as all would value them' (ibid.).

Furthermore, this price is also a just price which is commonly set 'by those who are sufficiently acquainted with both the merchandise and the market' (ibid.).

In fixing the natural price, consideration must be given to the labour and expense, which merchants undergo in importing and handling their wares. Pufendorf discusses what kind of expenses merchants in commerce can included in the natural price, and what expenses are not. If a merchant broke his leg or became ill when he brought his wares to the market such incurred expenses cannot be charged to the price. 'But, merchants can include in their estimation the time they have spent, the plans they have formed, and the troubles they have met in acquiring, preserving, and distributing their merchandise, as well as all necessary expenses for the labour of their servants' (V.i.10: 688). Furthermore, costs that accrues because of difficulties or risk in the transport, the length of transport, 'as well as different value of money and goods in different places' can be included in the natural price (ibid.).

Pufendorf also stresses the point that merchants are in the market to make profit and that a certain profit is necessary as incentives for the functioning of the market. 'And it would surely be inhuman, and likely to destroy the industry of men, to try to allow a man for his business, or any other short of occupation, no more profit than barely permits him to meet his necessities by frugality and hardship' (ibid.).

Finally, the natural price also varies with market conditions that is 'according to the manner of buying and selling'. For those who sell goods by retail can demand a somewhat larger price than those who sell wholesale. In a retail market, where goods are sold in small amounts, those who sell will experience more trouble in the buying and selling than those who sell in wholesale. It is also more profitable to receive payments in large sum than to collect in small amounts (ibid.).

In the natural price can be included any loss ensuing, or foregoing profit, which befalls the seller by virtue of such a sale. Merchants can therefore include the loss or increase of profit, which 'follows upon delayed or prompt payment'. The opportunity cost is recognized. 'For surely the day as well is part of price, and it is of more consequence to pay on the spot than after some time, since some further profit can be made of the money in the meantime' (ibid.: 689).

In their cost can also be included the abundance or scarcity of workers, who will be employed in the production and transport of these goods. Their abundance is again affected by the price of labour, which in turn depends on the dexterity required of such labour, usefulness, and necessity and labourers' freedom to work when they choose.

Changes in Market Price

The natural price is not the market price; this price will be determined by the interactions of what today will be called changes in demand and supply. 'But it is also well known how subject a market is to sudden and frequent changes from the plenty or scarcity of purchasers, money and commodities' (V.i.10: 688).

If for some particular reason a decrease in the number of purchasers or their income occurs while we have an abundance of commodities, the price will fall. On the other hand, an increase in the number of buyers, when we have a scarcity of goods, will increase the price. An increase in the quantity for sale, *ceteris* paribus, will have a reduction in the market price as an effect. This assertion is supported by a quote from the Roman historian Cornelius Tacitus: 'The quantity for sale brought about a fall of price' (ibid.). On the other hand, a decline in the quantity of goods, what Pufendorf calls a scarcity of goods, will increase the price.

Pufendorf is also aware of what we call buyers' and sellers' market. Buyers' market is when sellers have trouble selling all their wares at anticipated prices. He explains in the following way. 'So also it makes for a lower price if sellers hunt out purchasers and offers them his wares, that is, when the merchandise seeks purchasers' (ibid.). A mode of selling, when there is scarcity of purchasers that leads to a fall in price, has passed into the proverb 'proffered wares stinks' (ibid.).

From this discussion, it is clear that the market price is determined by an interaction between the utility of all buyers, and the scarcity of a commodity or service, in modern parlance, supply and demand. The price will rise towards a level where it covers the normal costs that accrue during the production and transport of that good, that is the natural price. Lack of need or demand of a good, caused by a scarcity of purchasers, lowers the price. But the price will also be lowered if the number of suppliers increases. He therefore expresses a rudimentary Marshallian demand and supply analysis.

Question of Information

Pufendorf also brings up for discussion the question of what kind of information a seller has to give possible buyers about the product he sells or about the market conditions for this particular product.

Equality is the key word. All parties should have the same kind of information and if inequality is found the party, who has received less, acquires the right to demand, 'that what he lacks to be made up to him' (V.iii.1: 708). From this it follows that 'he who by contract wills to transfer a thing to another, should indicate not only its qualities that can be estimated, but also its shortcomings and faults, insofar as they are known to him; for unless this is done, it is impossible to fix clearly a just price' (V.iii.2: 709). However, this does not mean that a man has 'to disclose to every one the condition of his affairs, or to communicate to another all his knowledge' (V.iii.3: 710). If he is not under contract, he can hide many things from others even though he may be the only one to enjoy profits from his silence. 'For instance, if I know that gems are found in a deserted place belonging to no one, I am not obligated to tell this to another that he also may share with me the profit' (ibid.).

Pufendorf also draws attention to another issue. Just as there is no doubt that notice should be given of possible faults with some merchandise that is being contracted, there has been a discussion among the ancients whether other things as well, which did not concern the actual matter at hand, and yet have some bearing on its value, should be indicated as much by the buyer as the seller. He uses an example the Merchant of Rhodes, as it is referred to by the Roman orator Cicero. A merchant from Alexandria has brought a shipload of grain to Rhodes, where there at this time was a famine among the Rhodians. The merchant also knows that many other merchants have sailed from Alexandria with grain, bound for Rhodes, and that they will arrive shortly. The question is if he should reveal this information to the Rhodians, or keeping silent and sell his own grain at as high price as possible (V.iii.4: 711).

Different authors at different times have brought up, discussed and given different answers to this question. Pufendorf claims that from a strict market point of view the merchant does not have to reveal this information because at the time of the contract nothing was concealed. The quality of the grain was apparent and it was worth as much as it was being sold for, although it would have been worth less a short time afterwards. Furthermore, the Rhodians had no right to this information, 'in the proper sense of the word, to learn this from the merchant, since they had no pact with him on that point' (ibid.: 712).

There is another question that Pufendorf 'would not hasten to answer in the affirmative' (ibid.). Did the merchant act against what he calls the law of beneficence and humanities? There are three reasons why the merchant in this case was not obliged to reveal his knowledge. First, for an obligation to come from the law of beneficence and humanity it is necessary that the other person is in great need 'of having it done him gratis'. This was not the case since the Rhodians needed grain but had no lack of money. They could certainly pay a high price. Second, a person is not obliged to do a kindness when he as the giver loses more than the receiver gains. In this case the merchant would have lost more profit by informing of the coming fleet, that the buyers would have gained in grain. Third, the general custom in business is not to stick to a too close observance of duties in transactions of this nature. The necessity of beneficence in the case of merchants 'can be easily overlooked' (ibid.).

Furthermore, Pufendorf contends that no one should be forced into a contract; 'neither of the parties may use unjust fear upon the other to make the contract' (V.iii.6: 713). Contracts made by cohesion should be declared null. However, a government can force a merchant to undertake a contract, that is, 'to sell something of which the state is in great need, or to let their services, wagons or ships' (ibid.: 714). This is entirely proper when the public service, or necessity requires it, and the price of the service or merchandise is justly met.

Finally, he adds, without further discussion, it is not uncommon for states to require that a man who wishes some particular thing, 'must buy from one person and from no one else' (ibid.).

Theory of Money and Trade

The Origin of Money

After completing his discussion of the factors that determine the value or price of a commodity or service, known as the ordinary or market price, Pufendorf turns to the origin of money as a common measure of value, known as the eminent price. The eminent price follows, in large extent, the metal value. This corresponds roughly to what we today call the monetary value. When the price of a good changes, we must distinguish between change in the price of the good itself or a change in the value of money. The first occurs if a greater or smaller quantity of the good is available, given an unchanged quantity of money. The other occurs if the quantity of money changes while the supply of the good is constant.

In simple primitive societies 'commerce used to consist only in the exchange of goods, and the works of others could be paid for only in the work or in kind' (V.i.11: 690). However, in more advanced societies people's more luxurious desires led to a lack of many things, and they were no longer satisfied with what was produced at home but yearned for the products of other countries. In such a situation, it was not easy for a person to exchange the goods and services he had in abundance for the goods or services he wanted. One particular good or service that he wanted had to be exchanged for just another good or service, or a combination of goods and services he had. The introduction of money is therefore closely linked to the development of commerce and international trade. 'Money is created the better to aid commerce, not merely between citizens of the same state, but between those of different states' (V.i.14: 693).

Obviously, it will not be easy to find the combination that makes exchange possible in this way. It is 'perfectly plain that those nations which are unacquainted with the use of currency have no part in the advances of civilization' (V.i.11: 690). Therefore, most nations, 'which enjoy a higher level of culture', have agreed to set an eminent or money price on a good which will serve as a measure for what it is worth when measured against other goods. When the volume of exchange increased, it became impractical to exchange one commodity for another. From this, a need arose to find something that could be used to measure the value of different commodities. Fine metals were practical for this purpose. Because of their scarcity, they have a high value in comparison to their weight. Fine metals could therefore also be handled and defended with some ease. Such metals could therefore be used as money.

By using money, a person could 'secure for himself anything that was for sale and carry on all commerce and fulfil every agreement with perfect convenience' (V.i.12: 690).

Another reason for the introduction of money was that we also know today what we will want in the future. Money was therefore introduced so that we could make sure in advance that we would have the means to secure what we should need in the future. It is a surety so that when a person presents it, he can get anything that is for sale. To deepen his exposition Pufendorf quotes again from several of Aristotle's works.

What Can Be Used as Money?

Most nations have found it most convenient to use the nobler and comparatively rare metals, such as gold, silver or bronze as this measurement. The reason being that money had to be of a substance that was convenient to carry. The money commodity must also be divisible and durable, so it can easily be divided into smaller units, and the metals should not easily wear out by usages. However, since the functioning of money is 'not given it by any necessity arising from its nature, but by the imposition and agreement of men', it is also clear that other materials can be used either because of 'stress or circumstances or by preference' (V.i.13: 692). Several examples are given of how other materials, such as leather or paper, but also materials such as grains of salts and seashell have served the purpose of money.

Can Heads of State Change the Value of Money?

Pufendorf thereafter goes on to discuss how far the heads of states can proceed in determining the value of money. Although the value depends upon the imposition and agreement of men 'the governors of states' do not have the freedom to change the value at their own will. They must bear in mind certain considerations. First, the value of money when different noble metals are used must, as a general rule, follow the ratio of the value of these metals. Second, money is created to make commerce easier, not merely between citizens of the same state, but between those of different states.

Debased Money Detrimental to Trade

Pufendorf warns sovereigns against fixing the values arbitrary. If the head of a state has set an outrageous value on his own coinage, it is of no use for trade between nations. Furthermore, the introduction of debased coinage will be detrimental to domestic commerce. To support this argument, he quotes the Greek historian Lucius Flavius Arrian (AD 86–160). 'Neither the banker nor the greengrocer can refuse the Emperor's currency, but, if you show it, he must part, willy nilly, with what the coin will buy' (V.i.14: 694).

He emphasizes that when the size and value of coins is not properly fixed, so it at least is not inferior to the coinage of foreigners that we trade with, it will check the trade between citizens and foreign partners when it is confined entirely to exchange of commodities: 'And this alone will not sustain commerce, except in so far as we export more than we import, and those whose wares we on our part do not need, still stand in need of ours' (ibid.).

It is the responsibility of the authorities to make sure that its citizens do not suffer because of debased money. The interest the Senate of Venice demonstrates for their subjects deserves every commendation.

> For when a great number of smaller debased coins had slipped in and could in no way be gotten rid of, a decree of the Senate was finally passed, that those who brought such to the treasury at an appointed time would receive their equivalent in silver or gold. To meet this there was drawn from the treasury over five hundred thousand crowns.
>
> (Ibid.: 695)

Who Can Change the Value of Money?

Pufendorf emphasizes that the heads of state should, as a rule, not change the value of money. Even fluctuations of the value of money, which arise from natural causes, without any interference by law, can be injurious to the economic system of the states. In this respect, it is irrelevant whether an abundance of goods depresses the prices, or plenty supply of gold and silver lowers the value of money and raises the prices. It is therefore only when the highest interest of the state makes it necessary that the value of money can be changed. 'Since money is the measure of the price of other things, it is easy to see that there should be no change in its value, unless the highest interests of the state advise it, then the slighter this change the less it will disturb the business affair of the citizens' (V.i.15: 696).

Quantity of Money and the Price Level

For the promotion of commerce, it is also important to select a kind of money, which has a permanent value to obviate the difficulties of exchange. On the question of the permanent value of money, attention should be given to the observation of Grotius: 'Money acquires its function naturally, not by reason of its material alone, nor by reason of a special name or form, but because it has a more general character by which it is compared either with all things, or with the things that are most necessary' (ibid.). The meaning is, Pufendorf claims, that if a certain coin today has a certain value, this is not only because it has so much gold or silver, nor whether it is called a ducat, crown, thaler, florin, 'or because it bears a certain stamp'. Its value results from the comparison of it 'as to scarcity and abundance with other things, and especially with those which are the most necessary for life' (ibid.). So again, it is the market conditions together with the alloy content of the coin, which determines the value of money.

Most of the products which sustain human life, today and in the future, come from land. Moreover, since these products in an average year have stable prices, and since it is 'highly agreeable' that other prices in general are raised and lowered according to the price of land itself, it is fair that the value of money should 'rise and fall according as it is found to be scarce or plentiful in respect to land' (ibid.). In a time of great abundance of money, the price of land and its products should be low, while if money is scarce the price will be high.

In addition, when the price of one and the same thing is said to be changed, a careful distinction must be drawn as to whether the value of the thing itself is changed, or if it is the value of money[10] (V.I.16: 698).

The Value of Money is Subject to Change

Pufendorf claims that it will now be possible to answer the question whether a farm, which some hundred year ago was rated at 100 pieces of gold, should not today be rated for more, everything else being equal; and whether the wages which before were comfortable enough are now evidently too low. The answer lies in the fact that, although our present currency is in weight and fineness equal to the old, in the last 200 years a great quantity of gold and silver had been brought into Europe from Africa and the Indies. Consequently little by little the value of money has fallen notably. Pufendorf quotes the French political writer Jean Bodin (1530–1596), who in his *On the Republic* from 1576 concludes that 'because of the abundance of gold and silver, the prices of things are now ten times as high as they were. Therefore, everything else being equal, the old prices of land and salaries would have to be increased in the same proportion' (V.i.16: 697).[11]

Using the same principle, we can conclude that when there is a scarcity of money compared with other things, a small amount of money can buy many things. On the other hand, if the volume of money increases, more money has to be paid for the same things. 'For since bullion can and does come into trade, just like other merchandise, according to ordinary price, its value will rise or fall with its scarcity or abundance' (ibid.: 697–698). In addition, the money value will out of necessity follow the ordinary or market price of metals since it is improper that same amount of silver in a country should have one value as bullion and another when it is coined.

So when it has been said that the price of a commodity has changed it is important to make a careful distinction whether it is the price of the commodity itself, the ordinary price in Pufendorf's word, or if it is the value of money.[12]

> For it is the former case when the thing itself begins to be found in greater or less abundance than usual, while the supply of money remains the same; but the latter when the coinage in general increases or decreases, while the supply of things remain as usual.
>
> (Ibid.: 698)

Money and the Rate of Interest

Pufendorf is fully aware of the connection between the amount of money and the rate of interest. He quotes the Roman antiquary and biographer Suetonius (70–130):

> By bringing the royal treasures to Rome in his Alexandrian triumph he (Augustus) made ready money so abundant, that the rate of interest fell, and the value of real estate rose greatly.
>
> (Ibid.)

Furthermore, when the amount of money increases the rate of interest falls and the value of real estate rises greatly. However, normally these changes happen slowly over a long time. And when such a fluctuation occurs slowly and imperceptible it did not destroy the character of money as a standard of value. It is only arbitrary and sudden changes in currency that shake the foundation of the system.

The Value of Money when the Exchange Value Varies

Pufendorf returns to the problem involved in a change in the value of a currency. He discusses the case when a consumable thing is given to a person on condition that he returns the same kind in the same quantity and quality. His starting point is that the exchange value of money varies. The question is then whether the value of money should be considered at the time when a loan was contracted or at the time of payment. Most authorities are, Pufendorf contends, of the opinion that a distinction should be drawn between the intrinsic and extrinsic value of money. The intrinsic value lies in the material or weight of the coins. The extrinsic value in the public assessment, that is in the market value, or the value set by the state.

If the change is in the intrinsic value, which is the money becoming debased, the loan should be paid back at the value it bore at the time the loan was granted. If money has been reduced in its intrinsic value by for example 25 per cent, then for 100 units by the old reckoning 125 by the new will have to be returned. 'Likewise, if I have lent a man 100 pieces, of which one half is alloy, only 50 has to be paid, should the issue be recalled and silver take the place of the alloy' (V.vii.6: 750). Pufendorf recognized that it is within the power of the state to raise or lower the value of money of the same metal. However, a state has to be very careful because considerations have to be given to our trading partners. Otherwise we have to be willing to see our trade with them reduced to mere barter. Neither is the sovereign authorized to change the value, or in modern parlance, to devaluate or revaluate, the currency except when the requirements of the state make this course imperative.

But what if the intrinsic value is unchanged and the external value of money changes due to changes in the market conditions? It is then felt, Pufendorf argues, that the value of money should be considered as it is at the time when the loan should be repaid. It would then be the debtor that would have a profit if the external value of money increases and a loss if the external value decreases.

Yet the affair is not entirely clear. The creditor that has given the loan in Imperials, may rise the point in the first case that if he had kept his Imperials the increase in value would have gone to him. Moreover, if he now loses it, another person is profiting from his loss. In the second case the debtor will raise the same complaint (V.vii.7: 751). However, in the end Pufendorf agrees with what Walter Simons (1934: 38a) calls the prevailing opinion of the time. Assume that a loan has been granted in a currency at full value, and that in the time before it should be repaid the currency has been debased or devaluated by the sovereign authority of a state. The loan should then have to be repaid in an amount where the currency has been revaluated to the original value.

Monopolies

Pufendorf starts this discussion by asking whether all kinds of monopolies are opposed to the law of nature (V.v.7: 738–740). The reason being that both the name monopoly is odious, and that the laws of many states censure the practice. However, many things do not deserve this negative characterization of being termed a monopoly. He claims that many cases should be exempted from the blame of being a monopoly since they are not truly monopolies.

So, what is a monopoly? 'For a monopoly means that if one man has secured for himself alone the power to sell certain goods, no others may have the same power' (ibid.). This means that a man who for example is the only one to import a certain commodity from a remote region does not exercise a monopoly, if no one else is forbidden to import the same commodity from that region. This is what we today will call a contestable market situation.

It can also be lawful for a nation, which has a large supply of a commodity, to agree with another to sell to it alone that kind of commodity. 'For every one is free to sell his own goods when and whom he pleases' (ibid.). However, if it should be the case that this nation has this commodity in abundance and that others cannot do without it; in such a case the law of humanity will require that the conditions for the others should not be made worse by such an agreement (ibid.).

Furthermore, it is against the law of nature if a man can secure from himself the sole right to sell a commodity and is able 'to prevent by force or secret machinations' others from selling the same commodity, such that all other men would have to purchase it from him. It is also clear that 'he both sins against the law of humanity, and malevolently infringes upon the liberty of the rest of mankind' (ibid.).

In some cases, state authorities will have granted privileges to 'a single person or a guild of merchants' to import certain kinds of goods from specific places. Others will then be excluded from this trade. There might be good reasons for granting such privileges:

1 There might be great expenses to establish such a trade and it might involve great risk. The first one to establish such adventures must therefore have the security that all their initial work and expenses should not fall gratis into the hands of others.
2 If needed such privileged companies, by their wealth, can be of more help to the state than individuals.
3 Trade carried out by such companies, can also lead to a greater imported quantity.

A prudent government that grants such privileges should do so only in the case that commodities are imported from very remote places at great risk. Furthermore, merchants should not be given the opportunity 'to mass great wealth at the expense of the rest' unless the state receives from this a special advantage. Finally, the state should not grant privileges to monopolies that use their monopoly power to force the providers to sell to them. In this case, 'the wealth of a state flows into the hands of a few to the oppression of the rest'. To underscore his point, he takes an issue against Grotius example of how Joseph when viceroy of Egypt created a monopoly. 'For the king had not forbidden others to lay up grain in the fruitful years, and no one was prevented from selling any of his surplus supply' (ibid.: 739).

Pufendorf then explains how private citizens can construct and maintain monopolies *by clandestine frauds and conspiracies.* They can for example by deceit prevent others from buying the commodities they sell, or they can hinder them from bringing their commodities to the market. They can also form an association and buy up all of a commodity, then hold back the quantity, create a scarcity, and sell to an unjust price. 'The wickedness of such men should be restrained in the same way as those, who in the oil-sellers' market, act together to raise the price of things too high by secretly agreeing among themselves not to sell their wares below a certain price' (ibid.).

On Interest

Pufendorf was writing in an era in which some kind of interest taking was an accepted commercial practice, but one that was still viewed with an utmost suspicious eye of both the Catholic, Lutheran and Calvinist churches. Schumpeter (1954) points out that theologians in the sixteenth and seventeenth centuries continued to repeat Scholastic arguments both for and against interest taking. In an interesting working paper *Usury, Calvinism, and Credit in Protestant England*, John Munro (2011) claims that it is myth that the usury doctrine of the late-medieval Scholastic era 'ceased to be observed in Protestant lands from the sixteenth century'. He points out that most followers of Luther or Calvin in the sixteenth and early seventeenth centuries were more hostile to usury than contemporary Catholics.

Pufendorf starts his discussion on interest with a summary of how the ancient Hebrews explained the divine law on usury using the elaboration set forth by the English jurist John Selden. Then he goes on to inquire whether the rules on usury observed by the Hebrews belongs to natural law, or to the positive divine law and furthermore if these rules were laid down for all people. The answer is that these rules belong to positive law for the Jewish people, whereas according to natural law a rate of interest may be agreed upon for a loan in proportion to the gains expected from the money loaned (V.vii.9: 754).

The reason for the fact that we are willing to lend someone our money is 'that we may secure the means to increase our wealth in some notable degree, or to get something that can bring us profit'. Moreover, when a man negotiates a loan for this end, 'there is no reason why a person should accommodate him gratis' (ibid.: 756).

Why can we charge usury or interest? Pufendorf discusses and rejects many arguments forwarded by Greek and Roman scholars, by representatives of the churches, and by some modern writers against interest. One reason for his rejection was the fact that although they could not accept interest, they accepted all kinds of payments that in the end had the same result as interest. Furthermore, he claims that there is no reason why a person should lend out his money gratis to a second person, who by using this money seeks his own gain and advantage. When the first person in the meantime might either have made the same gain or else certainly was undergoing the risk of losing his principle by the misfortune or dishonesty of the second person.

He also emphasizes that money is not a barren thing, since surely by means of money other things can be most easily acquired. Interest was also in these days payment for borrowing capital. Why do we want to take up a loan? Because, by borrowing money we may secure the means to increase our wealth, or to buy something that can bring us increased profit in the future. However, not only would interest benefit the individual lenders and borrowers it would also benefit society as such. 'And men of means, being unwilling for their money to lie idle, will either take up business themselves, or lend their money to those who will, whereby commerce will be quickened to the great advantage of the state' (V.vii.9: 756).

Pufendorf does not discuss how much interest a lender can charge. The lender and the borrower should nevertheless, negotiate the interest, and it should be moderate. Neither does he discuss in any detail if it is a task for the government to set the interest rate. But he ends his discussion on interest claiming that 'those civil laws are worthy of entire commendation, which do not allow men free play in the exaction of usury, but set for them a fixed rate, save that it does not appear unjust to exact a little higher interest when a loan is required for but a short period' (V.vii.12: 762).

Notes

1 The Greeks Aristotle, Demosthenes (384–322 BC), Plutarch (46–120 BC), the Jew Philo of Alexandria (20 BC – AD 50), the Romans Ovid (45 BC–AD 17), Seneca the Younger (4 BC – AD 65), Pliny the Elder (AD 23–79), Quintilian (AD 35–100).

2 He wrote in Latin under the name Ianus Nicius Erythraeus.

3 Pufendorf uses the Latin word *pretium*. The translators Charles H. Oldfather and William A. Oldfather have in *De Jure Naturae et Gentium* translated *pretium* with *price*. In *De Officio* the translator Frank Gardner More translated *pretium* with *value*. In *Elementorum Jurisprudentiae Universalis* the translator William A. Oldfather translated *pretium* with *worth*.

4 In Basil Kennet's translation he uses the word 'proper'.

5 According to Hutchison (1988: 97), Pufendorf with this distinction appears to develop a precursor of those subsequently drawn by Richard Cantillon (1680–1734), Adam Smith and others between 'natural' (or 'intrinsic') price and market price.

6 It is clear from Grotius' treatment of the theory of price in *De Jure Belli ac Pacis*, ch. 12 'On contracts' p. 351, that need is not the only measure of value.

7 The word 'demand' did not come into English language before Gershom Carmichael used it. See Chapter 15.

8 Strabo's work is a major source of knowledge of the ancient world. He lived in Amascia, now Amasya, Turkey. He wrote 47 books of *Historical Sketches* and his *Geographical Sketches* defines the aims and methods of geography.

9 *Theory of the Leisure Class* from 1899. This is also noted by Gaertner (2005:241).

10 This is what Bo Sandelin (1987: 577) calls elements of the quantity theory of money.

11 Joseph Schumpeter (1954: 311) claims that Bodin 'is universally voted the "discoverer" of the Quantity Theory of Money'.

12 According to Terence Hutchison (1988: 99), Pufendorf called attention to this fundamental distinction later emphasized by Carl Menger (1840–1921).

10 The Foundation of States and Councils

Pufendorf's views concerning the origin of the state is outlined in *De Jure Naturae et Gentium*. He presents his doctrines on the contractual nature of the state, how the will of the state can function, and how the decisions in a council are resolved. He uses and refers to many writers to prove his points.[1]

On the Establishment of a State

Pufendorf's starting point for the origin of the state is the presumption that man, by nature, loves himself more than society. In his view man's sociability, or inclination for society, led to the formation of 'first (or prime) societies'. However, these societies are not synonymous with a state or commonwealth. He claims that the reason why man, living in families, formed a state will be clear when we have examined both the nature of civil society and the inclination of human character (VII.i.1: 949).

In his usual way, he claims that it would be profitable to set forth what is commonly said about this matter. Most writers fall back on the nature of man, 'which is so drawn to civil society that without it he neither wishes to nor can exist' (VII.i.3: 949). These writers argue that it is man's social nature that is decisive. It would be miserable for man to live a solitary life. The faculty of speech was also given to humankind for no purpose other than socialization, the love of associating with men, the advantage of companionship with others, and the like. Hobbes, on the other hand, attempts to show 'that man is in fact an animal which loves first and foremost himself and his own advantage'. He would prove this by the fact that man is not induced to love the society of another by the mere fact that he is a man, but that he hopes to seek some advantage from this company. This point Pufendorf supports and illustrates by reference to particular societies. One example is drawn from business practices.

> Those who unite for business purposes have an eye to their own profit, which they hope they can obtain better by taking partners than by conducting their business separately. When they have been deceived in this expectation, every one will consider them fools, if they do not withdraw from such a losing partnership at the earliest opportunity.
>
> (VII.i.2: 950)

Nevertheless, he adds that although we presume in man a love for society, it does not at once follow that man is led by his nature to form a civil government. For this love can be satisfied by less developed societies and by friendship with one's equals. In addition, such fellowship can be attained without states. It should be observed outside the border of a state that there can be many people close to a man: parents, children, wives and friends. This matter will be clearer, if we consider what condition is assumed by men upon the formation of states, what is required for a man to be called a political creature, i.e. a good citizen and what is there in the nature of man that is repugnant, so to speak, to a civil life? (VII.i.4: 953).

Why would man give up his natural liberty and subject himself to sovereignty when his natural inclination is 'to be subject to no one, to suit all his actions to his own pleasure, and to seek his own advantage in all his undertakings'? (VII.i.4: 953–954). There must be reasons important enough to have the force to overcome such inclinations. Pufendorf concludes that 'man did not enter states by his own free will, led, as it were, by nature, but that he did so to avoid greater evils' (ibid.: 954).

What is required by the nature of a man for him to be called a political animal, which for Pufendorf is a good citizen? The answer is not that a natural aptitude can be found in each one to act the part of a good citizen, but that at least a part of humankind by nature has this aptitude. In addition, when humankind increases in number it can only secure its safety and preservation in civil societies. 'Into these, nature always intent upon its own preservation, impels men to enter, just as also it is the first fruit of civil society, that in it men may accustom themselves to lead an orderly civil life' (ibid.: 956).

What in the nature of man is repugnant to civil life? There are inclinations in the nature of man that works against the formation of states. For example, there is love among brothers, but they would like to be equals and no one would like to be subject to the sovereignty of the other. 'And so the primitive conditions of mankind as it multiplied, led more to their separation and scattering into different parts of the earth, than to their collection into larger groups' (VII.i.5: 957).

Therefore, the real and principal reason why men 'left their natural liberty and undertook to establish states, was in order that they could surround themselves with defences against the evils that which threaten man from his fellow man' VII.i.7: 959. So states were established as 'a seemly precaution against future evil' (ibid.). States are therefore established to gain security and protection from the evil or wickedness of men.

On the Internal Structure of States

Pufendorf's next task is then to examine the intrinsic structure of states in some detail. The purpose of this investigation is to determine whether the state provides sufficient protection against the wickedness of its inhabitants. This protection has to be so strong that an attack of one person upon another would be made so dangerous, that the attacker would feel it safer to restrain himself than to fight:

> For the wickedness of man's character and his proneness to injure others can in no way be restrained more effectively, than by thrusting in his face the immediate evil which will await him upon his attacking another, and by removing every hope of impunity.
>
> (VII.ii.1: 967)

This rather derogatory description of man's character emerges at various times in all his natural law works.

Accordingly, man created a state because the safety and preservation of mankind can be secured only by civil societies. Pufendorf concludes that there can be found no better guarantee against the danger that threatens man from man 'than that afforded by man himself, in pooling resources, mutually intertwining their safety, and warding off perils by a common confederacy' (VII.ii.1: 968).

He emphasizes that a confederacy of a few cannot offer man the security he seeks. There has to be a sufficient number of citizens so they can repel any injuries from their neighbours. He quotes Plato who 'requires for his state a number of citizens sufficient to repel any injuries from their neighbours, and to offer them succour when they are in turns the victims' (VII.ii.2: 968, Plato Laws, Bk.V:737). Here he also makes a reference to what the Greek historian Polybius (200–118 BC) set forth on the weakness of the Athenian democracy. Polybius claims that unions of many men will not prevail for a long time if they are not held together 'by some common fear'. Pufendorf argues that hence it follows that the concord of many men even if it is confirmed by a pact or an agreement will not give the necessary security. It is not enough that a group of people form a society for mutual aid, and promise each other that they will use their strength 'to the same end and the common good'. There must be added something else so that those who agreed to such a union for the sake of the common good would 'be prevented by fear from later department from that agreement, when they conclude that their own private advantage differs from that of the group' (VII.ii.3: 969).

Contractual Nature of the State

So when a sufficient number of men have come together to establish a state, they have to make a pact or an agreement with sufficient strength so that the state does not fall apart as soon as the immediate treat has disappeared.

> But something else must be added in order that those who have once agreed to peace and mutual aid for the sake of the common good will be prevented by fear from later departing from the agreement, when they conclude that their own private advantage differs from that of the group.
>
> (Ibid.)

It is therefore necessary to establish something more solid which can defy the many divergent wills or interests of men.

In the first place, it is not possible to create a union of wills of all, by throwing together all wills into one. Second, a union cannot be created when there is only one person who will be willing, and all the others are ceasing to be willing. Third, it is not possible to create a union by eliminating in some way the natural variations of people's wills and people's tendency to disagree with another (VII.ii.5: 972).[2]

So, what is it then that for a long time will bind together the consent of many men? Pufendorf's answer is a union of wills, where the will of every individual is subordinated to one man or a single council 'so that whatever that man or council shall decree on matters necessary to the common security, must be regarded as the will of each and every person. For whoever voluntarily grants his power to another is held to agree with his will' (ibid.).[3]

And finally: 'When such a union of wills and strength has been made, then there finally arises a state, the most powerful of moral societies and persons' (ibid.).

When men have come together to form such a union, they must also agree on applying the means suitable for that end. This union of individual wills within a state must be regulated by intervening agreements.

What Agreements Are Needed?

Pufendorf claims that two agreements and one decree are needed to create a state. First, there must be *an agreement* among many individuals that they desire to unite and administrate the safety and security through common council and leadership (VII.ii.7: 974). This can be called an agreement of association. It is entered either absolutely or conditionally. Absolutely, when every man pledges for himself to remain with the group, whatever government the majority will choose. Conditionally, when he reserves the right to approve or disapprove the chosen form of government. When this pact is entered, it is necessary for each and all to give their consent. Whoever does not give their consent remains outside the future state and is not required to join their government, but must take care of his own safety. Pufendorf does not discuss how this eventually can be done in practice.

Second, after this *agreement* has been decided upon it is necessary for *a decree* to be passed, by the agreement of the majority, on the form of government that shall be introduced, whether it should take the form of a monarchy, aristocracy or democracy. 'For until this decision is reached, it will be impossible to take consistent action on matters concerning the common safety' (ibid.: 974).

If the first *agreement* is entered into *absolutely* the matter is closed. Everyone will be forced by the agreement of the majority to consent to the form of government which the latter have agreed upon. However, if it was entered into *conditionally*, a man can withdraw if he does not agree with the chosen form of government.

Finally, after the form of government has been decided, a new *agreement* will be necessary between the rulers, that is the individual or body to whom the government is entrusted, and the others: the ruled or the subjects. In this pact, which can be called a pact of subjection, 'the rulers bind themselves to the care of common security and safety', and the ruled, i.e. the citizens, must give them their obedience, 'that subjection and union of wills, by reason of which the state is looked upon as a single person' (VII.ii.8: 975). This agreement of subjection between rulers and the ruled is required not only in monarchies and aristocracies but also in democracies. Although in the latter this is not so clear cut, since the same individuals are, in different aspects, both rulers and subjects because the power of command is vested in the people. In a monarchy, a pact is necessary by which the ruler or the ruler's council takes up the care of common security and safety, and requires the people to render them obedience. If democracy is chosen, each citizen is understood to have subordinated his will to the will of the majority, 'while it appears that sufficient necessity is, at the same time, laid upon each individual, by his love for himself and his possessions, to labour with all his strength for the public good, with which his own safety is also intertwined' (ibid.: 976). A tacit consent is therefore required.

From the two agreements, one of association and one of subjection, and one *decree* in between, a finished state is constructed.

Pufendorf presents in some detail the views of Hobbes, who in his formation of states recognizes only a single contract between individuals.[4] In his presentations there is no pact between a king or nobles and citizens. According to Pufendorf the reason that led Hobbes to hold such a view is outlined in Leviathan. Here he attacked 'all those seditious men' who took away the royal power and 'placed it under the control of subjects', or 'even do away with it altogether'. He took from their excuse for rebellion, namely, 'that the pledge between the king and citizen is reciprocal, and that when the former does not keep the promises he made by a pact, the latter are freed from obedience'. So Hobbes, 'to prevent turbulent citizens from making a case of broken faith out of any actions of a king which do not suit them', denied that there was any pact between a king and his subjects (VII.ii.9: 977).

However, it is of course important for the welfare of the people that the power of the prince or the king should be held sacrosanct, and that it should be protected from attacks by citizens that are not satisfied with how they use the power. However, it is also clear that there exists a bilateral contract between the prince (or the king) and the citizens. According to this agreement, the prince owes the citizens protection and the citizens owe the prince obedience. Simons (1934: 42a) claims that Pufendorf unswervingly pursues this idea and always carefully refutes the arguments of Hobbes. 'Therefore he applies the axe to the roots of the absolute power of princes whom he had served all his life.'[5]

Pufendorf claims that this method of forming a state by the intervention of two pacts or agreements and one decree is 'in the highest accord with nature, and common to all forms of states'. Now by the two pacts or agreements and the decree a multitude of men unite to form a state. This state can be conceived as a single person with both intelligence and will. This person can again be seen performing other actions that are peculiar to himself and separate from 'those of individuals' (VII.ii.5: 983).

The Will of the State

Pufendorf then goes on to discuss how the will of the state can function. It can function either through one simple person or through a single council depending on whether the supreme control has been secured in the former or the latter.

In an absolute monarchy, the will of the king is the will of the state. However, Pufendorf presupposes that the king is of sound reason. On this assumption, he makes it clear that if a monarch passes bad laws or expresses bad judgements, appoints unfit officials, or starts unjust wars they are still acts of the state. However, not so if he carries out purely private acts 'eats, drinks, sleeps, marries or indulges in vices' (VII.ii.14: 985). A distinction can therefore be drawn between the public and private will of a monarch. Pufendorf then asks the question if the acts of the monarch or the senate, who represent the will of the state, *passes bad laws, pronounces wrong judgements, appoints unfit officials, or starts unjust wars*, are still acts of the state? He answers this way: 'the inconveniences which fall upon innocent citizens from such public misdeeds are to be classed among those evils to which man in his mortality is exposed, and which he must bear, like drought, floods, and all other acts of nature' (ibid.: 986). Society's precautions against such bad deeds are to have good laws, good education and morals through religion.

Council Decisions and Voting Procedures[6]

If the power of the state is expressed through a council composed of several men, where each of them has retained their own will, there must be an agreement right from the beginning, how decisions shall be reached. First he asks how 'great part of it, when agreed, shall represent the will of the entire council, and so of the state' (VII.ii.15: 986).

Veto Rights

Pufendorf makes it clear that no man is bound to follow the opinion of a council more than his own unless he has subjected his will to the will of the council. Suppose a man has declared that he will not be bound if he disagrees. Suppose further that we have a veto structure where one member of a council can block the agreement of all the others. If the person that blocks an agreement of the council has entered the council on the condition that he under no circumstances would be bound by the decision of the majority, he has of course this right. However, he is bound by the general law that a man should conduct himself to the advantage of others, 'and that a part should conform to the good of the whole' (VII.ii.15: 987).

Unanimity Vs Simple Majority

When universal assent is required, Pufendorf maintains that business is carried out with utmost difficulty. This is especially the case when the council is composed of many. Often it would not be possible at all to have an outcome because of differences of opinion arising from what can be called 'the invincible obstinacy of some members' (ibid.). Furthermore, it is presumed that when a man joins a council he cannot demand of all the others that they follow his views or give up what they think is right, therefore he has 'obligated himself to follow and approve what the great majority of his associates have agreed upon' (ibid.).

It is therefore normally presumed that when a man joins a council, he cannot demand of all the others that they follow his views, since he has pledged himself to follow and approve what the great majority of the council has agreed upon. A person who has joined a council has to respect the decisions made by the majority.

Pufendorf discusses the difficulties that can rise when some members are not willing to bind themselves to the decision of the majority and concludes that in all councils the votes of majority have the force of those of all members. The reason being that although there is no necessity by nature for it to be so, 'there is scarcely any other way for them to carry out their business' (VII.ii.15: 988).

Furthermore, he claims that it is by this general rule that the passage by Aristotle must be understood. 'In all of them there exists the right of the majority. For both in an oligarchy, and a democracy, and in the gathering of a people, whatever seems good to the majority of those who share in the government has authority' (ibid.).

Weighted Voting

Although it might sometimes occur, that the opinion of the few would have been in the best interest of the state, it is not possible to construct arrangements that will have no shortcomings. A consequence of accepting the will of the majority is that it can happen that the more prudent are outnumbered by the less prudent, and that the latter then will undertake an act of folly.

He claims that when decisions are made about the truth of a theory, opinion should be considered not by numbers but by weight. He quotes several Greek and Roman scholars in support of such a view. Among them the Roman rhetorician Quintilian: 'And those who wish to appear learned to fools are decidedly pronounced fools by the learned' (VII.ii.15: 989). However, he realizes that to attach weights to opinions, cannot be applied when business is conducted in a council where all the members enjoy equal rights. 'For who will render the decision as to which opinion is the more prudent?' (ibid.). It cannot be one of the parties involved. Furthermore, it is not easy to leave the decision to a third partly since either party can question the prudence and integrity of an arbitrator. It is therefore important to follow a method 'which admits of no difficulty or obscure judgement'. Moreover, none can be found more practicable than just counting the number of parties supporting each opinion.

Furthermore, Pufendorf assumes that whoever is accorded a vote in a council is assumed to have enough prudence to enable him to understand the issues discussed. Optimistically, he argues that 'this is true at least of those councils to which men are not admitted without some choice of election' (ibid.). In a final note on this matter, Pufendorf warns against councils in which the president has been given the power by his vote to favour the majority or the minority or to reject both and select his own plan. In that way the control of affairs will be in favour of such a president, just as absolute princes can follow even the minority of the councillors, or he can 'follow the opinion which is different from any that has been proposed' (ibid.).

Qualified Majorities

In some councils, it is not enough for a decision to be made with a majority of votes. Numbers of votes in favour have to exceed those against by a certain number. The pope, for example, is elected upon receiving the votes of two-thirds of the cardinals. He also quotes the fifteenth century Italian historian Andrea Morosini (1558–1618), who in his *Historia Veneta* (Venice), noted that according to a decree of the Senate banishing the Jesuits, the clause was added that for the decision to be executed 180 senators had to be present and five-sixths had to favour it.

If there has not been made an agreement beforehand favouring a special voting rule, 'the opinion which has but one vote more shall be considered the stronger, and the view of the whole body' (VII.ii.16: 990).

Equality of Votes

In the case that the votes are equal Pufendorf holds that no action should result because the movement for change is not strong enough to warrant it. He is not in favour of giving a double vote to the president of the council. 'Nor would it always be a wise thing if some one man of the council, for example, the presiding officer, should be given the power to declare by his vote which plan is the better' (VII.ii.15: 989).

Some trial cases where the accused was acquitted when the votes were tied are discussed. In support of his argument, he quotes the Greek Orator Antiphon (480–411 BC): 'A stand-off arms the defendant rather than the plaintiff, since also in counting votes a tie helps the defendant rather than the plaintiff'

(VII.ii.17: 991). The possibility that the leader of a council, in such cases, should have a double vote is not discussed.

The Paradox of Voting[7]

Finally, Pufendorf brings up for discussion the case where there are more than two opinions or proposals. In such a case, the question arises as to what kind of rules we should use. A decision must be made if each opinion should be voted on separately. In such a case, the opinion that commands most votes is selected. Alternatively, two or more opinions, although they are opposed to each other, may be combined to be voted against a third opinion. If the third opinion is defeated then the two opinions, which were combined, may then be voted against each other. The one of these two that has the majority of the votes will then be selected.

Gaertner (2005: 236) points out that while the first of the two aggregation rules comes close to the plurality rule, where each voter casts one point for his top-ranked alternative and zero points for all the others, the second procedure is a variant of successive pair-wise majority voting. However, it is not quite clear whether Pufendorf had a ranking over all alternatives in mind.[8]

Pufendorf continues his account, and distinguishes between opinions that are entirely different from each other and those where one opinion includes part of another, which is where the opinions are combined (VII.ii.18: 991). He argues that one should distinguish between cases where the alternatives differ qualitatively, and cases where the alternatives differ only in quantity. He gives an example where opinions differ only in what he calls quantity. There are three judges, who are going to decide on the punishment of an accused. There are three alternatives: one, the accused should be fined twenty units of value: two, the accused should be fined ten units of value; three, the accused should be acquitted. One judge prefers a fine of twenty to a fine of ten or to acquittal. Another judge has the opposite preference. Acquittal prefers to a fine of ten or to a fine of twenty. And, the third judge prefers a fine of ten to both a fine of twenty or to acquittal.

From this, it follows that a majority prefers a fine of ten or more to the minority that prefers no fine at all. It is not said, that there is also a majority against the maximal fine of twenty. Nor does Pufendorf say explicitly that a fine of ten is the only alternative. However, according to Gaertner (2005: 237), 'this observation is visible behind the formulation used. Pufendorf states that the defendant will be fined ten units. In other words, the median voter wins.'[9]

By quoting Seneca the Younger, Pufendorf also argues that this was the reason for the custom of the Roman senate to urge a member to 'divide the motion' if it embraces two parts and only one of them is favoured: 'I think we ought to do in philosophy as they are wont to do in the Senate; when some one has made a motion, of which I approve to a certain extent, I ask him to make his motion in two parts, and I vote (for the part which I approve)' (VII.ii.18: 992). It is therefore clear that he recommends that such ambiguities should be reduced to a minimum by dividing complex proposal in parts, which could be voted on separately.

However, if the judges as in a court case are divided about how to sentence a defendant, the situation becomes complicated. Some of the judges vote to exile the indicted, some others want to execute him, and others want to set him free. In this case, the ones that want to exile will surely not want to join the ones that want to execute, against the ones that wants to set him free. Nor would the last ones want to join the ones that favour exile against the ones that wants to put him to death. Pufendorf argues that the reason is that these sentences are entirely different from each other. There is no exile in death, nor is it part of death. Although the ones that favours exile and the ones that wants to set free should agree that the accused should not be put to death, 'their sentence does not produce this effect directly, but only by consequence. Yet they are in themselves, as a matter of fact, different, for whoever votes for acquittal frees him of all punishment, while a banisher favours a punishment' (ibid.). When there are such ambiguities, Pufendorf's recommendation was referring to the custom of the Roman senate, that they should be reduced to a minimum by dividing such proposals into parts which could be voted on separately.

Manipulation

Pufendorf is fully aware of the possibilities that voting agendas can be manipulated. Referring to the Greek Polybius, who reported that when certain Achaeans were held captive in Rome and the question of what should be done with them was laid before the Senate there were three opinions: one to release, another to condemn, and a third to hold them for a while. The senators were so divided that those in favour of freeing them were more numerous than the others taken separately. The Praetor of the Imperial Senate, Lucius Postumius Albinus, who was an enemy of the Achaeans, employed a trick in their disfavour. When the time for voting came, the Praetor passed over one opinion, and asked for a vote on only two, ordering that the one that wanted the Achaeans to be released should move to one side, and those who opposed that view to the other side. Then it turned out that those who wished them to be held for a while, joined the ones who wished them condemned, and these two groups together had more votes than those who urged their release. So as pointed out by Lagerspetz (1986: 181–182), the Praetor 'simply omitted the second alternative, which, apparently, was the Condorcet-winner, and put the first alternative against the third in order to get a condemning result'.[10]

An Insoluble Problem?

At the end of this discussion, Pufendorf presents us with a problem that during his time was seen as insoluble. Starting with an outline of a debate by the Roman author and grammarian Aulus Gellius (125–180):

> Suppose seven judges try a prisoner – that judgement is to prevail which the greater number shall determine – the seven judges presided – two of them thought the prisoner should be banished; two of them that he should be fined; the remaining three that he should be put to death. Punishment is demanded according to the decision of the three, for which the prisoner appeals.
>
> (VII.ii.18: 992)

Furthermore, he claims that the same argument was used by the Roman Quintilian who, among other things, quite rightly says: 'You cannot add together those who disagree. Compare those who agree' (ibid.). As an example of an outcome of plurality voting he mentions how, according to the Bishop of Tricca Heliodorus (–395), 'Cenemon is said to have been condemned to death by 1700 votes, to banishment by 1000. But since some of the former had voted for stoning, others for casting him into a pit, the thousand who voted for exile formed a larger number' (ibid.: 993).

This has also been observed by Grotius:

> that when several persons do not constitute an all-inclusive body, properly speaking, but are only joined together in consideration of certain thing in which they do not share equally, not only should their order be fixed in accordance with the manner of their participation, but their votes should be counted in a geometric proportion.
>
> (Ibid.)

It is clear from the ideas discussed by Pufendorf in the previous sections that he is an eclectic, who builds and develops his own theories and presentation on the ideas expressed by others before him. His thoughts on these subjects and the examples that he draws our attention toward are, as noted by Gaertner (2005: 236–238) in the previous mentioned article, 'particularly illuminating with respect to modern social choice theory'.

Notes

1 Included in his references are many Greek and Roman historians, philosophers and orators as well as the moderns: the Dutch Grotius, the English Cumberland, Sir Kenelm Digby (1603–1665) and the French Pierre Charron (1541–1603), the Italian Petrus Suavis (1552–1623), the Germans Boecler and Johann Friederich Horn (1629–1665), and the Spanish Francisco López de Gómara (1511–1557).

2 John Chipman (2012) claims that this 'sentence asserts the impossibility of aggregating individual preferences – an intuition preceding the famous theorem of Arrow (1951)'.

3 Chipman (2012) claims that 'this sentence asserts a logical consequence of this impossibility [see footnote before]; the need for an agreement to transfer decision-making power to a government body – in order to avoid the alternative chaos'. Wulf Gaertner (2005:234) points out that this shows that Pufendorf did not believe

in an ideal union of wills or, as social choice theorists would express it in an effective way of aggregating preferences.

4 Hobbes single contract was named 'contrat social' by Rousseau.

5 Here it can be added that when the newly elected Norwegian Parliament met in 1814, and wrote a constitution and declared its independence, it used this argument. It refused to accept the Treaty of Kiel, where the absolute King Frederik VI of Denmark-Norway ceded Norway to Sweden. By doing this, the Parliament argued that the king had broken his part of the agreement that gave the king absolute power in 1660. The Parliament declared Norway an independent country, but was forced to accept a personal union with Sweden that is with the same king but separate parliaments and governments.

6 In researching this part, I have made valuable use of Wulf Gaertner (2005).

7 The term 'paradox of voting' is used by Marquis de Condorcet (1743–1794) in his article *Essai sur l'application de l'analyse a la probabilté des decisions rendues a la pluralité des voix*. This is discussed in an article by Erik Lagerspetz (1986). Furthermore, Melissa Schwartzberg (2008) contends that Rousseau built closely on Pufendorf and that Condorset again built on Rousseau.

8 Gaertner (2005: 236).

9 Gaertner also claims that these are single peaked preferences as claimed by Duncan Black (1948).

10 Lagerspetz claims that Pufendorf in his own pre scientific way 'seems to have recognized that all methods of collective decision-making can produce counter-intuitive results'.

11 Division of State Powers and Principles of Taxation

Pufendorf express his views on the nature and function of the state and he discusses the supreme sovereignty and the division of the highest powers of the state. This includes the legislative power, the punitive power, the judicial power, the power of war and peace and concluding treaties, and the constituent power, that is, the right of setting up magistrates. He discusses both the regular and the irregular forms of states. The attention will be on his discussion of the three regular forms of states, democracy, aristocracy and monarchy. He also discusses the supreme sovereignty over property, the sovereign's right to levy taxes and the different forms of taxes. He uses many authors to prove his points, among them Greek and Roman philosophers, but also some of the moderns.[1]

The Supreme Sovereignty

Pufendorf claims that a state is a moral body, which is understood to have one will. But, how could this be when a state is made up of many individual people with each person having his own inclination and will? It is not possible to combine the individual wills of many people into one will. He therefore contends that a unified will of a state can only be produced by having 'All the persons in the state submit their will to that of one man, or of a council, in whom the supreme sovereignty has been vested' (VII.iv.2: 1010). Furthermore, since all individual citizens of the state must adapt themselves in accordance with the will of the state, 'that will must be set before them by clear signs' (ibid.: 1011). It is therefore the duty of the supreme sovereignty, the one man or the council, to make clear and prescribe for the citizens of the state what can be done and what should be avoided. Furthermore, since all the individual citizens must adapt themselves in accordance with the will of the state, the will of the state must be made clear to them by distinct orders or prescriptions.

The Division of Responsibilities in a State

Although the supreme civil sovereignty is 'a single and undivided thing', it functions in different acts, and is therefore, Pufendorf argues, understood to have six parts. The first part is the legislative power. It is concerned with 'prescribing general rules of conduct'. The second part is the power to inflict penalties if someone has violated the rules of conduct. The third part is the judicial power. It is concerned with settling 'the controversies of its citizen by those rules' set by the legislative power. As to the fourth part of the supreme sovereignty that 'arms citizen against foreign foes, or orders them to keep the peace', it is called the right of war and peace. The fifth part is the constituent power. It is concerned with hiring 'ministers for the business of the state', and it is also called the right to set up magistrates. Finally, the sixth part is the power to levy taxes (VII.iv.1: 1010).

The Legislative Power

It is the task of the legislative power of the supreme sovereignty to make the laws with clear rules and directives and to prescribe what can and should be done and what should be avoided. It would of course be impossible to issue special directives for each decree for each citizen since there are such a multitude of citizens. General rules therefore should be outlined about what must be done and what must be avoided. These rules and regulations should be made known to all men and for all time. Among men there can be observed 'the greatest diversity of judgements and desires' and therefore 'an infinite number of disputes can arise.' It is therefore required that property rights be publicly defined, that is what each man should consider his own and what belongs to another. It should also be made clear what is considered lawful and what is not, and what is honourable and what is not. Furthermore, it should be made evident what an individual in a state retains of his natural liberty, that is, how to balance individual liberties with the need for state tranquillity. Finally, it needs to be revealed what every citizen by his right can require from other citizens and in what manner (VII.iv.2: 1011).

The Punitive Power

Pufendorf makes it clear that to be able to coerce men to observe both the common precept of natural law and the laws and regulations for each state, there is a need of both a fear of punishment and the power to inflict punishment if laws are broken. The punishment has to be proportional to the laws broken or crime committed.

> That the punishment may meet this end, it should be made so severe that it obviously involves a greater hardship to have broken the laws than to have observed them, and that in this way the severity of the punishment surpasses the satisfaction or gain which is secured or anticipated from an injury.
>
> (VII.iv.3: 1012)

This power to punish those who transgress the commands of the ruler is understood to have been given by the act where men submitted the use of their strength to the state.

The Judicial Power

Experience demonstrates that when even the most explicit laws are put into writing, disputes arise over what is the proper application of a certain law to a particular case. The function of the judicial power is to take jurisdiction and 'to decide between disputes of citizens, to examine individual cases which are accused of being unlawful and to pronounce a sentence appropriate to the laws' (VII.iv.4: 1012).

The Power of War and Peace

It is not enough to have the necessary implements to preserve the security of a citizen or a group of citizens against other fellow citizens. Nevertheless, it is of little use for men to foster peace among themselves, when they cannot protect themselves against foreign foes. Furthermore, this is not possible if they cannot unite their strength. It is due to such a union of strength that many are stronger than one.

> And so, for the security and safety of all mankind, there must exist in a state a power whose function is to assemble, unite, and arm as many citizens, or hire in their place as many mercenaries, as seem required for the common defence against the unknown numbers and strength of enemies, and also, when it seems advantageous, to conclude peace with enemies.
>
> (VII.iv.5: 1013)

Leagues are useful both in periods of peace and of war. When entering such treaties resources of different states can be combined to effectively repel or counter a common enemy. It shall therefore lie within the province of a supreme sovereign to enter such leagues both in a time of peace and in a time of war. Furthermore, leagues should require all their members to observe these treaties and 'at the same time to secure from them some advantages for the state' (ibid.).

The Constituent Power

The constituent power or the right to set up magistrates is an absolute necessity for a state, the reason being that the business of a state cannot be carried out, in a time of war or in a time of peace, by a single man without the aid of subordinate ministers and magistrates. A state will also need men that have the power as judges 'to look into disputes of citizens'. It needs diplomats that can 'search out the policies of neighbouring nations'. Furthermore, it needs officers that can train soldiers. It is also necessary that it has magistrates that can 'collect and dispense the resources of the state, and, finally, in every way to look out for its advantage' (VII.iv.6: 1013). This power can also compel appointed officials to fulfil their functions and duties and demand from them an account on how they have carried out their duties.

The Power to Levy Taxes

Pufendorf notes that the business of a state, in a time of peace or war cannot be carried out without expenses. The state therefore requires access to a certain part of the resources held by its citizens that are judged necessary to meet the expenses of the state. This is the power to levy taxes on its people. These taxes can be collected on the wealth held by its citizens or it can be collected on the produce of the country. Furthermore, the state has the right to levy taxes on imports and exports and on the consumption of goods at home (VII.iv.7: 1013).

What Parts Are Naturally United?

Pufendorf then goes on to explain that these parts of supreme sovereignty are naturally united together and bound up with one another. If we should imagine that some of them are within the control of one man and some within the control of others, the regular form of a state would be destroyed. To understand this, he contends that there are two chief bonds by which the wills of several persons or groups are intertwined, so that they think together as one, namely an agreement and sovereignty.

If those who are held together only by an agreement willingly perform what has been agreed upon, and as long as each party keeps to its agreement, 'there can be concord and unity among them to a sufficient degree'. However, if one person or one group with evil design, goes back on what has been agreed upon, to the determents of the others, there is nothing they can do since the guilty party often is as strong as the injured (VII.iv.9: 1016).

However, Pufendorf claims that sovereignty is a far stronger bond to bind several people or groups into one body. The reason being that whoever is controlled by sovereignty is no longer equal to the one man or council in 'whom is vested the sovereignty'. The power given to the sovereign can be used to inflict penalties upon those who have failed to meet their obligations. 'A far greater necessity of obedience lies upon all than if they were bound simply by a pact, which had not done away with the equality among associates, and then had to decide on their own affairs according to their own judgement' (ibid.).

There is such a close union between all the parts of the supreme sovereignty 'that one cannot be torn from another without destroying the regular form of state'. If we, for example, allot one-person legislative power and another punitive power, independent of each other, it will not function. To enact laws that cannot be enforced is arrant folly. It is also clear that the right of war and peace or the right to raise money cannot be separated from the judicial right. 'Therefore, each power must necessarily depend upon one and the same will' (VII.iv.11: 1017).

Problems of Divisions of Prerogatives

Pufendorf then examines the different kinds of such a division of prerogatives and the problems that arise from such a division. He starts out with an example: 'Let there lie, therefore, with the prince the power of war and peace, with the senate the right to pass laws and execute justice, with the assembly of the people the right to levy taxes' (VII.iv.12: 1018). After having discussed some of the problems that can arise with the division of responsibilities he concludes:

> Therefore, if any man should want entirely to separate the parts of sovereignty, he will under no circumstances establish a regular state, but an irregular body, the members of which, in possessing separate parts of the sovereignty, are held together not by a common sovereignty but only by an agreement.
>
> (Ibid.: 1019)

However, it will be possible to preserve concord in such a group if the opinions of the members of the state 'agree on the public good', and every citizen is ready to do his part toward meeting this end.

Forms of States

Pufendorf claims that supreme sovereignty is found in every regular state. Whether it resides in one man, in one council composed of a few, or in all the citizens, it gives rise to different forms of states. He discusses three forms of government in a regular state based upon supreme sovereignty. The first is democracy, with supreme sovereignty vested in a council, which is made up of all the citizens. In this council, every citizen has the right to vote. The second is aristocracy, with the supreme sovereignty being vested in a council made up of selected citizens. The third is monarchy or kingdom. It has the supreme sovereignty vested in one man alone. 'In the first that which hold the reins of government is called the people, in the second the nobles, and in the third the monarch' (VII.v.3: 1024). He then goes on to examine each of these three forms of government.

Democracy

Pufendorf begins with an examination of democracy. He makes it clear that the reason for this choice is not that a democracy surpasses the other two forms of governments in 'dignity, outward splendour, or convenience', but rather that democracy was chosen because it is the oldest form of government among nations. In addition, it is reasonable to assume that when a number of men 'endowed with natural liberty and equality' decided to unite into one state they first wished to 'administer their common affairs by a common council, and so to establish a democracy' (VII.v.4: 1025). Pufendorf claims that in the beginning democracy was held to be the fairest form of government. Matters that concerned all should be the care of all. Such a form of government should last either until the majority of the people had relinquished that status voluntarily or until some citizens or enemies forced a different form of government on the people. To support this view Pufendorf quotes the Greek philosophers Plato and Isocrates, on their positive opinion on democracy in the Athenian State. Furthermore, democracy is not denied by ancient history even when there were kings. In the most cases people enjoyed the authority of persuasion, rather than the power of command. So in ancient times people lived under a popular regime.

There have been scruples raised about the point that the will of the majority prevails in popular assemblies. This hesitancy arises because the votes of some individuals at times will contribute to the majority and under other circumstances be among the ones that constitute a minority. Such considerations will by no means destroy the unity of all, which may be attributed to the entire body (ibid.: 1028).

He also rejects all claims that true sovereignty cannot be attributed to a multitude, 'since a multitude is not obliged to observe for ever what once pleased them, and the multitude of all members of a state is not obliged' (ibid.).

After a state, has been set up by a gathering of people according to the agreements it becomes a democracy when the right to decide 'upon matters touching the common welfare' has been conferred upon a council made up of the entire citizenry, which is an assembly (VII.v.6: 1030).

What is then necessary for a democracy to function? First, a time must be decided and a place has to be found where the assembly can meet, deliberate and decide upon the affairs of the state. The times between meetings should not be too far apart. In addition, the votes of the majority must pass for those of all. Finally, certain magistrates or what today we would call a government should be appointed. These magistrates should carry on the daily business with the authority of the entire group. They should also investigate matters of importance and lay before the assembly any affairs that might have serious consequences (VII.v.7: 1030–31).

Aristocracy

An aristocracy is established when a group of people have united into some rudimentary form of state, using the first agreement of association, and have decided to commit the direction of their affairs to a council composed of a select number of men. The members of this council are designated either by their names, or by their positions, 'or by some other sign whereby they can be distinguished from the rest' (VII.v.8: 1031). These council members have accepted this designation on the condition that all others are submitting themselves to their will. On this condition, they accept the supreme sovereignty.

Pufendorf contends that Hobbes is incorrect in seeking the origins of aristocracy in democracy if his meaning was that all aristocracies had their origin in and were established by changes in perfect democracies. Experience proves, and reason does not deny, that from the first pact or agreement among men to unite and administrate their safety and security through common council and leadership, men were able to pass directly to aristocracies or monarchies. What is necessary for a democracy to function is also necessary for an aristocracy.

Monarchy

A monarchy is established by an agreement and a decree, when the supreme sovereignty is conferred upon one man. Pufendorf makes it clear that a group of people could not confer sovereignty upon a person on the condition that if he was not better in procuring the common protection than their previous democratic government, he could be removed. In such a case, they had not appointed a monarch but an eminent magistrate, who depended upon 'the fickle breath of the people'. Therefore, such a ruler had not received the supreme sovereignty (VII.v.9: 1033).

Pufendorf rejects the idea maintained most emphatically by many absolute monarchs that their supreme sovereignty was a creation of God Almighty. God could not by greater right be claimed to be the creator of monarchies than of any other form of governments. Moreover, a person who lives in a free state has to be just as much an obedient subject as the ones who live in a kingdom.

For the exercise of sovereignty in both democracies and aristocracies it requires appointed times and places for their deliberations and decisions. In an absolute monarchy such deliberations and decisions can take place at any time and place.[2] Pufendorf quotes the third-century Greek historian Herodian who claimed that: 'Rome is wherever the Emperor is' (ibid.: 1033). For Pufendorf this is a reason for preferring monarchy to other forms of government.

Comparative Advantages of Different Forms of States

Finally, Pufendorf discusses the comparative advantages of the different forms of states and claims that reason should decide what form should be preferred to another. The form of a state should be preferred that 'procures more easily and surely the safety of the state, or that the force of sovereignty is less open to abuse'. This much is clear: 'That no form of state can be so buttressed with laws but that, from the very form of government which is established for the safety of the citizens, some inconveniences can befall them by reason of the slothfulness or the wickedness of the rulers' (VII.v.22: 1052). The reason is that rulers are not immune to the vices by which they are incited to do harm to others. In spite of the fact that the supreme sovereignty is established to protect citizens from their fellows, the sovereignty is conferred on men with some proclivity to cause harm. To support this view, he quotes the Roman Tacitus: 'There will be vices so long as there are men.' Consequently, we sometimes experience from men the very things that they should have defended us against. Therefore, as has been pointed out by the Roman poet Quintus Horatius Flaccus (65–8): 'for every folly of their princes the Greeks feel the scourge' (ibid.).

Since the conditions of human affairs are not perfect, many disagree on what form of state will give the minimum of evils. However, Pufendorf claims that looking at the problem in this light the majority will cast their vote for a monarchy. Here he refers, without quoting, to the Greeks, Euripides (480–460), Herodotus (484–425), and Isocrates (436–338), to the German physician Henningus Arnisaeus (1580–1636), and to the French political writer Bodin.

There are also arguments against monarchies. Here Pufendorf refers to an unknown Dutch author of the book Bilanx Politica, without bringing up his opinions. However, he adds that many of his arguments can be turned against the author by what Thomas Hobbes set forth in his De Cive. Pufendorf contends that it is not his purpose to discuss these various positions but he suggests that every good and loyal citizen should contemplate on a remark by the Roman Tacitus:

> He [Marcellius] was not mindful on the times on which he had fallen, on the form of government established by their ancestors: he admired the past, and accommodated himself to the present system, devoutly wishing for virtuous princes, but willing to acquiesce under any sort.
>
> (Ibid.: 1053)

The Greek states were usually small city-states. In Pufendorf's opinion the most agreeable form of government in such states was in this order: a democracy, a mildly administered aristocracy, and finally, a kingdom of the Aristotle 'heroic' type. That is a principate, which asserts its authority by persuasion. If somebody seized the power as a monarch in these states, against the will of the people, it soon developed into a tyranny with all its awful protuberances. Pufendorf found it absurd to establish a monarchy in a state, which consisted of just a small city, but on the other hand, he also found it absurd to establish a democracy in a nation that occupies a large territory.

It is clear from his discussion, that Pufendorf favours an enlightened absolute monarchy. He does not discuss constitutional monarchies.

Principles of Taxation

The Right and Power to Levy Taxes

After having discussed the main responsibilities of the state Pufendorf makes it clear, as mentioned above, that the business of a state, both in time of war or peace, cannot be carried out without expenses. It is therefore necessary for the supreme sovereign of a state to have both the right and the power to either reserve for its use a certain part of the wealth or produce of a country, which is held by its people, or it may require individual citizens to contribute as much of their wealth 'as is judged necessary to meet the expenses' (VII.iv.7: 1013).

The supreme sovereignty has therefore the right to lay hands on a part of the citizens' possessions by way of taxation. The reason being that taxes 'when levied in just measure and honestly expended', are the price that each and every citizen pays to the state to meet the expenses for the defence of their life and property.

This can be done in the same way as it may command and exact whatever services are required of its citizens. In addition, a state has the right to use other means to increase its revenue. The most important is the right to levy taxes on all imports and exports, and to appropriate some part of the cost of goods consumed at home (ibid.).

Pufendorf claims that the supreme sovereign of a state has the right to pass laws, which interfere with the use citizens can make of their possessions. It is a condition that these laws are beneficial to the welfare of the state. The usual moralistic and mercantilist view are maintained. He also lists sumptuary laws against excessive expenditures and luxury. This is, according to Pufendorf, necessary because both private and state resources would be depleted when money flows out of the country for luxuries, caused by an urge for the delights furnished by foreign hands. He supports this argument by a quote from Pliny the Elder, who claims that the Arabians are the wealthiest since practically all the wealth of the Romans and the Parthians ends in their possession: 'For they sell whatever they secure from the sea or forest, and buy nothing in return'. The same is the case with India that imports from the Roman Empire half of what she exports (VIII.v.3: 1278).

It is also a further disadvantage when men have wasted their resources on luxuries, because then they will not be able to meet the expenses of the state. Those who spend all their incomes on luxury must also pay something to the state, they are therefore forced to either draw on their capital or cut down their scale of living. Here Pufendorf mentions the Roman laws against spendthrifts and luxurious spending. To the same class belongs also laws against gambling. These laws were enumerated by the Italian Manunzio and the similar laws in Greece by Plato. He also makes references to the second- and third-century Greek essayist Claudius Aelianus and the Spanish Garcilaso de la Vega, and a few more without quoting them.

Furthermore, he makes it clear that the duty of governing a state as well as the right of raising revenue to cover the expenses cannot be separated from the state's judicial rights. For no one can rightfully force its citizens to assume the cost of maintaining the state but him, who can rightfully punish those who refuse to pay.

Pufendorf emphasizes the need for a state to have the necessary revenue. Here he refers to the Roman Tacitus, who pointed to the Emperor Nero, who debated whether he should abolish custom dues altogether. Such a benefaction, he thought, would make him popular among his subjects. However, his advisers, who pointed out that the reduction in revenues 'by which the state was supported' would entail the breaking up of the empire, restrained this impulse (VIII.v.4: 1279).

He claims that it is not possible to determine in advance, exactly what the expenses of the state will be. This is particularly the case in a situation of war. Here references are made to several Roman authors who support this view. Pufendorf also quotes but finds very little truth in the historian Titus Livius (59–17), who maintained that 'War maintains it self' (ibid.: 1280).

The Duties with Respect to the Levy of Taxes

Pufendorf discusses the duties of the Supreme Sovereign with respect to the levy of taxes. In this connection, he also discusses how taxes should be collected and how they should be honestly spent. His starting point is that citizens are required to bear taxes and other burdens, which are necessary to meet the expenses of the state.

First, the duty of the supreme sovereign is not to exact more in tax than 'the necessities or the real advantages of the commonwealth require' (VII. ix.10: 1123–1124). To support this view, he quotes Grotius, who contends that it is the duty of princes to make sure that the burdens of the public should be held up against the necessity of a prudent government.

Second, it is the duty of the sovereign to make sure that the amount in taxes is justly proportioned among the citizens. Everybody should pay their share of the tax burden. No citizen should be granted exemption, 'with the result that the rest are defrauded and overburdened' (ibid.: 1124). However, Pufendorf advocated only symbolic taxes for the poor.

Third, it is the duty of the sovereign to crack down on tax evaders. This basic point of fairness he brought up when discussing the making of trusts. He made it clear that it is against natural law to form trusts to evade the law. '… for instance, if a man who does not pay taxes should be willing to, for another's goods to be made over to him for a time, so as to avoid the tax collectors' (V.x.8: 775).

Fourth, it is the duty of the sovereign to select trustworthy, non-corrupt, persons to serve in public positions. Pufendorf explains what kind of people that should not take the lead in public affairs with a passage from the Greek Polybius: 'It was impossible for a man to take the lead in public business with honour who neglected his own private affairs; nor again to abstain from embezzling public money if he lived beyond his private income.' This is also supported with an observation by the Greek Lucian: 'Whoever has misused his private affairs cannot be trusted with those of others' (VIII.v.3: 1278).

The Economic Responsibility of a Sovereign

The size of the revenue that can be collected by taxation depends on the size of the resources and wealth of the citizens of a state. In addition, the vigour of a state will depend on the strength and resources of its citizens. Pufendorf contends that since it is vexatious for sovereigns to rule in poor countries, they therefore have obligations, to the best of their abilities, to carry out policies that will make the private fortunes of their citizen's flourish (VII.ix.11: 1125).

These policies should also encourage its citizens to gather the richest possible harvest from fields and waters, and to utilize their resources in the best possible way. Furthermore, it is of great importance in maritime countries that these policies foster commerce, exchange of products and navigation.

He also prescribed moralistic mercantilist laws favouring frugality, forbidding laziness and superfluous expenses and especially such laws that prevented the wealth of nations, such as gold, to pass out of the country. He quotes the Greek historian Cassius Dio (165–229): 'Great wealth is gathered not so much by acquiring a great deal as by not spending a great deal' (ibid.).

He also contends that the health and stability of states comes from the union of its citizens. It is therefore the duty of the supreme sovereign to secure peace and 'to see to it that there arise in the state no factions from which it is an easy step to uprisings and civil wars' (VII.ix12: 1126).

Budget Discipline

Pufendorf emphasizes that what has been collected in revenues should be spent on the state, 'and not dissipated on luxuries, largesses, vain parade or empty trappings' (VII.ix.10: 1124). Budget responsibility and discipline is therefore important. He makes it clear that if the disbursements are higher than the income, the balance should be made up by economy and a reduction in the expenses. 'For splendour is fraught with ruin when it exceeds income' (VII.ix.10: 1124). Pufendorf drives home this point with references to the Italian Machiavelli and the Roman Pliny the Elder (ibid.).

He further supports his view with a reference to the Archbishop of Capua Girolamo Connestaggio, who points to the bad financial policy of Portugal. Furthermore, nor will any man be moved by a remark of the Roman Cicero: 'To be called a thrifty man confers no great honour on a king' (ibid.).

How Should Taxes Be Collected?

Because of the principle that citizens should not be overburdened by taxes and the importance of budget discipline, Pufendorf put great emphasis on tax collection. He claimed that taxes should be raised and collected with the least possible frictions and commotion. Here he observes that 'Indeed, the mass of mankind feel it to be a far greater hardship to part with something which they once numbered among their possessions, than not have received something at all' (VIII.v.5: 1281). Gaertner (2005: 239) finds this latter statement interesting, since it shows that Pufendorf was 'aware of an asymmetry with respect to gains and losses that men may incur, an aspect which only recently has been widely discussed in behavioural economics'.

Furthermore, he stresses that the state's tax revenues should be collected with the least possible expense. In addition, with a reference to Hobbes, the organization of the tax collection should be such that they are collected with the least possible expense and in such a way that no large amount sticks to the fingers of the collectors. Without using the word, Pufendorf warned against corruption in tax collection. The experience of the treasury should not be similar to what happens when people are trying to put out a fire by using jars and buckets passing down a long line. The jars and buckets, which are drawn full at the source, are scarcely half-full when they reach the place, where the water is to be poured on the fire. The passing from hand to hand and being shaken is the reason. He claims that there are many examples confirming similar results from the collection of taxes (VII.ix.10: 1124).

Therefore Pufendorf gives considerable attention to how taxes or other burdens are collected and levied on the citizens. Taxes should be publicly posted. This important principle he supports with a quote from the Roman historian Tacitus, who praised an edict by the Emperor Claudius Nero (37–68): 'That the regulation for each tax, hitherto kept secret, should be publicly posted up; that arrears should not be recoverable after one year; that suits against publicans should be heard out of the ordinary course' (VIII.v.5: 1282).

Finally, the exaction by tax collectors should be carefully monitored by the supreme sovereignty, so that possible harassment of the taxpayers does not take place. Pufendorf emphasizes that it is absolutely necessary to select well qualified people for public business. It is important that people who take the lead in public business, do not neglect their private affairs. There is reason to believe that a person, who lives beyond his private income, cannot abstain from embezzling public money. The Assyrian writer Lucian wrote: 'Whoever has misused his private affairs cannot be trusted with those of others' (VIII.v.3: 1278).

Furthermore, Pufendorf underlines the importance of having tax collectors, who are honest. 'It is also a duty of the supreme sovereignty to put a stop to the exactions of tax-collectors, which they make for their own profit, as well as to the ways in which they harass and vex subjects – a burden more intolerable than the very taxes' (VIII.v.5: 1282).

Taxes Should Be Equal and Just

When taxes or other burdens are levied, special care should be taken so that taxes are equally laid upon citizens and that subjects are given 'no just cause for complaints'. They will have such cause, 'if the burdens of the state should be laid upon citizens unequally' (Viii.v.6: 1282). For as Hobbes so well observes: 'For as a rule, out of grief or at the injury, or from envy of others, men complain not so much of the burden itself, as of the inequality' (ibid.: 1283). The ones that pay complain out of grief at the injury, and from envy of the ones that do not pay.

Pufendorf finds it reasonable that those who share equally in the peace should pay equally for it in money or services. The immunities from paying tax and other privileges, which exist in many states, can only be defended if they are balanced by the quality of the services these people provide.

How should the term equality be understood? It should be observed that the kind of equality he discusses is not equality paid in money. Equality is understood to be that the burden assigned to each man 'should not lie more heavily on one than another'. This will be the case 'if an equal ratio is maintained between the burdens and the benefits of peace' (ibid.). Although all citizens enjoy peace equally, not all of them share equally in its benefits. Some individuals have more property than others, and some have greater wants than others.

Should Taxes Be Proportional?

In general, Pufendorf believed that taxes should be proportional. Since every man's wealth receives its defence from the state, it can be argued that the burden should be laid in proportion to the citizen's income. This is illustrated by a statement of the Roman Grammarian Servius Tullius (fourth and fifth century) recorded by a quote from the Greek Dionysius of Helicarnassus in defence of the institution of the census: 'And I look upon it in itself to be both just and advantages to the public, that those who have great possessions should pay great taxes, and those who have small possessions, small ones' (ibid.). So also extraordinary demands made by a state in times of stress should be based upon capital.

However, since every man's life is defended by the resources of the state, and since life is as dear to the poor as to the rich it can in certain cases be argued for 'a small equal tax, such as the poll-tax, where a rich man pays no more than a poor' (ibid.).

Nevertheless, the principle of proportionality should not be carried too far. Pufendorf emphasizes that the poor should not be burdened by taxes. However, it is important that they also pay a small tax, even if it is just symbolic. He refers to the Spanish Garcilaso de la Vega, who tells us that the Incas of Peru ordered the very poor each year to render to their governors a certain amount of the horns of vermin, in order that no one could claim to be free of taxes (VIII.v.10: 1285).

Taxes on Income or Consumption

It is generally accepted that it is to the benefit of the state that citizens have the opportunity to increase their wealth by their own industry. However, citizens have different resources, that is, capital and labour skills; therefore, their income will probably be different.

It is also a problem that some people have equal incomes but not equal capital or wealth. In addition, some people spend their income carefully and other people waste their income on luxury. It could also be argued that if two men earn the same, for example, an annual income of 100 units of value, but one spends 40 and the other 80, they still share equally in the peace and it could be argued that they should therefore pay the same tax (VIII.v.6: 1284).

Occasionally, Pufendorf misses the distinction between tax on income and a tax on property or wealth. He admits that an income tax would involve several practical problems, and claims that one such problem is that a general property census cannot be taken so often. It would also be most difficult for the state to find out each year the amount of every citizen's income. If the tax should be set at the end of the year when every man would submit an account of his total receipts and expenses, and if then the tax is levied upon the surplus from the preceding year, one would pay twice as much as the other, notwithstanding the fact that they share equally in the benefits of the peace. Another important result from an income tax would be that one taxpayer would suffer from his frugality and the other profit from being a spendthrift. From this point of view, the most convenient course seems to be to tax citizens according to consumption and not income.

Indirect Taxation

Therefore, Pufendorf favoured indirect taxes, which are excise taxes on goods consumed. However, excise taxes should be moderate on necessities, since these goods are consumed by ordinary people, and higher on luxuries, since the wealthy people consume these.

Customs on Imports

With respect to customs we should bear in mind whether the imports constitute necessities of life for the inhabitants of the state or merely serve the requirements of luxury. If the imports are luxuries, customs may be increased, to prevent luxurious living. In addition, such imports are customarily used by people of wealth or people that are the recipients of many privileges and therefore contribute little to the common cause.

Another motive for laying a heavy custom on imports of certain commodities is what today is called the infant-industry argument. Native workers might turn their attention to these products, and start domestic production of these goods. For this reason, it is proper to lay heavy customs on foreign goods, especially the ones that only serve luxury.

Customs on Exports

Regarding exports, we should distinguish between commodities, which are the only means for some citizens of the state to make a living and the commodities which, if forbidden, would help the commonwealth prosper. In the first case customs duties should be taken off and in the latter case they can be increased. If foreign nations are in great need for these commodities we can levy a higher custom than if they can secure them from other markets.

A State of Emergency

There are times of crisis in the life of every state when great need, for example in the case of war, makes it impossible to collect strict quotas from each citizen. This is the case when something that belongs to one or a few citizens is required for the necessary use of the commonwealth. In such a case, the supreme sovereignty will be able to take over that thing for the necessities of the state on the condition, that whatever exceeds the just share of its owners, must be refunded them by the other citizens.

In such cases, it is emphasized that no one should be given special privileges. Furthermore, Pufendorf argues that: 'Yet the claim that those who have in this manner paid out or lost their fortune for the public weal, should, so far as possible, have it restored to them, or be properly recompensed by the entire state, rests on the most manifest equity' (VIII.v.7: 1286).

Note

1 The Dutch Grotius and Erycius Puteanus (1574–1646), the English Francis Bacon, Thomas More, and Thomas Hobbes, the French François Bernier (1625–1688), Jean Bodin (1530–1596), Isaac Casaubon (1550–1614) and Montaigne, the Germans Johann Christoph Becmann (1541–1617), Boecler, Gunther of Paris (1150–1220), Horn, and Michael Piccart (1574–1620), the Italians Girolamo Connestaggio (1530–1618), Niccolò Machiavelli (1469–1527), and Paolo Manuzio (1512–1574), the Jewish Josephus (AD 37–95) and the Spanish Garcilsso de la Vega (1535–1616).

2 An example, the absolute Swedish monarch Gustav Adolf signed the deed establishing the University of Dorpat (Tartu) the day before he was killed in the battle of Lützen in 1632.

Part IV

Diffusion of Pufendorf's Economic Ideas

From the previous discussion, Pufendorf developed extensive doctrines of political economy. The focus in this part will first be to sketch how his doctrines were dispersed through the spread of his natural law books, and how natural law became a university subject and thereby influenced the students.

Although Pufendorf in his *De Jure Naturae et Gentium* overwhelmed his readers with references to his sources he did not managed to set the standard for other writers in the seventeenth and eighteenth centuries. Unfortunately, no code of scholarly practice existed by which authors felt obliged to mentioned their use of the ideas of their predecessors when they developed their own. The truth is that most authors in this era only to a very limited extent listed their sources. It is therefore very difficult to detect the transmission of ideas from one author to the next.

12 A Great Popularizer

When *Elementorum Jurisprudentiae Universalis* was published in The Hague in 1660, it made Pufendorf known and earned him a chair at the University of Heidelberg. The book has been called the first real textbook in natural law and it was used at some universities. Thomas Behme (1999: ix) claims that seven editions of the Latin text had been published in Pufendorf's lifetime: The Hague 1660, Cygneae (Zwickau) 1668, Jena 1669 and 1680, Cantabrigae (Cambridge) 1672, Frankfurt am Main 1669, 1680 and 1694.[1]

His second book, *De Statu Imperii Germanici* (On the constitution of the German Empire), was published in 1667. It became, as earlier mentioned, an instant bestseller and was published in numerous editions.[2] It enhanced Pufendorf's reputation to non-academic circles.

In 1668, Pufendorf moved to Lund, where he had been invited to a chair in natural and international law at the newly established university. Here he in his first years, in addition to his new teaching assignments, researched, wrote and completed the manuscript he had brought with him from Heidelberg. A comprehensive exposition of the state of the art in natural law, which also included political economy, *De Jure Naturae et Gentium*, in eight books was published in 1672. A year later, he published an abridged, popularized version, a so-called 'student edition' entitled *De Officio Hominis et Civis* (On the duty of man and citizen) in two small books. This 'student edition' became in modern parlance an international bestseller. As well as being adopted as a textbook in natural law at many universities, it made the author famous in the European academic circles. The focus will be to trace the circulation of this book, and how important it became for the establishment of natural law including political economy as a university subject.

What Were the Reasons for his Popularization?

De Officio is 'excerpted almost entirely' from his major work, but it does not include the long and often tedious arguments that support its conclusions.[3] In his major work we are almost overwhelmed by his numerous quotations from ancient writers and contemporary sources. This is not the case with this abridged 'student edition'.

What was Pufendorf's motivation in publishing this popularized version? His own answer can be found in the dedication of the book to the first chancellor of the University of Lund, Lord Gustaf Otto Stenbock (1614–1685), and in his preface entitled 'To the benevolent reader – greetings'. His dedication is a tribute in return for the protection the chancellor gave him when he was grievously criticized by his colleagues. Lord Stenbock had granted Pufendorf tenure in his university position, and thereby made it clear that he had the support of the highest authority of the university. In the dedication, he makes an apology for having produced such a small work. However, his excuse is that it is a work for beginners, 'as it can furnish some use perhaps to those who are undertaking the first step to that study'. Accordingly, the content embraces merely 'the first rudiments of moral philosophy'.

This position he also made clear in the preface, which reveals his persistent pedagogical intent. His purpose was to produce an introductory textbook for students and lay people, which 'set forth for beginners the chief headings of natural law, briefly and I think in a clear compendium'.[4] In addition, he thought that the education of students would be to the greater public advantage, 'that the minds of studious youths be imbued with moral doctrine of this character, in order that its manifest use in civil life might be considered'.

Furthermore, it is also clear that Pufendorf had another reason for his popularization. He wanted to counter and refute his previously mentioned detractors, who had written 'a bull of excommunication' against him. At first the effect of his counterattack was like throwing petrol onto a fire but ultimately the dispute strengthened his reputation tremendously. *De Officio* contributed greatly to this development.[5]

With Pufendorf's natural law works and the reputation he had accomplished, the study of natural law became fashionable among academic scholars, students and educated people.

De Officio: An International Bestseller

De Officio, when it was published in 1673, 'hit the market' at the right time. It became an international bestseller. It spread Pufendorf's doctrine of natural law, which includes ethics, jurisprudence, society and political economy, on the European continent, the British Isles and the North American colonies. New editions, with or without commentaries, appeared in the most important European countries. It was reprinted innumerable times, and thousands of copies were produced and sold.

Latin was the lingua franca of the educated classes and used as a language of instruction at all universities in the seventeenth and eighteenth centuries, but *De Officio* was also translated into all the major European languages. The first translation and publication of *De Officio* into German as *Über die Pflicht des Menschen und des Bürgers* by the German historian, jurist and professor in Giessen Immanuel Weber (1657–1726), appeared in 1691. The first English translation, as *The Whole Duty of Man, according to the Law of Nature*, by the English scholar and professor at Gresham College, Andrew Tooke (1673–1732) appeared the same year. It was reissued in 1698, 1705 and 1716.

Although the Catholic Church placed Pufendorf's natural law works on the index, they found their way into university libraries, state libraries and libraries of the intellectual classes, also in French, Italian and Spanish speaking parts of Europe.

French was not only the spoken and written language in France and parts of Switzerland; it was the first foreign language across Europe, after the classical languages Greek and Latin. If readers had difficulties with a text in the classical languages, they turned to the French translations. These translations were also in many cases used as basis for translations into other foreign languages. Translation of books into French, originally written in Latin, was therefore very important for the circulation of new ideas.

Only two years after its publication in 1667, Pufendorf's political work *De Statu Imperii Germanici* was translated to French by François-Savinien d'Alquié (fl. 17th c.) and published in Amsterdam.[6] The first translation into French of *De Officio et hominis et civis* as *Les devoirs des hommes et des citoyens suivant la loi naturelle* by Antoine Tessier (1632–1715) appeared in Berlin in 1696. The translator was a French jurist who, as so many other Huguenots, had to escape from Catholic France after the revocation of the Edict of Nantes in 1685. As a consequence of the revocation, the French Huguenots lost their legal existence in France. Huguenot (Calvinist) churches were closed, their right to emigrate was denied and Catholic upbringing was made compulsory for their children. However, more than 500,000 Huguenots managed to emigrate.

Tessier first went to Calvinist Switzerland, but after a stay of seven years, he moved to Berlin in 1692. Here he, like Pufendorf, became counsellor and historiographer, first to Prince Elect Friederich III, who from 1701 became King Friederich I of Prussia. Nothing is so far known about the circulation of Tessier's translation.

Jean Barbeyrac: The Preeminent French Translator

One person is very important in this context. It is the French jurist and philosopher Jean Barbeyrac. Being a Huguenot, he and his family had to escape France in 1685. After spending some time at Geneva and Frankfurt am Main, he became professor of belles-lettres at the French school of Berlin. In 1711, he was called to be professor in history and civil law, at the University of Lausanne, before finally settling as Professor of Public Law at the University of Groningen. Barbeyrac became the preeminent eighteenth-century translator of Latin natural law works into French.

In Berlin Barbeyrac translated Pufendorf's major work *De Jure Naturae et Gentium* into French. His translation contained a substantial number of comments and was published in Amsterdam in 1706.[7] He dedicated his translation to His Majesty the King of Prussia. This translation had a tremendous effect on subsequent editions, both in Latin and translations into other languages, since many of them included and used Barbeyrac's comments. The year after he translated the *De Officio Hominis et Civis*, also with an extensive preface and many comments.[8] He did this translation since he was not satisfied with the translation by Tessier. Barbeyrac's translations saw many editions and reprints. In addition, to a great extent they were used as the basis for translations into other languages.

Barbeyrac's translations, together with his recommendation for their use, had a tremendous effect on the circulation of Pufendorf's natural law books and the diffusion of natural law including political economy. The French public, but also people from other parts of Europe who were familiar with the French language, became acquainted with the doctrines of natural law not only from Pufendorf's works but also from his translations of *De Jure Belli et Pacis* (Le droit de la guerre et de la paix) by Hugo Grotius from 1724, and *De legibus naturae disquisition philosophica* (Traité philosophique des lois naturelles) from 1744 by Richard Cumberland. The works of Grotius and Cumberland was also reissued my times in the eighteenth century and became the sources for many important scholars.

Barbeyrac should therefore be given a great deal of honour with regard to popularity of natural law or moral philosophy as a university subject, and the use of Pufendorf's *De Offico* as a textbook. His own fame rests chiefly on the preface and annotations to his translations. John Christian Laursen (1995: 1–14), Simone Zurbuchen (1998: 415) and Fiammetta Palladini (2011), acknowledged the major role the Huguenot diaspora played both in the socio-economic development in Brandenburg-Prussia at the end of the seventeenth and the beginning of the eighteenth century, and the role Barbeyrac played in the diffusion of natural law.

Editions and Translations of *De Officio*

Sieglinde Othmer (1970: 129) and Klaus Luig (1972: 539–557) have both made investigations into the diffusion of natural law by looking at the number of editions and translations of both Pufendorf's major work *De Jure Naturae* and his popularized 'student edition' *De Officio*.

The combined major results of Luig's and Othmer's studies of editions and translations of *De Officio Hominis et Civis* until the 1770s are shown in Table 12.1.

Othmer's emphasis was on Barbeyrac's translations of Pufendorf's works into French, and included an analysis of their readership. In her study, she claims that Barbeyrac translated Pufendorf for the younger generation of students and for those pupils who were in preparation for university studies. These young people learned and spoke Latin, but their knowledge of the language was not sufficient for the study of such an important but also difficult subject as natural law. Barbeyrac proposed that all university programmes in the French-speaking parts of Europe should have textbooks in their mother

Table 12.1 De Officio Hominis et Civis, editions and translations

	In Latin	*In local languages*	*In French*
The Netherlands	12 (4)	3 (1)	8 (7)
Germany/Austria	59 (37)	7 (1)	3 (1)
British Isles	10 (9)	7 (6)	1 (1)
Switzerland	5 (1)	—	2 (1)
France	—	6 (4)	—
Sweden	10 (4)	—	—
Italy	8	4 (1)	—
Denmark	—	1 (1)	—
Russia	—	2 (2)	—
Poland	2 (1)	—	—
Spain	—	1 (1)	—
Total	**106 (56)**	**31 (17)**	**14 (10)**

Sources: Klaus Luig (1972: 546) and Sieglinde Othmer (1970: 140).

Note: Othmer's results in brackets.

tongue at the beginning. When he himself held his inaugural speech as rector of the University of Lausanne in 1715, it was in French.

According to Luig, by the 1770s there were around 150 identified editions and translation of *De Officio*. However, though his survey is more comprehensive than earlier accounts, it does not claim to be complete.[9] Luig re-examined Othmer's study and claimed that, although her investigation was correct with respect to the editions and translations of Pufendorf's major work, she had missed many editions of the popularized 'student edition' *De Officio*.

De Officio was published in many editions and printed in tens of thousands of copies. In all, according to Luig's study, this work has been published in more than 151 editions. Of these, 106 are in Latin and 45 in other European languages, Danish, Dutch, English, French, German, Italian, Russian and Spanish. There are thirty-one editions in the local language as well as fourteen editions in French, but published in another country than France; eight in the Netherlands, three in Germany/Austria, two in Switzerland and one on the British Isles.

Most of the twenty editions in French can be attributed to Barbeyrac. In addition, it should be mention that several of the translations into other local languages are based on one of Barbeyrac's French editions, not the Latin original. His extensive commentaries are often added to other editions and translations. This is for example the case of Basil Kennett's 1729 translation of *De Naturae et Gentium* into English.

Although Luig's investigation is extensive, even this study is not complete. For example, a Swedish translation from 1747 has been missed by both Othmer and Luig.[10] Sæther (2009) concludes that *De Officio* has, at least, been translated into nine European languages.

Since many of these translations are, as mentioned, not from the original Latin text but from Barbeyrac's French translation, Pufendorf's original meanings could easily have been distorted in such translations. Unfortunately, it is also a fact that many translators took a great freedom in their translations and 'adopted the text' if they did not agree with the original. David Saunders (2003: 477) asserts that Andrew Tooke, the English translator of *De Officio* did adjustments so that his translations coincided with his own views. He also contends that Barbeyrac did more than just translate the text: he manipulated it systematically to be better in line with his own convictions and that he in his notes deliberately directed the opinions of his readers against the original text (ibid.: 482). Maurizio Bazzoli (1979) contends that Giambattista Almici's (1717–93) translation of *De Jure Naturae* into Italian in 1757–59, on the basis of Jean Barbeyrac's translation as well as Pufendorf's text, was unreliable and that Almici purposely misrepresented Pufendorf's work. However, he adds that it was necessary for Almici to remove from the text sentences that were, or could be interpreted, as being against the Catholic Church. If not, he would not have been able to get permission to print.[11]

Of the professors who adopted the *De Officio* as a textbook, many published their own comments, sometimes separately, but usually together with the text. It should also be noted that some professors published their own books on natural law or moral philosophy that closely shadowed Pufendorf's work. Therefore, several imitations of *De Officio* have been published. Some authors admitted that they built closely on Pufendorf, while others tried to disguise their source.[12]

Of the eighty-three editions of *De Officio* that were included in Othmer's study, sixty-four were published after 1706. The last edition in the Netherlands, and the last edition in Germany; both date from 1769. The last in England is from 1758, the last in Switzerland from 1748, the last in France from 1830, the last in Sweden from 1748 (missed by Othmer), the last and only one in Italy from 1761, the last and only one in Denmark from 1742, the last in Russia from 1726, the last and only one from Poland in 1682 and finally, the last and only one from Spain was published in 1834. From this, it can be concluded that the popularity of Pufendorf's 'student edition' lasted well into the second half of the eighteenth century.

Interestingly enough, some more recent editions, reprints and translations of this book have been found, which are not included in Othmer's investigation from 1970. There is the edition in Latin with a translation into English by Frank Gardner Moore published by Oxford University Press, New York in 1927. Furthermore, Cambridge University Press published a new translation into English by Michael Silverthorne in 1991. In addition, there is a reprint of the translation by Andrew Tooke *et al.* from 1735, with *Two Discourses and a Commentary* by Jean Barbeyrac, translated by David Saunders, and published by Liberty Fund Inc., Indianapolis 2003. Furthermore, there is a reprint of Bayberac's 1735 translation into French by Olms Verlag, Amsterdam in 1992. A German edition and translation by Klaus Luig (1994) published by Insel

Verlag, Frankfurt am Main, and another German edition by Akademie Verlag, Berlin 1996. There is also a new Swedish edition by the City University Press, Stockholm, from 2001.

Editions and Translations of *De Jure Naturae et Gentium*

The popularity of Pufendorf's 'student edition' also led to many translations and new editions of his major natural law work *De Jure Naturae et Gentium*

In all, forty-four editions of this work have, according to the investigation by Othmer been published. In Latin twenty, the Netherlands four, Germany twelve, Switzerland, one and Sweden three. In local languages thirteen, Germany three, England and Scotland seven, France two and Italy one. In the French language outside France eleven, the Netherlands five, Germany two, England and Scotland one and Switzerland three. The number of editions in French are all based on Barbeyrac's work. Of the forty-four editions that were included in this study, thirty-one were published after 1706.

The first translation into English was done by Basil Kennet (1674–1725) and others in 1703.[13] It was based on Pufendorf's 1688 edition. The second edition of Kennett's translation from 1710 was 'corrected and compared' with Mr Barbeyrac's French translation and his notes from 1706. The fourth edition from 1749 included Barbeyrac's Prefatory discourse.[14]

By the middle of the seventeenth century Pufendorf's natural law works could be found in university and state libraries across Europe and North America. For more than 100 years, these books were among the most read academic books in Europe and the New World.

In Protestant Europe, these works could be found in the libraries, because they were used by the professors, and were part of the curriculum for those studying jurisprudence, philosophy or ethics. In Catholic Europe Pufendorf's natural law books were in many cases blacklisted and in some cases banned. However, they were needed by scholars so that they could counteract and refute the dangerous ideas presented in these works. Therefore, Pufendorf's books could also be found in most Catholic university libraries across Europe, although students in the seventeenth and eighteenth centuries were in principle not permitted to read them.

Knowledge of Pufendorf's natural law works was also, according to Jan V.M. de Vet (1996: 209–35), disseminated through reviews in the learned journals in the Netherlands and elsewhere.

It should be emphasized that *De Officio* was not only read by university students and scholars. It was a book that was known and spread among the educated classes from emperors and kings to aristocrats, landowners, bureaucrats, and people of the clergy, business people and others who could read and write. It could therefore also be found in many large and small private libraries and book collections throughout Europe. These private libraries could in special cases contain several thousand volumes but they might also just have a handful of books.[15]

In her study, Othmer mentions that Friedrich the Great (1712–1786) had Barbeyrac's translation of *De Officio* in his library. The Emperor Joseph II (1741–1790) of the Austrian-Hungarian Empire was required to study it, as part of his education. The Emperor Peter the Great (1672–1725), initiated and followed closely the translation to Russian of *De Officio* in 1726. Furthermore, Othmer emphasized that Barbeyrac's personal work and influence in Lausanne was very important for the spread of natural law in general and the works of Samuel Pufendorf, particularly in Switzerland. She also mentions Jean-Jacques Burlamaqui (1694–1748) from Geneva, who had listened to Barbeyrac's lectures in Groningen, and Emerich de Vattel (1714–1767). Both were well-known Swiss philosophers and jurists that carried a great deal of influence. Petter Korkman (2006: xv–xvi) stresses that Burlamaqui in his teaching and writings built extensively on Pufendorf, but that they also differ on fundamental principles.[16]

Natural Law a University Subject

Pufendorf became, as earlier mentioned, Professor at the University of Heidelberg in 1661. Although he did not manage to get a professorship in natural law at the Faculty of Law, he taught the subject together with international law and philology. At University of Lund he became professor of natural law and taught the subject from 1668. Owing to his reputation and influence, and as a result of the popularity of his natural law works in general and his popularized version *De Officio* in particular, natural law, including political economy, became part of university studies in natural law or moral philosophy at most Protestant universities across Europe, and even at some Catholic universities.

Nokter Hammerstein (1986: 31) begins his article on the influence of Pufendorf's natural law at German universities, in the eighteenth century, with a rhyme from Friedrich Schiller (1759–1805). In the poem 'Die Weltwiesen' from the year 1795, he writes: 'Drum flieth der wilden Wölfe Stand/ Und knüpt des Staates dauerned Band!/ So lehren vom Katheder Herr Pufendorf und Feder'. This rhyme was used to show the undisputable influence of natural law not only in the faculties of law but also in other German academic faculties during the eighteenth century.

The introduction of natural law as a subject at German universities coincided to a large degree with the introduction of university reforms. Again, this was the century of the Enlightenment or the Age of Reason, and was characterized by a belief in progress that could be achieved through reason and the rejection of traditional, authoritative teaching. Pufendorf's natural law was at the forefront of this development and his popularized version *De Officio* was the book that, hit the market at the right time.

After the initial establishment of natural law at Heidelberg in 1660–61, study programmes and chairs in Pufendorfian natural law were established at many European universities.[17] In Germany, Heidelberg was followed by Jena

1665, Greifswald 1666 or 1674 (It had recently been conquered by Sweden), Königsberg 1673, Marburg 1674, Helmstedt 1675, Erfurt 1676, Altdorf 1680, Tübingen 1684 or 1686, Frankfurt an der Oder 1690, Giessen 1692, Halle 1694. A few years later came Rostock, Wittenberg, Leipzig 1711 and Göttingen 1734.[18] Moreover, this listing does not claim to be complete.

Knud Haakonssen (2012) for example contends that, at the end of the first quarter of the eighteenth century, all the fourteen Lutheran and nine Reformed universities, which functioned in the German-Roman Empire, had chairs in natural law either at the Faculty of Philosophy or the Faculty of Law or both, and often also at the Faculty of Theology. In addition, the Catholic universities had started early to react to this development and had created independent chairs in natural law. The first was Freiburg im Breisgau 1716 and Salzburg 1717. Numerous other Catholic universities all around Europe soon followed them.

In the Netherlands, natural law had been part of the curriculum at Leiden as early as the 1640s using the works of Grotius. From 1662 Pufendorf's *Elementorum Jurisprudentiae Universalis* was used as a textbook. The same year this book was also used at University of Groningen. In Switzerland, thanks to the afore mentioned Barbeyrac, natural law became part of the curriculum, first at the University of Lausanne 1711, and a few years thereafter at the universities of Geneva and Basel.

In the Nordic countries, the University of Uppsala was first 1665, then came Lund in 1668, and after a few years other universities took up the subject, that is Åbo and Dorpat (Tartu in today's Estonia) 1690, Copenhagen 1695 and the Universität Kiel, in today's Schleswig-Holstein, in 1665 and or 1689. Pufendorf's name became so familiar in the Nordic countries that the popular Swedish poet Carl Michael Bellman (1740–1795), just like Schiller, used his name in his songs and rhymes.

In the United Kingdom, John Locke at the University of Oxford first taught natural law in the early 1660s, but it was at the five universities in Scotland, first at Glasgow and Edinburgh, but soon followed by St Andrew and King's and Marischal Colleges in Aberdeen, that moral philosophy, as natural law was called, gained a strong position in the early eighteenth century. Fifty years after the first publications of Pufendorf's natural law works, natural law had become a university subject at almost all Lutheran, Calvinist, Anglican and Presbyterian universities across Europe and North America.

All major libraries in Europe and North America had copies of Pufendorf's natural law works in their collection. Pufendorf's *De Officio* was on the natural law curriculum of almost all universities in Protestant Europe in the beginning of the eighteenth century. For more than 100 years, this book was among the most read academic books in Europe and the New World. Horst Denzer (1987) tells us that students at some universities, such as Kiel, forced reluctant professors to accept Pufendorf's abridged 'student edition' as a textbook.

Although natural law did not become a university subject in the Catholic universities (with some exceptions), this does not imply that natural law, and

Pufendorf's works, were not known among scholars and students. At Catholic universities in general and Jesuit universities in particular, professors warned their students against the heretical writings of Pufendorf. These warnings probably stirred the interest of both professors and students.

Dissemination of Natural Law

With his natural law works, Pufendorf became famous as an enlightened academic scholar. Natural law including political economy became a fashion, and new chairs in this subject were created at many universities. *De Officio* was translated into nine languages, printed in thousands of copies and used as a textbook. It is therefore clear that many professor and scholars and thousands of students had an introduction to his natural law. The doctrines of natural law characterized by belief in progress, which could be achieved by a self-reliant use of reason and by a reaction to traditionalism, obscurantism and authoritarianism must have hit a nerve and stimulated the curiosity among some of these students and scholars. Many of them would turn to *De Jure Naturae et Gentium* where they could get a deeper insight into these topics. Here they could also find the references to further studies.

Pufendorf's ideas had a tremendous influence on the way of thinking in most European countries in the century between the English revolution of 1688 and the French of 1789. They contributed to the beginning of the Enlightenment and became part of the common knowledge to such an extent that it may partly explain why he has been almost forgotten and ignored by most contemporary philosophers, historians, economists, and finally historians of economic thought.

Notes

1 More recent editions are the Latin and English edition, Clarendon Press, New York, 1931 and London, 1934; the English edition by Oxford University Press, 1994; the Latin edition by Akademie Verlag, GmbH Berlin, 1999; and the English edition by Liberty Fund, Inc., Indianapolis, 2009.

2 A recent translation into English, with an introduction by Michael J. Seidler, was published by Liberty Fund Inc., Indianalpolis in 2007.

3 All quotations from DOH. Dedication. iii.

4 All quotations from DOH. Preface. v.

5 See for example Bo Lindberg (1983) who claims that the great dispute he had at Lund did not diminish his reputation.

6 *L'Estat de l'empire d'Allemagne de Monzambane, traduit par le sieur Fr. S. d'Alquié*, Amsterdam, J.J. Schipper, 1669. The translator, François-Savinien d'Alquié, was a French writer and doctor (physician) having practised in Kristiania (Oslo), Norway.

7 The French title *Le Droit de la Nature et des Gens ou Système Général des Principes les plus importants de la Morale, de la Jurisprudence et de la Politique, Traduits du Latin de feu Mr. Le Baron de Pufendorf*, Par Jean Barbeyrac, Amsterdam, Henri Schelte, 1706 (Dedication: A sa Majesté le Roi de Prusse).

8 The complete French title *Les Devoirs de l'Homme et des Citoiens, tel qu'ils lui sont prescrits par la Loi Naturelle, Traduits du Latin de feu Mr. Le Baron de*

Pufendorf, Par Jean Barbeyrac, Amsterdam, Henri Schelte, 1707. (The introduction by the translator is dated De Berlin le 1. Mars 1707). He based his translation upon the eleventh edition of the original, which was prepared in 1703 at Frankfurt am Main by Professor Immanuel Weber of the University of Giessen.

9 In the Dutch Tijdschrift voor Rechtsgeschiedenis from 1972.

10 *Twenne böcker om menniskians lefnads och samlefnads plicht*. Stockholm, 1747.

11 Maurizio Bazzoli (1979), 'Giambattista Almici a la diffusione di Pufendorf nel Settecento italiano', *Critica Storica* 16: 3–100. Almici's translation of Pufendorf's *De jure naturae et gentium* was published in Venice from 1757 to 1759 as *Il diritto della Natura e delle Genti, ossia sistema generale de' Principii li più importanti di Morale, Giurisprudenza e Politica di Samuele Barone di Puffendorf, rettificato, accresciuto ed illustrato* da G. B. Almici bresciano (4 vols).

12 Sæther (2005) has investigated two examples that fall into the former. The first is the previously mentioned Dano-Norwegian moral philosopher and professor at the University of Copenhagen, Ludvig Holberg, whose book *Moralsk Kierne* or *Kunskab om Natur og Folkeretten* (Moral source or knowledge of natural law and international law) was published in Danish in 1716. Danish was at that time the written language in Denmark- Norway. This book became, according to the Danish Professor Ditlev Tamm (1986: 83), very popular, and was published in six editions. It was also translated into German (Leipzig, 1748), and Swedish (Stockholm, 1789). The second example of this category is Francis Hutcheson (1694–1746), with his *A Short Introduction to Moral Philosophy* from 1747 (first published in Latin in 1742). Both Holberg and Hutcheson admit their dependence on Pufendorf, and a closer investigation shows that each follows him chapter by chapter. However, neither accepted Pufendorf's emphasis on self-interest as an important driving force behind human behaviour.

13 The others were the Reverend Mr William Percival (1674–1734) who translated Book V, and the Reverend William Itchiner (16–? – 17–?), who translated Book VIII.

14 There are also here more recent editions, reprints and translations of this work, which are not included in Othmer's investigation. It is the Latin and English edition by Oceana Publications Inc., New York and Wiley & Sons, London, 1933; the Latin edition by Akademie Verlag GmbH, Berlin, 1999; the English edition by The Lawbook Exchange, Clark, New Jersey, 2005; and the English edition by Liberty Fund Inc., Indianapolis from 2009.

15 As an example of how this book was known and read also by more ordinary people, there is a study by the Norwegian Professor Francis Bull (1916: 234–235). He investigated 58 book catalogues, from the rather small collections of books by deceased persons in the eastern part of Norway, in the second half of the eighteenth century. He found one or more of Pufendorf's works, most commonly his 'student edition', in 33 of these catalogues.

16 See also Petter Korkman (2013).

17 Natural law had been thought at universities or academies since the Middle Ages. But with Grotius' *De jure belli et pacis* from 1625 a change took place. The first chair in the subject was, according to Lindberg (1976), established at University of Uppsala in 1655.

18 The articles by Dufour (1986), Hammerstein (1986), Mautner (1986), Denzer (1987), Haakonssen (2012) and the book by Israel (2006)

13 John Locke

An Admirer of Pufendorf

When Pufendorf published *Elementorum Jurisprudentiae Universalis*, scholars belonging to what can be called the early Enlightenment, supported the opinions he expressed. They also saw the work as the first useful textbook in natural law. Others criticized the opinions expressed in it, and some Catholic and Protestant fundamentalist wanted it banned. Consequently, its reputation increased, and the use of the book became more common. The first scholar of any importance, to actively use Pufendorf's first natural law work in the development of his own ideas, was probably John Locke.

A Biographical Sketch

John Locke was born in Somerset, southern England in 1632. He attended the prestigious Westminister School before he matriculated at Christ Church College, Oxford in the autumn of 1652 as a King's Scholar. Here Locke made his home for more than thirty years, though he was occasionally absent from it for long periods.

The university Locke found when he entered, was in total disarray as a consequence of its involvement in the Civil War. William Letwin (1963: 149) in his *The Origins of Scientific Economics*, claims that 'Locke's education, like that of so many of his contemporaries, was deeply influenced by the accidents and dislocations of the Civil War.'

At Oxford, Peter Laslett (1964: 18) claims in his Introduction to the *Two Treatises*, that 'Locke was urbane, idle, unhappy and unremarkable, all these things at the same time and only just successful enough.' He was not satisfied with the state of learning at the university where he had to study scholastic metaphysics and logic. He preferred the French philosophers René Descartes and Pierre Gassendi (1592–1655). But despite this fact he managed, according to Henry Richard Fox-Bourne (1876, Vol. 1: 40), to satisfy the authorities, did reasonably well in his studies, and was awarded his Bachelor of Arts degree in 1656, and his Master's in 1659. He became Reader in Greek in 1660 and in Rhetoric in 1662. In 1663, he was appointed Censor of Moral Philosophy. Part of his duties, in this capacity, was to deliver a series of lectures, and Locke chose the topic: 'The Law of Nature'.

At the time of his lectures on natural law, Locke decided to switch to the study of medicine, a decision based on an interest he had cultivated for several years. Although he was never awarded a degree in medicine, he made a reputation for himself as a physician. In this capacity he in 1667 met and became the personal physician and adviser to Antony Ashley Cooper, later the first Earl of Shaftesbury (1621–1683). Consequently, his interest turned to politics and political economy. He was given the opportunity to serve as a secretary on important government boards. This gave him first-hand knowledge of how a government worked. When Shaftesbury fell from favour in 1675, Locke spent some time travelling across France, as tutor and medical attendant to a young pupil. In 1679 Shaftesbury's political fortunes took a brief positive turn and Locke returned to England. Around this time, he composed the greater part of his *Two Treatises of Government*, and furthermore started his writings on several essays.[1] However Shaftesbury became deeply involved in the abortive Monmouth Rebellion,[2] and in 1683 was forced into hiding in Holland. As a Shaftesbury sympathizer, Locke was in 1684, by a royal mandate, expelled from Oxford. As a consequence, he followed Shaftesbury, and went into exile in Holland. A request to extradite him was ignored by the Dutch government.

During his six years in exile, he completed several essays, among them *Essay Concerning Human Understanding*, which James McCosh (1875: 27) calls 'Locke's immortal essay', and *Thoughts Concerning Education*. Returning to England in 1689 he quickly published the first of these and in addition *Letter Concerning Toleration*. The year after, he published anonymously his *Two Treatises of Government* (TT), in which he discusses the state of nature, natural rights, natural law, and political economy including the social contract and problems concerned with property.[3]

After returning to England, the new government recognized his services to their cause. Consequently, he was offered important posts, as for example ambassador to Berlin and Vienna. These he politely refused because of his fragile health, but he did agree to serve in some important offices at home. In 1688, he become secretary to the Lords Proprietors of Carolina and a year later, he helped to draft the *Fundamental Constitution for the Government of Carolina*. Later, when his fame had spread and the 'Glorious Revolution', with the fall of the Stuarts, had brought influence and power to his friends, his career reached a peak when he was appointed Commissioner of Appeals in 1689. He also served as Commissioner of Trade and Plantations from 1696 to 1700. Although these and other official duties demanded him to stay in London for periods, he was in 1691 able to make a permanent home at Oates in Essex, at the house of his friends Sir Francis and Lady Masham. He continued to live with them until his death in 1704.

John Locke was an Oxford scholar, medical researcher and physician, political operative, political economist and ideologue for a revolutionary movement, as well as being one of the great philosophers of the late seventeenth and early eighteenth centuries.

Pufendorf Locke's Primary Source

Like most of his contemporaries, Locke listed only a few of his sources. It is therefore very difficult to establish exactly whose ideas Locke used when he put his own thoughts into writing. Laslett (1964: 130) claims that Locke had a deliberate policy of making as few references as he could.[4] In his *Two Treatises* he mentions only six writers by their names and two others by the titles of their works.

Locke is considered one of the most influential philosophers in the history of modern thought.[5] Therefore, a great number of academic scholars have discussed his contributions and commented on whom he built his theories on, and who in turn took over his theories and built on them. Unfortunately, only a few have carried out an investigation into his use of Pufendorf's works. The reason being that very few writers on society or political economy have read Pufendorf's natural law works and are aware of his contributions. This is particularly true of economists. Historians of economic thought have only occasionally found any connection between Pufendorf and Locke. There are, however, a few scholars, who have included Pufendorf's natural law works when analysing Locke's essays and treatises, and compared them with the texts of the authors Locke had studied.

Although Locke was born in the same year as Pufendorf, attended university at about the same time, and became a very productive writer during his life, it is a fact that the publishing of most of his writings took place later in his life. Laslett (1964: 16) writes that he was 'a reluctant author, a professed "enemy to the scribbling of his age" ' He was 57 years old before a word of the works which have given him renown was published in print. By then, Pufendorf had written and published many essays, three great natural law works, and numerous books of history.

However, Locke's writings actually started as early as the beginning of the 1660s. It was during the preparation of his lectures on natural law that he wrote, in Latin, a manuscript containing these lectures. He even revised this manuscript a few times. Locke never published these lectures himself. They were not published until Wolfgang von Leyden translated, edited, and published them in 1954 as *John Locke: Essays on the Law of Nature*. These essays are, according to James Gordon Clapp (1967, Vol. 3: 498) in his article on *Locke* in *The Encyclopedia of Philosophy*, considered his earliest known political writings.

When Locke prepared his lectures, and wrote these essays both von Leyden (1954: 39) and Roger Woolhouse (2007: 38) claimed that he had a copy of Pufendorf's first book *Elementorum Jurisprudentiae Universalis* in his possession and that he had procured this book just after it was published in 1660. Michael Zuckert (1994: 243), in his book *Natural Rights and the new Republicanism*, also claimed that it was 'a book Locke admired'. Later in 1681, Locke also bought a copy of the edition of 1672 of *this book*, together with a copies of *De Jure Naturae et Gentium* and *De Officio Hominis*.[6] Consequently, there can be little doubt that Locke consulted Pufendorf when he wrote his essays and treatises, and that he used Pufendorf's works, together with the works of others, such as Grotius and Hobbes, as a point of departure in his analysis. In Pufendorf Locke found all the references to the Greeks, the Romans and the modern writers that he used in his later works.

This reliance on Pufendorf is also confirmed by von Leyden (1954: 39), who contends that there can be little doubt that Locke consulted Pufendorf's *Elementorum*, 'for a number of points raised in it are discussed by him'. Moreover, he points to a few cases where Locke and Pufendorf disagree and to others where they agree. Von Leyden also asserts that Locke's first essays became a foundation that he built his later works on, and that these essays over the rest of his life provided him 'with topics and inspiration which he turned to account in the building of his own philosophy'. Nevertheless, surprisingly and wrongly he claims that Pufendorf was mainly concerned with an examination of specific legal points, and that these attracted little of Locke's attention. His conclusion is peculiar: 'Thus, since the fields of their special inquiries did not coincide, a further comparison of their doctrines could hardly be fruitful' (ibid.: 82). It was the Cambridge Platonist, Nathanael Culwerwell (1619–1651), who provided Locke with an important stimulus and who had a direct influence on the formation of Locke's mature doctrines.[7]

In his introduction to Locke's *Two Treatises of Government* Laslett (1964: 74) finds it idle to look for the source to Locke's political thinking.

> But of the writers he consulted when engaged on his book Samuel Pufendorf was perhaps of the greatest use to him, in spite of the fact that their views of constitutional matters were in such contrast. He took advantage of Pufendorf's arguments, he reproduced his positions, and he described his major work as 'the best book of that kind', better than the great Grotius on War and Peace.

In several footnotes, Laslett shows how Locke used and built on Pufendorf. From his discussion, it is clear that Pufendorf was his primary source.

How John Locke rose to dominance, within the context of seventeenth-century Anglo-American thought, is discussed by Zuckert (1994: 187–188). He claims that Locke when he held his Oxford lectures not only presented Locke's views as from 1664, but also his considered judgements on the many important natural law theorists, both the ones that preceded him, like Richard Hooker (1554–1600) and Grotius, and the more recent such as, Hobbes and Pufendorf. Locke had, when he was writing his *Essays*, access to the works of all the mentioned authors and he used their works extensively, without citing them, in his own writings. Zuckert points out, for example, that 'It might seem quixotic to treat the Essays as a critique of Grotius, for Grotius never once appears by name in Locke's book. Nonetheless Grotius has an unmistakeable presence there' (1994: 188). According to Zuckert, Locke also quotes and refers to the more recent ones including Pufendorf, without mentioning their names or citing their books. Many examples are given by Zuckert of how Locke makes use of Pufendorf, in what manner he was influenced by him, and by what means he breaks with him. When Locke, for example, attempts 'to justify his definition [of law] in terms of criteria essential to all law', the criteria is clearly adapted from Pufendorf's discussion of law. 'Locke identifies three or perhaps four such characteristics of law … all taken from Pufendorf' (ibid.: 192). John Locke and his debt to Pufendorf is also discussed by Michael Crowe (1977), James Tully (1980) and Helge Hesse (2009: 436).

It is therefore reasonable to claim that Locke was probably the first important scholar who actively used Pufendorf when he did his own writings. This also strongly indicates that Locke early in his life acquired a good theoretical knowledge of natural law, which included a state of the art exposition of ethics, jurisprudence, society and political economy, from Pufendorf.

Locke's Writings on Political Economy

Letwin in his *The Origins of Scientific Economics* from 1963 analyses the development of English economic thought in the period 1660–1776. He outlines the contributions of several English scholars, among them John Locke. Neither Grotius nor Pufendorf is mentioned as a predecessor or contemporary of Locke or the others. This is particularly surprising since Letwin recognizes that the doctrine of natural law, 'with its fusion of scientific principle and moral standard', was the foundation that Locke built his works on and that this also carried over into economics (1965: 176).

Locke's writings on applied economics have also been investigated by Karen Vaughn (1980) in her *John Locke Economist and Social Scientist*. Locke was, in Vaughn's opinion, a far more sophisticated economist than most historians of thought have given him credit for, and that he was an early social scientist with a consistent view of social action in both his economic and political writings. Her declared objectives in her study were therefore first to provide 'a comprehensive treatment of John Locke's position in the development of economic thought', second 'to establish the influences on his thought and his relationship to his contemporaries', and last to make 'the connection between his economic theory and his theory of political society' (1980: x). In her study, the second objective is only superficially treated.

Although she claims (1980: 18) that the real influence on Lock's economic thought comes primarily from 'a combination of his reading of Aristotle, the Scholastics, and his contemporaries Grotius and Pufendorf on the one hand, and his own personal observation of economic problems on the other', there are no discussions or examples of how Locke built on any of these authors.[8]

In one footnote Vaughn has a reference to Pufendorf's *De Jure Naturae*. Locke claims, like Pufendorf that fashion is for the most part, 'nothing but the ostentation of riches', and therefore a high price increases the demand (1980: 24). With this exception, there are no references to Pufendorf and no indication that she has studied his natural law works or his price theory in any detail. Nevertheless, she sees it as a problem that Locke 'gives no indication of which of his ideas are new and which are borrowed' (1980: 18). Furthermore, she asserts that 'This is true not only of Locke, but of most seventeenth-century writers. Footnoting is a mania of our age of widespread literacy' (1980: 141). Unfortunately, Vaughn leaves it at that and makes no investigation of Locke's use of Pufendorf in his writings on political economy.[9]

Neither does Vaughn make any attempt to assess the influence Locke had on later economic thought. She only mentions in passing that Richard Cantillon (1680–1734) had read his essays before he wrote *Essai sur la nature du commerce en general* between 1730 and 1734, and that Ferdinando Galiani (1728–1787) is reputed to have introduced himself to economics by translating Locke's first essay before he in 1741, wrote his own essay *On Money* and that Adam Smith made reference to Locke's essay in *The Wealth of Nations.*

Writings on political economy can be found in most of Locke's works. It certainly goes back to his *The Law of Nature* based on his Oxford lectures in the early 1660s. His work on what can be called purer political economy goes back to 1668, when he wrote a paper, or manuscript, on the consequences of *Lessening of Interest.*[10] From 1668 to 1774 Locke corrected and added to this manuscript, but he did not publish it. However, Letwin (1963: 273–300) published it as an appendix called *Locke's Early Manuscript on Interest.* When Locke wrote this manuscript, Letwin (1963: 156) contends that he had not read any of the economic tracts that were published at the time. However, he later became an avid collector and reader of such tracts. Furthermore, in spite of the fact that Letwin points to Locke's 'disposition to consider moral and political problems from the standpoint of "natural law"' he is not aware of the fact that Locke was well acquainted with Pufendorf's *Elementorum*, when he first wrote this manuscript, and later became familiar with *De Jure Naturae et Gentium.* Pufendorf is not mentioned at all in Letwin's book.

Henry William Spiegel (1983: 155) in his book *The Growth of Economic Thought* has a different opinion. He claims that it was Josiah Child with his pamphlet *Brief Observations Concerning Trade, Interest and Money* published in 1668 that was responsible for bringing Locke 'into the discussion of economic matters'. Furthermore, he claims that Locke had 'carefully perused', a tract by Thomas Manley (1628–76) from 1669, in which Manley argued that a low rate of interest would cause an increase in drunkenness, and that Locke employed some of his arguments.[11] Surprisingly, Spiegel writes that Locke 'may have found more food for thought in Pufendorf', but leaves it at that, and does not discuss it further (ibid.: 232).

When Locke came to compose, and publish *Some Considerations of the Consequences of the Lowering of Interest, and Raising the Value of Money* in 1691, he incorporated pages of his original manuscript in it. Locke's essay was an attempt to convince the British Parliament to defeat a proposed bill designed to lower the real rate of interest from 6 to 4 per cent. However, his influence was insufficient to sway Parliament to his side. In 1695, he published *Further Considerations concerning Raising the Value of Money*, which again argued for recoinage at full value. These two essays along with a short pamphlet *Some Observations on a Printed Paper Intituled, For Encouraging the Coining of Silver Money in England and After for keeping it here*, and a few scattered papers comprise Locke's total published output on issues of what can be termed pure economics. However, his writings on political economy, such as human behaviour, private property, theory of value and money, foundation of states, and division of state power and taxation can also, as already mentioned, be found in *Essay Concerning Human Understanding*, in his most important and influential work, the *Two Treaties of Government* and in several of his smaller works.

Theory of Human Behaviour

In his *Essay Concerning Human Understanding* Locke outlines his theory of knowledge and his philosophy of science. In addition, he discusses other issues such as ethics and philosophy of mind.

Although Locke was a devoted Christian, he followed Pufendorf in criticizing and rejecting the widely held view about the origin of our knowledge. According to this view, which was strongly advocated by all the different Christian dominations, our fundamental theoretical and practical principles and ideas are innate. They are there from birth. Locke saw this doctrine as a threat to freedom of thought and inquiry. Like Pufendorf, he held the opinion that knowledge must be acquired. Our mental faculties and our ability to use them may be said to be innate, but it is only by using these faculties that we can acquire knowledge. He said that at birth our mind has no innate ideas, it has not yet been affected by experiences and impressions, it is blank, a *tabula rasa*. As our mind gains simple ideas from sensation, it forms complex ideas from these simple ideas by processes of combination, division, generalization and abstraction.

In his *Two Treatises*, Locke starts discussing the state of nature. Like Pufendorf, he considers what state all men are natural in (TT.II.ii.4). His answer is that men are in a state of perfect freedom to decide their actions 'as they think fit, within the bounds of the Law of Nature', without having to depend on other people.[12] He continues by claiming that the state of nature has a law of nature to govern it. This obligates everyone to reason, which in turn means for all mankind 'that being equal and independent, no one ought to harm another in his Life, Health, Liberty or Possessions' (TT.II.ii.6). Since all men are the workmanship of one wise creator, and are in this world to do his business, each one has to take care of his own self-interest. 'Every one as he is bound to preserve himself' (ibid.). When his own self-interest is not threatened, he ought, 'as much as he can to preserve the rest of Mankind' (ibid.). The allusions to Pufendorf's self-interest and sociability is clear.

Theory of Property

Locke uses, like Pufendorf, his theory of human behaviour to develop his theory of property. This theory is also outlined in the Second Treatise, in the chapter *Of Property*. His endeavour is to show how men come to have property 'in several parts of that which God gave mankind in common, and that without any express compact of all the commoners' (TT.II.ii.25).

The starting point is the same for Locke as for Pufendorf:

> God, who hath given the World to Men in common, hath also given the reason to make use of it to the best advantage of Life, and convenience. The Earth, and all that is therein, is given to Men for the Support and Comfort of their being. And though all the Fruits it naturally produces, and Beasts it feeds, belong to Mankind in common, as they are produced by the spontaneous hand of Nature; and no body has originally a private Dominion, exclusive of the rest of Mankind, in any of them, as they are thus in their natural state.
>
> (TT.II.ii.26)

However, the fruits of the earth did not fall into each mouth by themselves. Therefore, even if they were given for the use of man, 'there must of necessity be a means to appropriate them some way or other before they can be of any use, or at all beneficial to any particular Man' (ibid.). Pufendorf argues, as explained in an earlier chapter, that people in a state of nature must obtain the consent of their fellow men before the fruits of the earth can be privately appropriated. At first, this consent could be tacit but later it must give way to express agreements.

A Labour Theory of Property

Locke departs from Pufendorf and outlines his labour theory of property. He was a persistent champion of natural rights – the idea that 'every man has a Property in his own Person' (TT.II.ii.27). Nobody has any right to this person but himself. A person owns himself and should have certain liberties that cannot be expropriated by the state or anyone else. Locke claims that most things need cultivation before they can be used. This required the use of labour. When someone labours for a productive end, the results become that person's property. It would be improper that some, who had contributed no labour, should have the same rights as someone that used his labour and skills in the production. Ownership is therefore created by the application of labour. Here it should be emphasized that Locke could also have got this idea from Pufendorf, who claimed that 'it was improper that a man who had contributed no labour should have right to things equal to his whose industry a thing had been raised and rendered fit for service' (DJNG. IV.iv.6: 540).

The question is asked when particular things became a man's property. In answering, Locke uses an example from Pufendorf.[13] 'He that is nourished by the Acorns he pickt up under an Oak. Or the Apples he gathered from the Trees in the Wood, has certainly appropriated them to himself. No Body can deny but the nourishment is his' (TT.II.v.28). Did the fruits became private property when they were digested, or when he ate them, when he boiled them, when he brought them home or when he picked them up? Locke's answer was that it was man's labour that removed the fruits out of the common state and made them his property.

Locke claims, like Pufendorf, that property preceded government. Government can therefore not arbitrarily dispose of the estates of its subjects. How much could each person appropriate of land or other things? 'As much as any one can make use of to any advantage of life before it spoils, so much he may by his labour fix a Property in' (TT.II.v.31). A person can also appropriate what his employee has produced. It is possible that Locke got this appropriation idea from Pufendorf, who in his discussion of the causes of private property, emphasizes that most things require cultivation, and to cultivate you need the use of labour. However, there are limits to how much property one can own. Since nature is given to all of mankind, one cannot take more than his fair share.

Nicolas Jolley (1999: 205), in his book *Locke: His Philosophical Thought*, contends that Locke rejects Pufendorf's theory of property as a clumsy solution, which would effectively condemn the human race to starvation (TT.II.v.26). This can, however, be disputed.

Property by Agreement

Locke took over Pufendorf's view that introduction of property was a process in time, but it was a somewhat different process. Thus in the beginning it was labour that 'gave a Right of Property, where ever any one was pleased to employ it, upon which was common, which remained, a long while, the far greater part and is yet more than Mankind makes use of' (TT.II.v.45). At first men 'contended themselves with what un-assisted Nature offered to their necessitees'. Later land became scarce when population and stock increased. Then several communities settled their bounds of distinct territories. Laws were introduced and 'regulated the Properties of the private Men of their Society, and so, by Compact and Agreement, settled the Property which Labour and Industry began' (ibid.). It is therefore clear that Locke also had the use of an agreements in his theory of property. Hont and Ignatieff (1983: 40) expressed it in this way. 'Locke's improvement on Pufendorf, as Barbeyrac observed, was to have pushed back the moment in history when contract became necessary by virtue of a hypothesis of initial abundance, and then to have theorized the emergence of the inequality which would make necessary a pact establishing government.'

Private Property Creates Peace

Furthermore, it is clear that Locke like Pufendorf believes that the introduction of property would contribute to the creation of peace among men.

> For when Men by entering into Society and Civil Government, have excluded force and introduced Laws for the preservation of Property, Peace, and Unity amongst themselves.
>
> (TT.II.xix.226)

Locke also discusses the limitation of private property in the case of great needs. He makes it clear that nobody had the right to live comfortably from other people's labour. Hont and Ignatieff (1883: 38) conclude: 'Locke's position on charity was neither more or less generous than Pufendorf's.'

Theory of Value, Money and Trade

An inquiry into Pufendorf's treatment of the development of a commercial society and his theory of value and money, and a comparison with Locke's views and theories shows clearly his influence on Locke. Locke does not plagiarize Pufendorf, but he builds directly on his opinions and theories. Sometimes he agrees and sometimes he disagrees. The differences between the two, often found in Locke's emphasis on English conditions and a substantially more advanced quantity theory of money.

In *Some considerations* from 1691, he opposes, as mentioned, a bill before Parliament to lower the maximum legal interest rate from 6 per cent to 4 percent. Because interest is a price, and because the laws of nature determine all prices, he reasons, ceilings on interest rates would be counterproductive. People would evade the ceiling, and the costs of evasion would drive interest rates even higher than they would have been without the ceiling. Locke believes that governments should not regulate interest rates. Locke's reasoning on the subject, sophisticated for his era, has withstood the test of time: some economists make today the same objection to controls on interest rates.

Theory of Value

On the subject of value and price, Locke takes over and uses Pufendorf's theory of value. A comparison of Locke's writings on the theory of value and price in *Some Considerations* with Pufendorf's writings substantiates that he must have had his work close at hand. This is also recognized by Hutchison (1988: 68). Locke's account is a rudimentary demand and supply theory. He starts out using Pufendorf's treatment of the distinction between the intrinsic value and the market value of a good. Locke claims that the intrinsic worth of a thing consists in its fitness to supply the necessities or serve the conveniences of human life. The more necessary it is to our being or the more it contributes to our well-being, the greater is its worth.

Locke (1691: 16) used the terms 'quantity' and 'vent'. The vent of any good 'depends on its necessity or usefulness'. An estimation of the value of a good can be done by comparing its quantity to its vent. Quantity and vent are approximately equivalent to supply and demand, which also depend on the number of buyers and sellers. 'The price of any Commodity rises or falls by the proportion of the number of Buyer and Sellers' (1691: 15). Fewer buyers will lower the price; fewer sellers will increase the price. The allusions to Pufendorf are remarkable. As with Pufendorf, Locke is also aware of the fact that the most useful things, such as water and air, have no price or a small price. 'Hence it is, that the best, and most useful things are commonly the cheapest; because, though their Consumption be great, yet the Bounty of Providence has made, their production large, and suitable to it.' (1691: 21). From this Letwin (1965: 224) suggests that the paradox of value (the diamond-water paradox) although known 'since the time immemorial probably entered the stream of economic theory through Locke's Considerations'. However, Letwin had not studied Pufendorf's writings on value and price and his understanding of this paradox.

In the *Two Treatises* Locke changed his view on the theory of value and combined a labour theory of property with a labour theory of value. Of all the provisions of life, the ones that nature furnishes us with and the others, which our industry and pains prepare for us, a computation will make it clear 'how much labour makes the far greatest part of the value of things, we enjoy in this World' (TT.II.v.42). Labour is not only the origin of property, but also the determinant of its value and thereby the differences in value on everything. The contradiction between Locke's demand and supply theory and his labour theory of value is discussed by Spiegel (1983: 164–169). However, Hutchison (1988: 70) contends that Locke did not propose a labour theory of value that determined relative prices, and therefore there are 'no outright contradiction' between the two theories.

Karen Vaughn (1980: 17) starts her exposition of Locke's contribution to economics with his theory of value. She claims that his value theory forms the basis of his economic analysis and economic policy. 'It was his one tool, his one model for dealing with all economic problems.' He applied this model consistently to economic problems and his analysis mostly yielded satisfactory explanations. Vaughn claims that Locke's account of the determination of prices often has been described as an early version of supply and demand analysis, where *quantity* was his term for *supply* and *vent* his term for *demand* (ibid.: 19). However, she adds that it was a supply and demand analysis of a most primitive kind. Furthermore, Vaughn claims that Locke's analysis can best be described as an analysis of shifts in demand and supply. His treatment of what determines the demand of goods, vent, is rich but his treatment of supply and quantity is scanty (ibid.: 21). It can be argued that her statement also applies to Pufendorf's theory of value.

Money and Trade

From his theory of value, Locke goes on to develop his theory of money. As with Pufendorf, his theory can be divided into the origin of money, the requirements and functions of money and what determines its value. Locke distinguishes, like Pufendorf, two functions of money, as a 'counter' to measure value, and as a 'pledge' to lay claim to goods. He believes silver and gold, as opposed to paper money, are the appropriate currency for international transactions. Silver and gold, he says, are treated to have equal value by all of humanity and can thus be treated as a pledge by anyone, while the value of paper money is only valid under the government, which issues it.

The quantity theory of money forms a special case of this general theory. His idea is based on 'money answers all things' or 'rent of money is always sufficient, or more than enough,' and 'varies very little … '. Regardless of whether the demand for money is unlimited or constant, Locke concludes that as far as money is concerned, the demand is exclusively regulated by its quantity. He also investigates the determinants of demand and supply. For supply, goods in general are considered valuable because they are scarce, and can be exchanged or consumed. For demand, goods are in demand because they yield a flow of income. Locke develops an early theory of capitalization, such as land, which has value because 'by its constant production of saleable commodities it brings in a certain yearly income.' Demand for money is almost the same as demand for goods or land; it depends on whether money is wanted as medium of exchange or as loanable funds. As a medium of exchange, 'money is capable by exchange to procure us the necessaries or conveniences of life.' For loanable funds, 'it comes to be of the same nature with land by yielding a certain yearly income … or interest'.

As with Pufendorf, Locke understands that changes in money supply had a direct influence on prices. However, he goes further and is not far from stating the quantity theory of money as it is formulated today: 'This shows the necessity of some proportion of money to trade, but what proportion that is hard to determine, because it depends not barely on the quantity of money, but the quickness of its circulation' (1691: 12).

A comparison of Locke's writing on the theory of value and money, in his *Some Considerations* with Pufendorf's writings on this issue, proves that he must have used his works, Locke does not plagiarize Pufendorf, but he builds directly on him. The notion that a change in money supply will lead to changes in prices, he probably borrowed from Pufendorf. Another example is the idea that abundant money will lead to a fall in interest.

In his essay on money, Locke also brings up for discussion another problem; the deteriorating state of the British coinage. He participated actively in calling in all debased coinage. Locke's claim that the authorities should not debase money because it is against the law of nature comes clearly from Pufendorf. The only difference between the two is that Locke dwells on English conditions.

He believes that debased coinage should be recoined at full value, i.e. according to standard weight, and that the cost should fall upon the Exchequer. The recall and reissue finally took place in 1696. This recall was in accordance with Pufendorf's strong view that debased coinage would be detrimental to domestic commerce.

Foundation of States

Locke's views on the foundation of states or what he calls commonwealth starts out with a statement of man in a state of nature.

> God having made Man such a Creature, that, in his own Judgment, it was not good for him to be alone, put him under strong Obligations of Necessity, Convenience, and Inclination to drive him into Society, as well as fitted him with Understanding and Language to continue and enjoy it. (TT.II.vii.77)

He then discusses how men chose to live in prime societies that is marriages and extended families.

The next step is then to explain why they wanted to establish states. Locke starts out, like Pufendorf, claiming that since man being born 'with a Title to perfect Freedom, and an uncontrolled enjoyment of all the Rights and Priviledges of the Law of Nature, equally with any other Man in the World' man also have by nature a power. With this power he can 'preserve his Property, that is this Life, Liberty and Estate, against the Injuries and Attempts of other Men'. Furthermore, he can also 'judge of and punish the breaches of that Law in others' (TT.II.vii.87).

But since 'men being by Nature, all free, equal and independent' no one can be forced out of this estate and 'subjected to Political Power of another, without his own consent' (TT.II.viii.95). There is only one way whereby man is willing to divest himself of his natural liberty and 'puts on the bonds of Civil Society'. This is by agreeing with other men to join and unite into a state. The purpose of this state is peaceable living, security of property and security against any that is not a member of the state. Any number of men may establish such a state because it injures not the freedom of the one that are left outside; 'they are left as they were in the Liberty of the State of Nature' (ibid.).

So when any number of men, by the consent of every individual, have made a state, they have also made it 'one Body, with a Power to Act as one Body', by the will and determination of the majority. Everyone in this state is bound by the majority. 'The act of the Majority passes for the act of the whole' (ibid.: 96). Locke calls this the 'Original Compact'. It corresponds to Pufendorf's pact of association.

Men therefore have to come together in a community or commonwealth. This commonwealth is a political or civil society and it will then have the legislative and executive power to make decisions on behalf of all its members.

An extensive discussion of the beginning of political societies follows. Locke concludes: 'And thus much may suffice to shew, that as far as we have any light from History, we have reason to conclude, that all peaceful beginnings of Government have been laid in the Consent of the People' (TT.II.viii.112).

The theory that the state exists only to guaranty security and legal protection was advocated by Pufendorf, and thereafter taken over by Locke.

Division of State Powers, Corruption and Taxation

Like Pufendorf, Locke discusses three forms of governments: democracy, oligarchy and monarchy. When the majority have the whole power of the community, when they employ that power in making laws for the community, and when they execute these laws with officers that they have appointed, then this form of government is called perfect democracy. When the power of making laws is placed in the hands of a few selected men, and their heirs and successors, this form is called oligarchy. If this power is in the hands of one man it is called different forms of monarchy. It can be absolute or constitutional; it can be hereditary or elective (TT.II.x.132).

However, from his discussion, it is clear that Locke finds that absolute monarchy is inconsistent with civil society and that he himself prefers moderate monarchies where legislative and executive functions are in different hands (TT.II.xiv.159).

The legislature is the key:

> This Legislative is not only the suprema power of the Common-wealth, but sacred and unalterable in the hands where the Community have once placed it; nor can any Edict of any Body else, in what Form soever conceived, or by what Power soever backed, have the force and obligation of Law, which has not its Sanction from the Legislative, which the public has chosen and appointed.
>
> (TT.II.xi.134)

However, there are restrictions or bounds on the legislature. First, it cannot act arbitrary over the lives and fortune of the people. Second, it cannot assume to itself a power to rule by extemporary arbitrary decrees. Third, it cannot take from any man any part of his property without his own consent. Fourth, it cannot transfer the power of making laws to any other hands. These bounds have been set by society to the legislative power of every state in all forms of government (TT.II.xi.142).

Since it is not necessary that the legislature is constantly in session there is a need of 'a Power always in being, which should see to the Execution of the Laws that are made, and remain in force', that is the executive power. It takes care of all the domestic affairs of the state. The management of the security and interest of the state with other state Locke calls the federative power. Both the executive and the federative powers are subordinate and accountable to the legislative power (TT.II.xiii.143). This relation is therefore close to Pufendorf's pact of subjection, between the rulers and the ruled.

On Corruption

Locke as well as Pufendorf considers corruption an evil that all have an obligation to resist. He argues that corruption is a violation of trust. Men enter society for the preservation of their property. That is why they authorize a legislative to make laws and rules, set as guards and fences to the properties of all members of society. These laws and rules should also limit the power and moderate the dominion of every part and member of the society. If the legislators endeavour to take away the property of the people or to reduce them to slavery under arbitrary power, they put themselves into a state of war with the people. If the legislators transgress this fundamental rule of society; 'and either by Ambition, Fear, Folly or Corruption,' it is a breach of trust and they forfeit the power the people has put in their hands. (TT.II.xix.222). What is said here concerning the legislative in general holds also true for the supreme executor, who have a double trust put in him, both to have part in the legislative, and the supreme execution of the law. He acts against both when he sets up his own arbitrary will as the law of the society. He also acts contrary to the trust when he either:

> imploys the Force, Treasure, and Offices of the Society, to corrupt the Representatives, and gain them to his purposes: or openly pre-ingages the Electors, and prescribes to their choice, such, whom he has by Sollicitations, Threats, Promises, or otherwise won to his designs; and imploys them to bring in such, who have promised before-hand, what to Vote, and what to Enact.
>
> (Ibid.)

On Taxation

Locke does not have a detail theory of taxation as Pufendorf did. However, he claims that governments cannot be supported without great charge. Everyone that enjoys his share of the protection should pay out of his wealth his proportion of the maintenance of this protection. This tax must be with each person's consent, that is the consent of the majority of all, or by the majority of the representatives, they have chosen.[14] Should any claim the power to 'lay and levy' taxes on the people, by his own authority and without the consent of the people, he thereby 'invades the Fundamental Law of Property, and subverts the end of Government' TT.II.xi.140. It is also clear that the government cannot raise taxes on the property of the people without the consent of the people, given by themselves or their deputies. His overriding interest in taxation is, like Pufendorf, to clamp down on arbitrary taxation and its iniquities.

Locke and the Diffusion of Pufendorf's Natural Law

Two scholars are central to the spread of natural law or moral philosophy as it was later called: the previously mentioned French translator, Jean Barbeyrac, and John Locke. For some years, these two corresponded. They also had a tremendous respect for Pufendorf and considered him one of the greatest scholars of their times.

It is clear from the earlier treatment that Locke used Pufendorf's natural law work extensively in the development of his own theories of government and political economy. He had, towards the end of his life, become a highly venerated scholar, known across the British Isles, Continental Europe and North America. Locke became, according to Udo Thiel (1999: 323) in his article on *Locke* in the *Penguin Dictionary of Philosophy*, one of the first and leading figures of the Enlightenment. His ideas had a substantial effect on both the development of the science of philosophy, psychology and educational theory, government and political economy. In addition, his work influenced the development of freedom, tolerance, democracy and governments accountable to their constituency. Locke was an admirer of Pufendorf. He spoke highly of him, recommended his works to others, and used his natural law works in developing his own theories. Indirectly the spread of Locke's thoughts therefore also had tremendous effects on the diffusion of Pufendorf's ideas.

Education on all levels and in most European countries in the sixteenth and seventeenth century was in glaring need of reform. During his exile in the Netherlands 1683–89, Locke wrote a number of letters to a friend giving him practical advice on the education of his son. These letters he adapted as *Thought Concerning Education*, an essay that could have been inspired by Pufendorf's emphasis on education in his *De Jure Naturae*. It was published four years after his return to England in 1693 as an *Essay Concerning Education*. Further enlarged editions were published later in his lifetime as an *Essay on Education*. It had a remarkable influence on education in many European countries, and in particular on university education in Scotland. It became a very popular reading among educators and politician concerned with the improvement of education. In it Locke gives advice and made proposals for what authors, and which books should be recommended reading for the education of a gentleman.

> When he has pretty well digested Tully's Office, and added to it 'Puffendorf De Officio Hominis et Civis', it may be reasonable to set him upon 'Grotius de Jure Belli ac Pacis' or, which perhaps is the better of the two, 'Pufendorf De Jure Naturae et Gentium', wherein he will be instructed in the natural rights of men, and the original and foundations of society, and the duties resulting from thence. This general part of civil law and history are studies which a gentleman should not barely touch at, but constantly dwell upon, and never have done with.[15]

James Gordon Clapp (1967: 500) in his article on Locke in the *Encyclopaedia of Philosophy* wrote that his educational proposals were pragmatic, and based on considerable psychological insight into the motives needs and passions of parents and children. He claims that Locke's letters were written in response to 'so many, who profess themselves at loss how to breed their children', and that they furthermore displayed 'clearly the liberal bent of his mind as well as his love of freedom, tolerance, and truth'. He could also have added concepts that he could have found in Pufendorf's lengthy discussion of education and learning. Pufendorf strongly emphasizes the duties that lie in the cultivation of the mind, and the duties of those who have laid upon them the education of others (DJNG.II.iv: 231). Furthermore, Pufendorf discusses in some length useful learning and 'the evils of pedantic learning'. Addled pedagogues are not to be laid at the door of letters (ibid.: 251).

However, with his writings in general and his essay on education in particular, Locke had a tremendous influence on educational thought and practice in many European countries. His writings often led to reforms in education on all levels from elementary schools to universities.

There can be no doubt that Locke's recommendation of Pufendorf's natural law works contributed to the use and diffusion of both *De Officio* and *De Jure Naturae* across Europe and North America. In recommending Pufendorf, Vere Chappel (1994: 229) in an article in *The Cambrdge Companion to Locke*, claims that Locke was linking himself to a type of natural law thought that only had begun to develop in England, because of the influence of the works of Grotius.

Notes

1 It has been claimed by Laslett (1964: 67–78) that his *First Treatise* was written against the views of Sir Robert Filmer (1588–1653). Filmer's views were expressed in *Patriarcha*, which had the subtitle *The Natural Power of the Kings*. It was probably written in defence of the authority of the state in 1638. It circulated from that year, but was not published before 1680. In it Filmer argued that political authority was derived from religious authority, also known as the Divine Right of Kings, which was a very dominant theory in seventeenth-century England. Pufendorf argued strongly against this doctrine.

2 It was called the Monmouth Rebellion after the Duke of Monmouth, who claimed the English throne, and led an unsuccessful rebellion against the Roman Catholic King James II in 1685. However, three years later James II was forced to give up the English throne to William of Orange and fled the country.

3 It has been published in numerous editions and reprinted repeatedly. And it has at least been translated into French, German, Hebrew, Hindi, Italian, Norwegian, Russian, Spanish and Swedish.

4 This was also in accordance with Pufendorf's view in his first book *Elementorum Jurisprudentiae* where he claims that he has drawn much on Grotius and Hobbes, whom he cites there 'once for all', but otherwise he has no citations. However, his lack of references in his first work was in sharp contrast to his main work where the readers are overwhelmed with citations.

5 Although Laslett (1964: x), claims that Locke did not write as a philosopher.

6 Von Leyden (1954: 39) writes 'Locke possessed two copies of the Elementa, the edition of 1672, which he had bought together with *De Jure Naturae*, in 1681 and the edition of 1660, which he may have acquired shortly after it was published. There can be little doubt that he consulted this book when he wrote his essays.' This is also confirmed by Woolhouse (2007: 38): He states that in October and November of 1660 Locke was in Pensford. From his correspondence, it is clear that Locke was occupied with 'what was called the "law of nature"'. 'Two important books on the subject had been published during the year. One of these, *De Officiis secundum Naturae Jus*, was by Robert Sharrock, and ... it is very possible that

Locke had read it; the other, which he evidently did read, was Samuel Pufendorf's *Elementa Jurisprudentia Universalis.*'

7 The Cambridge Platonists believed strongly that reason is the proper judge of disagreements, and they advocated dialogue.

8 In a chapter *John Locke, Social Scientist* Vaughn (1980: 108–109) mentions that Schumpeter noted Locke's contributions to the seventeenth-century theory of natural law, 'and ranked Locke along with Hobbes, Grotius and Pufendorf, among others, as philosophers who despite their Protestantism, were in the Scholastic tradition'.

9 Karen Vaughn (1980:141) claims that her first professor Joseph Soudek, in a personal correspondence, contended that: 'In earlier times, it was taken for granted that the reading public, which was small, was well enough educated to be able to supply the source of non-original ideas. Only the really obscure writers tended to be credited for their ideas.'

10 The full title was 'Some of the consequences that are like to follow upon lessening of interest to 4 per cent'.

11 Tim Keiren and Frank Melton (1990) have surveyed this debate.

12 There has been much discussion as to whether or not Locke did believe in natural law. Vaughn (1980: 154–155) sumarizes this discussion, up to the date of her book. See also James Tully (1991: 625–629).

13 DJNG IV.iv.13: 554. 'An oak-tree belonged to no man, but the acorns that fell to the ground were his who have gathered them.' See also the comment in a footnote of Peter Laslett (1964: 306).

14 The majority of the elected representatives meant the majority of those elected by the property owners.

15 All Locke's writings on education have been collected and edited by James Axtell (1968). Quotation from footnote in ch. 13, p. 25. Quotation here from *An Extract from* … In R. Wynne (1761: 84–85). 'When he has pretty well digested Tully's Offices, and added to it Puffendorf de Officio Hominis & Civis, it may be reasonable to set him upon Grotius de Jure Belli & Pacis, or, which perhaps is the better of the two law works, Puffendorf de Jure Naturali & Gentium; wherein he will be instructed in the natural rights of men, and the original foundations of society, and the duties resulting from thence.'

Part V

Early French Philosophers and Pufendorf

14 The First French Followers

The great French and European philosophers of the eighteenth century were all importantly indebted, directly and indirectly, to a diverse group of French scholars, among them the Augustinian theologian and moral essayist Pierre Nicole, to a lesser extent the legal philosopher Jean Domat, a magistrate from Normandy Pierre de Boisguilbert, Pufendorf's French translator Jean Barbeyrac, the unoriginal plagiarist Jean-Jacques Burlamaqui and the editor Denis Diderot.

The Distinguished Moralist

Pierre Nicole was born at Chartres in Eure et Loir. He studied at the University of Sorbonne in Paris from 1642, became Master of Arts in 1644, followed courses in theology from 1645, and became Bachelor of Theology in 1649. He also studied and taught at Port-Royal Abbey in Paris, the centre of Jansenism.[1] Here he also worked together with another philosopher and theologian, Antoine Arnauld (1612–94).

Among philosophers, Nicole is considered a distinguished moralist writer and a vigorous controversialist.[2] He wrote many books and essays, among them *Essais de Moralis* (Essays on Ethics), which was published from 1671. In his first essays, there are no references other than to the Bible. These essays became too controversial for the authorities, and in the beginning of 1679 they were stopped. Fearing the Inquisition, he had to escape to the Austrian Netherlands (today's Belgium). However, he managed to become reconciled with the authorities and returned to Paris in 1683.

In his essays, he offered an enlightened defence of self-interest. Hutchison (1988: 101) contends that Nicole in his view of human nature agreed with Hobbes, seeing man as basically selfish, greedy and aggressive. However, through an enlightened ordering of society, ordinary men, who primarily pursued their own interest, could 'nevertheless be brought to cooperate in achieving a peaceful, orderly and prosperous existence, based on commercial mutuality in serving and exchanging with one another.' Nicole found that the answer to the problem of reconciling the aggressively selfish nature of individuals with their economic interdependence in meeting one another's needs and wants required a taming of self-interest so it became relatively enlightened. Furthermore, he maintains that it is a divine law that one should do unto others what one would have done onto oneself. All these ideas he could have found in Pufendorf's *Elementorum Jurisprudentiae Universalis*, which was available to him when he started to write his essays.[3] Later Pufendorf's major natural law work would also have been accessible to him.

It should, however, be mentioned that Nicole's views could also, according to Hont (2005: 47) in his book *Jealousy of Trade*, have emerged, not from natural jurisprudence but from Augustinian political theory in France. Nicole was a widely read author. His *Essais* appeared in an English translation and Henry W. Spiegel (1983: 226) in his *Growth of Economic Thought* claims that even Locke had tried to translate a few of them. Finally, it should be noted that Hutchison (1988: 101–102) claims that Nicole anticipated Smith's famous observation about 'the benevolence of the butcher, the brewer, or the baker'.

The Legal Philosopher

Jean Domat was born at Clermont in Auvergne, He studied first the humanities in Paris and then law at the University of Bourges. After his promotion in 1645, he practised law in Clermont and was appointed a crown prosecutor there in 1655. He held the prosecutor position until he retired in 1683.

He is principally known for his elaborate three volumes legal digest, the *Lois civiles dans leur ordre naturel* (Civil laws in their natural order) from 1689 to 1694. A fourth and fifth volume, *Le Droit public* (Public law) was published posthumously in 1697. A second edition with all the five volumes was published in 1702. It is a restatement of Roman law considered as a system derived from ethical theory and natural law. He endeavours to base all law upon ethical principles in these works. These five volumes are considered the most important works on the science of law that France has produced, and more than sixty editions have been published. They were translated into English in 1722.

In Domat's law works there are a large number of references to French and Roman law and the Bible. There are no references to any of the natural law philosophers, Grotius, Hobbes or Pufendorf. However, there can be no doubt that Domat had Pufendorf's natural law works at hand when he structured and wrote his legal works. The allusions to these works are strong. This is also confirmed by André-Jean Arnaud (1969: 144), who, in his *Doctrinal Origins of the French Civil Code* explains that a synthesis of Domat's work is even closer to the work of 'the natural law from across the Rhine'. If we are not only looking at the 'lois civiles', but consider all his works: 'They form, indeed a complete system which by its structure calls for certain parallels with for example Pufendorf.'

Hutchison (1988: 102–103) contends that Domat was sympathetic to the Jansenists. In the introduction to his vast legal treatise he expresses similar views on human behaviour as Nicole. It was his analysis of 'the mutuality of a commercial society, based on a realistic, if pessimistic, view of human nature, which laid the foundation of the case for commercial freedom and economic liberalism, developed by Boisguilbert and Mandeville, and elaborated later in Scotland and France.'

In his book, Hutchison does not investigate Nicole's and Domat's sources. The fact that it is unlikely that they were ignorant of Pufendorf's writing on natural law in general and his theory of human behaviour has not been addressed.

The Magistrate from Normandy

Pierre Le Pesant de Boisguilbert was born in Rouen, northern France, in 1646.[4] He received his classical education in a Jesuit college there. Later he was taught in Paris at the Petites écoles de Port-Royal, the centre of Jansenism, where he could have met Pierre Nicole. He completed his education after three years at École de droit (School of Law), obtaining the title of Avocat. With all his years of study, it would seem implausible that he was not acquainted with all the natural law philosophers and Pufendorf in particular.

After completing his law studies Boisguilbert became a magistrate in his home city of Rouen. Thereafter he entered the magistracy and became a judge in a small town near Le Havre. In 1690, he became president of the 'bailliage' of Rouen, a post which he retained almost until his death.

He was disgusted by the economic situation in France and wrote numerous letters and memoranda to officials attacking present policies and advocating reforms. This also brought him into trouble with the authorities, and in 1715 he was exiled from Rouen for six months.

In 1695 Boisguilbert published his major work, *Le détail de la France; la cause de la diminution de ses biens et la facilité du remède* (A detailed account of France; the reason for the reduction of its goods and the easiness of the cure). Hutchison (1988: 107) contends that the subtitle in some editions was *La France ruinée sous la règne Louis XIV* (France ruined under Louis XIV). In this work he outlined the deplorable conditions for all classes of Frenchmen. These conditions had been created by the disastrous policies of the different governments. These policies had detrimental effects on agricultural production.[5] The major remedies, Boisguilbert claims, were a reform of the tax system, making it more equal, abolishing most of the internal customs, which strangled domestic commerce, and liberalizing foreign trade. These measures would increase consumption of the poor people, raise production and thereby the general wealth of the country.

His *Factum de la France* (The factum of France) was published in 1705, the *Traité des grains* (The treaty of the grains) in 1706 and finally the *Dissertation sur la nature des richesses, de l'argents et des tributs* (A dissertation on the nature of wealth, money, and taxes), was published in 1707.

Hazel van Dyke Roberts (1935: 186–187) in her dissertation *Boisguilbert: Economist of the reign of Louis XIV* from 1935, outlines his system. It was based upon what may be termed socialized-individualism. Individuals must voluntarily submit to the group.

> The foundation of his social philosophy is that the interest of the individual must give way to the general interest when the two come into conflict. This subordination of self-interest to the general interest would be utilized to produce economic equilibrium. In essence, his idea was that, although man is dominated by self-interest, in his ignorance of the fundamentals of economic principles he does not comprehend wherein his true interest lies. He thinks it is in the economic destruction of others, whereas in reality it lies in saving of others from this annihilation. He must consider the interest to others in preserving his own welfare.

The similarities with Pufendorf's self-interest and sociability is striking, but is not seen by Roberts.

Roberts contends that one of Boisguilbert contributions is that he saw domestic commerce as an exchange of surpluses of different areas. He also recognized that exchange could be profitable both to the buyers and sellers. 'Indeed he declared that it must be profitable to both if commerce is to continue' (ibid.: 259).

Furthermore, she argues that Smith had read and built directly on Boisguilbert's theories when he wrote his two books *The Theory of Moral Sentiments* and *The Wealth of Nations*. At first glance, it looks like they are only in superficial agreement with regard to self-interest: 'that the former considered it as the foundation of an economic and social philosophy, whereas in the theory of the latter it appeared to constitute little more than a human attribute underlying the desire for gain' (ibid.: 315). Nevertheless, she contends that a closer inspection shows that Smith had in mind the doctrine of modified self-interest utilized by Boisguilbert. Roberts complains that no one that had investigated Adam Smith's originality and his sources had looked at the writings of Boisguilbert. This is true, but as will be discussed in a later chapter, Smith's investigators have rarely any references to Pufendorf either. Moreover, what is important in this context is that Boisguilbert himself was not in favour of revealing his sources. In his *Détail*, Boisguilbert drew a picture of the general ruin of all classes of Frenchmen caused by the bad economic regime. Hutchison (1988: 108–113) asserts that Boisguilbert started from the idea of interdependence of men in an exchange economy. 'Man cannot survive alone but must engage in exchange, and by mutual help provide reciprocal utility.' He emphasizes how individuals, who were moved by their own interests, contributed to the general good of society. From this starting point, he developed his theories. He wrote about money as a medium to facilitate exchange of goods. He claimed that it was necessary to have a complete reshaping of the tax system based on principles very similar to those proposed by Pufendorf. Moreover, Hutchison claims that 'Quesnay and the physiocrats were explicitly and considerably indebted to Boisguilbert' and that he could, to an important extent, be seen as 'a precursor of both Adam Smith and Keynes – though, of course differing from these in significant respects' (ibid.: 114–115). Gilbert Faccarello (1999) in his *The Foundation of 'Laissez-Faire': The Economics of Pierre Boisguilbert*, makes a survey of the studies of Boisguilbert's work, from Roberts' 1935 dissertation. He shows that the concept of 'laissez- faire' can be found in *Le détail de la France*.

Although it is clear that the students at *École de Droit* must have known Pufendorf and his natural law writings, he is not mentioned by Hutchison or Roberts as a source for Boisguilbert. Boisguilbert (1851 [1707]), in his *Dissertation sur la nature*, has no references to any authors at all.[6] However, the similarity between Boisguilbert's writings on human behaviour, value, money and taxation, and Pufendorf's accounts of these themes are striking.

Pufendorf's French Translator

Jean Barbeyrac was born in Béziers, Languedoc in southern France. As explained his family had to move to Switzerland to escape religious persecution. In 1688, Barbeyrac entered the College in Lausanne, where he studied Hebrew, Greek, philosophy and theology. There he also attended some private lectures on the natural law of Pufendorf. After spending some time at Geneva and Frankfurt am Main, he became professor of belles-lettres in the French Gymnasium of Berlin.[7] This is where he translated into French, Pufendorf's main natural law work *De Jure Naturae* and his student edition *De Officio*. In 1711, Barbeyrac was called to the University of Lausanne, where he became the first holder of the newly created 'Chaire de Droit et d'Histoire' (Chair of history and civil law). Finally, in 1717 he received his doctorate and moved to the University of Groningen, where he settled as professor of public and civil law. Both at Lausanne and Groningen, he taught natural law and introduced Pufendorf's work to a large audience. It should also be repeated here that Barbeyrac as early as 1702 had begun a correspondence with John Locke. They both influenced each other.

Barbeyrac became the preeminent eighteenth-century translator, from Latin into French, of the most important natural law works of the seventeenth century. All his translations were accompanied by extensive prefaces, annotations and comments in footnotes, where he expressed his own thoughts on natural law. These writings were always motivated by his desire to guarantee human liberty against arbitrary rule. He works out with great skill the theory of moral obligation, referring to it as the command or will of God. Likewise, he indicates the distinction, later developed more fully by Christian Thomasius and Immanuel Kant, between the legal and the moral qualities of action. The principles of international law he reduces to those of the law of nature, and in so doing opposes many of the positions taken up by Grotius. Furthermore, he rejects the notion that sovereignty in any way resembles property, and makes even marriage a matter of civil contract.

In Barbeyrac's own book, *Traité de jeu* (Treatise of games), from 1709, he builds on Pufendorf *De Jure Naturae* (Bk. IX: 766–770) in his chapter *On contracts subject to chance*, and argued that games involving skill and chance were not prohibited, either by Christian morality or natural law. Daniel Brühlmeier (1995: 60) in his article on natural law and Barbeyrac and Vattel claims that it is 'an elegant treatise, showing remarkable qualities for a writer who is sometimes regarded as a footnote-warrior'.[8]

Finally, in his book *Traité de la morale des perès de l'Eglise* (Treatise on the moral teaching of the Church Fathers) from 1728, Barbeyrac counters what he saw as the dubious moral teachings of the Church Fathers. This caused quite a stir, particularly in the Catholic countries. David Saunders (2003) contends that Barbeyrac was a philosopher in his own right, who actively took part in the European debate, and that he was something quite other than a neutral mediator of Pufendorf, as many writers had asserted. He was considered an advocate of the '*dignitas et utilitas juris ac historiarum et utriusque amica conjunctio* (the dignity and utility of law and history, and both [law and history] lovingly united)'. His natural law writings were motivated by his desire to guarantee human liberty against arbitrary rule and he denounced a clergy prejudiced in favour of political and spiritual tyranny.

Furthermore, it should be mentioned that Barbeyrac defended Pufendorf's separation of natural religion and natural jurisprudence, against some violent attacks from Gottfried Leibniz. There can be no doubt that he, because of his translations, his commentaries and his own writing, also became a well-known European scholar.

In fundamental principles and particular in the issues of political economy, Barbeyrac follows Pufendorf almost entirely, but there can also be found examples where he deviates from him. In the case of Pufendorf's remarks on the priceless character of certain goods and services, Barbeyrac rectifies him by saying there is nothing for which a price cannot be found. He was also sceptical to the necessity of Pufendorf's first pact of association in the establishment of the state.

Moore and Silverthorne (1983: 81) claim that Barbeyrac was well-acquainted with Locke's political ideas and that he corresponded with Locke in the last years of Locke's life and exchanged opinions with him.

An Unoriginal Plagiarist

Jean-Jacques Burlamaqui was a Swiss legal and political theorist who greatly publicized and popularized several ideas propounded by other thinkers. In 1719, 25 years old, he was designated honorary professor of ethics and the law of nature at the University of Geneva. Thereafter he made a study tour of the Netherlands and England, where he visited Oxford for a few months and in addition met people of political influence. On his return journey in 1723, he met Barbeyrac at Groningen. Back at the University of Geneva, he became a full professor. The earlier mentioned Daniel Brühlmeier (1995: 63) contends that 'with a full professorship in the subject of natural law and civil law, Burlamaqui dominated legal thought and the natural law tradition in Geneva from 1723–1740.' Peter Korkman (2006: x) claims in his study on *Burlamaqui and Natural Law* that Burlamaqui was a well-respected and popular lecturer that drew many foreign students to Geneva. Here he lectured until 1740 when he unfortunately was compelled to resign because of ill health. In Geneva he was also elected a member of the Council of State and he gained as high a reputation for his practical sagacity as he had for his theoretical knowledge.

Burlamaqui Borrowed from Pufendorf

His work, *Principes du droit naturel* (Principles of natural law), based on his lecture notes, was published in Geneva in 1747. This was the only work he published himself. It was intended for his students and other beginners. His treatise of law became very popular and was translated into Danish, Dutch, English, Italian, Latin and Spanish and published in more than sixty editions. The English translation became a standard textbook at University of Cambridge and the foremost American colleges. His treatise represents a digest of the thoughts of like-minded theorists, Grotius, Cumberland, and in particular Pufendorf, who is by far the most-quoted author in the book. Korkman (2006: xi) claims that Barlamaqui in this work borrowed extensively from Barbeyrac's French translations of the main natural law treatises of his time, especially from Pufendorf's *De Officio* and *De Jure Naturae*, but also from Grotius' natural law work. Often Burlamaqui omitted to mention his sources, so the typical reaction, of many of his commentators, has been to call him, 'an unoriginal plagiarist' (ibid.: xi). However, in footnotes Korkman gives many examples where there are disagreements between the three: Pufendorf, Barbeyrac and Barlamaqui.

Three years after Burlamaqui's death, some of his colleagues edited and published in 1751 a manuscript he had written, as *Principes du droit politique* (Principles of politic law). This manuscript was also based on a series of notes from his lectures. Burlamaqui himself had entrusted the manuscript to his sister and his daughter with instructions that it should not be published (ibid.: xii). It is therefore quite clear that this manuscript was meant only for his students as a commentary to his lectures on natural law philosophers in general and Pufendorf in particular. It is therefore too harsh a judgement to contend that he was a plagiarist. In 1754 his friends also published a manuscript of his lecture notes in Latin, which in 1773 was published in French as *Élémens du droit naturel* (Elements of natural law).

Burlamaqui on Political Economy

Burlamaqui (2006) had a more optimistic view of human behaviour than Pufendorf. He insists that: 'The desire to happiness is essential to man, and inseparable from reason' (2006: 66). This was different from Pufendorf, who stresses man's inclination for evil and who saw natural law as rules needed for men to survive each other's company. Furthermore, Burlamaqui asserted, according to Korkman (2006: xvii), that natural laws are rational egoistic principles for finding the shortest road to happiness, while Pufendorf contends that natural laws impose absolute duties, telling us what we must do, not what we, by the use of reason, are motivated to do. He agrees with Pufendorf's human attribute of self-love, and that society is necessary for men. 2006: 150–155. The true principle of the duties, which the law of nature prescribes to us in respect of other men, is called *sociability.* However, Burlamaqui claims that the Creator has imprinted 'a sentiment of benevolence for our fellow creatures' (ibid.: 156). This is absent in Pufendorf. Nevertheless, he agrees with Pufendorf that the understanding of the law of nature is not innate.

> For to think with some people, that law of nature is innate, as it were, in our minds, and actually imprinted in our souls from the first moment of our existence; is supposing a thing that is not at all necessary, and is moreover contradicted by experience.
>
> (Ibid.: 164)

In his short treatment of private property Burlamaqui contends, in a manner similar to Pufendorf's, that the introduction of property is an important establishment, which produces a new adventitious state.

> It modifies the right which all men had originally to earthly goods; and distinguishing carefully what belongs to individuals, ensures the quiet and peaceable enjoyment of what they possess; by which means it contributes to the maintenance of peace and harmony among mankind.
>
> (Ibid.: 61)

He continues, in accordance with Pufendorf, that since all men originally had the right to common use of the earth's fruits, it is evident 'that if this power is actually restrained and limited in divers respects, this must necessarily arise from some human act' (ibid.: 62).

In his very short treatment of property, Burlemaqui emphasizes that among states established by an act of man there is none more considerable than the civil state, and that this state and property of goods gives rise to several other adventitious states.

Burlamaqui treats his theory of value in his *Éléments du droit naturel.* This book has not been translated to English. However, Leon Walras (1977 [1874]: 201–5) brings this theory forward with a long quotation from it in his treatment of the origin of value in exchange. It is clear that Burlamaqui with his emphasize on scarcity builds very closely on Pufendorf. Hutchison (1988: 322) claims that Burlamaqui did no more than 'accurately restating the master's doctrines'.

The foundation of states has an important place in Burlamaqui's analysis. Although he has a much more positive opinion than Pufendorf of how people lived in the state of nature, he eventually agrees with him. The remedy that ended the inconveniences in the state of nature, men found in the establishment of civil society and a sovereign authority.

> But this could not be obtained without effecting two things equally necessary; the first was to unite together by means of a more particular society; the second to form this society under the dependence of a person invested with an uncontrollable power to the end that he might maintain order and peace.
>
> (2006: 282)

Later he discusses the essential constitution of states and the way they are formed and he found it necessary, as Pufendorf, to have two different covenants and one general decree (ibid.: 293). These are exactly Pufendorf's pacts of association and subjection and his decree made for settling the form of government.

Burlamaqui does not discuss council decisions and voting procedures. However, he stresses as did Pufendorf that:

> It must be established for a rule, that the plurality of suffrages shall pass for the will of the whole; otherwise no affair could be determined, it being impossible that a great number of people should be always of the same opinion.
>
> (Ibid.: 329)

In his discussion of the division of state power and taxation, Burlamaqui starts out, with strong allusions to Pufendorf, explaining that in every government it is necessary to have a supreme power, the sovereign. He discusses the role and duties of the sovereign and the various forms of government. Sovereignty is the right of commanding civil society, 'in the last resort' (ibid.: 296). Following Pufendorf he discusses the different forms of power, the legislative power, the coercive power (that is, the right to ordain punishment), the judiciary power and the right to appoint magistrates (ibid.: 323–329). He also discusses three forms of government (democracy, aristocracy and monarchy) as well as the advantages and disadvantages of each. He does not follow Pufendorf's claims that monarchy is the best form of government. He favoured the Genevan mixed system of aristocratic democracy. Geneva was ruled at the time by a small council of 25, a large council of 200, and the general council of all citizens. Burlamaqui supports increased power to the small council. With a reference to the last chapter in Pufendorf's *De Officio*, he also discusses the duties of the subjects (ibid.: 364–368).

Burlamaqui, like Pufendorf, contends that the sovereign has the right to raise taxes. This will be evident if we consider that taxes are a contribution that individuals pay to the state for the preservation and defence of their lives and properties, and for the ordinary and extraordinary expenses of government. People cannot refuse to pay tax without prejudicing their own interests. It is, however, the responsibility of a prudent civil government to make sure that people are not overcharged, 'but also that taxes should be raised in a gentle and imperceptible a manner as possible' (ibid.: 436).

On the question of specific taxes Burlamaqui follows Pufendorf. Taxpayers should be equally charged so they have 'no just reason to complain' (ibid.: 436). There must be a just proportion between the burden of the tax and the benefit of the peace. The advantages are not equal. Every man ought to be taxed in proportion to his income, but the best way to levy taxes is to lay them on things daily consumed.

Imported merchandise that is not necessary can have very high duties justly laid on them. If foreign goods consist of things that can be grown or produced at home, taxes ought to be raised higher upon these articles. If exported goods are of the kind that should be consumed at home, it may be right to raise the customs upon them. If it is to the public advantage that they be sent to a foreign country, the customs should be reduced. In all these cases, the sovereign must take all proper measures to make commerce flourish (ibid.: 437). The governing power ought to attend to the conduct of the tax collectors to hinder their 'importunity and oppression' (ibid.: 438).

Burlamaqui's Influence

Burlamaqui had quite an influence on students across Europe and America. His treatise on law *Principes du droit naturel* became a very popular textbook for students of law and was translated into Danish, Dutch, English, Italian, Latin and Spanish and published in more than sixty editions. The English translation of *Principles of Natural Law* was done by Thomas Nugent (1700–1777) in 1748. He also translated *Principles of Politic Law* in 1752. The first combined two-volume *Principles of Natural Law and the Principle of Politic Law*, was published in London in 1763. It became a standard textbook at the University of Cambridge and the foremost American colleges. The Liberty Fund 2006 edition is based on Nugent's 1763 translation. It is clear from Korkman's introduction and extensive notes in this edition that Burlamaqui uses Pufendorf, with Bayberac's comments, widely in his representation.

Waddicor (1970: 100) claims that Burlamaqui passed on the ideas of the natural law philosopher to August Walras (1801–1866) and his son Leon Walras (1834–1910). 'August Walras was amply justified in complaining how neglected the natural law concept of scarcity had become in the nineteenth century.' Hutchison (1988: 323) shows us how Barlamaqui, in his natural law, passed on Pufendorf's formulation of economic concept to August and Leon Walras. He mentions that Walras senior in his *De la nature de la richesse et de l'origine de la valeur* complains of the 'eclipse of the natural law-theory of Pufendorf and Burlamaqui'. Walras then goes on to explain the theory of value stating that the 'doctrine of Burlamaqui is mine'. This theory was in due course taken over by his son Leon.

Finally, it should be mentioned that Burlamaqui's vision of constitutionalism had a major influence on the American Founders. For example, his understanding of checks and balances is much more sophisticated and practical than that of Montesquieu, in part because Burlamaqui's theory contains the seed of judicial review. He was frequently quoted or paraphrased, sometimes with attribution and sometimes not, in political sermons during the American pre-revolutionary era. He was the first philosopher to articulate the quest for happiness as a natural human right, a principle that Thomas Jefferson later restated in the *Declaration of Independence.*

The Editor

Denis Diderot was born in the eastern French city of Langres. He went to school at the Lycée Louis le Grand in Paris. In 1732, he earned a Master of Arts degree in philosophy. He abandoned the idea of entering the clergy and decided instead to study law. His study of law was short-lived. In 1734, Diderot decided to become a writer and in doing so, he became a prominent figure during the Enlightenment.

In 1749, Diderot was approached by a bookseller and a printer named Andre Le Breton (1708–1779), who wanted him to take part in the translation into French and the publishing of Ephraim Chambers' *Cyclopaedia, or Universal Dictionary of Arts and Sciences.*[9] During his work Diderot came up with the idea to expand the project from a reproduction into a major French Encyclopédie. He served as the co-founder, together with Jean le Rond d'Alembert (1717–1783), as well as the chief editor and major contributor to the *Encyclopédie.* In 1750, a prospectus announced the project to the public, and the year after the first volume was published. The *Encyclopédie ou dictionnaire raisonné des sciences, des arts et des métiers* (Encyclopedia, or a rational dictionary of sciences, art and craft), had many unorthodox and forward-thinking articles by many prominent authors and experts in their respective fields. With the project, Diderot wanted to give information about all-important issues to the common people, who had the ability to read.

The work, however, was plagued by controversy from the very beginning. For a period, it was suspended by the court, and it was accused of seditious content because of its entries on religion and natural law. Diderot was also detained by the authorities for some time. With the support of important well-placed people, the work resumed, but the controversies stayed with it. Its popularity and influence increased, and also the number of subscribers. Nevertheless, the number of enemies also grew with its popularity. It threatened the governing aristocracy with its emphasis, in the spirit of Pufendorf, on religious tolerance and freedom of thought. In 1759, the antagonists were strong enough to formally suppress it. The work continued but important contributors no longer dared to make known their support.

Diderot was left to finish the task as best he could. He wrote several hundred articles, some very short, but many of them laborious, comprehensive, and long. He damaged his eyesight correcting proofs and editing the manuscripts of less competent contributors. He was incessantly harassed by threats of police raids. It took many years before the subscribers in 1772 received the final 27 folio volumes of the *Encyclopédie.* Today it is considered one of the great works of the Enlightenment.

All this work did not bring Diderot any wealth. Although his work was broad and rigorous, he could not secure for himself a decent income. He obtained none of the posts that were occasionally given to needy men of letters. When the time came for him to provide a dowry for his daughter, he saw no alternative other than to sell his library. When the Empress Catherine II (1729–1796) of Russia heard of his financial troubles, she commissioned an agent in Paris to buy the library. She then requested that the philosopher retained the books in Paris until she required them, and that he acted as her librarian with a yearly salary. In 1773 and 1774, Diderot spent some months at the empress's court in Saint Petersburg. When he died in 1784, his vast library was sent to Russia, where the Empress had it deposited in the National Library.

Diderot an Admirer of Pufendorf

It is clear from numerous entries that when Diderot wrote, he had Barbeyrac's translations into French of Pufendorf's *De Officio* and *De Jure Naturae* in his library and that he extensively consulted and used these works. Sometimes he only copied what Pufendorf had written. Other times he made critical assessments of Pufendorf's views. His admiration for Pufendorf is evident.

During his stay at the court in St Petersburg, Diderot wrote *Plan d'une Université pour le gouvernement de Russie* (Plan of a university for the government of Russia). Here he recommends the use of Barbeyrac's translation of Pufendorf's *De Officio* together with Burlamaqui's *Traité Elements de droit Naturel* and Hobbes' *De Hominis* and *De Civis* for the first class of the second course of studies as well as a guidance for the Professor of Natural Law for the first year of studies at the Faculty of Law. Diderot's many references to the natural law philosophers and Pufendorf in particular contributed to the diffusion of Pufendorf's views on ethics, jurisprudence, government and political economy. It was not only Diderot that used Pufendorf and referred to him. Pufendorf and his writings on natural law were known to most contributors to the *Encyclopédie.* One contributor, the renowned French lawyer of that time, Antoine-Gaspard Boucher d'Argis (1709–91), wrote an article under the headword *Droit des gens* (Law of nations) where he describes Pufendorf's legal work and claims that *De Jure Naturae et Gentium* is much better for the understanding of natural law than Grotius's *De jure belli et pacis.*[10] In another headword, *Citoyen* (Citizen), he also makes a reference to Pufendorf.

Notes

1 The theological principles of Cornelis Jansen (1585–1638), Bishop of Ypres (*Cornelius Jansenius Yprensis*), from whom Jansenism derives its origin and name. It was a puritanical revival within the Catholic church and it emphasized predestination, denied free will, and maintained that human nature was incapable of good. They were condemned as heretics by the Church. Port Royal Abbey was the main centre of Jansenism in France. It stood as a symbol of the resistance to the royal power of Louis XIV.

2 Recommended reading on Pierre Nicole and his influence: Edward Donald James (1981), Jill Vance Buroker (ed.) (1996) and Istvan Hont (2005).

3 EJU II.O.iii and iv.

4 A study of Boisguilbert, his ideas and his writings can be found in Jaqueline Hecht (1966).

5 Economic historians generally agree that the second half of the seventeenth century was a period of economic decline for France. The plight of France was partly due to the costly wars and extravagances of the degenerate courts of Louis XIV, but also because of the mercantilist policies that were pursued. The prohibition of grain export had detrimental effects on agricultural production and income. A system of oppressive taxation, which was arbitrarily assessed and administered, and which exempted the aristocracy and the clergy, became an almost intolerable burden for the poor.

6 Boisguilbert (1851 [1707]).

7 Fiammetta Palladini (2011).

8 Barbeyrac's starting point is probably DJNG Book V, chapter IX 'On contracts subject to chance'.

9 Ephraim Chambers (1680–1740) was an English writer and encyclopaedist. He is primarily known for having produced the Cyclopedia. It had the full title: *Cyclopedia: or a universal dictionary of arts and sciences, the whole intended as a course of ancient and modern learning compiled by the best authors, dictionaries, journals, memoirs, transactions, ephemerides, in several languages.* First published in London, 1728.

10 Denis Diderot and Jean le Rond d'Alembert (eds), *Encyclopédie ou Dictionnaire raisonné des Sciences, des Arts et des Métiers*, Bibliothèque National, Paris, 1755, vol. 5, p. 128.

15 Charles Montesquieu

A Great Philosopher

Charles-Louis de Secondat, baron of La Brède (near Bordeaux) and later of Montesquieu got his first education at home. Thereafter, he was educated at the famous Oratorian College de Juilly near Paris and finally at the Faculty of Law at University of Bordeaux. After graduation in 1708, he went to Paris for a few years to gain legal experience. He returned to Bordeaux and became counsellor at the Parliament of Bordeaux in 1714, and in 1716, he inherited from his uncle the office of *president a mortier* at the Parliament. The same year, he was admitted to the Academy of Bordeaux and he became its *directeur* in 1717. From 1728 to 1731, he travelled in Europe, visiting many countries among them Austria and Hungary. He stayed one year in Italy and one and a half years in England. There he met many important men and interested himself in political and constitutional questions. Returning to France, he divided his time between Bordeaux and Paris.

In 1721, Montesquieu published *Lettres persanes* (Persian letters), a satire that sharply criticized the absurdities of contemporary France. It made him famous, but he also received hostility from conservative quarters. An English translation by John Ozell (d.1743) appeared in London as early as 1722.

Anne M. Cohler (1989: xvi) in her Introduction to Montesquieu's *The Spirits of the Law* asserts that he, as a member of the Academy, wrote and presented papers primarily on scientific observations. However, he also offered several papers on social practices in other countries and other times, and on duties, according to natural law. In 1725, he read notes from a work in progress to the Academy. The work to be called *Traité des devoirs* (On compulsion), was aborted and not published by Montesquieu.

What became his most influential work *De l'Esprit des Lois* (The spirit of the laws) was first published in Geneva in 1748, anonymously because of censorship. A revised and corrected edition was published in Amsterdam in 1749. The work on this book had taken almost twenty years. With its title Montesquieu meant, Maurice Cranston (1967: 370) claims 'the *raison d'être* for laws, or the rational basis for their existence'. It is therefore a study of the laws of different countries in the light of their constitution, history, and geographical position. Hutchison (1988: 221 claims that Montesquieu took the title from a chapter in Jean Domat's *Traité des Lois.*

In France, the work was met with an unfriendly reception from both supporters and opponents of the regime. His opponents accused him of putting forward a deterministic philosophy that undermined religion and natural law. The work was violently attacked by representatives of the Catholic Church. However, it received the highest praise from the rest of Europe, especially Britain. The book was an unqualified success and it sold 22 editions in less than two years. In 1752, Thomas Nugent published the first English translation.

In 1751, the Catholic Church banned the *Esprit des Lois*, and many of Montesquieu's other works. Along with them was also Pufendorf's *De Officio* and a work by Abbé de Chauvelin (1714–1770). These books were all included in the *Index of Prohibited Books.* This happened despite Montesquieu efforts to defend himself and to turn back the accusations against him. The result of his efforts was his *La défense de 'L'Esprit de Lois'*, which he published in 1752.

Montesquieu was for many years troubled by poor eyesight. and in his last years he was completely blind. He died from a high fever in 1755 and is buried in the *Église Saint-Sulpice* in Paris.

Montesquieu Stands Indebted to Pufendorf

In *Montesquieu: A Critical Bibliography*, Robert Shackleton (1961: 72) tells us how Pufendorf was utilized by Montesquieu when he delivered a paper called *Traité des devoirs* (On duties) to the Academy as early as 1725. 'For a model Montesquieu seems to have had recourse to the short treatise De officio hominis of the German Pufendorf, a work which he possessed in the French translation of Barbeyrac.' The copy of this book in the library at La Brède has several annotations by Montesquieu. 'To find him already in 1725 reading, studying and using Pufendorf is of capital importance' (ibid.). Shackleton forwards a number of references to Pufendorf and other natural law philosophers.

In his *Montesquieu and the Philosophy of Natural Law*, Mark Waddicor (1970: x) claims that 'the time has surely come for a less prejudiced and more detailed study than hitherto has been attempted on Montesquieu's debt to the philosophy of natural law'. This is necessary if Montesquieu's contribution to the history of ideas is to be properly assessed. He then attempts to carry out such a study. His study also includes a survey of many Montesquieu bibliographies. Of the natural law writers, most references are to Pufendorf, Grotius and Locke. Furthermore, Waddicor claims that although there is no proof of Montesquieu's acquaintance with the works of Pufendorf before he made some readings to the Academy in 1725, 'it is at least possible that the young Montesquieu may have been tempted to open the works of these modern theorists of natural law' (ibid.: 15). Furthermore, Waddicor emphasizes that Montesquieu, in one of his notebooks, *Pensées*, writes in eulogistic terms of his predecessors: 'I give thanks to Messr. Grotius and Pufendorf, who have achieved what a great part of that book requested from me, with a loftiness of genius that I could not have reached myself' (ibid.: 35).[1] This tribute seems to have been intended for the *Preface* to *The Esprit des Lois*, but even if this was not the case, it clearly expresses that he owed much to them. When Montesquieu gave these thanks, Waddicor contends that he:

> was not trying to flatter anyone, but was expressing his sincere thanks to the fact that they had prepared the way for his inquiry. But it was above all the more sophisticated empiricism of Pufendorf – with his unmoralistic approach to many controversial problems, and his acceptance of the fact that civil law can, indeed must, vary from country to country – which seems to foreshadow Montesquieu's aim in the Esprit des Lois.
>
> (Ibid.: 195)

In the Introduction to a new edition of *Défense del'Esprit des Lois*, Robert Derathé (1973: 425) claims that Montesquieu often refers to the thoughts of Pufendorf when speaking about natural law. This is particularly the case in his *Défense* when he follows Pufendorf's formulation of 'man fallen from heavens totally abandoned to himself'.

Alan Baum (1979: 15) in his *Montesquieu and Social Theory*, mentioned that Montesquieu's library housed over 3,000 volumes including 349 important works on Jurisprudence and many treatises by Grotius, Hobbes, and Pufendorf. These works he had either inherited or acquired before 1732.[2] Baum writes that the form of Montesquieu's *De Esprit des Lois*:

> bears a strong resemblance to that of the treatises of Grotius and Pufendorf: his book divisions correspond to their book or chapter divisions, and his multitudinous and oft-criticised chapter divisions, to their paragraph divisions. The most obvious difference is that his chapter headings are sometimes more witty, but less informative than theirs.
>
> (Ibid.: 23)

To support his view, Baum refers to Cecil Courtney (1968: 30–44): 'It is futile to try to disguise, as the positivists and their followers do, Montesquieu's debt to the philosophers of natural law for his general conception of social and political science'. However, he adds that it is equally futile to disguise the fact that he surpassed them. Baum also discusses the importance of Montesquieu's early work *Traité des devoirs* (On duties) and contends that 'It was his first wholly serious book, building on the concepts of natural Law of the German Pufendorf' (ibid.: 27).

Alfred Dufour (1986: 104), in an article on Pufendorf's influence on the French and Anglo-American culture, tells us how the classicists Locke, Rousseau, Montesquieu and many more had studied Pufendorf's natural law works. They considered his works to be fundamental and necessary for the study of civil law and politics, and they used his theories when they developed their own theories. Dufour therefore finds it surprising that Montesquieu in his extensive reference list has only a few references to the natural law philosopher.

Anne M. Cohler (1989: xx) in her Introduction to the English edition of *The Spirit of the Laws*, claims that this work is handicapped by an excess of evidence. 'He seems to have read everything.' In the *Esprit des lois*, he cites some 300 works in over 3,000 references. However, hardly any references can be found to the natural law philosophers. There is no reference to Grotius, only one to Hobbes, and only a couple to Pufendorf. His references to Pufendorf are only to his historical works.[3] However, this does not mean that Montesquieu was not familiar with or didn't use the works of the natural law philosophers, and Pufendorf in particular.

Rebecca Kingston (1996: 134) in her *Montesquieu and the Parliament of Bordeaux*, discusses the importance of Montesquieu's *Traité des devoirs* for his development and claims that this work was 'a development of the classical reflection of Cicero and of the modern scholarship of Pufendorf on the theme of duty'.

There can therefore be no doubt that Montesquieu stands strongly indebted to Pufendorf.

Montesquieu on Political Economy

Montesquieu touches on political economy in almost all of his writings. The focus here will be on his exposition in his *De l'Esprit des Lois* from1748.[4]

Human Behaviour

In the *Preface* Montesquieu (1748: xliii) declares: 'I began by examining men, and I believed that, amidst the infinite diversity of laws and mores, they were not lead by their fancies alone.' In the first chapter; On laws in their relation with the various beings, he claims that prior to all laws are the laws of nature, and they are derived 'uniquely from the constitution of our being' (ibid.:1.2: 6–7).

The first idea of man in the state of nature is to think of the preservation of his being that is of his self-interest. Montesquieu, like Pufendorf, rejects Hobbes' idea that man's first desire is to subjugate one another, and that men live in a state of war. On the contrary, man would, because of his weakness and his feeling of inferiority, seek peace with his fellow men. Furthermore, Montesquieu contends that weakness and mutual fear would persuade them to approach one another. They will also be inclined to peace by the pleasure of being together. The charm of the sexes would add to this pleasure. By being together, they also succeed in gaining knowledge, and this gives them another motive for uniting and a desire to live in society. The allusions to Pufendorf's self-interest and sociability are strong.

It is clear, as also Waddicor (1970: 66) has pointed out, that Montesquieu like Pufendorf and Locke did not believe in the existence of innate ideas. 'A man in the state of nature would have the faculty of knowing rather than knowledge.'

Property and the Four-Stages Theory

Montesquieu contends that the political laws provided liberty for people and the civil or private laws sanctioned property. Furthermore, he stresses that we must not apply the principle of one to the other. Private property, according to Montesquieu, is a natural right not derived from the state, but on the contrary one that the state must protect. Political law must in no way retrench on private property, because no public good is greater than the maintenance of private property. If it is necessary to build 'some public edifice' on private land, compensation must be paid to the owner (ibid.: 26.15: 510).

Montesquieu, unlike Pufendorf, has no rudimentary theory of how private property was progressively introduced as men under pressure of growing population and depleted resources moved from one stage of development to another. However, he compares the relationship of laws to the ways various people procure their subsistence:

> There must be a more extensive code of laws to people attached to commerce and the sea than for a people satisfied to cultivate their lands. There must be a greater one for the latter than for people that live by their herds. There must be a greater one for these last than for people who live by hunting.
>
> (Ibid.:18.8: 289)

There is no further discussion of these stages, but he discusses in the next chapters the relationship of population to the way of procuring subsistence.

From this it is hard to understand, how some authors, for example Ronald Meek (1971: 33), Alix Cohen (2014: 763) and Margaret Schabas (2014: 739), can claim that Montesquieu was one of the first to anticipate that changes in the condition of mankind took place in different stages. It looks more like he is just summarizing Pufendorf's rudimentary four-stages theory.

Value, Money and Trade

Montesquieu does not develop a theory of value, but he outlines a theory of money and trade. 'The cultivation of the land requires the use of money. Cultivation assumes many arts and much knowledge, and one always sees arts, knowledge, and needs keeping pace together. All this leads to the establishment of a sign of value' (ibid.:18.15: 292). When money is introduced, one is forced to have good civil laws.

Montesquieu uses Pufendorf's ideas and argues in the same manner as him. People, who have little in the way of commodities of commerce, trade by exchange. However, when they deal in a large number of commodities, there must necessarily be money (ibid.: 22.1: 398). Money is a sign representing the value of all commodities. Some metal is chosen, so that the sign will be durable, will be little worn by use, and can be divided many times without being destroyed (ibid.: 22.2: 399).

Also, following Pufendorf, he warns against debasement of money when part of the metal is withdrawn from each piece of money. He maintained that 'in order to remove the source of abuses in every country, where one wants commerce to flourish,' there should be a law that orders one to use real money and to perform no operations that debase the value of their money (ibid.: 22.3: 401).

However, Montesquieu also develops his own ideas. He gives, for example, a rather extensive description of how an exchange determines the value of money in various countries and what influences these values. In this context, he gives a description of the system, instituted by John Law that led to a chaotic economic collapse in France (ibid.: 22.9–11: 405–412). He emphasizes that the establishment of commerce requires the establishment of an exchange. Moreover, he discusses the aid the state can draw from banks; he discusses public debt and the payment of such debt.

Montesquieu supports Pufendorf's view that interest should be permitted. He argued that: 'To lend one's silver without interest is a very good act, but one senses that this can be only a religious counsel and not a civil law' (ibid.: 22.19: 420). The interest should be small. If the interest is too high, a trader, who sees that it would cost him more in interest than he could gain in his commerce, will not trade at all. If the interest is zero, no one lends money and there will be no trade. Furthermore, he contends that when the risk is great, the rate of interest could legitimately be increased. It is hard not to see the allusions to Pufendorf.

It should be emphasized that Montesquieu has an extensive discussion of the nature and distinction of commerce. In addition, there is a lengthy argument on what influence commerce has had on many countries of the world: (ibid.: 20–21: 337–397). It is his general view that the development of commerce was the most effective safeguard against arbitrary and despotic government, and it would lead to peace.

Foundation of States and Council Decisions

Montesquieu claims that the desire to live in society is one of the natural laws. As soon as men enter a state of society, they lose their feeling of weakness, the equality that existed among them ceases, and a state of war begins between people and between nations. These two states of war bring about the establishment of laws, respectively, civil law and laws of nations. Since the number of inhabitants on the earth is large, men have laws bearing on the relations they have with another. This is the law of nations. The allusion to Pufendorf's first pact of association is striking. Living in a society they must also have laws concerning the relation between those who govern and those who are governed, that is the political law. It seems to correspond with Pufendorf's pact of subjection. Finally, they have laws concerning the relations citizen have with each other that is the civil law (ibid.: 1.3: 7).

The laws men experience in a state of nature will be the laws of nature. In the state of nature, each human feels himself both weak and inferior, and such men will not seek to attack each another. Peace is therefore the first natural law. The second is the inspiration to seek nourishment. The marks of mutual fear would persuade people to approach each other and feel the pleasure of being together. This is therefore the third natural law. The desire to live in society is the fourth natural law (ibid.: 1.2–3: 6–7).

All nations have a right of a nation, claims Montesquieu. In addition, there is a political law for each one. 'A society could not continue to exist without a government.' To strengthen the expression, he quotes the Italian man of letters and jurist Giovanni Vincenzo Gravina (1664–1718) 'The union of all individual strengths forms what is called the political state' (ibid.: 1.3: 8). Like Pufendorf, he contends that the strength of the whole society may be put in the hands of one, or in the hands of many. However, individual strengths cannot be united unless all wills are united. Again, he quotes Gravina: 'The union of these wills, is what is called the civil states' ibid.: Books II and III). Montesquieu does not discuss the problems of council decisions and voting procedures.

Division of State Powers and Principles of Taxation

Montesquieu wrote that the main purpose of government is to maintain law and order, political liberty, and the property of the individual. As Pufendorf, he discusses three categories of government; democracy, aristocracy and monarchy. He discusses the laws in relation to each of those types and the principles of them (ibid.: 2–4). Mark Waddicor (1970: 106–107) claims Montesquieu, in his discussions on forms of government, contends that 'the majority of evidence indicates that he believed in the superiority of monarchy'. However, it was not an absolute monarchy such as Pufendorf favoured; his was more a monarchy where the monarch had to share his power. Montesquieu thought monarchy 'to be more practical than democracy' and that it most likely would produce political freedom. For Montesquieu, this fact gave it a most important advantage over other regimes. He held two monarchies, the English and the 'Gothic' in special favour, because of the amount of freedom they ensured their subjects. He believed that in the case of the English Constitution, freedom was more or less protected by the limitations imposed on the monarch's power by the privileges of the nobility and of Parliament. Nevertheless, he denied that it is necessarily suitable in other countries (ibid.: 106–107).[5]

Montesquieu (1989 [1748]:156–166) discusses, in the spirit of Pufendorf, the legislative power, the executive power and the judicial power.[6] However, he writes that the best form of government is one in which the three powers are separate and keeps each other in check to prevent any branch from becoming too powerful. If these powers are held in one hand as in an absolute monarchy it would lead to despotism. Montesquieu's view is taken over by Francis Hutcheson's view in his *A Short Introduction to Moral Philosophy* from 1747.

In the matter of political liberty, Waddicor (1970: 135), Montesquieu's superiority over his predecessors is clear. Although they refer to a contract as a means of guaranteeing liberty, he goes further and describes the separation of powers as a more practical safeguard, and this is not found in the works of Grotius or Pufendorf, although it is found in somewhat similar terms in Locke.

As Pufendorf, Montesquieu warns against corruption in democracies, aristocracies, and monarchies. He brings forward many examples. Greek and Roman sources he illustrates by referring to many countries. Furthermore, he returns again and again to the problem of public virtue, and he was understandably equally focused on its opposite which he called corruption (ibid.: 8.1–15: 112–125).

In his discussion of revenue and taxation, Montesquieu brings up the same themes as Pufendorf. Whatever government is chosen for a state; revenue is necessary for the government to be able to carry out the duties of the state. 'The revenue of the state is that portion each citizen gives of his goods in order to have the security or the comfortable enjoyment of the rest' (ibid.: 13.1–20: 213–227). To determine the revenues both the necessities of the state and the necessities of its citizens should be considered. To collect its revenue, the state must levy taxes on its citizens.

Montesquieu discusses different forms of taxes in different countries and under different governments. In a state, where all individuals are citizens 'and each one there possesses by his domain that which the prince possesses by his empire', taxes can be of three categories: they can be placed on people, or on land, or on commodities, or on all these (ibid.: 215). A tax on people can be such that they must give up part of their income to the state. The income can be in money as well as in produce. In the assessment of lands, registers are made for the various classes of land, but it will be very difficult to recognize these differences. Duties on commodities are least felt by the people. This is particularly the case when the seller collects the tax. He will know that he is not paying it himself and the buyer, who ultimately pays it, confounds it with the price. Montesquieu concludes: 'An impost [tax] by head is more natural to servitude; the tax on commodities; more natural to liberty because it relates less directly to the person' (ibid.: 13.14: 222).

A tax on people will be an unjust tax if it is levied in strict proportion to income Montesquieu claimed. Contrary to Pufendorf, he supported a progressive income tax. He refers to Athens, where the citizens were divided into four classes. The tax on an income of 500 was one talent, on 300 it was half a talent, and on 200 one-sixth of a talent. Those of the fourth class paid nothing. It was therefore not a proportion of income system, but a progressive proportion of needs (ibid.: 13.7: 216).

However, like Pufendorf, he claims that taxes should be clearly established and be so easy to collect that they could not be changed by the tax collectors Tax collectors did not belong to the most popular profession among citizens of different countries. Montesquieu ends his treatment of taxation, in the spirit of Pufendorf, with a warning about tax collectors. 'All is lost when the lucrative profession of tax-collectors, by its wealth comes to be an honoured profession.' He points to the many wrong doings made by people in this profession and concludes: 'Respect and esteems are for those ministers and those magistrates who, finding only work upon work, watch day and night over the happiness of the empire' (ibid.: 13.20: 227).

Hutchison (1988: 224) claims that Montesquieu's views on taxation have much in common with the four maxims subsequently enunciated by Adam Smith. It is surprising that he does not see the link between Pufendorf and Montesquieu and furthermore between Pufendorf and Smith.

Montesquieu's Followers

The conclusion in Waddcor's analysis is clear: when Montesquieu studies human customs and laws he draws extensively on the tradition of natural law. In the *Esprit des lois*, where he attempts to reconcile the eternal law with human diversity, his greatest debt is to Grotius and Pufendorf.

Montesquieu's *De Esprit des Lois* sees numerous editions and is translated to many languages. It had an enormous influence on the work of his descendants, among them the Continental and the British philosophers and politicians, the founding fathers of the United States Constitution, and Alexis de Tocqueville (1805–1859) in his *Democracy in America*, published in 1835 and 1840. *The Federalist Papers* written by James Madison (1751–1836), Alexander Hamilton (1755–1804) and John Jay (1745–1829) have frequent citations from this work. Therefore, Montesquieu became an important figure in the European and American Enlightenment. He passes on his own ideas and thereby also the ideas of his predecessors on political economy to many of his descendants. Elisabeth Fox-Genovese (1976: 139) in her *The Origin of Physiocracy*, asserts that, *even those who doubt Montesquieu's influence on Quesnay do not question his profound impact on Mirabeau.*

It is important to note that Montesquieu in the British colonies was recognized as a fighter for freedom, although not for American independence. Donald Lutz (1984: 193) in a study on the influence of European writers on American thoughts, claims that Montesquieu was the most-quoted philosopher in the American colonies in the second half of the eighteenth century. This is also confirmed by Bernard Bailyn (1992: 345), who contends that his name 'recurs far more often than that of any other authority in all the vast literature of the Constitution'.

Notes

1 Translation into English our responsibility.
2 See also Waddicor (1970), footnotes 65 and 66.
3 *Histoire de Suède*, Chatelaine, Amsterdam, 1748; *Introducion à l'histoire générale et politique de l'univers*, Chatelaine, Amsterdam, 1743.
4 All references to the Cambridge University Press edition of 1989.
5 See also *The Spirit of the Laws*. 3.1–10.
6 Thomas Hueglin (2008: 141) in his *Classical Debates of the 21st Century*, contends that 'Montesquieu expanded Locke's separation of legislative and executive power by adding the judiciary as an important third power in its own right, which had to be separate by all means.' Hueglin has no references to Pufendorf.

16 Jean-Jaques Rousseau

A Political Thinker

Jean-Jaques Rousseau was born in Geneva. Orphaned in 1722, he was sent to a boarding school at a neighbouring village, Bossey, where he learned Latin and the Calvinist catechism. He spent two happy years at this school, but never advanced further in formal or classical education. Out of school, he lived a wandering existence for five years. In 1728, he converted to Catholicism and entered the Seminary of St Lazare but he had so little formal education that he had to leave. In 1729 he became employed by Françoise-Louise de Warrens (1699–1762), also called Madam de Warrens, who became his benefactress and later his mistress. The Durant's (1967 X: 10) in their *The Story of Civilization*, asserts that she gave him books to read, among them Pufendorf's works, 'presumably the De jure naturae et gentium, or conceivably its crib the De officio hominis et civis both available in a French translation by Jean Barbeyrac'.

In the beginning of the 1740s Rousseau moved to Paris where he made a precarious living by tutoring and writing, but also by arranging music, which was his passion. In 1752, he wrote a play with eighteenth acts, *Narcissus or The Self Amirer.* It was published with a preface in 1753. He became secretary to the French ambassador in Venice in 1743. Here he contrasted the Venetian government with the Genevian and the French, and he studied Plato, Grotius, Pufendorf and Locke. In 1750, he wins the prize from the Academy of Dijon for his so-called first discourse, *Discourse sur les science et les arts* (Discourse on Sciences and Arts). It was published in 1751, and made according to Gourevitch (2007: xxxiii) in his *Introduction to Rousseau*, 'an immediate, resounding success throughout Europe'.

Rousseau visited Geneva in 1754 and reconverted to Calvinism. In 1755, his most famous and most influential work the so-called second discourse, *Discours sur l'origine et les fondements de l'inégalité parmi les hommes* (Discourse on the origin and basis of inequality among men) was published. It elaborated on the arguments in his first discourse. Here he notes that Pufendorf, in company with Cumberland and Montesquieu, differs from Hobbes in his conception of human nature (2008: 179). Rousseau leaves Paris in 1756 and settles in a cottage, Les Charmettes (the hermitage), on the estate of Louise Florence d'Épinay (1726–83). Here, in 1762, he writes and publishes first,

Émile, ou de l'éducation (Émile, or treatise on education) and later, his main work, *Du Contrat Sociale, ou Principes du droit politique* (The social contract or principles of political law). It became one of the most influential works of political philosophy, and in it he further develops some of the ideas from a 1755 article *Economie Politique* (Discourse on political economy), featured in volume 5 of Diderot's encyclopedia. In this article, he also cites Pufendorf, by way of support for the contention that the right to transfer property may only be enjoyed by the living (2007: 24).

Du Contrat Sociale, which was published in 1762, opens with: '*L'homme est né libre, et partout il est dans les fers*' (Man is born free, and everywhere he is in chains) (2007: 41). Both *Émile* and *The Social Contract* were condemned and publicly burned both in Geneva and in France. The French government ordered his arrest and he fled to Neuchatel, which was then governed by Prussia. After a brief and unhappy spell in England, he returned to France and lived under an assumed name, Renou. In 1772, he wrote the *Considérations sur le government de Pologne* (Consideration on the government of Poland). Rousseau died suddenly in 1778. After his death in 1782, an autobiographical book, *Les Confessions* (Confessions), which he had completed in 1770, was published.

Did Pufendorf Influence Rousseau?

In his works, Rousseau gives only a few direct references to the natural law philosophers. Two direct references in his *Discourse on the origin of inequality* and one reference in his *Economic Politique.*[1] His infrequent references to Pufendorf are uniquely to *De Jure Naturae et Gentium*. In his *Du Contrat Sociale* where he mentions Grotius twice, there are no references to Pufendorf.

However, in a memorandum he wrote as early as 1738, *Projet pour l'éducation de M. de Sainte-Marie*, Rousseau expresses his views on Pufendorf in the following way:

> Lastly, should my pupil stay long enough in my hands, I would take the risk to give him some knowledge about moral and natural law through the readings of Pufendorf and Grotius, because it is an honnête homme and a sensible man worthy to know the principles of good and evil and the grounds on which the society he belongs to are set.

Lois Robert Derathé (1970: 16) in his work on Rousseau and political science, contends that one thing is clear regarding Pufendorf himself: 'no one writing on law and morality for more than half a century after 1672 could afford to ignore him'. Moreover, he added: 'Nor, indeed, can anyone writing on this period today.'

In an article *Rousseau's Pufendorf*, Robert Lucian Wokler (1994: 381) investigates in detail Pufendorf's influence on the writings of Rousseau. Although he, in all of Rousseau's works, finds only five references to

Pufendorf he writes: 'I should add that apart from these direct references to Pufendorf, there are a number of obvious, and perhaps many more not so obvious, allusions to Pufendorf's ideas or Barbeyrac's interpretations of them in Rousseau's writings.' After having discussed some of these references and allusions, he concludes:

> Until a few years ago I believed the direct influence of Pufendorf upon the intellectual formation of Rousseau's ideas was slight, but I now hold that view to be false. Although his citations from Pufendorf are scanty, the themes they pursue form prominent features of both his philosophy of human nature and his theory of the foundation of the state, and I have come to see some of his principal arguments as quite centrally designed to challenge Pufendorf's natural jurisprudence, to the extent that it gave warrant to what Rousseau judged was the miserable history of human society and the despotic establishment of state power.
>
> (Ibid.: 382)

Another author, who claims that Rousseau extensively used the works of Pufendorf when he wrote, is the already mentioned Victor Gourevitch (2008: xii):

> In his [Rousseau's] day, the most systematic, comprehensive compendium on political philosophy was Pufendorf's Right of Nature and Nations, especially in Barbeyrac's learnedly annotated French translation, *Droit de la nature et des gens.* He seems to have kept its massive two tomes at his elbow whenever he undertook a major project in political philosophy.

Rousseau's Writings on Political Economy

Theory of Human Behaviour

Rousseau was convinced that man's original nature was good, but that it had been corrupted by the development of society. His *Discourse on the Arts and Sciences*, which was a response to the prize essay question: has the restoration of the sciences and the arts helped to purify morals? Here he argues that it had not. It led to the decline of virtue. This he pursued in his *Discourse on Inequality.* In the *Preface* Rousseau (2008 [1755]: 124) starts out with the statement: 'The most useful and the least advanced of all human knowledge seems to me to be that of man and I dare say that the inscription on the Temple of Delphi alone contained a more important and more difficult Precept than all the big Books of the Moralists.' It is clear, Gourevitch claims, that he has had Pufendorf's (DJNG.II.iv.5: 238) reference to the inscription in the temple 'Know thyself' at hand (2008: 352).

Rousseau sees two principles (before reason and independent of sociability): man's interests in his self-preservation and man's pity for other people, that is the spontaneous, natural disinclination to hurt or harm others (2008 [1755]: 127). He believed that as reason improved, when society moved forward, it weakened the natural sentiment of pity. In nature, man was independent, but as society advanced, he became dependent on other people.

From his book, Émile, it is also clear that Rousseau (2014 [1762]: 21), along with Pufendorf, does not believe in innate ideas, e.g. that man from birth knew what was right and wrong; he had to be taught. 'We are born weak, we need strength; helpless, we need aid; foolish, we need reason. All that we lack at birth, all that we need when we come to man's estate, is the gift of education.' This becomes even clearer later: 'It is no part of a child's business to know right and wrong, to perceive the reason for a man's duties' (ibid.: 273).

Theory of Property

In part II of his *Discourse on Inequality*, Rousseau opens with the following statement:

> The first man who having enclosed a piece of ground, to whom it occurred to say this is mine, and found people sufficiently simple to believe him, was the true founder of civil society. How many crimes, wars, murders, how many miseries and horrors Mankind would have been spared by him who, pulling up the stakes of filling in the ditch, had cried out to his kind: Beware of listening to this imposter; You are lost if you forget that the fruits are everyone's and Earth no one's: But in all likelihood things had by then reached a point where they could not continue as they were: for this idea of property; depending as it does on many prior ideas which could only arise successively, did not take shape all at once in man's mind.
>
> (2008: 161)

He then goes on to tell us, how this idea of property develops in man's mind, and the allusions to Pufendorf are strong. Much progress had to be made, industry and enlightenment acquired, transmitted and increased from one age to the next, before this last stage of nature was reached (ibid.) Man's first sentiment was that of his existence, his first care was that of his preservation. The earth's products provided the nascent man with all necessary support. However, soon some difficulties presented themselves, like the height of the trees, or competition from ferocious animals. Man, learned to overcome these and other obstacles. As humankind increased and spread, difficulties multiplied. Differences in terrain and climate led to differences in living. People discovered fire, invented tools for hunting and fishing, and improved their dwellings. Dealings with other people lead to the invention of language. This initial process finally enabled man to make more rapid progress and the more the mind became enlightened the more industry was perfected, that is better tools and better dwellings were created.

When agriculture was gradually introduced, it followed from the cultivation of land that its division was necessary:

> and from property, once recognized the first rules of justice, necessarily followed; for in order to render to each his own, each must be able to have something; moreover, as men began to extend their views to the future and all saw that they had some goods to lose, there was no one who did not have to fear reprisals against himself for the wrongs he might do to another.
>
> (Ibid.: 169)

Labour is the origin of property: 'Since labour alone gives the cultivator the right to the produce of the land he has tilled, in consequently also gives him a right to the land … is easily transformed into property', is all the more natural as it is impossible to conceive the idea of property emerging in any way other than in terms of manual labour (ibid.). The allusion to Locke's labour theory of property, which he could have got from Pufendorf, is clear. The first effect of property, as claimed by Rousseau, was negative. Men with property became knavish, and with some people imperious, and harsh with others. The division of land and labour transformed the natural equality in the natural stage into inequality of rank.

The three stages are also outlined in his third discourse or an *Essay on the Origin of Languages*, posthumously published in 1781. Human industry expands with the needs that give rise to it. There are three ways of life available to man, 'hunting, herding and agriculture' (2008: 271). This division corresponds to the three states of man considered in relation to society. 'The savage is a hunter, the barbarian a herdsman, the civil man a tiller of the soil' (ibid.: 272).

Theory of Value, Money and Trade

Rousseau develops neither a theory of value nor a theory of money or trade. In his *Discourse on Inequality*, the *Social Contract* and his essay on *Political Economy*, he sees the introduction of money, at best, as a necessary evil. For Rousseau, the worst kind of modern society is that in which money is the only measure of value. In his *Social Contract* it is expressed in this way:

> It is the hustle and bustle of commerce and the arts, it is the avid interest in gain, it is softness and love of comforts that change personal services into money. One gives up a portion of one's profit in order to increase it at leisure. Give money, and you will soon have chains. The word finance is a slave word; it is unknown in the City. In a truly free State the citizens do everything with their hands and nothing with money.
>
> (2007: 113)

Foundation of States and Council Decisions

In the *Social Contract*, Rousseau claims that there comes a point in the state of nature where the conflicts between people are so great that the primitive life in the state of nature can no longer subsist,[2] 'humankind would perish if it did not change in its way of being'. A society should be formed for humankind to survive (2007: 49).

Since men cannot come up with new forces, but only unite and direct the ones that exist, men have no means of self-preservation other than to form, by aggregation, a sum of forces that will be strong enough to overrule the conflicts, and make them act in concert. The sum of men's forces can only arise from the cooperation of many: 'but since each man's force and freedom are his primary instruments of self-preservation, how can he commit them without harming himself, and without neglecting the cares he owes himself?' (ibid.). This difficulty Rousseau states in the following terms. 'To find a form of association that will defend and protect the person and goods of each associate with the full common force and by means of which each, uniting with all, nevertheless obey only himself and remain as free as before' (ibid.). This is the fundamental problem to which the social contract provides a solution. This contract can be reduced to the following terms: 'Each of us puts his person and his full power in common under supreme direction of the general will; and in a body we receive each member as an indivisible part of the whole' (ibid.: 50). The public person thus formed by the union of others is called a state when it is passive, sovereign when active.

It is important to note that when a man joins the contract he loses the freedom to act on his own personal appetite, but he gains liberty via the limitation of reason and the general will placed on his behaviour. Rousseau's social contract is close to Pufendorf's agreement of association.

Rousseau contends that the political aspect of society ought to be divided into two parts, the sovereign and the government. The sovereign consists of all, and it represents the general will. It is also the legislative power. The government carries out the laws and decisions made on the authority of the sovereign. If it oversteps its boundaries, it can be removed. The relations between the government and the sovereign correspond roughly with Pufendorf's agreement of subjection.

In a chapter 'Of Suffrage', Rousseau contends that 'the way in which general business is conducted provides a fairly reliable indication of the current state of morals and the health of the body politics' (ibid.: 123). Furthermore, like Pufendorf, Rousseau claims that there is only one law, which by its nature requires unanimous consent. That is the social pact. 'If then, at the time of the social pact there are some who oppose it, their opposition does not invalidate the contract, it only keeps them from being included in it; they are foreigners amongst the Citizens' (ibid.). When the state has been constructed, consent has to be reached. Residents in the state are to submit to the sovereignty and obey (ibid.: 124). Rousseau argues that 'except for this primitive contract, the vote of the majority always obligates the rest; this is a consequence of the contract'. As with Pufendorf, the obligation to abide by a majority decision requires a prior unanimous decision.

Rousseau also discusses the proportional number of votes needed to declare the general will, that is the question of supermajorities (ibid.: 125). A difference of a single vote breaks the tie, a single opponent destroys unanimity, but between unanimity and a tie there are various uneven divisions, at any one of which this proportion of majority can be fixed, taking the state and the needs of the body politic into account. He puts up two general maxims that can help to guide these ratios of majority. First, the more important and serious the deliberations are, the closer to unanimous should be the opinion that prevails. Second, the more rapidly the business at hand has to be resolved, the narrower should be the prescribed difference in weighing opinions. 'In deliberation which have to be concluded straight away a majority of one should suffice' (ibid.). In Rousseau's opinion, the first of the two maxims appear better suited to laws, the second to business. However, he adds that it is by a combination of these two maxims that the best reasons for a deciding majority are determined.

Rousseau also has a brief discussion on voting by secret ballot or by voice (ibid.: 135). Furthermore, he discusses the case when an assembly consists of tribes. In each tribe, the majority of votes determine the vote of that tribe, a majority of votes of the tribes determines the vote of the people.

The question of supermajorities is discussed in his *Consideration of the Government of Poland*, from 1772. He accepted the veto right of each member of the Sejm, the Polish Parliament, when applied to fundamental laws. In such a case, the constitution will be made solid and the laws will be strong. However, in Poland, acts of government and administrative decisions were also governed by veto which hindered necessary changes. Therefore, the veto should only be applied to fundamental laws. For administrative decisions, a simple majority should prevail. In between, depending on the importance of the matter under consideration, any proportion of a supermajority is possible. Rousseau claims that one might require a three-quarters majority in legislation, a two-thirds majority in matters of state, and a simple majority in administration and daily business. No doubt that Rousseau had Pufendorf's major work close at hand when he wrote his decision rules (2007: 217–218).[3]

Division of State Powers and Principles of Taxation

In the *Social Contract*, in the chapter 'Of Government in General', Rousseau claims that every free action has two causes, which join in producing it: one moral, namely the will which determines it, the other physical, namely the power which executes it. The same is the case with a state. 'The body politic has the same motive causes; here, too, a distinction is drawn between force and will: The latter being called legislative power, the former executive power' (1997: 82).

The legislative power belongs to the people and can belong only to it. The legitimate exercise of the executive power is the government or supreme administration. The government is an intermediate body established between subjects and the sovereign 'so that they might conform to one another, and charged with the execution of laws and the maintenance of freedom both civil and political' (ibid.: 83).

Rousseau discusses, like Pufendorf, three major forms of government. He claims that the sovereign can entrust the charge of government to the whole or the majority of the people. This is given the name democracy. Alternatively, the government can be left in the hands of a small number of people. This bears the name of aristocracy. Finally, it can concentrate governing in the hands of a single magistrate i.e. a monarchy. He discusses different forms of these governments and the advantages and disadvantages of each of them. He stresses that not every form of government is suited to every country. He rejects the first two forms, democracy and absolute monarchy, but settles for an elective aristocracy. 'It is Aristocracy properly so called' (ibid.: 93).

Carl Friederich (2002: 19) asserts in his *Corruption Concepts in Historical Perspective* that Rousseau was deeply concerned with what he believed to be the corruption of his age and he considers himself the wise man who must rise a warning voice. He believes that the right kind of guidance could shape public opinion to avoid such corruption.

Rousseau touches upon the evils of corruption in several of his writings. In the first *Discourse* from 1750 he starts out with the question: 'Has the restoration of the Sciences and Arts contributed to the purification of Morals' but adds 'or to their corruption' (2008: 5). In this discourse, he holds for example the view that the necessary consequence of luxury is the dissolution of morals, which in turn leads to the corruption of taste (ibid.: 20). Furthermore, that a senseless education adorns our mind and corrupt our judgement (ibid.: 22). In his *Discourse on Inequality* corruption is closely related to that of nature. It is something that he must strip away to get to the real nature of man. Corruption is also an important part of the process of human development. His view is rather pessimistic, when human reason develops man is corrupted and declines from the state of nature. In his *Social Contract* he discusses, as Pufendorf, corruption in democracies, aristocracies and monarchies. He warns against corruption of the lawgiver in a democracy and claims that luxury corrupts.

> Finally, little or no luxury; for luxury is either the effect of riches, or makes them necessary; it corrupts rich or poor alike, the one by possession, the other by covetousness; it sells out the fatherland to lexity, to vanity; it deprives the State of all its Citizens by making them slaves to one another, and all of them slaves to opinion.
>
> (2007: 91)

In a monarchy, the lack of continuous successions may create situations were; 'intrigue and corruption will play their part' (ibid.: 97).

Rousseau's principles of taxation are laid down in his *Discourse on Political Economy* from 1755 and in his *Considerations* from 1772. His principles are very close to Pufendorf's principles in *De Jure Naturae*. The legitimate basis for taxation can be found in his *Discourse*, Rousseau 'On the other hand, it is no less certain that the maintenance of the state and the government involves costs and expenditures; and since anyone who grants the end cannot refuse the means, it follows that the members of society must contribute to its upkeep with their goods' (2007: 23). He claims that it has been generally recognized, by 'all philosophers and jurisconsults, who have achieved any reputation in matters of political right', that taxes can be established legitimately only by the consent of people, the sovereign, or its representatives (ibid.: 30).

Taxes levied on the people are, Rousseau claims, of two kinds: one that are levied on things i.e. property, and ones that are personal, which are paid by the head (ibid.). In his *Considerations* from 1772 he changed his mind and makes it clear that although the most convenient and least costly is without question a per capita tax, it is also the most forced, the most arbitrary, the most unjust and unreasonable. 'Taxes on property is always preferable to a tax on persons' (2007: 231). The best tax that will not be subject to fraud is therefore a proportional tax on land, and on all land without exception, for all what produces ought to pay. With 'all land', he also meant land owned by the kings, the nobles, the Church, and land held in common. A general land registry is necessary but the expense can be avoided, to good advantage, by assessing the tax not directly on the land but on its produce (ibid.: 232).

Rousseau discusses, in the manner of Pufendorf, three factors that should be considered when deciding on how much tax people should pay. First is the question of proportionality. A tax should be equal, that is proportional, in the sense that someone who has ten times more goods than another should pay ten times as much in tax. Second is the issue of need. A person with only the bare necessities for life should not pay anything in tax. However, if a person consumes many luxuries he should, if need be, pay a tax; 'up to the full amount that exceeds his necessities'. A third factor is the utility that each person derives from social alliances. This is never considered, and it favours the rich, the privileged and the powerful. Rousseau claims that all advantages and benefits of society, the lucrative posts, all exceptions, all exemption etc. are reserved for the rich. Another, no less important point to note is that the losses of the poor are far more difficult to make up for than those of the rich, and that the difficulty of acquiring always grows in proportion to need (2008: 32).

When all this is taken into consideration:

> the conclusion will be that in order to distribute taxes in an equitable and truly proportional fashion it should be imposed not solely in proportion to the taxpayers' goods, but in a proportion that takes account of the difference in their stations as well as how much of their goods is superfluous.
>
> (Ibid.: 33)

There is also another inconvenience of the personal tax. It is often felt too directly and furthermore it is collected to harshly, which does not prevent its being evaded in many ways. 'It is easier to hide one's head than one's possessions from tax-rolls and from prosecution' (ibid.: 33).

Duties on imports, i.e. customs, can, also in the manner of Pufendorf, be set on foreign goods, which the population craves, but the country does not need. Furthermore, customs can be set on the export of domestic goods of which the country has no excess, and which foreigners cannot do without. It is not hard to understand why the privileged classes in France reacted so hatefully towards Rousseau after having read his principles of taxation.

Rousseau's Influence

Gourevitch (2008: xv) writes: 'The First Discourse had won the Academy's Prize and had made him famous. The Second Discourse did not win the Prize, but made him immortal.' In France, as in most other European countries, Rousseau's name and many of his works were known to the intellectual part of the population. He was loved by many, and they used his arguments to promote their own ideas. He was, however, hated by the classes that held the power. They thought his ideas undermined the present order and encouraged radical changes in the governing system. Ronald Grimsley (1967: 224) in his article *Jean-Jacques Rousseau* claims that his powerful influence on later generations, was 'partly due to his vision of a regenerated human nature, but unlike merely utopian thinkers he seemed to promise a transfiguration of everyday existence, not the pursuit of a hopeless chimer'.

There has been some discussion about the extent of Rousseau contributions to the French revolution. Robert Wokler (2006: 25–56) brings this up in an article called *Rousseau on Rameau and revolution*. He could not find that Rousseau had any direct influence. However, there can be no doubt that Rousseau influenced the intellectual climate in France and thereby was instrumental in promoting change.

Like Locke in England and Scotland, Rousseau became an instrument for change in the way education was looked upon. In America, Rousseau became a familiar name, and his work was read by the elite. When he wrote the American Declaration of Independence, Thomas Jefferson is known to have used the works of the natural law philosophers in general and Pufendorf together with Locke, Montesquieu, Burlamaqui and Rousseau.

Notes

1 In Rousseau (2008 [1755]) *Discours sur l'origine* the references to Pufendorf are found on p. 135 and 179, and in Rousseau (2007 [1755]) *Economie Politique* the reference is found on p. 24.

2 How Rousseau tackles this problem and a comparison between his views and the views expressed by Pufendorf can be found in Melissa Schwartzberg (2008).

3 See also footnote 93, p. 93.

17 The First Economic Model Builders[1]

Introduction

It was not only Boisguilbert, who spoke out against the appalling economic conditions and the oppressive economic policies of the French government. A group of French intellectuals, known in their own days as *Les économistes*, but later called themselves Physiocrats, also wrote and spoke out against the deplorable situation.[2] Many economists agree that this group were the first economic model builders.

Ronald Meek in his *The Economics of Physiocracy* from 1962 claims: 'The French Physicrats are at once the most exciting and the contemporary group of economist in the whole history of economic thought.' He continues: 'The most exciting, because the birth of Physiocracy was in fact the birth of the science of economics in the broad general form in which it has come down to us today' (1962: 9). He also adds the most contemporary because their major preoccupation was strikingly similar to those of present-day economists.

The group's undisputed intellectual leader was François Quesnay, court physician to Madame Pompadour and the King Louis XV. The Physiocratic group has therefore also been identified as a court party, although a radical one. The inner circle of the group included as its most important members: Victor Marquis de Mirabeau, a close associate and collaborator of Quesnay, Paul-Pierre Mercier de la Rivière (1720–1793), and Pierre Samuel du Pont de Nemours. The French minister, Anne Robert Jacques Marquis de Turgot, expresses sympathy for their doctrine, but does not consider himself a member of the close group around Quesnay.

In the beginning the Physiocrats published in the *Encyclopédie* but later the monthly *Ephémérides du Citoyen, ou bibliothèque raisonnée des sciences morales et politiques* (The Citizens Chronicle, a library-based science of morals and politics), which was published from 1767 to 1772, almost became their official medium. The journal's publisher and chief editor was Nicolas Baudeau (1730–1792), a French theologian and canon, therefore also often called '*abbé Baudeau*', economist and journalist.[3] He had many international contacts and was well-informed. He had considerable influence through his popularizing of the doctrines of the Physiocrats. Furthermore, he was also responsible for the diffusion of their ideas in France, the rest of Europe and America. However, it also went the other way, he informed his fellow Physiocrats, and other subscribers in France, about important books published in other countries.

When and how did the Physiocratic group start their activity? Elizabeth Fox-Genovese (1976: 13) points to du Pont, who claimed that, 'the history of physiocracy began in 1756 with the publication of the article "Fermiers" [The farmers] in volume VI of the Encyclopéde'. Du Pont also recounted how its author Quesnay in 1757 acquired as collaborator Marquis de Mirabeau, 'the flamboyant author' of the year's bestseller *L'Ami des hommes, ou Traité de la population* (The friend of men or a treaty on population).[4]

Sources

The Physiocrats like most other writers in the eighteenth century did not overwhelm us with quotations. There are scarcely any references to the sources of their ideas in the articles and books comprising what can be termed the Physiocratic library.

Surprisingly, the impression is that few of the authors that have been analysing the doctrines of the Physiocrats have been particularly interested in their predecessors. One example is the above-mentioned Ronald Meek, who in his thorough inquiry into the economics of Physiocracy makes no references to their predecessors.

Joseph Schumpeter (1954: 138) not only contends that Quesnay is a philosopher of natural law. He also asserts that the term Physiocracy denotes 'rules of nature' (ibid.: 228).[5] However, he does not investigate how Quesnay or the other Physiocrats eventually used the doctrines of the major natural law philosophers when they developed their own theories.

Fox-Genovese (1976: 22) in her book about Physiocracy asserts: 'That the physiocrats like Rousseau, use, misuse and reinterpret Pufendorf, Grotius, Hobbes, Locke, Barbeyrac, Burlamaqui, Felon, and many other without direct references.' Furthermore, she claims that the roots of the Physiocratic ideas have not been satisfactorily investigated.

> Nearly two centuries of scholarly interest have failed to produce a satisfactory view of the chain of Quesnay's thought. He has been variously identified as a rationalist and an empiricist, as a Cartesian and a Lockeàn. His thoughts have been linked to that of Plato, the Schoolmen, Shaftesbury, Cumberland, Descartes, Leibniz and Wolff.
>
> (Ibid.: 77)

She claims that Quesnay was 'deeply immersed in the current natural law debates' and that Quesnay owned the work of Richard Cumberland, 'as well as the works of the German political theorist, Pufendorf, and those of Pufendorf's French translator, Barbeyrac' (ibid.: 86). Although she includes a short review of contemporary literature that Quesnay was familiar with in her study, no investigation into the predecessors of the Physiocratic ideas can be found. Only in rather vague general terms does she mention Pufendorf as a source for the Physiocrats.

The monthly *Ephémérides* features many articles that point to the natural law philosophers in general and Pufendorf in particular. For example, in volumes 1 and 2 of the journal, for the year 1767, the editor Baudeau reviewed a long essay on Pufendorf in a book by Martin Hübner (1723–95). The book had originally been published in London, but republished in Paris in the beginning of 1767.[6] In volume 2 he made it clear that he could not follow Hübner in his critizism of Pufendorf.

From all this, it is reasonable to conclude that Pufendorf was a well-known philosopher whose doctrines on natural law, including political economy, have been appreciated and used in the milieu of the Physiocrats.

Foundation of Physiocratic Economic Thought

What did the Physiocrats themselves understand with political economy and what was the foundation for their doctrines? Fox-Genovese refers to a letter du Pont de Nemours sent to Jean-Baptiste Say in 1815.[7] Du Pont asserts that for all the Physiocrats, political economy was 'the science of natural law applied, as it should be, to civilized societies', and of 'enlightened justice in all social relations – internal and external' (1976: 10). It was not possible for the Physiocrats to directly and openly criticize the existing abuses of the present system since they, as a group, were attached to the inner circle of the king's court. However, they talked relatively openly about the economic problems of France, but they had to hide their views on political and social matters. Since they had to work from within, and their only option was to appeal to laws that were above the law of the realm. The underlying philosophy for the development of their economic ideas was therefore that of natural law.

The Physiocrats asked themselves whether the nature of things did not tend towards a science of political economy. Under Quesnay's leadership, the Physiocrats devoted their efforts to the discovery of the principles of this science and the disassociation of political economy from the general body of natural law.

In his writings on political economy, Quesnay claimed that wealth came entirely from the land, that nature was fertile and that man could tie together its reproductive forces. Agriculture was therefore the industry that created wealth. Hard labour and investments in agriculture would create surplus that would circulate to other sectors of the economy. His *Tableau économiqué*, which was first published in Versailles in 1758, is the first presentation of a circular flow between the different sectors of the economy in the history of economic thought. Today's historians of economic thought therefore generally agree that this *Tableau* had in it the origin of modern ideas of the circulation of wealth and the nature of interrelationship in the economy. Hutchison (1988: 285) contends that:

> It was the first school of economists in the history of the subject, and probably the most closely knit of all such groups, much more than the Ricardians, or the Keynesians, or the Austrians, though perhaps rather less dictatorially directed than the Marxians.

Heinz Kurz (2008: 267) claims that Karl Marx (1808–83) considered the Physiocrats ‘the true fathers of modern political economy’ and dubbed the Tableau ‘an extremely brilliant conception’. It is outside the scope of this inquiry to discuss the influence of the Tableau on contemporary and future philosophical and economic thinking. This investigation will concentrate on the Physiocrats view on the themes of political economy, where they could have been influenced directly by Pufendorf or indirectly through his French followers.

Theory of Human Behaviour and Private Property

Fox-Genovese contends that the Enlightenment represented an emerging ideology, it sought to liberate all men in all countries. ‘Its most generous aspect embodied a view of universal human equality, which rested upon the concept of uniform human nature’ (1976: 44). The Physiocrats usually insisted upon the dictates of nature. It was the material condition that was the prime determinate of human behaviour (ibid.: 47).

The Physiocrats saw both political and economic theory as integral parts of a single science grounded on private property. Private property, in Physiocratic thought, constitutes man’s first natural right (ibid.: 48). Man arrives in the world with a fundamental obligation to keep himself alive, and his survival depends upon his right to property. The original obligation to live can only be fulfilled by eating. To eat with moral sanctions, ‘man must have a natural right to the fruits of the earth’. The Physiocrats defended that right in order to refute Hobbes’ contention that society rests on struggle. The first man simply collected the fruits freely offered by nature. Later, men turned into active cultivation of the earth, which required the use of labour. However, as everyone can recognize from his own experience, or in Quesnay’s chosen phrase, no one in his right mind willingly undertakes hard labour without being assured of the absolute fruits of that labour. Quesnay’s theory of property has elements of both Pufendorf’s theory of right and Locke’s labour theory of property.

The Physiocrats claimed that society must approve human action, efforts and tools, and must positively sanction property as a social good. In this defence of individual’s right to property, in contrast to the traditional notions of the community’s right to preserve social harmony, lies the heart of the Physiocratic ideology, which they summed up in the words: property, liberty, and security. Spiegel (1983) claims that it was in this connection that the phrase *laissez faire, laissez passer* was coined, ‘a maxim that to this day has served as an affirmation of economic individualism’. The Physiocrats made a distinction between natural and positive order.

> Only in the natural order, the ideal, would harmonious individualism reach its full flowering. In the positive order of the world of reality the free play of individual forces might well be frustrated, with disadvantages that result in economic conflict rather that harmony.
>
> (1983: 186)

The allusion to Pufendorf is not easily avoided. Furthermore, society must recognize individual self-interest as a most respectable motive for social action. However, it was not an egoistic self-interest. Mirabeau states, according to Fox-Genovese (1976: 206), that our intellect enables us to channel our unbridled passions into the socially acceptable paths of enlightened self-interest. Her description of the Physiocratic view of self-interest is very close to Pufendorf's self-interest and sociability.

She also claims that Quesnay had learned from Locke to mistrust the notion of innate ideas, but she does not mention that Locke had found this idea in Pufendorf's writings (ibid.: 85).

From the extract from '*Rural Philosophy*'[8] it becomes clear, according to Meek (1963: 57–64) that Quesnay was familiar with the development in stages, although the order was different. When the fruits of the earth had been used and population increased, men had to cultivate the land, 'whence arose agricultural nations' (ibid.: 60). Men also had to herd together and rear domestic animals, which was the origin of herdsman. Furthermore, men had to hunt and set trap for wild animals and do the same for fish, which was the origin of hunters and fishermen. Using examples from the Genesis he explains how these societies developed. From the interrelationships of these societies there 'is born a new kind of secondary and artificial societies that is commercial societies'. These societies are 'less secure so far as its basis and duration are concerned, less capable of extension, and unable to form a great empire, but nevertheless free, wealthy, and powerful within its narrow boundaries' (ibid.: 62). The distinction between 'thine and mine' was here established in relation to the land.

Theory of Value

Quesnay's *bon prix* forms, according to Spiegel (1983: 193), part of his value theory. His theory is not fully developed but it has a number of interesting features. The *bon prix* stands in a certain relationship to the '*prix fondamental*', which is the cost of production. Market price will normally be above the cost of production. If it falls below it, it will create losses for the producers. However, on the other hand, if the market price is excessively high, it will constitute a 'burden'. The *bon prix* is located between these extremes. It yields a profit and is therefore an incentive to maintain or expand production. The allusion to Pufendorf's discussion of natural price and market price is there.

Foundation of States and Council Decisions

The Physiocrats maintained that natural law governed the economy. Individual rights, and the justification of private property based on these rights, was part of this natural law. The laissez faire principle was the basis for the harmony-of-interest doctrine in which individual pursuit of an enlightened self-interest by each member of society would lead to the maximum social good. The allusion to Pufendorf is easily seen.

Society must approve human action, effects, and tools, and must positively sanction private property as a social good. The Physiocrats claim, according to Fox-Genovese (1974: 49), that without security, property would be a theoretical right constantly violated in practice. The need for security of private property therefore justifies government. The principle duty of the government is therefore to guarantee private property.

Mirabeau in his investigation of the origin of society explains it this way. 'All social organization rests upon the desire to harvest the fruits of one's labour. That desire, illuminated by reason, affords the basis for the recognition that union offers the best means of implementing individual desires. The union itself is what we call society' (ibid.: 206).

Division of State Powers and Principles of Taxation

The Physiocratic views concerning the nature of the state and the best form of government is not easy to grasp. The Physiocrats invented for example the name 'legal despotism' to describe the government they favoured. It included a sovereign assisted by administrators and a group of magistrates to serve as custodians of the fundamental laws· of the realm. Although the views of the Physiocrats generally were relatively homogeneous, their views on the state and government were not constant but evolved over time. Being a group connected to the court, they were also in an awkward position. The Physiocrats saw both their political and economic theories as integral parts of a science founded on private property, personal liberty and individual self-interest, although an enlightened one, as the driving force in the economy. Personal security is also very important as a foundation for society. These concepts are closely related to Pufendorf's natural law philosophy.

In 1760 Mirabeau published his *Théorie de l'impôt* (Theory of taxation). It outlined the Physiocratic theory of taxation, criticizing the present system in general and in particular the abuse of the tax farmers (tax collectors). It shocked public opinion. The author was imprisoned, but got out after eight days because of the groups connections. However, exiled to the countryside for two months. Mirabeau proposed that the tax farmers should be replaced with a system of a single direct tax on landed property *l'impôt unique*. His critic of the present system has allusions to Pufendorf's criticism of the tax collection abuses.

Despite his criticism of the present tax system Mirabeau was not a revolutionary. He defended noble privilege and tax exemptions (ibid.: 143). The prince, with his absolute power, enjoys the undisputed right to demand subsidies from his subjects, who on their side have no right to refuse. If the prince requires financial assistance for the upkeep of the public domain, his purposes serve the interest of all. If the prince misuses the funds he receives, then he abuses his powers (ibid.: 215).

Considering all this it is therefore not surprising that several historians of economic thought – for example Fox-Genovese (1976), Ekelund and Hébert (1990), Rima (1991) and Landreth and Colander (1994), point to natural law in general as a source for Quesnay and his fellow Physiocrats. However, so far, no one has been found, who points to a direct link between the Physiocrats and Pufendorf's writings on natural law and political economy.[9]

The Influence of Physiocracy

The first publication of the *Tableau* was almost not noticed outside the inner circle. However, it was republished in 1761, in the second part of the sixth volume of a new edition of Mirabeau's *L'Ami des Hommes*. It created quite a stir and gave rise to debates in France lasting until the revolution. Their influence was therefore short-lived. They advocated and wanted reforms, but these reforms still preserved the old regime albeit with a less absolute king. This was not possible. Their emphasis on agriculture, according to Spiegel (1983: 199), 'was already obsolete in an age that saw the dawn of the industrial revolution'.

Economists and social reformers in other countries, particularly where they had an absolute but enlightened monarchy, hoped to copy some of these reforms. They would look to France and see a group of eager reformers, the Physiocrats, who worked with considerable freedom close to the king. However, there were obvious and hidden limitations to their freedom. If their proposals for reforms infringed on the rights of the privileged or the Church, there was a swift reaction to stop these proposals.

A discussion of the impact of Physiocratic ideas in Hungary, Poland, Russia, and Sweden can be found in the booklet *Physiocracy Yesterday and Today*, edited by Janina Rosica, from 1996. Among some rulers, Physiocracy became the fashion of the day. Empress Catherine II of Russia, King Stanislaus of Poland, King Gustav III of Sweden, Emperor Joseph II of Austria, Grand Duke Leopold of Toscany, together with many other political personalities tried to understand its principles. Ganni Vaggi (1987: 871) in his article *Physiocracy* mentions that Empress Catherine II invited Mercier de La Rivière to St Petersburg to spread the new ideas. How the Physiocratic ideas could have been implemented in the Russian feudal system is another question? Physiocracy had, according to Lluch and Argemi (1994) in their article *Physiocracy in Spain*, considerable influence in Spain, particularly before 1815. They also mentioned that Physiocracy was transmitted from Spain to Argentina.

One practical experiment to adopt a Physiocratic system should be mentioned. In 1763, the enlightened absolute ruler Grand Duke Karl Friederich of Baden-Durlach (1728–1811) made such an effort. He appointed the leading representative of the Physiocrats in the Roman-German Empire, Johann August Schlettwein (1731–1802) as a superintendent to his court at Karlsruhe. They were committed to achieve practical improvement of agriculture and started the world's only known attempt to introduce the Physiocratic system, with the 'impot unique' in three villages of Baden. In one village, the experiment lasted thirty years before it was abandoned.

Adam Smith's (1976 [1776] Bk. IV) *The Wealth of Nations*, had high regards for what he calls the agricultural system:

> This system, however, with all its imperfections, is perhaps, the nearest approximation to the truth that has yet been published upon the subject of political economy, and is upon that account well worth the consideration of every man who wishes to examine with attention the principles of that very important science.
>
> (Ibid.: 199)

This system was developed by a numerous sect, which followed implicitly, 'and without any sensible variation, the doctrine of Mr. Quesnai'. Smith found the most distinct and best connected account of the doctrine in a little book by Mr Mercier de la Rivière (ibid.: 200).

Notes

1 In writing this part, I am much indebted to the writings of Ronald Meek (1962), Elizabeth Fox-Genovese (1976) and Liana Vardi (2012).

2 Schumpeter (1954: 228) claims that the term was used by du Pont de Nemours in 1767, but might have been used earlier by Baudeau and was perhaps due to Quesnay himself.

3 Baudeau travelled to several other European countries. For example, he stayed in Poland and Russia in 1768–1769, and then again in Poland in 1774.

4 F.A. Hayek in his *The Trend of Economic Thinking* (*The Collected Works of F.A. Hayek*, vol. 3, The University of Chicago Press, 1991), claims very convincingly that Mirabeau plagiarized Richard Cantillon's *Essay on the Nature of Trade in General* from 1755 [1731].

5 The term was invented by du Pont de Nemours. It is derived from two Greek words and means the rule of nature.

6 Martin Hübner (1723–1795), born in Hanover and died in Copenhagen, was the Danish author of *Essai sur l'Histoire du droit naturel* (Essay on the history of natural law). It was published in London in two volumes, the first in 1757 and the second in 1758. There is no publisher mentioned in the book. Martin Hübner was professor of history at the University of Copenhagen, member of the Royal Society of London, of the *Académie des Inscriptions et Belles Lettres* of Paris and adviser to the King of Denmark. A copy of the Paris edition can be found in Bibliothèque National, Paris. In vol. 2 of the *Essai*, he devotes a large part to Samuel Pufendorf (pp. 223–298).

7 A letter dated 22 April 1815.

8 Philosophie Rurale first appeared in 1763.

9 See Sæther, 'Samuel Pufendorf's Natural Law and Physiocracy', in Jaina Rosicka (ed.), *Physiocracy Yesterday and Today*, Cracow Academy of Economics, Cracow, 1996.

Part VI

Scottish followers of Pufendorf

18 Gershom Carmichael brought Pufendorf to Scotland

It was Gershom Carmichael (1672–1729), who introduced the natural law tradition into Scotland. Carmichael was born in London to Scottish parents. His father was a Presbyterian minister who had been exiled from Scotland.[1] Carmichael, however, returned to Scotland and graduated Master of Arts from University of Edinburgh in 1691. Thus, he became Regent at St Andrew's University. His task was to introduce the students to all aspects of the curriculum. In 1694 he applied and obtained, by public trial, a regentship at the University of Glasgow. Here he introduced natural law as a subject in the curriculum for the students. When the University carried out a reorganisation and abolished the Regent system in 1727, Carmichael became the first professor of moral philosophy.

For the use of his students in his philosophy classes Carmichael produced lecture notes. These lecture notes were published as compendias, *Theses Philosophicae* (Philosophical theses), from 1699 and 1707, and *Ethicae Jurisprudentiae Naturalis* (Ethics of natural law) from 1702 to 1703 are examples.[2] Besides these compendia's, his published works included *Breviuscula Introduction ad Logicam* (A short introduction to logic) from 1720 and 1722, and *Synopsis Theologiae Naturalis* (Synopsis of natural theology) from 1729.[3]

As David Murray (1927: 507) notes in his *Memories of the Old College of Glas*gow, it was Carmichael) that 'brought the teaching of philosophy abreast'. In his moral philosophy course, which included ethics, jurisprudence, government and political economy, he used Pufendorf's 'student edition' *De Officio Hominis et Civis* as a textbook and it was 'for long an exceedingly popular textbook'.

Hans Medick (1973: 300) claims in his book about the natural state and natural history, that Carmichael had a very high opinion of both Grotius and Pufendorf. He claims that their works should be studied 'day and night'. He used Pufendorf's *De Officio* as a textbook and in 1718 he published in Glasgow an edition in Latin for the use of his students. It saw a second edition in Edinburgh in 1624 and a third posthumously in Leiden in 1769 (reproducing the 1624 text). This book included his own extensive *Notes and Supplements* (also in Latin).[4] With Carmichael, natural law or natural jurisprudence was designated moral philosophy:

> The discipline which teaches the prescriptions of the natural law in themselves … which directs human actions in conformity with that law is that very discipline, which is called ethics or moral philosophy; and therefore we find no reason to distinguish it from natural jurisprudence.
> (2002 [1718]: 29)

Thomas Mautner (1996: 191) in his book *Carmichael and Barbeyrac*, writes that Carmichael's edition was met by general approval. He mentions Eberhard Otto (1685–1756), professor of jurisprudence at Utrecht, who in his comments to his edition of *De Officio*, from 1740, praised Carmichael's *Notes and Supplements.* Carmichael was only one of many that published editions of Pufendorf's *De Officio*, with their own commentaries, for the use of their students. He himself refers to two, the professor of Roman law at University of Leipzig, Gottlieb Gerhard Titius (1661–1714) and the professor at Groningen, Jean Barbeyrac.

Why did Carmichael Select *De Officio* as a Textbook?

It is not known precisely why Carmichael selected Pufendorf's *De Officio* as a textbook. In his book *The Scottish Philosophy* James McCosh (1875: 22) contends that the Parliament of Scotland in 1690 had appointed a *Commission for visiting the universities to implement reforms in the curricula*. Locke's essay on education was known to some of the commission members, and it clearly affected the committee's proposals for reforms, including changes in curricula and later the abolishment of the regent system. A change was therefore in the air. He also emphasized the strong influence Locke had on the intellectual developments in Scotland., Locke was, as discussed, for long an admirer of Pufendorf, and there is no doubt that Carmichael was familiar with Locke's view when he made his choice of a textbook. In his commentaries, there is, claims Stephen Buckle (1991: 194), 'a powerful Lockian component'. Buckle also refers to an unpublished paper by James Moore where he notes that 'Carmichael referred his readers repeatedly to improvements made by Locke on themes addressed by Pufendorf, improvements which consistently defended the individual against the power of the magistrate.' 1980: 19. Carmichael's use of *De Officio* as a textbook for his students was met with suspicion from theologians, but was accepted when he made it clear that he was not an uncritical follower of Pufendorf's ideas, and that he disagreed fundamentally with his view that natural law must abstract from belief in the immortality of the soul and an afterlife. Jennifer Herdt (1997: 28) claims that Carmichael thought the secularizing trends in natural law were deplorable. He insisted that natural religion and natural jurisprudence could not, as claimed by Pufendorf, be separated. Natural law could not abstract from belief in immortality of the soul and an afterlife.

In his commentaries, Carmichael elaborated on Pufendorf's writings and claims that his doctrine on natural law 'has long been criticized by many grave and learned men as unsatisfactory and inadequate to the end it seeks to achieve'. He, therefore, 'will attempt to give some idea, in the most summary form possible, of a doctrine of the precepts of Natural Law which may be seen to be less open to those criticisms' (Moore and Silverthorne 2002: 46). Furthermore, Carmichael claims that Pufendorf built his natural law on one precept, but that he, in contrast, builds it on three fundamental precepts; 'that God must be worshipped, that everyone must seek his own harmless advantage, (utilitate) so far as it does not injure others, and that sociability must be fostered' (ibid.: 51). However, as also noted by Moore and Silverthorne (1984: 8), Carmichael may have overstated his differences with Pufendorf in respect to the three laws of nature. Pufendorf claimed in his *De Officio* (1673 [1927] I.iii.13: 20–21) that the duties incumbent on man, in accordance with natural law, can be classified under three main headings: 'according to the dictate of sound reason alone, a man should conduct himself toward God, the second, how toward himself, the third, how toward other men'. Carmichael claims that self-interest was not a prime driving force and that men did not become sociable from insecurity to be safe, as Pufendorf asserted (1673 [1927] I.iii.13: 19).

Likewise, Carmichael could not accept Pufendorf's opinion that 'no one would practice works of pity or friendship without having the assurance of fame or emolument' (1927 [1673] I.iii.13: 26). In his supplements, he argues, as claimed by Peter Stein (1982: 669) that 'man's ability to live with others in society depends on natural feeling of sympathy for others, which men could never have invented themselves and which must have been implemented in them by the Supreme Being'.

On how things become property, Carmichael argued, as Locke and Barbeyrac did, that the right of property had its origin in labour (Moore and Silverthorne 2002: 94). They found this more satisfactory than Pufendorf's account, which made it dependent on consent.

Carmichael makes only a few remarks on Pufendorf's chapter on value but discusses the contracts it is built on in some detail. Neri Naldi (1993: 457) investigates Carmichael's ten notes on quasi contracts and claims that 'we can recognize an attempt to transform Pufendorf's list of causes influencing price determination into a compact and significantly original scheme'.

The manner in which Pufendorf proposed that men unite in society under government by mutual agreement and consent was, as pointed out by Moore and Silverthorne (1984: 1–12), attractive to Carmichael and other supporters of the Revolution Settlement, since it excluded the claim of hereditary rights for the monarch.[5] However, they could not accept his theory that the duty of sociability recognizes that the sovereigns should enjoy absolute power over their subjects. This could not be reconciled with the rights that British subjects had won by the Glorious Revolution.[6] Carmichael sought to revise the absolutist implication of Pufendorf's theory by restating their obligations to be sociable in terms of a duty to respect the natural rights of others.

Carmichael's Influence

Carmichael became a scholar of some renown. Robert Wodrow (1843: 95–96) claims that he 'was exceedingly valued both at home and abroad, where he had considerable correspondence with learned men, such as Barbyrack; and he brought a great many scholars to Glasgow'.[7] William Hamilton (1872: Vol. 1: 30n) writes that Carmichael 'may be regarded, on good grounds, as the true founder of the Scottish school of philosophy'.[8]

It was largely due to Carmichael's efforts, William Taylor (1955: 251–255) wrote, 'that speculative economic inquiry initiated by Hobbes, Grotius and Pufendorf, formally entered Scottish universities, and before very long, British political economy'. This is also supported by Hutchison (1988: 192) who claimed that Carmichael played a vital role both in the history of Scottish philosophy and in the history of economic thought. He is today considered one of the founders of the Scottish Enlightenment. Moore and Silverthorne (2002: xvi) claim that Carmichael's work 'contributed, very fundamentally, to shape the agenda of instruction in moral philosophy in eighteenth-century Scotland'.

Carmichael became a very popular teacher who also attracted many students from England, Ireland and Wales to the University of Glasgow. This in spite of the fact that Michael Brown (2002: 22) in his study *Francis Hutcheson in Dublin* contends that Carmichael found lecturing a chore and he 'attended his duties by simply reciting passages of Pufendorf and amending and commenting upon it as he saw fit'.

With Carmichael's use of Pufendorf's *De Officio* as a textbook, he started the process of transforming natural law into moral philosophy.

Notes

1 Stein (1982) claims that this is the reason for his unusual first name, Gershom. It is derived from the name of Moses' son: 'a stranger in a strange land' (Exodus 2:22).
2 Carmichael not only introduced Pufendorf's natural law to Scotland. In his lectures 1702–1703 he also, according to Moore and Silverthorne (1983: 81), made references to Locke.
3 These works were published in Moore and Silverthorne (2002: 223–286 and 286–324).
4 John N. Lenhart compiled and Charles H. Reeves translated in 1985 Carmichael's Supplements and Appendix, but not the Notes, from the 1718 edition. Also, *The Introduction* to the 1769 edition and the January 1927 review of Gershom Carmichel's notes to the *De Officio* in *Acta Eruditorum* has been translated by Charles H. Reeves and privately published by John N. Lenhart, Cleveland, Ohio. Furthermore, James Moore and Michael Silverthorne have edited and Michael Silverthorne has translated Carmichael's writings in 2002. The quotations are from this last translation.
5 The Revolutionary Settlement was a series of Acts passed by the English Parliament in the years 1689–1701. It limited the power of the king but also the authority of the Parliament.
6 It is also called the Revolution of 1688 where King James II was overthrown and William III and his wife Mary II became jointly king and queen of England.
7 Quotation taken from Brown (2000: 17).
8 The quote is from McCosh (1875: 36) or Taylor (1955: 253).

19 Francis Hutcheson a User of Pufendorf

In 1710 an Irish student, Francis Hutcheson (1694–1746), matriculated in the University of Glasgow. James McCosh (1875) claimed that he enjoyed the privilege of 'sitting under the prelections' of Carmichael, who introduced him to the moral philosophy of Samuel Pufendorf. Pufendorf's influence on Hutcheson therefore started with Carmichael's lectures. Here it should be noted that Brown (2002: 16) claims that it is unclear whether Hutcheson ever attended Carmichael's lecture on jurisprudence. But Brown does not have McCosh (1875) on his reference list.

Hutcheson was born into a Scottish-Irish family in Northern Ireland, where his father, a Presbyterian minister, brought up his children in the Calvinist branch of Presbyterianism. He therefore received his first education at a dissenting school and thereafter at a dissenting academy. Being a Presbyterian, he was unable or unwilling to attend the Trinity College in Dublin, or Cambridge or Oxford; he therefore entered the University of Glasgow at the age of 16. His education and training had been directed towards establishing himself as a minister of the Presbyterian Church in Ireland or Scotland. After a year of study, followed by a year's break, and after having completed the Master degree in 1712, he began the study of theology the following year,

During his six years at Glasgow, his original orthodox Calvinist views underwent fundamental changes due to the influence of two of his professors, Carmichael and John Simson (1668–1740). The latter was Professor of Divinity. They both promoted tempered and moderate views on Christianity. These views also brought the professors in conflict with the orthodox Presbyterian leaders. Charged with heresy, Simpson was suspended from teaching duties at the University and Carmichael had to admit to his deviations from the 'right thoughts'.

Hutcheson left the University of Glasgow in 1716, with a licence from the Presbyterian Church and returned to Ireland. Here he was actively engaged in church controversies, but this did not prevent him from becoming pastor of a congregation. In 1721 or 1722 he was invited to Dublin, by a group of Presbyterian clergymen, and asked to open a dissenting Academy for conformist students. Brown (2002: 78) suggests that the Academy, under his leadership 'contained a broadly humanist education', and became an academic rival to

Trinity College, which was supported by the official Church of Ireland. His years at the Academy were very productive, both as a teacher and as a writer. In Dublin, Mautner (1993: 3) claims that he became associated with the circle around Viscount Robert Molesworth of Swords (1656–1725). Consequently, he took active part in the philosophical debate and wrote letters and articles concerned with ethical questions to the *London Journal* and the *Dublin Weekly*. His article *Reflections on our common system of morality* was published in the *London Journal* in 1724.

In 1725, Hutcheson published several scholarly works on ethics. The first was *Three Essays on Reflection upon Laughter* where his point of departure was criticism of Hobbesian egoism. His second piece on ethics was *Observations on the Fable of the Bees*, where he discussed and attacked polemically the ethical questions found in the work by the notorious Bernard Mandeville (1670–1733).[1] The third was *An Inquiry Concerning Beauty, Order, Harmony and Design*, and the fourth is *An Inquiry Concerning Moral Good and Evil*. In all these works he refers to and uses Pufendorf's natural law writings and he talks highly of him who, because of his distinct intelligible reasoning, is recognized as 'the grand instructor in morals to all who have of late given themselves to that study' (Hutcheson 1725: 103).

Three years later, he published *An Essay on the Nature and Conduct of the Passions and Affections*, and *Illustration of the Moral Sense*. In these works, he turns his attention to the more respectable Pufendorf, elaborates on the ethical questions he raised in his natural law work and treated him, as noted by Hont (2005: 51), 'as the apostle of commercial sociability and modern Epicureanism'. These works enhanced Hutcheson's reputation as a moral philosopher.[2]

Due to illness, Carmichael retired from his chair of moral philosophy in 1729 and died of cancer a few months later. Hutcheson was chosen to succeed him. When he took up the position in the autumn of 1730 he held his inaugural lecture 'On the Social Nature of Man'.[3] In this lecture he made it clear that he had high regards for Pufendorf, although he disagreed with his emphasis on self-love and called him in this respect a follower of Hobbes (Hutcheson 1993 [1730]: 134–135).[4]

Hutcheson brought with him several young gentlemen from his Academy 'and his just fame drew many more both from England and Ireland'.[5] His importance as a professor, teacher and author was recognized even in his own time. It has been said that he was 'the personality most responsible for the new spirit of enlightenment in the Scottish universities'.[6] According to his biographer William Scott (1900: 69), he was among the first to lecture in English, and with eloquence. The university made him serve on numerous university committees. He carried substantial, although controversial, weight in the creation of a more liberal 'forward university policy'. He was the guardian and friend of his students and his care for 'the wild Irish teagues' among them was recognized. Hutcheson was, as Carmichael before him, a user and an admirer, but also a critic of Pufendorf.

According to Elmer Sprague (1967: 99), Hutcheson 'devoted himself in Glasgow to enriching the culture and softening the Calvinism of his fellow Presbyterians'.[7] The Presbytery of Glasgow tried him for 'false and dangerous' doctrines. However, he managed to brush aside the charges of his accusers, although for a time the situation was quite serious.

Even if there are few direct references, there is no doubt that Hutcheson had used Pufendorf's writings extensively in his early works in Dublin. His articles and essays during his years there emanate from his studies of moral philosophy and theology at Glasgow. He had studied Pufendorf's works in detail both in class, in the library and later in Dublin.[8] In these articles he criticizes Hobbes and Mandeville for their egoistic theories of morality and Pufendorf for his claim that 'no understanding had been implanted by nature'. However, his starting point was always the questions raised by Pufendorf. Here it should again be pointed out that he, like Carmichael, could not accept Pufendorf's emphasis on self-interest or his view that there were no moral obligations without rewards and penalties. Hutcheson put his emphasis on man's passions towards altruism and cooperation.[9]

Therefore, it was natural that, from the outset, Hutcheson continued Carmichael's practice and based his teaching upon *De Officio*. He used Carmichael's edition with his *Notes and Supplements*. He held Carmichael in high regard and claimed that he was 'by far the best commentator on that book [Pufendorf's De Officio]' and that his lecture notes were so good that they were 'of much more value than the text'. Hutcheson (1747: i). It is therefore clear that he was greatly influenced by both Pufendorf and Carmichael. Brown (2002: 18) quotes a student in Hutcheson's class in the beginning of the 1740s 'He teaches Mr. Carmichael's Compend on Pufendorf, and speaks with much veneration of him [Carmichael]'.[10]

David Murray (1927: 508) contends that Hutcheson lectured on Pufendorf's *De Officio* until 1742. During these years, he developed his own lecture notes, which were published as a compendium, *Philosophiae Moralis Institutio Compendiaria*. This student textbook was, as pointed out by William Scott (1900), first published as a compendium in 1742, without his authorization. A new edition, with his consent, was published in 1745. This edition was translated by Hutcheson, or supervised by him, and published in English in 1747 as *A Short Introduction to Moral Philosophy*. As a student textbook, it became very popular and was published in three editions in Latin and four editions in English. To sum up, Hutcheson made his students read and study Pufendorf's *De Officio*. When he lectured, first using as a textbook *De Officio* and later his own compendium, he makes it clear to his students where he deviated from Pufendorf. Furthermore, he urged his students to find the sources and study them carefully.

By 1734–35, Hutcheson had already begun writing a manuscript called *A System of Moral Philosophy*, which he used in his lectures. It contains, according to Mautner (1999: 261), 'an attempt to give a utilitarian interpretation of the current ideas of natural law and natural rights'. It rejects Hobbes's view of man's unsocial nature. This work was, as also noted by Daniel Carey (2000: v), 'by no means identical' with his compend.[11] However, it remained un-published during his lifetime despite the fact that an almost complete version had circulated among friends from 1737. His son, Francis Hutcheson MD, published it posthumously in 1755, nine years after his death.

Moral Philosophy becomes Ethics, Government and Political Economy

With Carmichael and Hutcheson's use of Pufendorf's works on natural law in their classes, the term 'natural law' was replaced by 'moral philosophy'. The transformation of natural law into moral philosophy, which also included political economy, was complete. However, this was not the only change that took place. Hutcheson's textbook, *A Short Introduction to Moral Philosophy*, was divided into three parts: Ethics and the Law of Nature, Economics, and Politics (Hutcheson 1747: i). Although the topics under each heading do not fully coincide with what would have been the division today, this division was important for the development of political economy as a science.

Hutcheson's textbook was based, as the preface candidly acknowledged, on Carmichael's edition of Pufendorf's *De Officio*. Hutcheson himself had no problems admitting this fact. In the preface, entitled 'To the Students in Universities' he writes:

> The learned will at once discern how much of this compend is taken from the writings of others, from Cicero and Aristotle; and to name no other moderns, from Puffendorf's smaller work, De officio hominis et civis, which that worthy and ingenious man the late professor Gerschom Carmichael of Glasgow, by far the best commentator on that book, has so supplied and corrected that the notes are of much more value than the text.
>
> (Ibid.)

He also asked the question why write a new 'compend' on a subject when there already exist many good ones. His answer was pedagogical: each lecturer must use his own judgement, his own methods, and create the best account of the subject that he thinks will appeal to his students. Furthermore, he also explained why he does not make references in this 'compend':

> The author once intended to have made references all along to the more eminent writers, ancient or modern, who treated the several subjects. But considering that this could be of no use except to those who have the cited books at hand, and that such could easily by their indexes find the corresponding places for themselves: he spared himself that disagreeable and unnecessary labour.
>
> (Ibid.: iii)

Hutcheson makes it clear that this elementary book is for the use of students and not for the learned. When a student has studied this introductory book well he should 'go on to greater and more important works' (Ibid.: iv).

A comparison has been made (Sæther 2016) between the chapters in Pufendorf's 'student edition' *De Officio* and the chapters in Hutcheson's *A Short Introduction to Moral Philosophy* which was published in 1747, and *A System of Moral Philosophy*, which was published by his son in 1755.

It is clear that Hutcheson in his books follows the outline and structure of Pufendorf's *De Officio* almost chapter by chapter. This is also noted by Stephan Buckle (1991: 54), in his *Natural Law and the Theory of Property*. However, it is not only the outline of Pufendorf he follows; a closer inspection shows that Pufendorf's influence is much stronger. The contents of many chapters are simply a free translation of Pufendorf *De Officio* with the addition of some parts from *De Jure Naturae et Gentium*. Where he deviates, Hutcheson follows in many instances Carmichael's comments, or the comments of Pufendorf's French editor and translator Barbeyrac, in his French editions of Pufendorf's natural law works. Here it is important to remember that Pufendorf's *De Officio*, is an abridged version of his major work, *De Jure Naturae et Gentium*. Hutcheson was familiar with this work and used it in both his lectures and his writings.

Not many authors have studied the relationship between Pufendorf, Carmichael and Hutcheson. However, a few important sources should be mentioned. Richard Teichgraeber (1986: 21) writes that the chief sources of Hutcheson's and Smith's thinking were two seventeenth-century figures who, until very recently, have not figured prominently in the history of eighteenth-century English-speaking thinkers, Grotius and Pufendorf. They both reflected in their writings 'a great debt to these highly revered natural law jurists'.

Enzo Pesciarelli (1989: xviii) claims that Pufendorf's influence on Hutcheson through his teacher, 'Master Carmichael', who she calls 'a divulger in Scotland of the works and thoughts of Pufendorf', was important. Hutcheson's dependence on Pufendorf is also emphasized by Knud Haakonssen (1996: 65): 'It is incontrovertible that Hutcheson in his published work both criticizes the theory that morality is dependent upon law and expounds a system of natural jurisprudence which is largely derived from that of Pufendorf.'

Hutcheson built on Pufendorf

There has also been some discussion of how much Hutcheson built on Pufendorf, and if their deviations and disagreements were of such magnitude that they should not be considered belonging to the same school of thought. Mautner (1996: 194) has examined this issue and concluded:

> An underlying consensus between the various commentators is, however, to be expected, even if there are disagreements on particular points. A professor who radically disagreed with Pufendorf would have no reason

> to adopt and lecture on De officio in the first place. The disagreements, therefore, are of the kind that arise within a school of thought, not the kind that divide different ones.

Few economists or historians of economic thought today seem to be aware of, or are unwilling to acknowledge that, Hutcheson's writings, as pointed out above, are directly influenced by Pufendorf's natural law works. This direct influence is also clearly indicated by William Taylor (1965) and Mautner (1986).[12] The influence from Pufendorf is particularly noticeable when Hutcheson discusses issues of political economy. Table 19.1 shows where the topics of political economy can be found in Pufendorf's and Hutcheson's texts.

Although Hutcheson mostly followed Pufendorf, this inquiry will acknowledge some important issues where their views departed and he developed his own theories.

Theory of Human Behaviour

Hutcheson departed from Pufendorf when he developed his theory of human behaviour. He could not agree with Pufendorf's emphasis on self-interest as a driving force in human behaviour. Mautner (1986: 129) and Ian Simson Ross (2010: 49) have examined Hutcheson's inaugural lecture *On man's natural sociality.*[13] Hutcheson made it clear that he wished to continue the tradition of his former teacher Carmichael, in making the staple of his courses the classical Stoic tradition, revived in the seventeenth century by Grotius' and Pufendorf's analysis of the social nature of man. Here he argues that there are altruistic tendencies in the human frame, which cannot be reduced to or derived from motives of self-interest. He mentions the Epicureans, Hobbes

Table 19.1 A comparison of political economy in *De Officio* with Hutcheson's two books

Topic of political economy/Books	*De Officio Hominis et Civis*	*A Short Introduction to Moral Philosophy*	*A System of Moral Philosophy*
Theory of Human Behaviour	Book I. Ch. 1–7	BI. Ch. I–VI, BII. Ch. V	BI. Ch. 2,3,4,5,9,10,11
Theory of Property and the Four-Stage Theory	Book I. Ch. 12,13	BII. Ch. V, VI	BII. Ch. 7, 8
Theory of Value and Money	Book I. Ch. 14,15	BII. Ch. XII, XIII	BII. Ch. 12,13
Foundation of States and Councils	Book II. Ch. 5–10	BIII. Ch. IV–VIII	BIII. CH. 4–9
Division of State Powers and Taxation	Book II. Ch. 11, 12	BIII. Ch. VII, VIII	BII. Ch. 3 BIII. Ch. 9

and Pufendorf, as holding the opposite view. In this lecture Hutcheson publicly expresses criticism of Pufendorf. This was probably necessary since, there was a lot of scepticism towards Pufendorf's ethical views. among the clergy of different denominations. Hutcheson therefore put his emphasis on man's passion towards altruism and cooperation which, he argued, are the major sources of society and of the capacity of human beings to live together amicably and constructively.

> There are other still more noble senses and more useful: such is that sympathy or fellow-feeling, by which the state and fortune of others affect us exceedingly, so that by the very power of nature, previous to any reasoning and meditation, we rejoice in the prosperity of others, and sorrow with them in their misfortune; as we are disposed to mirth when we see others cheerful, and to weep with those that weep, without any consideration of our own Interest.
>
> (1969 [1747]: 14)

He also maintained that human motivation and man's conception of right and wrong are innate and not acquired. This was also the view expressed by Carmichael, but in sharp contrast to Pufendorf's, who claimed that 'no actual understanding of those things has been implanted by nature'. For him, man had to be educated to be able to act well in society.

Theory of Property

In his theory of property, Hutcheson (1969 [1747]: 150) departed from Pufendorf and, following Carmichael, built on Locke's labour theory of property. 'Now no man would employ his labours unless he were assured of having the fruits of them at his own disposal; otherways, all the more active and diligent would be a perpetual prey, and a set of slaves, to the slothful and worthless.' This is also noted by Stephen Buckle (1991: 54) in his book *Natural Law and the Theory of Property Grotius to Hume.*

A stadial theory of development cannot be found in Hutcheson's work, but it is of interest to note that he, in *A System of Moral Philosophy* (ibid.: II.iv), discusses the advantages of the division of labour. This he could not have found in Pufendorf, who only stresses the importance of cooperation among men in a commercial society, but does not develop this any further.

Theory of Value, Money and Trade

Hutcheson outlines his theory of value and money in *A Short Introduction to Moral Philosophy.* His chapter *Of the Values of Goods and of Coin* (1747: II.xii) is for example, with some small adjustments, mostly taken from Carmichael's *Commentary*, more or less a free translation of Pufendorfs *De Officio* (Book I, ch.14).[14] One of the adjustments is that he explicitly uses the term 'demand', which Carmichael had introduced in brackets in his Latin edition of *De Officio*. Like Pufendorf, he is aware of the 'Paradox of value' and he also warns against debasement of money. 'No state which holds any commerce with its neighbours can at pleasure alter the values of their coin in proportion to that of goods' (II.xii.14: 212).

Foundation of States and Council

Pufendorf's theory of the foundation of states has a rather pessimistic starting point. People took to founding states because 'they might fortify themselves against the evils which threaten man from man' (*De Officio* II.v.7). This was changed by Hutcheson to a more positive view: 'Tis highly probable therefore that not only the dread of injuries, but eminent virtues, and our natural high approbation of them have engaged men at first to form civil societies' Hutcheson (1747: III.iv:280). Thereafter, Hutcheson follows Pufendorf closely in his belief that two contracts and a decree in between the two are necessary.

> First a contract of each with all, that they shall unite into one society to be governed by one council. And next a decree or ordinance of the people, concerning the plan of government, and the nomination of the governors; and lastly another covenant or contract between these governors and the people, binding the rulers to a faithful administration of their trust, and the people to their obedience.
>
> (1747: III.v: 286)

In *A Short Introduction* Hutcheson (2000 [1747]: III.vi.292) claims that when power is committed to a council, the will of the state is determined by the majority unless a supermajority is required. He also touches on the problem when a question of three or more parts are put to the vote. This is very close to Pufendorf in his *De Officio* (II.vi.12.108). In his *System*, built on his lecture notes 1734–35, he has some more illustrative descriptions, probably derived from Pufendorf's *De Jure Naturae* (VII.ii.16–18, 990–993). It is always understood that if there are no special limitation in the constitution 'the majority of the council have the right of determining the matters proposed' (1747: III.vi.1: 240). The will of the council is that 'which has the plurality of votes'. However, he recommends that a certain number of the council members should be present to make the council the proper representation; 'otherwise different small cabals at different times may make the most contrary decrees' (ibid.: 241). It is also highly prudent that, when decisions are going to be made in affairs of great importance, more than a bare majority should be requisite, 'such as two-thirds, or three-fifths; 'particularly in altering any of the ancient laws, or in condemning any person impeached' (Ibid.). He also stresses that precautions should be taken against an obvious fallacy if there are three propositions to be voted on. In a council of a hundred there might be thirty-four favouring one proposition and thirty-three favouring each of the other two. The result being that thirty-four might decide against sixty-six. Such cases may generally be reduced; first into a simple question of two parts, and when one of these have been determined, it may be subdivided again into another question of two parts if necessary. The same method should take place in the elections to offices where there are three or more candidates. There should first be a vote to decide the two candidates with most votes. The candidates with fewest should be left out in the decisive vote between the other two.

Division of State Powers and Principles of Taxation

The powers that are requisite for governing a people are the power of making laws, the power of exacting revenues, the executive power, and the power of making treaties (ibid.: 288–289).

The forms of states that Hutcheson discusses are the same as Pufendorf's: monarchy, aristocracy and democracy, although he subdivides them differently. A monarchy can be either absolute, when the whole administration 'is committed to the prudence of the monarch', or limited, when 'certain rights are reserved for the people' (1947: III.v: 298). Each of these can be subdivided into hereditary or elective. The elective princes can be chosen for life or for a certain term. Likewise, there can be several kinds of aristocracy. It can be absolute or limited, hereditary or elective, perpetual or temporary. If it is temporary and new senators are elected by the people and any free citizen may stand as a candidate, the council is rather democratic. There are also, he claims, different kinds of democracies.

After a discussion of the advantages and inconveniences attending each of the forms of government, Hutcheson expresses a preference for a mixed form of government. A brief outline may be of interest. Hutcheson's government consists *of a council of delegates*, an *assembly*. This assembly should be duly elected by a general popular vote. Furthermore, he contends that 'it seems advisable that a large share of the civil power should be lodged in such a body; such as that of enacting laws and even determining definitively the most weighty affairs of deliberation' (ibid.: 300). It should also have *a senate of a few*, whose members should have approved their abilities and fidelity 'in discharging the great offices of the common-wealth' (ibid.). This senate should be entrusted 'with the sole right of deliberating, debating and proposing business to the popular assembly' (ibid.). In both the assembly and the senate it may be proper to contrive a rotation, new members gradually succeeding the old so that neither of the councils have more than one-third inexperienced members. And lastly to take care 'for sudden unexpected exigencies or dangers, and for secret and speedy execution of what the publick interest may require', some sort of *regal power* is requisite. The regal power has its foundation in the laws of the country and its power 'may be committed to the command in war and the execution of laws'. This branch may also be an arbitrator and hold the balance between the assembly and the senate (ibid.: 301).

When a state has been established with its proper government, Hutcheson follows Pufendorf and claims that it had the right to exact tributes from its subjects by law. However, this right is not unconditional. What is exacted should not be more than what is requisite for the prudent administration of public affairs.

In his *System of Moral Philosophy* Hutcheson outlines his principles of taxation.[15] Here he mainly follows Pufendorf's theories in *De Jure Naturae et Gentium*. In a short and concise sentence, he explains that taxes should preferably be levied on luxuries rather than on necessities, on imports rather than exports. 'As to taxes for defraying the publick expenses, these are most convenient which are laid on matters of luxury and splendour, rather than the necessaries of life; on foreign products and manufactures, rather than domestic' (1755. III.7: 340). He stresses that duties on imports are often necessary to encourage industry at home. 'Goods prepared for export should generally be free from all burdens of taxes' (ibid.). Unmarried people should pay higher taxes than married since 'they are not at chance of rearing new subjects to the state' (ibid.: 319).

Taxes, as also emphasized by Pufendorf, should be economical in the sense that they should be; 'easily raised without many expensive offices for collecting them.' Hutcheson emphasized that taxes should be just. 'But above all, a just proportion to the wealth of people should be observed in whatever is raised from them' (ibid.).

To obtain a just tax system it will be necessary with a census or 'an estimation made of all the wealth of private families'. Such a census should be carried out at frequently recurring periods, once in five, six or seven years. Hutcheson's view on the necessity of a census is interesting since Pufendorf contends that it would be most difficult for a state to find out every citizen's yearly income, 'nor could a general property census be taken so often'.[16] Hutcheson claims that with a census, it would be conceivable to have a tax system where all are 'burdened proportionally to their wealth' (ibid.: 341). Furthermore, it would be possible to have a tax system that is not oppressive and that no one pays more than their neighbours do.

Hutcheson's Influence

Hutcheson was a reformer and a libertarian who believed like Pufendorf that the world could, and should, be better organized by application of reason. It was, according to Edwin George West, Hutcheson and not Jeremy Bentham (1748–1832) who originated the famous phrase, 'the greatest happiness of the greatest number' (1976: 42–43).

We know that Smith and David Hume (1711–1776), also a friend of Hutcheson, had a very high opinion of their mentor, and both were greatly influenced and inspired by him. There is good reason to believe that Hutcheson made not only Smith but all his students familiar with the works of the natural law philosophers in general and Pufendorf's works in particular. Alec

Lawrence Macfie (1952: 127) writes that Smith's indebtedness to Hutcheson 'is certainly greater than a mere reference to sources can show.' West (1976: 42) in his book *Adam Smith the Man and his Works* wrote that there is no doubt that Smith was greatly influenced by several of his teachers at University of Glasgow, the most influential being 'his never to be forgotten teacher' Professor Hutcheson. 'It is certainly from him that our economist seems to have acquired the feeling and respect 'natural liberty and justice'. Pesciarelli (1989: xix) claims that Hutcheson transmitted to Smith, Pufendorf's way of thinking, and in particular; 'a view of society represented as an enormous arena of dealers, buyers and sellers'. Hutcheson, being Smith's predecessor in the Glasgow chair exerted positive influence on his students in general and Smith in particular.

Hutcheson's importance as an author, a professor and successful teacher at the University of Glasgow was recognized even in his own time. The university made him serve on numerous university committees. He carried substantial, although controversial, weight in the creation of a new, more liberal 'forward university policy'.

As mentioned, Hutcheson drew many students to the university and to his own lectures in moral philosophy. Many of these students, who also belonged to important families with power, took up later in life, important positions in politics, public administration, and college or university education, both in the United Kingdom and in the colonies. One student that entered the university in 1737 and took up a seat in Hutcheson's class in moral philosophy was Adam Smith. There can be no doubt that Hutcheson had a profound influence on Smith, and this will also be discussed in some details in the next chapter.

Here it should, however be mentioned that Robert William Scott (1900: 230–33) in his Hutcheson biography, compares his *Introduction to Moral Philosophy* (1747) and *System of Moral Philosophy* (1755) with Adam Smith's works. He found that the economic topics such as division of labour, theory of value, money, state and foreign trade, and maxims of taxation discussed by Hutcheson are repeated by Smith in his *Lectures on Jurisprudence* and again in *The Wealth of Nations.* Scott realized that Hutcheson's *System of Moral Philosophy* contained many reproductions of the views of Pufendorf, Grotius and Locke upon 'Politics and Economics'. However, he seems to be unaware of how closely Hutcheson builds on Pufendorf. His argument is rather weak:

> It might, of course, be contended that Smith consulted the authorities direct; but when it is remembered that he heard these very passages read and expounded in the Glasgow classroom, and further that the System of Moral Philosophy was published a few years after his appointment to the Chair of Moral Philosophy, when he would be preparing his own lectures, it seems reasonable to trace Hutcheson's influence here.
>
> (Ibid.: 231–232)

Today Hutcheson is by many seen as the forerunner of the social theories of the Scottish Enlightenment. These theories gained influence far beyond the borders of Scotland. According to many, e.g. Donald Winch (1978) and David Norton (1982), he influenced both Hume's *A Treatise of Human Nature* and Smith's *Wealth of Nations.* The question of who influenced Adam Smith will be discussed in the next chapter.

His influence in America was considerable. Hutcheson's compendium, *A Short Introduction to Moral Philosophy*, was used as a textbook at several American colleges, e.g. College of Philadelphia, College of New Jersey (Princeton University), Harvard College, in the second half of the eighteenth century. Norman Fiering (1981: 199) in his *Moral Philosophy at Seventeenth-Century Harvard* claimed that Hutcheson was 'probably the most influential and respected moral philosopher in America in the eighteenth century'.

Several of the Founding Fathers therefore had a good general knowledge of the ideas of the moral philosophers and in particular Pufendorf and Hutcheson. Garry Wills in his *Inventing America* from 1978 argues that the phrasing of the Declaration of Independence was due largely to Hutcheson's direct influence. A comparison of Hutcheson's favoured government with the constitution of the United States unveils also an astonishing degree of compatibility.[17]

Notes

1 Bernard Mandeville was born in Rotterdam and studied philosophy and medicine at University of Leiden in the 1690s. He married an English woman and moved to England in 1699. There he took up the practice of what today probably would be called psychiatry. Mandeville is best known for his pamphlet *The Grumbling Hive* from 1705. From this small poem he developed his major work *The Fable of the Bees: or Private Vices, Public Benefits* which first appeared in 1714. This was expanded in subsequent editions in 1723, 1724 and 1725. In this fable, a beehive, where all lived virtuously, was poor, while a beehive, where all lived in vice driven by self-interest, was rich. This view came under severe criticism and it was denounced as immoral. Outrage and condemnation came from churches of all denominations across Europe. Mandeville sought to vindicate himself from these severe attacks in *The Fable of the Bees, Part II 1714–1729*, and in some smaller publications. Like most of his contemporaries, Mandeville made few references to his sources or to other writers. There can, however, be no doubt that during his studies at Leiden he had been acquainted with Pufendorf's natural law works. A quotation clearly indicates this: 'Men are naturally selfish, unruly creatures, [and] what makes them sociable is their necessity and consciousness of standing in need of other's help to make life comfortable. And what makes this assistance voluntary and lasting are the gains for profit accruing to industry for services done to others, which in a well-ordered society enables everybody, who in some thing or other will be service able to the public, to purchase the assistance of others.' Here quoted from Hutchison (1988: 117). The argument of the fable, expressed in the subtitle *Private Vices, Public Benefits*, created from 1730 and onwards a heated debate all over Europe. In the 1924 edition of Mandeville's Fable of the Bees, the editor F.B. Kaye (1924: cxxxiv) claims that Mandeville had a profound influence on Smith. 'Mandevlle's treatment of division of labour must have Made an especial impression on him, for one of the most famous passages on this matter in *The Wealth of*

Nations – that about the labourer's coat – is largely a paraphrase of similar passages in the *Fable*.'

2 Peter Kivy (1973), in his 'Note on the text' to *An Inquiry Concerning Beauty, Order, Harmony and Design* argues that the view held by some 'that Hutcheson was not a first-rate moral theorist in his own right can no longer be sustained'.

3 Francis Hutcheson *On the Social Nature of Man* (*De Naturali hominum Socialitate Oratio Inaugurlis*) 1730. It was reprinted by the Foulis Press in 1756.

4 It can be claimed that Hutcheson had no choice. He had to dissociate himself from some of Pufendorf's opinions if he wanted a position at the university.

5 Leechman 1754 in the Preface (xi) to Hutcheson's *A System of Moral Philosophy.*

6 Gladys Bryson (1945: 8): *Man and Society; the Scottish Inquiry of the Eighteenth Century.* Here quoted from Hutchison (1988: 35).

7 *The Encyclopedia of Philosphy*, 1967, Vol. 4.

8 The University of Glasgow Library confirms that Pufendorf's natural law works, in all probability, were parts of its collection when Hutcheson was a student.

9 A. Sæther (1994), 'The Model of Human behaviour in Adam Smith and Samuel Pufendorf'. Paper presented at the History of Economic Society Meeting, Babson College, Boston, 1994.

10 Wodrow (1843: 191): 'About this time [i.e. 1730] Mr Hutcheson comes to Glasgow … He teaches Mr Charmichaels's compend and Puffendorf and speaks with much veneration of him, which at least is an evidence of his prudence.'

11 Hutcheson (2000 [1747]), Introduction by Daniel Carey.

12 Thomas Mautner (1986: 130) discusses the differences between Pufendorf and Hutcheson on jurisprudence. He points to some important differences and claims that Hutcheson, maybe without knowing it, has no genuine right theory. He concluded his analysis with these words: 'On its arrival in Great Britain modern natural law theory was quickly and quietly pruned. What was presented as jurisprudence was in fact almost from the outset a utilitarism in disguise.'

13 Hutcheson, *De naturali hominum socialitate oratio in auguralis*, 1730, pp. 10–11.

14 This view has also been noted by Luigi Cossa, *An Introduction to the Study of Political Economy*, London, 1893, p. 251, here taken from Raymond de Roover (1974: 303). Terence Hutchison (1988: 194) confirms this view when he writes that Hutcheson's chapter on value and price follows Pufendorf's 'fairly closely, indeed almost word for word at some points'.

15 Short Introduction III, ch. 8: 329.

16 DJNG VIII.v.6: 1284.

17 The claim that there has been such a direct and distinctive influence has been hotly disputed, according to Mautner (1993: 5).

20 Pufendorf as a Predecessor of Adam Smith

A Biographical Sketch

An investigation into Adam Smith's important sources should start with a short biography. Smith matriculated, at the late age of 14, in the University of Glasgow. Here he took up a place in Professor Hutcheson's class in moral philosophy in 1737. The textbook used was Carmichaels edition of Pufendorf's *De Officio*.

At Glasgow Smith studied under several members of the academic staff, but two had, in particular had a major influence on him. These were Professor Robert Simson (1687–1768), who taught mathematics, including Eucludean geometry,[1] and, most notably in this connection, Professor Francis Hutcheson, who taught moral philosophy.

Smith completed his course for the Master of Arts degree and graduated in 1740. Being one of the best students, he won a Snell Exhibition Scholarship to Balliol College, Oxford. The scholarship was for eleven years, and a candidate was expected to take up a position in the Presbyterian Church on completion. Smith, however, changed into a study course of civil law, and furthermore decided to leave in the sixth year. His years at Oxford were long and not very happy with apparently no visits home in the interim. Later he spoke very harshly of the anti-Scot prejudice of the professors. He also mentioned that their rather boring lectures could not inspire him. Balliol College at that time was not the institution it is today. James Mosh (1885: 164) tells us in his *Scottish Philosophy*, that when the heads of the college found Smith reading Hume's *Treatise of Human Nature*, they seized the work and reprimanded the youth.

However, Smith used the libraries to read Greek, Roman and modern literature, studied the works of the natural law philosophers and in particular Samuel Pufendorf, and expanded his language knowledge, particularly French. In August 1746 he returned to Scotland as a well-educated academic.

The next two years he spent quietly at home, but undoubtedly continuing his studies. In 1748, he was invited by a local philanthropic society to give a series of lectures in Edinburgh. He moved to Edinburgh and in the next years, he delivered lectures on rhetoric, belles-lettres and jurisprudence.

In 1751, Smith accepted an offer of a chair in logic at the University of Glasgow. After only a year he moved to the chair in moral philosophy, which his former teacher Hutcheson had occupied. In the moral philosophy course, he lectured on the same topics as Hutcheson before him. Thomas Mautner (1986: 121) points out that parts two and three of Hutcheson's compendium *A Short Introduction to Moral Philosophy*, in which natural jurisprudence is expounded, was the text that Adam Smith agreed to teach when he was appointed to the university. He adds, 'there is unmistaken traces of it in his later lectures on jurisprudence'. Smith therefore used Hutcheson's compend together with his notes from his lectures in Edinburgh. In the next few years, he developed his own lecture notes, and based on these, published *The Theory of Moral Sentiments* in 1759. This book covered the ethical part of his course. The book turned out to be a success.[2] It was widely praised and gained quite an audience and it saw six editions in Smith's lifetime.

The book ends with a promise to produce a further book on jurisprudence but unfortunately he did not keep his promise. However, in 1895 Professor Edwin Cannan (1861–1935) became aware of a manuscript, which according to the title page consisted of jurisprudence or 'Notes from the lectures in Justice, Police, Revenue and Arms' delivered by Adam Smith. This manuscript relates to lectures he held in 1763–64. In 1958, the late Professor John M. Lothian (1896–1970) discovered two sets of lecture notes made by former students of Smith. One related to Smith's lectures on rhetoric and belles-lettres as delivered in 1762–63, and the other to his lectures on jurisprudence delivered at the same time.[3] It should also be mentioned that another important manuscript has been found. It probably dates from before 1763[4] and has been given the title 'An Early Draft of Part of the Wealth of Nations'.[5]

During the 1750s and 1760s Smith produced some smaller dissertations and essays, the best known being 'A dissertation on the Origin of Languages and an Essay on the History of Astronomy'. Smith held many important positions at the university and was, for example, elected both Dean and Vice Rector.

In 1764, he resigned from the university and accepted a position as tutor to the young Duke of Buccleuch. Together, they toured France, Switzerland and Italy. The last nine months they stayed in Paris where he met and discussed political economy with François Quesnay, Anne Robert Turgot and others belonging to the Physiocrats. Smith returned to his home town in 1767.

A generous pension from the Duke enabled Smith to spend the next years writing. This led to the publication of *An Inquiry into the Nature and Causes of the Wealth of Nations*, in 1776. In his lifetime, Smith saw five editions of this book in English, and translations into German, Danish/Norwegian and French.

In 1778, at the request of the Duke of Buccleuch, Smith was appointed Commissioner of Customs for Scotland and he moved to Edinburgh, taking his mother with him. He held this appointment until his death in 1790. Finally, it should be mentioned that Smith in 1787 was elected to the honorary position as Rector Magnificus of the University of Glasgow.

Who Influenced Adam Smith?

Adam Smith's *The Wealth of Nations* earned him tremendous fame and a reputation as The Father of Modern Political Economy. It was also in 2012 named among the 100 Best Scottish Books of all time. An investigation into the sources that Smith used in his writings has been carried out by Sæther (2017). Since Smith's biographers and editors of his books can reveal important clues of the sources he used, four biographers and five editors have been examined and a short summary is presented.

Biographers and Editors of Adam Smith

The biographies in this investigation were Dugald Stewart (1794), John Rae (1895), William R. Scott (1937) and Ian Simpson Ross (2012). They all stress that Smith was influenced by his teacher Francis Hutcheson. The two first, Stewart and Rae, do not at all look into the texts that Hutcheson used. Scott acknowledged that Hutcheson used Pufendorf's *De Officio* as a textbook but claims that the economic sections in this book are few. Ross claims that Smith had been stimulated by Hutcheson's analytical treatment of economics and he allows that Hutcheson had been inspired by Pufendorf's treatment of the principles of political economy, However, this does not lead to an investigation into Pufendorf's possible influence on Smith.

This investigation also surveyed the introduction written by five editors of Adam Smith's *Lectures on Jurisprudence, The Theory of Moral Sentiments* and *The Wealth of Nations.* These editors are: Edwin Cannan (1904), Andrew Skinner (1970), Ronald L. Meek, David D. Raphael and Alec L. Macfie (1978), David D. Raphael and Alec L. Macfie (1982), and finally David D. Raphael (1991).

In his edition of *The Wealth of Nations* from 1904 Cannan sets out to trace Smith's sources. First he absolves the Physiocrats. Thereafter he points out that Smith might have evolved his theories entirely in his own mind. He dismisses Hutcheson as a major source, since he could not accept self-interest as a driving force behind human behaviour, but stops with Bernard de Mandeville. Cannan does not seem to be aware of Pufendorf's emphasis on self-interest and that both Smith and Mandeville had studied his works. Cannan's edition was reissued in 1937 with an introduction by Max Lerner and in 1976 with a preface by George J. Stigler. These economist's point to self-interest as the foundation of Smith's analysis. However, neither Lerner nor Stigler speculate on who could have been his source. Pufendorf is not mentioned.

A new edition of parts of *The Wealth of Nations* was published in 1970 with Andrew Skinner as editor. Skinner successfully tries to elucidate the interconnections that exists between Smith's two books and he concludes that his *The Theory of Moral Sentiment* has much in common with his Scottish contemporaries. In his treatment, he does not include any thorough discussion of Smith's sources. He seems to believe that Smith's basic ideas were home-grown. None of the natural law philosophers or other continental philosophers are mentioned.

In 1991 David D. Raphael edited a new edition of *The Wealth of Nations.* He claims that Smith received his initial stimulus from Hutcheson. He also mentioned David Hume but concludes that it was the Physiocrats that had most influence on Smith's economics.

David D. Raphael and Alec Lawrence Macfie were co-editors of a new edition of *The Theory of Moral Sentiments* published in 1982. The primary source of Smith's ethical thoughts, they claim, is predominately Stoic and he often refers to Plato, Aristotle and Cicero. In addition, they claim that Smith could have been stimulated by his disagreement with Hume, and there were a few issues on which he could have been affected by other lesser-known contemporaries. Faint echoes of Mandeville and Rousseau are also in evidence. They also mention that Smith draws on the natural law philosopher's Grotius and Pufendorf. However, there are no further investigations or discussions of how he was influenced by these scholars.

In 1978 Ronald L. Meek, David D. Raphael and Alec L. Macfie were co-editors of Smith's *Lectures on Jurisprudence.* They have investigated Smith's sources in these lectures using textual analysis, and they found clues to Grotius, Pufendorf, Locke, Montesquieu, Hume and Hutcheson. There are, however, only a few of these clues where Smith treats issues of political economy. Furthermore, they seem to be unaware of the fact that Grotius was Pufendorf's most important source and that he was the main source for Locke, Montesquieu and Hutcheson.

Pufendorf – Adam Smith's Primary Source

Pufendorf is not seen as a primary source for Adam Smith by any of the explored biographers or editors, although Pufendorf's natural law works must have been familiar to Adam Smith. Attention should therefore be focused on the evidence of Smith's knowledge of Pufendorf.

First, Carmichael's Latin edition of *De Officio* was Smith's textbook in his first year obligatory course in moral philosophy, taught by Hutcheson. Smith therefore had to study this book carefully. When Hutcheson deviated from the textbook, which he did on the question of self-interest as a driving forces behind human behaviour, he probably urged his students to investigate the sources.

Second, in his last year at Glasgow, Smith benefited from Hutcheson's teaching of 'a private class' on the lessons of the law of nature and nations. No textbooks are mentioned but it is not unreasonable to assume that the major natural law works of Grotius and Pufendorf were referred to. Books that could be studied in the university library.

Third, in his fourth year at Oxford Smith chose to follow the path of a student in civil law. In this direction, the study of the natural law philosophers was compulsory. Their natural law books could be found in both the Balliol and the Bodleian Library.

Fourth, it is important to point out that Smith acquired a copy of Pufendorf's major work *De Jure Naturae et Gentium* before he gave his lectures in Edinburgh. A French translation with Barbeyrac's comments could also be found in his private library. In this work, which is a jewel, not only because of its scholarship but also because it serves as a reference for the works of the moderns, the Scholastics, the Greeks, the Romans as well as the writings in the Old and New Testament and the Koran. In this work Smith could find both the inspiration and the first access to important references for his own works. It is therefore reasonable to assume that Smith had Pufendorf's natural law works ready at hand when he prepared his lectures and wrote his books.

Fifth, Smith in his Edinburgh freelance lectures in 1750–51 taught the Grotius-Pufendorf tradition of the laws of nature and nations. He therefore had to use the works of these scholars when he prepared his lectures. In addition, he had his notes from Hutcheson's classes, the books Hutcheson had authored, and Locke's *Two Treatises of Government*, all of which were strongly influenced by Pufendorf.

Sixth, in Smith's first lectures on jurisprudence at the University of Glasgow from 1752 he used Hutcheson's Latin *Compendium* from 1742 as his textbook, together with his own Edinburgh lecture notes. This compendium built very closely on Pufendorf's natural law works and in some sections Hutcheson just copied him.

All these points, one by one and together, *suggest* that Adam Smith, early on, became familiar with Pufendorf's natural law works, including substantial tracts of political economy, and that he used them extensively when he prepared his lectures in Edinburgh and Glasgow.

It is recognized by most writers who discuss Smith's sources that his books have their point of departure in his lecture notes. Therefore, it is surprising that only a few authors point to Pufendorf as one of his primary sources.

Adam Smith, as with most of the eighteenth-century authors, very reluctantly relinquished the names of the literature that he had at his disposal and used. He was not a writer that overwhelmed his readers with numerous citations and references in his books. Therefore, the lack of such citations and references do not communicate anything about his use of the literature he had at his disposal in general and in particular Pufendorf's works.

Smith refers only twice to Pufendorf in *The Theory of Moral Sentiments.* He presents him first together with Mandeville as a follower of Hobbes, who claimed that man is driven to take refuge in society, not by any natural love to his own kind, 'but because without the assistance of others he is incapable of subsisting with ease or safety'.[6] Second, he presents him together with Barbeyrac and Hutcheson, in a discussion of how different authors have treated the practical rules of conduct.[7] In his *Lectures on Jurisprudence*, in which Pufendorfian natural law including political economy, is predominant, there are five direct references to Pufendorf. First, in a discussion about a man's natural rights. Second, in a discussion of how Hutcheson follows Pufendorf on rights. Third, in a discussion about the property of the state.

Fourth and fifth, in a treatment about testamentary succession in *The Wealth of Nations* we do not find any direct references to Pufendorf. Although strong elements of Pufendorfian natural law also can be found in this work.

The lack of recognition of his use of Pufendorf does not, however, tell us anything about Pufendorf's influence on Smith. There are paragraphs, sections, and other clues and allusions in all of Smith's work that point directly to both Pufendorf's *De Officio* and *De Jure Naturae et Gentium*. Pufendorf must therefore have had a strong influence on Smith.

At the time when Smith wrote his books, Pufendorf's natural law works had been translated into several European languages. They were also published in new editions with or without commentaries and reprinted repeatedly. His views were known not only to university academics but also to many educated people outside the closed university circles. Smith could therefore have assumed that his readers would have known his sources without him explicitly making references to them.

Pufendorf and Smith on Political Economy

Table 20.1 shows where the topics of political economy can be found in Pufendorf's natural law works and in Smith's *Lectures on Jurisprudence* and *The Wealth of Nations.*[8]

A comparison of Pufendorf's and Smith's doctrines of political economy are outlined in the next sections.

Table 20.1 Political economy in Pufendorf's and Smith's works

Topics	*De Jure Naturae et Gentium*	*De Officio Hominis et Civis*	*Lectures on Jurisprudence*	*The Wealth of Nations*
Theory of Human Behaviour	Book I. i–iv Book II i–iv Book III i–ii	Book I. Ch. 1–7	A: iii.1–147 B: Pt.II.203–209, 326–333	Book I.i–ii
Theory of Property Four-Stage Theory	Book IV. iii–v Book V. v	Book I. Ch.12–13	A: i.16–167, iv.23–40, 113–179 B: Pt.I.19–75, 149–175	Book I.x–xi Book V.i.2
Theory of Value and Money	Book V. i, iii, v, vii–viii	Book I. Ch. 14–15	A: vi.1–171 B: Pt.II.203–306	Book I.i–vii, ix–x Book II.ii
Foundation of States & Councils	Book VII. i–ii	Book II. Ch. 5–10	A: i.66, iv.1–122, v.1–149 B: Pt.I.12–99	—
Division of State Powers & Taxes	Book VII. iv–v Book VIII. iv–v. Book V. x	Book II. Ch. 11–12	A: iv.1–179, v.100–139, vi.84–86 B: Pt.I. 18–99, Pt.II.310–321	Book IV. ix Book V. i. Pt. i–iv V. ii. Pt. i–ii

Notes: In the column on the *Lectures on Jurisprudence* 'A' relates to his lectures 1762–63 and 'B' relates to his lectures 1763–64 (The so-called 1766 report).

Theory of Human Behaviour

Smith's *The Theory of Moral Sentiments* is an inquiry into the origin of moral approbation and disapproval that is moral judgement. He must have had *De Jure Naturae et Gentium* ready at hand when he wrote the book. He is clearly influenced by Pufendorf (DJNG II.iv.14–15) when he, at the outset, asks the fundamental question regarding how man, who is basically a creature that tries to pursue his own self-love or self-interest, can form moral judgements in which self-interest seems to be checked or transmuted to a higher plane? His answer is clear:

> How selfish soever man may be supposed, there are evidently some principles in his nature, which interest him in the fortune of others, and render their happiness necessary to him, though he derives nothing from it except the pleasure of feeling it.
>
> (TMS.I.i.1: 9)

This feeling for others, which he called sympathy, is to be found in all men. 'The greatest ruffian, the most hardened violator of the law of society, is not altogether without it' (ibid.). The term sympathy is clarified in the following way:

> Pity and compassion are words appropriated to signify our fellow- feeling with the sorrow of others. Sympathy, though its meaning was, perhaps, originally the same, may now, however, without much impropriety, be made use of to denote our fellow-feeling with any passion whatever.
>
> (Ibid.: 10)

Smith claims, like Pufendorf (DJNG II.iii.14), but contrary to Hutcheson, that self-interest is a primary drive in all human beings.

> Every man is, no doubt, by nature, first and principally recommended to his own care; and as he is fitter to take care of himself than of any other person, it is fit and right that it should be so. Every man therefore, is much more deeply interested in whatever immediately concerns himself, than in what concerns any other man; and to hear, perhaps, of the death of another person, with whom we have no particular connexion, will give us less concern, will spoil our stomach, or break our rest much less than a very insignificant disaster which has befallen ourself.
>
> (TMS.II.ii.2: 82–83)

Every man may be the whole world to himself, his own happiness may be of more importance to him than that of the rest of the world. However, it may be true that every individual in his own breast naturally prefers himself to all humankind, 'yet he dares not look mankind in the face, and avow that he acts according to this principle' (ibid.). Self-interest is therefore not the only human drive. Furthermore, self-interest is not incompatible with sympathy or benevolence. These basic motives live side by side, and each has its part to play at the appropriate time. This view is in sharp contrast to Hobbes, Mandeville and Hume, who argued that all our sentiments can be deduced from certain refinements of self-love. However, it is in accordance with Pufendorf's views on self-interest and sociability: 'By a sociable attitude we mean an attitude of each man towards every other man, by which each is understood to be bound to the other by kindness, peace, and love and therefore by a mutual obligation' (DJNG.II.iii.15: 208).

To explain how individual self-love is checked and brought down to something that can be accepted by all men in society, Smith introduces the concept of a supposedly well informed or 'impartial spectator' within everyone who would judge, approve or disapprove his actions along with the concept of 'fair play' that governs the interactions between all men in society (TMS.II.ii.2: 83). The allusions to Pufendorf (DJNG.I.iv.1), who introduced an 'internal moderator' or 'internal director' of a man's action that would make it possible for him to choose what would seem most suitable to him, are clear.[9] The impartial spectator of Smith's may then enter into the principles of man's conduct, 'which is what of all things he has the greatest desire to do, he must, upon this, as upon all other occasions, humble the arrogance of his self-love, and bring it down to something which other men can go along with' (TMS.II.ii.2.1: 83).

How this can be understood in business life, he explains in the following way.

> In the race for wealth, and honours, and preferments, he may run as hard as he can, and strain every nerve and every muscle, in order to outstrip all his competitors. But if he should justle, or throw down any of them, the indulgence of the spectators is entirely at an end. It is a violation of fair play, which they cannot admit of.
>
> (Ibid.)

Like Pufendorf (DJNG.II.i.5–6: 15), Smith contends that men are social beings, and social beings are dependent on each other: 'It is thus that man, who can subsist only in society, was fitted by nature to that situation for which he was made. All members of human society stand in need for each other's assistance, and are likewise exposed to mutual injuries' (TMS.II.ii.3: 85).

It is not possible for man to grow up to manhood 'in some solitary place'. When he is brought into society, he is able not only to view his own passions, guided by the 'impartial spectator', but also to adjust and moderate these passions in accordance with other members of society (TMS.III.1.3: 111).

According to Smith, man is not endowed by nature with an innate moral sense. He has to be educated, i.e. brought into society with others. This is again in opposition to Hutcheson but in accordance with Pufendorf (DJNG. II.iii.13).

Smith also discusses in what order individuals are recommended by nature to our care and attention.

> Every man, as the Stoic used to say, is first and principally recommended to his own care; and every man is certainly, in every respect, fitter and abler to take care of himself than of any other person. Every man feels his own pleasure and his own pains more sensibly than those of other people. The former are the original sensations; the latter the reflected or sympathetic images of those sensations. The former may be said to be the substance; the latter the shadow.
>
> (TMS.VI.ii.1.1: 219)

After him comes the members of his own family: his parents, his children, his brothers and sisters, his earliest friendships, the children of brothers and sisters and so on.

> After the persons who are recommended to our beneficence, either by their connection to ourselves, by their personal qualities, or by their past service, come those who are pointed out, not indeed to what is called, true friendship, but to our benevolent attention and good offices; those who are distinguished by their extraordinary situation; the greatly fortunate and the greatly unfortunate, the rich and the powerful, the poor and the wretched.
>
> (TMS.VI.ii.1: 225)

The question concerning what motivates human actions is also discussed in Smith's *Lectures on Jurisprudence.* In these lectures self-interest is also looked upon as a general universal principle. He discusses human motives whenever commerce is introduced into a country. These motives can be reduced to self-interest: 'that general principle which regulates the actions of every man, and which leads men to act in a certain manner from views of advantage'. The drive of self-interest is deeply implanted in 'an Englishman as a Dutchman' (LOJ.Pt.II: 327).

In *The Wealth of Nations*, Smith discusses the principle which gives occasion to the division of labour.[10] The allusion to Pufendorf (DJNG.II.iii.14: 207), who emphasized the importance of cooperation among men, is there when Smith stresses that men at all times and contrary to animals, who in their natural state have no occasion for the assistance of other living creatures, are 'in need of co-operation and assistance of great multitudes' (WN.I.ii.18).

Smith starts out claiming that the division of labour is not originally the effect of any human wisdom. 'It is the necessary, though very slow and gradual, consequence of a certain propensity in human nature which has in view no such extensive utility; the propensity to truck, barter, and exchange one thing for another' (Iibid.: 17). This propensity is self-interest, and it is common to all men. However, man has almost constant occasion for the help of fellow man, and he cannot expect this help from their benevolence only. 'He will be more likely to prevail if he can interest their self-love in his favour, and show them that it is for their own advantage to do for him what he requires of them' (ibid.: 18). When someone offers another a bargain, this is what takes place. If you give me what I want, I will give you what you want. Then he comes up with one of his most famous statements:

> It is not from the benevolence of the butcher, the brewer, or the baker that we expect our dinner, but from their regard to their own interest. We address ourselves, not to their humanity but to their self-love, and never talk to them of our own necessities but of their advantages.
>
> (Ibid.)

With his *Theory of Moral Sentiments* and *The Wealth of Nations* Smith made self-interest an acceptable drive for modern man. He used Pufendorf's theory of human behaviour, that is, his theory of the self-interested social man, who by satisfying his own needs also satisfies the needs of others, in a commercial society, to construct his own theory of economic growth in such a society. Hont in his *Jealousy of Trade* from 2005 claims that: 'Smith's contemporaries recognised that the famous passage on the benevolence of the butcher, the brewer and the baker was a direct comment on the central issues of natural law' (2005: 162).[11]

Theory of Property and the Four-Stages Theory

In his *Lectures on Jurisprudence* Adam Smith develops his theory of property. He starts out claiming that: 'The first and chief design of all civil governments, is, as I observed, to preserve justice amongst the members of the state and to prevent all encroachments on the individuals in it, from others of the same society' (1978 [1762]: 7). That is to maintain everyone in his perfect rights. He considers in the first place those rights that belong to a man as a man, 'as they are generally most simple and easily understood, and generally can be considered without respect to any other condition' (ibid.: 8). He contends and discusses that these rights correspond to what Pufendorf (DJNG IV.iii.1–6) calls natural rights. Furthermore, he observes the distinction, 'which Mr. Hutcheson, after Baron Puffendorf, has made of rights' (ibid.: 9).

One of the rights is the full right of property. By this right, a man has the sole claim to a subject, 'exclusive of all others', but he himself can use it as he pleases. By this right, he can, if he has lost a subject, claim it from any possessor and, though the possessor might have come justly by it, he cannot claim any restitution but must restore it to the owner. Property is considered as an exclusive right by which we can prevent any other person from using it (ibid.: 10).

How did the right to property originate? Smith asserts that: 'The only case where the origin of natural rights is not altogether plain, is in that of property.' He continues in the spirit of Pufendorf (DJNG IV.iii.1): 'It does not at first appear evident that, e.g. any thing which may suit another as well or perhaps better than it does me, should belong to me exclusively of all others barely because I have got it into my power' (ibid.: 13). He uses an apple as an example. Why should it be altogether appropriated to me and all others excluded merely because I had pulled it from the tree?[12]

Property may, according to Smith, have its occasion in five sources. First by occupation, we get a thing in our power that was not the property of another before. Second by tradition, property is voluntarily transferred from one to another. Third by accession, a man has, e.g. the right to the horse's shoes along with the horse. Fourth by prescription, a right to a thing that belonged to another, arising from long and uninterrupted possession. Fifth by succession, the nearest in kin or the testamentary heir gets the property left to him by the testator.

The Four-Stages Theory

Before considering these causes of how property are acquired, Smith asserts, like Pufendorf, that it is proper to observe that the regulations concerning them vary according to the state or age society is in at that time. What Smith had in mind was an inductive historical investigation, which could explain the fact that, while property was everywhere seen as an exclusive right, those goods men have allowed to be property, varied considerably 'according to the state or age society is in at that time' (ibid.: 14). He claims, like Pufendorf in his rudimentary theory (DJNG IV.iv.11–13 and V.v.11) that there are four distinct stages that humankind has passed through; '1st, the Age of Hunters: 2ndy, the Age of Shepherds; 3rd, the Age of Agriculture; and 4th, the Age of Commerce' (ibid.).

Smith, with strong allusions to Pufendorf, then explains in more detail each of these ages or stages and how a society, with limited resources 'in a process of time as their numbers multiplied' would move from one stage to the other and how property developed in each (ibid.: 14).[13] 'It is easy to see that in these several ages of society, the laws and regulations with regard to property must be very different' (ibid.: 16). Few laws and regulations are required in the age of hunters and shepherds, but in the age of agriculture and commerce many more laws and regulations are necessary. When flocks and herds come to be reared, property is introduced together with many more laws and regulations. They are necessary to prevent thefts and robberies since they are being easily committed in such an age. In the age of agriculture, they are perhaps not so easily exposed to thefts and robbery, but new ways are added whereby property might be disrupted. The laws might not be so rigorous but they will be of a far greater number than among a nation of shepherds. In the age of commerce, the subjects of property are greatly increased and the laws must be proportionally multiplied. 'The more improved any society is and the greater length the several means of supporting the inhabitants are carried, the greater will be the number of their laws and regulations necessary to maintain justice, and prevent infringements of the right of property' (ibid.).

Property as an Exclusive Right

Smith, like Pufendorf (DJNG.IV.iv.6), asks how occupation, that is the bare possession of a subject, comes to give us an exclusive right to the subject so acquired. How can a man by pulling down an apple have a right to that apple and a power of excluding all others from it, 'and that an injury should be conceived to be done when such a subject is taken for [from] the possessor' (ibid.: 17).

Here again Smith makes use of the impartial spectator. If someone has acquired a subject by occupation, and if others try to take it from him, the impartial spectator would support him in defending his property 'and even in avenging himself when injured' (ibid.: 17).

After having explained the foundation on which occupation gives the property to the occupant, he considers and discusses in some detail at what time property is conceived to begin by occupation. Thereafter he discusses in what circumstances property continues and at what time it is supposed to be at an end (ibid.: 18).

Property Based on a Common Consent or Agreement

Adam Smith does not directly use Pufendorf's tacit pact or agreement (DJNG IV.iv.4–9) as a foundation of his theory of property. However, there are allusions and clues that indicate that he comes close to it. He introduced the notion of common consent.

Among hunters, the notion of property seems at first to have been confined to one's person, his clothes and the tools that he needed. Their occupation led them to be continually changing their place of habitat. The introduction of shepherds made habitation more fixed but still very uncertain. By consent of the tribe, have their huts been, allowed to be the property of the builder. 'The introduction of the property of houses must have therefore been by the common consent of the severall members of some tribe or society' (ibid.: 21). However, property would still not be extended to land or pasture.

Even after the introduction of agriculture it took some time before the land was divided into individual properties. In the beginning, the land was cultivated in common and the produce distributed according to the size of families and the rank of individuals. The inclination of a single individual would not be sufficient to give him ownership of a piece of land. The rest of the community would protest against him who tried to make common land private.

The first origin of private property would probably happen when men started to live in cities, 'which would probably be the case in every improved society' (ibid.: 22). In time, property would be extended to almost every subject. Yet Smith, like Pufendorf (DJNG IV.v.2), claims that there are still some things that must continue to be held in common. He discusses wild beasts, the air, running water, the waters of rivers, and sailing on the open sea (ibid.: 23).

Later Smith divided the nature of rights into natural and acquired. The latter are divided into real and personal. Property is a real right. Among savage people, hunters and gatherers, property begins and ends with possessions, which are things close to their own bodies. Among shepherds, the idea of property is extended not only to what they carry with them, but also to what they have deposited in their hovels, including their cattle. When people started to cultivate the earth, there was initially no private property. However, when proper agriculture was introduced, land was divided and property begins when 'a division be made from common agreement' (ibid.: 460), The allusions to Pufendorf, who claimed that 'dominion presupposes absolutely an act of man and an agreement, whether tacit or express', are very strong (DJNG IV.iv.4: 536). Smith ends this discussion contending that property would, in time, be extended to almost every subject.

A Labour Theory of Property?

Smith has in his *The Wealth of Nations* one sentence concerned with property. 'The property which every man has in his own labour, as it is the original foundation of all other property, so it is the most sacred and inviolable' (1976 [1776]: I.x.136). This has by some authors been interpreted as an adherence to Locke's labour theory of property, a theory that Smith took over from Hutcheson and he again from Locke. However, Knud Haakonssen (1989: 106–107) has questioned this belief and contends that Smith does not subscribe to this theory. Furthermore, he posits that Smith was obviously very strongly indebted to the continental natural law tradition of Grotius, Pufendorf, and others, and especially to the form, which this tradition has been given him by his teacher Hutcheson. Pufendorf claims that cultivation, which requires the use of labour, is important for the establishment of private property (DJNG IV.iv.6).

Theories of Value, Money and Trade

Smith treats the theory of value and money in both his *Lectures on Jurisprudence* and *The Wealth of Nations.* It is clear that Smith in both books made good use of Pufendorf's natural law works. This is recognized by Marian Bowley in her *Studies in the History of Economic Theory before 1870*, from 1973 and Istvan Hont in his *Jealousy of Trade* from 2005. Bowley asserts that Smith was the conscious or unconscious heir in the direct line to the schoolmen with respect to the concept of the price mechanism and the natural prices of commodities. 'Indeed, since Hutcheson, his teacher, made him familiar with Pufendorf's work, which set out the views of the Schoolmen, the line of affiliation of thought seems obvious' (1973: 129). Hont points out that Smith's two books, *The Theory of Moral Sentiments* and *The Wealth of Nations*, 'together provide a complete analysis of market behaviour.' He adds that in these works 'Smith merged and reworked insights that were first adumbrated by Pufendorf, Nicole and other French moralists' (2005: 51).

Value and Money in Lectures on Jurisprudence

In his *Lectures* Smith (1978 [1762]: 353) discusses opulence. Here he first considers the rule of exchange, or what it is that regulates the price of commodities. Next, he notes that money can be considered the measure by which we compute the value of commodities (as a measure of value) or the common instrument of commerce or exchange. There can be no doubt that Smith must have had Pufendorf's main natural law work *The Jure Naturae et Gentium* (V.i) accessible when he prepared his lectures. The obvious reason being that he went further than Pufendorf's abridged *De Officio* and Hutcheson's *Introduction to Moral Philosophy*. The latter built, as discussed earlier, very closely on Pufendorf's works.

Natural Price and Market Price

As an introduction, Smith gives an account of the nature of wealth and the things in which the riches of the state might consist. He notes the need for cooperation in a commercial society, which was stressed by Pufendorf. But, Smith also asserts that a division of labour and an ample size of the market are crucial for economic development.

For every type of commodity Smith claims, as did Pufendorf (DJNG V.i.8–9), that 'there are two separate prices to be considered, the natural and the market price' (ibid.: 356). The first is the price that is necessary to induce someone to enter a business. This price includes the cost of production and the associated risk of going into production. The market price, which might differ considerably from the natural price, 'is regulated by other circumstances' (ibid.: 357). The other circumstances that determine the price are: '1st, the demand or need for it; 2dly, the abundance of it in proportion to demand; and 3dly, the wealth of the demand, or demanders' (ibid.: 358). Smith then discusses, in the same manner as Pufendorf (DJNG V.i.10), how changes in these circumstances will influence the market price. The market price and the natural price of commodities relates to each other. If the market price of a commodity is below the natural price, the suppliers cannot pay the cost of labour. This will have many effects. One being that the supply of the commodity is reduced and the price will increase. If the market price was above the natural price the effect will be the opposite.

The Paradox of Value

If a thing is of no use, such as a lump of clay, but is brought into the market, it has no price, as no one demands it. If it should have some use, the price will be determined by the demand and the availability of supply. Something like diamonds, which is hardly of any use but still has a demand, will have a high price since the quantity is limited. On the other hand, water is a necessity but will have no price because of its abundance (ibid.: 333). This description of what has become the 'paradox of value' cannot have been taken from Hutcheson but there are strong clues to Pufendorf's treatment (DJNG V.i.6).

Monopolies

Smith, like Pufendorf (DJNG V.i.6), claims that all monopolies limit the supply and raise the price of commodities and therefore are detrimental to the opulence of a nation. As an example, Smith mentions the Hudson Bay Company. In his view, such companies prevent free competition that free competition would have brought down the price to its natural level, a level consistent with production costs and the risk the company runs. All such companies are a public nuisance (ibid.: 363).

Money Promotes Commerce

As it was for Pufendorf, it is also clear to Smith that money facilitated exchange and promoted commerce. He uses the same arguments as Pufendorf (DJNG IV.i.12–14) when he claims that money serves two purposes. 'It is first the measure of value'. But 'it is also the instrument of commerce, or medium of exchange and permutation' (1978 [1762]: 368).

It is necessary that the government of a country should carry the trouble and expense of coining money out of gold and silver and put a stamp on it. The stamp given by the government 'gives no additional value, it merely ascertains the value' (ibid.: 373). The motive is that money promotes commerce, which will enrich the people and thereby also benefit the government, since it facilitates taxes. Reduction in the value coins has often been caused by either the necessities or frauds of government.

Debasement of Money

Smith therefore brings up for discussion the effects of debasement of money and its effects on the payments of debts and commerce. 'And here civil law of all countries and natural justice and equity are quite contrary' (ibid.: 100). It is therefore clear that Smith, as Pufendorf considered debasement of money to be against natural law. 'Justice and equity plainly require that one should restore the same value as he received without regard to the nominal value of money, and therefore he is to restore as much in the old coins or an equal value in the new as he received' (ibid.: 101). Smith adds: 'But the civil government in all countries have constituted the exact contrary of this' (ibid.). The reason for such conduct is that governments have had difficulties in raising money. He stresses and shows, like Pufendorf (DJNG V.i.14), that such steps are very detrimental to commerce. 'The effects of this operation is very prejudiciall to commerce. The great benefit of money is to give a plain, clear, and ready measure of value and medium of exchange for all commodities; but this is considerably disturbed by this means' (ibid.: 374). When an alteration is made in the value one does not readily know whether the new coin 'is equal to a certain value; this necessarily embarrasses commerce' (ibid.: 375). He claims that it is necessary that all debts should be paid by the value of the old money.

Money and Trade

Smith claims, as did Pufendorf (DJNG V.i.11–12) before him, that money is extremely necessary as an instrument for trade. 'The intention of money as an instrument of commerce is to circulate goods nec(e)ssary for men, and food, cloths and lodging' (ibid.: 377). He stresses that it is not the money, 'which makes the opulence of a nations, but the plenty of fodd, cloaths and lodging which is circulated' (ibid.: 378). He attacks the theory that placed the wealth of a nation on its amount of coin and money. Trade increases the wealth of a nation. The prohibition of exportation of coin and bullion is therefore one of these hurtful regulations that has been practised by many countries.

Money and Value in *The Wealth of Nations*

In *The Wealth of Nations*, Smith discusses both the origin and use of money, and the theory of value. His discussion is based on his *Lectures*. He contends that when the division of labour has been thoroughly established only a small part of what a man wants is the produce of what his own labour can supply. He will then exchange a part of his produce with what other people can supply. 'Every man thus lives by exchanging, or becomes in some measure a merchant, and the society itself grows to what is properly a commercial society' (1976 [1776]: 26). Different societies have used different commodities as a method of exchange; the most practical is money coined from gold and silver. Smith, like Pufendorf, warns also here against debasement of money, which is favourable to the debtor, and ruinous to the creditor.

In all civilized nations has money become the universal instrument of commerce, in which goods of all kinds are bought and sold, or exchanged for one another. The rules of exchange determine what may be called the relative or exchangeable value of goods. The word value has two different meanings. Sometimes it expresses the utility of some objects and sometimes the power of purchasing other goods with that good:

> The one may be called 'value in use;' the other, 'value in exchange'. The things which have the greatest value in use have frequently little or no value in exchange; and on the contrary, those which have the greatest value in exchange have frequently little or no value in use.
>
> (Ibid.: 32–33)

He then presents the 'paradox of value'.

> Nothing is more useful than water but it will purchase scarce any thing; scarce any thing can be had in exchange for it. A diamond, on the

> contrary, has scarce any value in use: but a very great quantity of other goods may frequently be had in exchange for it.
>
> (Ibid.: 33)

The Labour Theory of Value

However, Smith changes his mind from his *Lectures* and introduces, as did Locke, a rudimentary labour theory of value:

> If among a nation of hunters, for example, it usually costs twice the labour to kill a beaver which it does to kill a deer, one beaver should naturally exchange for or be worth two deer. It is natural that what is usually the produce of two days or two hours labour, should be worth double of what is usually the produce of one day's or one hours labour.
>
> (Ibid.: 53)

Since labour is not the same in all production he modifies this view; 'the produce of one hour's labour in the one way may frequently exchange for that of two hours labour in the other' (ibid.: 201).[14]

The Natural and the Market Price

Smith starts out claiming that in every society there is an ordinary or average rate for wages, profit and rent in every different employment of labour, stock and land. 'These ordinary or average rates may be called the natural rates of wages, profit and rent, at the time and place in which they commonly prevail' (I.vii.62). He then, more or less in the same way as Pufendorf (DJNG V.i.8), defined the natural price:

> When the price of any commodity is neither more nor less than what is sufficient to pay the rent of the land, the wages of labour and the profits of the stock employed in raising preparing and bringing it to market, according to their natural rates, the commodity is then sold for what may be called its natural price.
>
> (Ibid.)

The commodity is then sold precisely for what it is worth, or for what it really costs the person, who brings it to the market. This cost does not comprehend the profit to the person who is to sell it again. If he sells it at a price, which does not allow him the ordinary rate of profit in this society, he is evidently a loser by the trade. The price that includes the ordinary rate of profit is the lowest at which he is likely to sell for any considerable time. He adds, 'at least where there is perfect liberty' (ibid.: 63). Smith claims, like Pufendorf (DJNG V.i.9), that the actual price at which any commodity is commonly sold is called its market price. It may either be above, or below, or exactly the same as its natural price.

> The market price of every particular commodity is regulated by the proportion between the quantity which is actually brought to market, and the demand of those who are willing to pay the natural price of the commodity, or the whole value of the rent, labour, and profit, which must be paid in order to bring it thither.
>
> (Ibid.: 63)

Smith calls such people the effectual demanders and their demand the effectual demand.

Changes in the factors that determine the demand will change the market price. 'The natural price, therefore is, as it were the central price, to which the prices of all commodities are continually gravitating' (ibid.: 65). Sometimes the market price will be a little above and sometimes a little below, but the price will gravitate towards the natural price.

Smith then goes on to discuss what determines the wages of labour, the wages and profit in the different employments of labour, stock, and the rent of land.

Origin of Money and Debasement of Money

Smith's treatment of the origin of money follows his account in his *Lectures*, which built closely on Pufendorf's exposition. Money was introduced to facilitate exchange in a commercial society. 'It is in this manner that money has become in all civilized nations the universal instrument of commerce, by the intervention of which goods of all kinds are bought and sold, or exchanged for one another' (ibid.: 32). Smith takes a strong stand against the debasement of money. 'Such operations, therefore, have always proved favourable to the debtor, and ruinous to the creditor, and have sometimes produced a greater and more universal revolution in the fortunes of private persons, that could have been occasioned by a very great public calamity' (ibid.).

Smith makes it clear that the popular notion that wealth consists of money (or gold and silver) naturally arises from the double function of money, as an instrument of commerce and as the measure of value. However, it is not for its own sake that men desire money, but for the sake of what they can purchase with it.

Foundation of States and Councils

Smith claims in his *Lectures on Jurisprudence* that the first and chief design of a state or civil government is to preserve justice amongst the members of the state and to prevent all encroachments on the individuals in it from others in the same society (1978 [1762]: 7). He stresses that justice is violated whenever a man is deprived of what he had a right to and could justly demand from others. Then he discusses how many ways justice may be violated, i.e. in how many respects a man may be injured. He may be injured as a man, as a member of a family, and as a citizen or member of a state. The allusion to Pufendorf (DJNG VII.i.7), who claimed that states were established to gain security and protection from the evil or wickedness of men, is strong.

Smith came close to asserting, like Pufendorf, that private property arose from consent and agreement. However, he contended that the origin of government arose 'not as some writers imagine from any consent or agreement of a number of persons to submit themselves to such or such regulations, but from the natural progress which the men make in society' (ibid.: 207). However, from this starting point, he explains how a state and its different forms of government develop using the historical account of the four-stages theory of development, which he had inherited from Pufendorf. Numerous examples are described how different nations at various times have developed their governments and the powers of government, depending on what stage these nations have found themselves in.

There are two principles that explain why men enter into a civil society: a principle of authority and a principle of common or general interest.[15] With regard to the first principle, Smith claims that 'every one naturally has a disposition to respect an established authority and superiority of others, whatever they be' (ibid.: 318). With regard to the second principle, he claims that everyone sees that the magistrates not only support the government in general but the security and independence of each individual, and they see that this security cannot be attained without a regular government. 'Every one therefore thinks it most advisable to submit to the established government' (ibid.). In a monarchy, the principle of authority chiefly prevails. In a democracy, the principle of common or general interest is the most important. However, the principle of authority has some influence. In an aristocracy, the principle of authority is the leading one, but the other also has some effect. Smith stresses that all have a duty of allegiance to the sovereign: 'and yet no one has any conception of a previous contract either tacit or express' (ibid.: 321). He uses several lectures to argue against authors, such as Pufendorf, who believed in contracts.

Later in his 1763–64 lectures, Smith repeats this view: 'It has been a common doctrine in this country that contract is the foundation of allegiance to the civil magistrate' (ibid.: 402). Then he starts out arguing that this is not the case and gives several reasons for this. He concludes: 'Contract is not therefore the principle of obedience to civil government, but the principle of authority and utility formerly explained' (ibid.: 404).

Voting Rules

Smith brings up for discussion in one of his lectures the question of what determines the voice of the people in a republic that is an aristocracy or a democracy. It is clear that he used both Hutcheson[16]and Pufendorf[17] in the preparation of this lecture. 'It is a general rule that in every society the minority must submit to the majority' (ibid.: 290). However, it may often happen that the majority is not so easily determined. He uses the same numerical example as Hutcheson. There are three candidates A, B and C. A gets thirty-four votes out of hundred and B and C thirty-three each. A is chosen, although to sixty-six voters he might be the most obnoxious of all. Smith adds that this often happens in elections and that 'it is a very great grievance'. The solution when there are three candidates is to have a previous vote by which one candidate is excluded.

If this way of counting votes is used in a trial, it can have a grave result. Suppose someone is tried for murder and thirty-four out of a hundred find him guilty, thirty-three of manslaughter and thirty-three of chance-medley only. Although sixty-six absolve him from murder, he will be condemned if the questions are not made bipartite. First guilty of murder or not, the result will be acquittal. Next guilty of manslaughter or not, he will then be found guilty with sixty-seven votes.

If there is a draw when a council is voting, Smith claims, like Pufendorf (DJNG VII.ii.15), that no decision should be made. The question of super-majority, which is discussed by Pufendorf and Hutcheson, is not discussed by Smith.

In his *The Wealth of Nations* Smith discusses the duties of the sovereign and how sovereignty has developed. The first duty is that of defending the society from the violence and injustice of other states (1976 [1776].V.i.I: 213). The second duty is that of protecting, as far as possible, every member of society from the injustice or oppression of every other member in it (V.i.II: 231). The third and last duty is that of erecting and maintaining those public institutions and those public works, which may be in the highest degree advantageous to a great society (V.i.III: 244). Civil government supposes a certain subordination. The necessity of civil government gradually grows with the acquisition of valuable property. Some men will gain superiority or sovereignty over the greater part of their brethren. The leaders will have some or all of the four following characteristics; first, superiority of personal qualifications, of strength, beauty, and agility of body; of wisdom; and virtue, of prudence, justice, fortitude, and moderation of mind; second the superiority of age; third the superiority of fortune; fourth, the superiority of birth. Smith's discussion of the duties of the sovereign and subordination of the people gives allusions to Pufendorf's pact or agreement of subjection (DJNG VII.ii.7).

Division of Responsibility and Principles of Taxation

In his *Lectures* Smith gives numerous examples of how different nations at different times have developed their governments and the powers of government, depending on what stage these nations have been in. Like Pufendorf (DJNG.VII.iv.2–11), he treats the development of the executive power, the legislative power, the power of the magistrate and officers and the judicial power. He discusses the duties the subjects owe the sovereign power of whatever nature, 'the monarch in monarchy, the nobles in an aristocracy and the body of people in a democracy' (ibid.: 291). At length, he outlines the different forms of crimes that subjects might commit against the sovereign power. However, the subjects not only have duties they also have rights. He then discusses the duties that the sovereign owes to his people and he considers 'the crimes which the sovereign may be guilty of against the subjects' (ibid.: 304). The allusions to Pufendorf (DJNG VII.v.3–9) are everywhere to be found.

Taxation

In his *Lectures*, Smith starts out explaining why governments need revenue and he discusses the proper means of levying revenue, 'which must come from the people by taxes, duties etc.' (ibid.: 398). The allusions to Pufendorf (DJNG VIII.V.3–4) are numerous.

Smith's starting point is that revenue or taxes are one of the reasons 'that the progress of opulence has been so slow' (ibid.: 529). However, he continues and gives an account of how in the beginning there was no government revenue and no taxes, but when society developed 'magazines must be provided, ships built, palaces and other public buildings erected and kept up, and consequently a public revenue levied' (ibid.: 530).

There are many expenses necessary in a civilized country: 'Armies, fleets, fortified places and public buildings, judges and officers of the revenue must be supported, and if they be neglected disorder will ensue' (ibid.: 531). A land rent to serve all these purposes would be the most improper thing in the world.

Smith then claims that all taxes may be considered in two divisions: taxes upon possessions (land, stock and money) and taxes upon consumption. Subjects, therefore, can contribute to the support of the government through a land tax and/or a tax on commodities. In Britain, except for the land tax, most taxes are upon commodities. He discusses the advantages and disadvantages of these forms of taxation. It is easy to levy a tax upon land, but it is very difficult to lay a tax on stock and money 'without very arbitrary proceedings' (ibid.: 532). The land tax has the advantage that it is levied without great expense and tends not to raise the price of commodities, as it is raised in proportion to rent. Taxes upon possessions are naturally equal, but those upon consumption are naturally unequal. The advantage of taxes on consumption is that they are not felt, since they are 'being paid imperceptibly' (ibid.: 533).

The fifth book of *The Wealth of Nations* is devoted to public finance. It includes a review of considerable length of fiscal practices in England and other countries (1976 [1776]: 341–440). Harold Groves in his *Tax Philosopher* claims that Smith gave 'a great deal of advice on these matters, advice which was taken seriously by ministers and parliament' (1974: 18). In this exposition, Smith expands his treatment of taxation in his *Lectures*, for which Pufendorf (DJNG VII.ix.10 and VIII.v.3–7) was his major source.

Smith has both an extensive treatment of the sources of general revenue of the society and his principles of taxation. A society needs revenue for defence, for supporting the magistrates and for all other necessary expenses of government, for which the constitution of the state has not provided any earmarked revenue. The revenue, which must defray all the expenses of government, is the cost of defending the society and supporting the dignity of the chief magistrate and all other necessary expenses. The revenue that will cover these expenses comes from one of two sources. Either it comes from some funds, which belong to the sovereign, or commonwealth, and which are independent of the revenue of the people or it comes from the revenue of the people.

He then goes on to treat the funds, or sources of revenue, which belong to the sovereign or commonwealth. Next, he asserts that the private revenue of individuals arises from three sources: rent, profit and wages, and those taxes must be paid from some or all of these sources. He then endeavours to give an account of the taxes that will fall on each of these sources and those taxes, which will fall indifferently upon all these sources of private revenue.

Before Smith sets out to examine specific taxes, he informs his readers that many taxes are not ultimately paid from the sources of revenue, which they were originally intended. The reason, of course, is that market forces are at work.

As an introduction, he finds it necessary to put forward four maxims that apply to taxes in general. These maxims are very close to Pufendorf's principles of taxation expressed as the duties of the supreme sovereign (DJNG VII. ix.10). First, taxes should be 'equal and equitable'. They should fall on individuals 'like the expense of management to the joint tenants of a great estate, who are obliged to contribute in proportion to their respective interests in the estate'. Further, 'the subjects of every state ought to contribute to the support of the government, as nearly as possible in proportion to their respective abilities; that is in proportion to the revenues which they respectively enjoy under the protection of the state' (ibid.: 350). Smith, like Pufendorf, was a firm believer in proportionality in taxation and like Pufendorf (DJNG VIII. v.10) he supported a no tax or a minimal tax for poor people.

Second, taxes ought to be certain and not arbitrary. The time of payment, the manner of payment, and the quantity to be paid ought all 'to be clear and plain to contributor and every other person'. Otherwise, the taxpayer may be subject to extortionate administration. Smith claimed that the certainty of what each individual ought to pay is in taxation a matter of so great importance 'that a very considerable degree of inequality, it appears, I believe, from the experience of all nations, is not near so great an evil as a very small degree of uncertainty' (ibid.: 351).

Third, taxes ought to be levied at the time or in the manner in which it is most likely to be convenient for the contributor to pay it. Taxes on land or houses should be payable when rents normally are paid. Taxes on consumable goods and on luxury items are finally paid by the consumer, when he has occasion to buy the goods (ibid.).

Fourth, taxes should be economical to collect so that they take out of the pockets of the people, 'as little as possible, over and above what it brings into the public treasury of the state'. There are four reasons why taxes might be contrary to this principle. First, the levying of taxes may require a great number of officers, which have to be paid. Second, the taxes may obstruct the industry of the people. Third, the forfeitures and other penalties that tax evaders should have paid are in fact not paid since it ruined them, and hence no tax revenue is generated. Fourth, subjecting taxpayers to frequent visits and odious examinations by the tax collectors has a dampening effect on people's spirits and energy. Although this is not, strictly speaking, an expense it is certainly equivalent to the expense (ibid.: 351).

The clues and allusions to Pufendorf's treatment of taxation in his *De Jure Naturae et Gentium* are strong. Smith uses his four maxims on taxation and starts a comprehensive examination and evaluation of particular taxes, with examples from various political systems and different countries also using an historical context. His thoroughness in this exposition is impressive.

From this discussion, it should be clear that Adam Smith used Pufendorf's writings on political economy when he wrote his two books and when he held his lectures on jurisprudence at the University of Glasgow. Pufendorf's position in the history of economic thought should therefore be well established.

Notes

1 Mark Knell presented a paper entitled 'Isaac Newton, Robert Simson and Adam Smith', at the ESHET 2014 Conference in Lausanne. In this paper he claimed that Professor Simson had a profound influence on Smith's thought.

2 A second, revised edition appeared two years later in 1761.The third edition appeared in 1767, the fourth edition in 1774, and the fifth in 1781. These editions differ little from edition two. Edition six, which was published in 1790, contains extensive additions and changes.

3 Adam Smith's *Lectures on Rhetoric and Belles Lettres* has been edited by J.C. Bryce and was published by Oxford University Press in 1983. An exact photographic reproduction by Liberty Classics was published in 1985. The two discovered lecture notes on jurisprudence 1762–1763 and 1763–1764 have been edited by Meek, Raphael and Stein and published as *Lectures on Jurisprudence* by Oxford University Press, 1978. An exact photographic reproduction by Liberty Classics was published in 1982.

4 Ronald Meek and Andrew S. Skinner (1973: 1103) claim that it must have been written before 1763.

5 Published in William Robert Scott,*Adam Smith as Student and Professor*, 1965 [1937], pp. 317–356, or as an appendix to Meek, Raphael and Stein (eds), *Lectures on Jurisprudence*, 1982 [1762–1763], pp. 560–581. According to Raphael and Macfie (1982: 23), 'these documents show that Smith had gone a considerable way in his economic thinking by the time he left Scotland for France in 1764, and that this early material provided a sound foundation for developments which were certainly stimulated by the visit to France'.

6 TMS VII.iii.i.1.

7 TMS VII.iv.ii.11.

8 The *Theory of Moral Sentiments* is not included. However, it is this book that mostly contains Smith's Theory of human behaviour.

9 Pufendorf uses 'internal moderator' in his *Elementorum Jurisprudentae Universalis*, 2009 [1660, 1672], Book II, Obs. II.1, p. 306, and 'internal director' in his *De Jure Naturae et Gentium*, 1964 [1672] I.iv.1.

10 This chapter, Book I, ch. 2, is almost identical to the 'Early Draft of Part of The Wealth of Nations' from 1759 in *Lectures on Jurisprudence*, pp. 562–581.

11 Hont (2005: 162) mentions, as an example, Governor Pownall (1776), who wrote an open letter with comments to Smith after the publication of *The Wealth of Nations.* In the Danish-Norwegian edition and translation of *The Wealth of Nations*, 1779–1780, this letter is included.

12 Pufendorf used an acorn as an example (DJNG IV.iv.13: 554). Locke took over his example but extended it to acorns and apples (TT II.28: 306).

13 Ronald L. Meek (1976: 31–35) in his *Social Science and the Ignoble Savage* claims that the immediate source of Smith's 'four stages' probably was Montesquieu's *Spirit of the Laws*, Book XVIII. See also Ian Simpson Ross (2010: 121). This author disagrees with both Meek and Ross, since these stages are more developed in Pufendorf's *De Jure Naturae et Gentium*. In addition, Pufendorf was also Montesquieu's source. Another Scot who built on Pufendorf's four-stage theory was Lord Kames (1696–1782), who had studied law at Edinburgh. In his *Historical Law Tracts* from 1774 and in his *Sketches of the History of Man* he described human history as having four stages.

14 Pownall (1776: 341ff.) in his letter Adam Smith was the first to criticize his labour theory of value.

15 In his 1766 lectures he calls the second principle one of utility (ibid.: 401).

16 *A System of Moral Philosophy*, Book III.6: 241.

17 *De Jure Nanturae et Gentium*, Book VII.ii.15.987.

Part VII

How Could Pufendorf Be Overlooked?

Many authors have recognized Pufendorf's importance as a natural law or moral philosopher and his influence on many of his descendants. However, it is a fact that very few of these authors are economists, economic historians or historians of economic thought. The question why Pufendorf has been ignored by most authors of textbooks on the history of economic thought or by writers of books and articles concerned with Adam Smith's predecessors is not an easy one to answer.

This part has two objectives. The first is to analyse and evaluate to what extent Pufendorf has a place in textbooks of philosophy and in textbooks on the history of economic thought. The second is to survey a few books and articles concerned with the origin of classical economics, or more specifically, with Adam Smith's sources, and investigate to what extent Pufendorf is considered a source.

21 The Bedevilled Historians

It has previously been determined that Pufendorf in his *De Jure Naturae et Gentium* employed an eclectic method in which he defended man's ability to understand reality and to draw conclusions on the basis of observations from the reality of life. This ideal, or to be more exact, he uses this method of philosophy to develop his natural law theories, among them his theories of political economy. However, his way of reasoning was challenged.

At the end of the eighteenth century the German philosopher Immanuel Kant from Königsberg, East Prussia, lectured, researched and wrote on philosophy. Kant is considered one of the most influential critics of the natural law philosophy of the Enlightenment. Andreas Aure (2014: 70) contends that Kant in his famous tract on international law, *Zum Ewigen Frieden* (Perpetual peace) from 1795, scorned Grotius, Pufendorf and Vattel,[1] calling them miserable comforters because no state or ruler cares about their arguments.

More damaging to the natural law tradition, however, was Kant's denial of the possibility of making inferences from empirical reality or nature. Kant's major work, *Kritik der reinen Vernuft* (Critique of pure reason), first published in 1781, made him famous and he gained a tremendous influence on the development of philosophy. He claimed that: '*Jeder philosophische Denker baut, sozusagen, auf den Trümmern eines anderen sein eigenes Werk*' (Every philosopher built his work, so to speak, on the ruins of someone else's work).[2] Kant built on the apprehension that man does not have the faculty to comprehend reality and to draw conclusions from it. This view was in opposition to Pufendorf, who defended man's ability to understand reality, and to draw conclusions based on observations from the reality of life.

Unfortunately, Kant's view had a tremendous impact on the development of philosophy, on the writings on the history of philosophy, and unfortunately also on the writings of the history of economic thought.

The Bedevilled Historians of Philosophy

Richard Tuck (1987) claimed that the late eighteenth-century Europe witnessed, with the views of Kant and his followers, 'one of the greatest revolutions which have ever occurred in the writing of philosophy'. He boldly states: 'that the survival of the post-Kantian history into our own time has proved a great barrier to a genuine understanding of the pre-Kantian writers'. In his opinion, the character of this revolution is best appreciated by contrasting two works on the history of philosophy: first, Johann Jacob Brucker's (1796–1870) *Historia criticae philosophiae* (Critical history of philosophy) from 1742 to 1744 and second, Johann Gottlieb Buhle's (1763–1821) *Geschichte der neuern Philosophie* (History of recent Philosophy) in six volumes from 1800 to 1805. Both authors were recognized academics; Brucker was a parish minister and a member of the Academy of Sciences at Berlin, and Buhle a professor at Göttingen, Moscow and Brunswick. Their works were written to help philosophy students but both found a wider European audience. The structure and content of these two works are, however, startlingly different.

In Brucker's history his hero was Grotius, since he produced, in his *De Jure Belli ac Pacis*, a new system of ethics and advanced 'open eclecticism'. Grotius was closely followed by Selden, then Hobbes and, finally, Pufendorf. Brucker points 'to the strength of Pufendorf's genius, the clearness of his discernment, the accuracy of his judgment, and the variety and depth of his erudition'.[3] He ends it with a thorough discussion of Pufendorf's *De Jure Naturae et Gentium.*

A different story is told in Buhle's history of philosophy. He does not attempt to write a history of modern moral philosophy. The opposition of two schools, which are described as 'realists' and 'idealists', characterized modern philosophy, he asserts. According to Tuck (1987), these schools are 'empiricism' and 'rationalism'. They have, in his opinion, 'bedevilled the history of philosophy ever since'. Grotius, who was fundamental to Brucker's account of the modern theory of ethics, is treated with 'dramatic contempt' by Buhle. Pufendorf is cut off with a short life history and a summary of *De Officio.*

Tuck argues that it is in Buhle's account we find all subsequent general works on the history of philosophy. He continues: 'Grotius and Pufendorf have never re-emerged to take up places of honour in the history of modern philosophy. If they are mentioned, it is as late examples of scholasticism, and their modernity, which so impressed Brucker, is not taken at all seriously.' He concludes that a broader range of insights will be available to us once the post-Kantian history of morality is replaced with the pre-Kantian one. 'The moral theories of the late seventeenth- and eighteenth-century natural lawyers constituted, in many ways, the most important language of politics and ethics in Europe, influential over a huge area and in a wide variety of disciplines.'

Jerome B. Schneewind (1987) agrees with Tuck that Pufendorf was treated as a major figure in eighteenth-century writings on the history of ethics but unfortunately is 'largely forgotten by moral philosophers today'. As an example, he points first to a work by Christian Garve (1742–1799), *Ubersicht der vornehmsten Principien der Sittenlehre* (Overview of the principles of moral philosophy) from 1798. Here Grotius is the first modern philosopher. Pufendorf, as his follower, is treated at greater length. Schneewind then turns to Karl Friedrich Stäudlin (1761–1826)[4]and his *Geschichte der Moralphilosophie* (History of moral philosophy) from 1822, which he calls the first modern treatment of the history of ethics. Pufendorf is only given a page or two, as a follower of Grotius. Schneewind concludes: 'and that much, or less, is all that those interested in moral philosophy have gotten about him from their historians ever since'.[5] This unfortunate situation Schneewind wants to change – Pufendorf should be rescued from oblivion because knowledge of him is necessary if we wish to understand the history of ethics.

Tim J. Hochstrasser (2000) adds another writer W.G. Tennemann (1761–1819) with his *Geschichte der Philosophie* (History of philosophy), published in the years 1798–1819. He claims that Buhle and Tennemann only give extended discussions and summaries to those philosophers who have produced philosophical systems. In their works, 'there is no discussion of eclecticism for the simple reason that its very principles disqualify it. It does not conform to the epistemological system-building that these historians are looking for.' Pufendorf therefore has just a tiny place in their expositions.

The Hochstrasser view has been supplemented by Knud Haakonssen (2004). He notes that 'Samuel Pufendorf and Christian Thomasius, have not only been taken seriously as philosophers but have commonly been written out of the history of philosophy altogether, a process that had already begun with the Wolffian takeover of the German universities and has continued ever since.'

The German philosopher Georg Wilhelm Friederich Hegel (1770–1831), should also be mentioned in this context since he has had a huge impact on how the histories of philosophy have been taught. Hegel was not only a great philosophical thinker. He was also a committed teacher who had a firm idea of how to teach philosophy properly. Furthermore, he cherished the value of philosophy, not just to philosophers but also to society and culture as a whole. Philosophy was in his opinion the most important element in a liberal education. His lectures on the history of philosophy were delivered not to academic philosophers but to students. On this topic, he lectured students at the University of Jena 1805–06, the University of Heidelberg 1816–17, and the University of Berlin from 1819 to 1830.

Unfortunately, Hegel gave little attention to the philosophers who had been neglected by the Kantians. The reason was that, in his opinion, their thinking was insufficiently systematic. The eclectics were pre-eminent in this regard. In his *Vorlesungen über die Geschicte der Philosophie* (Lectures on the history of philosophy) published after his death, 1833–36, the natural law philosophers Grotius, Hobbes and Pufendorf are given respectively one, five and one page. Locke astonishingly dominates with twenty-three pages. However, it should be mentioned that Hegel had a low opinion of Locke's empiricism and eclecticism. Hegel believed that Locke's empiricism essentially denies the importance of metaphysics, and he also expressed only contempt for the eclectic tradition. Ironically, as Hochstrasser (2000: 219) has pointed out, Hegel *was* 'more than a little influenced by it [eclecticism] in the course of his education in the history of philosophy.'

A generation later, the German historian Christian Ueberweg (1826–1871) published in 1868 his massive multi-volume opus *Grundriss der Geschichte der*

Philosophie (Outline of the history of philosophy). In it he made do with merely nine lines for Pufendorf – in the chapter *Leibniz und gleichzeitige Philosophie und deutsche Philosophen des 18. Jahrhundert.*

Here it should be mentioned that there was another, but related, explanation why the philosophy of natural law was brought into discredit and almost disappeared for more than hundred years, i.e. the positivists and their followers, the Marxists. In the previous mentioned *Montesquieu and the Philosophy of Natural Law* Mark Adducer (1970) claims that the philosophy of natural law has 'suffered a fate that could hardly have been envisaged in the seventeenth and the eighteenth-century exponents of its universalities and eternity; it has become old-fashioned.' He contends that the positivists and the Marxists have been happy 'to throw eternal morality out of the window, confident that some magic temporal harmony would eventually follow Progress in by the front door.' Although their hopes may not have been fully realized, they did succeed in discrediting natural law.

Adducer emphasizes that what is often not appreciated is the extent to which we have adopted the tenets of the philosophy they despised, both in the fields of politics and in the field of personal and social ethics. This was what Barbeyrac called '*la science des moues*' and which the positivists rechristened 'social science'. Although we live in a world where freedom is largely a result of the popularization of the philosophy of natural law, and where conscious and unconscious standards are a result of that philosophy as it became combined with Christianity, the doctrine of natural law is largely forgotten or badly understood.

Furthermore, Adducer hoped that in view of the present trend toward a more balanced view of the Enlightenment the time had come for a less prejudiced and detailed study than hitherto have been attempted of Montesquieu's debt to the philosophy of natural law. Only then could his contribution to the history of ideas be properly assessed.

Philip Soper (1992: 2343) acknowledges a recent resurgence of interest in natural law, in both moral and legal theory. In legal theory, the return of natural law is a viable 'challenger' to positivism. In moral theory, however, the focus has been on natural law as 'a potential guide to fundamental question of morality or public policy'. Natural law has been assigned the role of a challenger to the reigning orthodoxy, rather than that of a defending champion.

Tuck (1987) in his article argued that the revolution in the writings of the history of philosophy, caused by Kant and his followers, almost eliminated the natural law philosophers, including Pufendorf, from the history of philosophy textbooks. What is not so familiar, he continues, is that the writing of the history of philosophy which was transformed about 200 years ago 'has remained in its new form ever since'. However, there are some optimistic signs. During the last twenty to thirty years it looks as though a new breed of philosophers has rediscovered the natural law writers and particularly Pufendorf. An increasing number of articles and books have been published where natural law, as it was presented by Grotius, Hobbes and Pufendorf, is given both a comprehensive and a systematic treatment. Hopefully, this will be reflected in future history of philosophy textbooks.

The Bedevilled Historians of Economic Thought

It is probably not only the historians of philosophy that have been bedevilled, in the sense that the natural law philosophers and Pufendorf in particular has been eliminated or reduced to what can be almost characterized as a footnote in their history of philosophy textbooks. This seems also to be the case with authors of textbooks on the history of economic thought.

A collection of forty-five textbooks on the history of economic thought has been investigated, Sæther (2017: 205–210). The purpose was to reveal to what extent authors of such textbooks are aware of Pufendorf's contributions to political economy and the influence he had on Montesquieu, Rousseau, Locke, Hutcheson and Smith.[6]

From this investigation, it can be concluded that the authors of thirty-one textbooks do not mention Pufendorf, the authors of seven books mention his name only in passing, another six finds it worthwhile to attach some importance to him, and in particular they mention his price-theory and that Smith could have gained something if he had paid attention to his views.

The author of only one out of the forty-five textbooks in this investigation has seriously discussed Pufendorf's important role in the history of economic thought. Terence Hutchison in his analysis *Before Adam Smith* (1988) tries, once and for all, to kill the myth that Adam Smith is the founder of economics as a science. He claims that Pufendorf deserves a significant place in the history of economic thought. 'The natural law doctrines expounded by Pufendorf, comprising ethics, law, politics and economics, amounted to a comprehensive theory of society.' However, surprisingly he only gives a detailed account of Pufendorf's theory of value.

From this study four conclusions can be drawn. First, not one of the surveyed forty-five textbooks gives a comprehensive exposition of Pufendorf's writings on political economy. Second, Samuel Pufendorf's writings on political economy, and his importance as a predecessor of, for example Locke, Montesquieu, Rousseau, Hutcheson, and not least Smith, are not generally recognized among the authors of these textbooks. Third, that most authors of such textbooks might have bedevilled, to use Richard Tuck's expression, the history in the way they have overlooked, underrated or downplayed Pufendorf's possible influence on Adam Smith, and his importance for the development of modern political economy. Fourth, of the nine textbooks published in this century six do not mention Pufendorf at all. Two mention his name in the passing. Only one, Sandelin *et al.*, finds it worthwhile to attach some importance to him and his works on political economy. This is, of course, unfortunate since most students of the history of economic thought get their first introduction by reading textbooks.

Notes

1 Emerich de Vattel (1714–1767), a Swiss philosopher and legal expert, known for his work *Droit des gens; ou, Principes de la loi naturelle appliqués à la conduite et aux affaires des nations et des souverains* (The law of nations or the principles of natural law applied to the conduct and to the affairs of nations and of sovereigns) from 1758. He was strongly influenced by the German philosopher Christian Wolff (1679–1754), who again was a follower of Pufendorf.
2 Immanuel Kant, *Gesammelte Schriften*, Band 9, Berlin, 1923, p. 25.
3 In W. Enfield (1837: 625). The English translation of Buhle (1744).
4 Karl Friedrich Stäudlin was, for thirty-six years, professor of theology at University of Göttingen. He wrote on Church history, moral theology and moral philosophy. On moral philosophy, he was a follower of Kant.
5 Schneewind points to several writers of the history of moral philosophy who ignore Pufendorf.
6 This is the author's collection of textbooks on the history of economic thought supplemented by some textbooks owned by friends and colleagues.

22 Have Economists Overlooked Pufendorf?

It is clear from this investigation that almost all authors of textbooks on the history of economic thought have neglected Pufendorf. His influence on Smith has only rarely been brought up. However, it is not possible from this fact to draw the conclusion that he has been forgotten by all or most economists that are engaged in exploring the sources of Smith's thought. It might be that their writings on the importance of Pufendorf's contributions to political economy and his influence on Smith, for reasons unknown, have not yet been discovered by authors of textbooks, and have therefore not been incorporated into their works.

In the 240 years since Smith published his *The Wealth of Nations* in 1776, many books and thousands of commentaries and articles have been published on the origin of classical economics and different aspects of Smith's writings. It is beyond the scope of this book to examine all these books and articles. A more limited task was to examine a small sample of prominent books that have been searching for the origin of classical economics. This examination will determine to what extent these authors recognize the importance of the natural law tradition for the development of political economy. Furthermore, whether these authors are aware of Pufendorf's contributions to political economy and his impact on Smith.

In addition, a sample of articles has been investigated. The Wood collection consisting of 225 articles concerned with Smith's writings was chosen. The purpose was to examine to what extent these articles discuss Smith's predecessors and if they recognize that Pufendorf had an important influence on his writings.

Books Examining the Origin of Classical Economics

Edgar A.J. Johnson in his book *Predecessors of Adam Smith: The Growth of British Economic Thought* (1937), surveys several authors whom he considers to be Smith's most important forerunners. In his otherwise thorough investigation there are no discussion of the natural law tradition and its influence on British economic thought. There is, amazingly, not a single reference to Pufendorf, or to his British followers Locke, Carmichael and Hutcheson.

William Letwin, in his *The Origins of Scientific Economics* (1963), starts out with the important question: how far back in the history of mankind should we investigate the origin of economics? He claims that a scientific theory must be a system produced by an act of invention and he concludes that: 'Before 1660 economics did not exist; by 1776 it existed in profusion.' He then, rather arrogantly, claims that the invention should have taken place in England, 'since seldom has a community been so fervently interested in both trade and science'. Several British authors belonging to what he calls 'the old style' are discussed. John Locke is included and he contends that: 'The doctrine of natural law, with its fusion of scientific principle and moral standard, Locke carried over into economics'. However, there are strangely enough no references to Locke's predecessor Pufendorf, whom he used extensively, or his Scottish followers Carmichael and Hutcheson.

Letwin ends his account with the following expression: 'All the efforts of seventeenth and eighteenth century economic writers culminated in the Wealth of Nations.' Smith incorporated everything useful that these writers provided. When they left something out, he accomplished it. However, it was partly due to luck that he found himself at the moment when all the materials lay ready at hand. Letwin does not recognize that Smith could have been influenced by Hutcheson his teacher, or Pufendorf, the author of textbooks he studied.

Milton Myers attempts in his study, *The Soul of Modern Economic Man Ideas of Self-Interest Thomas Hobbes to Adam Smith* from 1983, to answer the question: who is to be charged with influencing the ideas of the classical economist? Myers starts with Hobbes' doctrine of self-interest as a prime mover among the various motives of man. This very harsh doctrine, in which Hobbes saw human beings as destructive animals, created a heated debate. However, Myers sees only the British debate and does not make any attempt to describe it as an integral part of a broader European debate. The opposition to Hobbes from the Cambridge Platonists is in detail outlined by Myers. The fact that probably all of them had studied Pufendorf's natural law works is not recognized.

Given the rather ambitious title of Myers book, it is puzzling that his outlook is solely on the British tradition. What is stirring on the Continent is of no concern to him in his inquiry. There are no references to any of the continental natural law philosophers. Hobbes and his ideas are seen totally isolated from European philosophy. It is surprising, and hard to believe, that Pufendorf is not mentioned at all in Myers's otherwise comprehensive analysis.

Richard F. Teichgraeber III in his book *'Free Trade' and Moral Philosophy: Rethinking the Sources of Adam Smith's Wealth of Nations* (1986) contends that most 'modern readers' have come to see 'The Wealth of Nations as a giant machine assembled to drive home a very easily understood point – namely, the view that self-interested pursuit of gain, unregulated by legislation or popular prejudice, ensured the greatest benefit to society.'

It was Hutcheson who first instructed Smith in the philosophical meanings of morality, politics and economics. The central elements of Smith's account of politics, his explanation of rights, his theory of property, and his notion of justice, also had their immediate source in Hutcheson's lectures on natural law theories of government and jurisprudence. In short, like Hutcheson, Smith at the outset of his career conceived himself as a moral philosopher, a practitioner of that 'commanding art' that brought views on ethics, politics and economics into one final and harmonious system. Teichgraeber does not seem to know that Hutcheson built very closely on Pufendorf, but that he could not agree with his emphasize on self-interest as a primary human driving force.

Teichgraeber claims that the predominant intellectual influence on Smith's work 'must be traced back to the Glasgow moral philosophy curriculum that Smith studied at the feet of Francis Hutcheson'. The fact that Hutcheson used Pufendorf's *De Officio* as a textbook and that he urged all his students to explore the sources is not mentioned by Teichgraeber. Pufendorf is not discussed and not seen by him as a direct source for Smith.

Pierre Force in his *Self-Interest Before Adam Smith – A Genealogy of Economic Science* (2003) has as his objective to study the history of the concepts of self-love and self-interest in order to understand what these concepts meant when Adam Smith decided to use them as a foundation for the system he constructed in *The Wealth of Nations*.

Force only mentions Pufendorf once. He writes that Smith in his *Lectures on Jurisprudence* gives an account of 'that science which inquiries into the general principles which ought to be the foundation of the Laws of all nations' and in this context, mentions his predecessors Grotius, Hobbes and Pufendorf (2003: 228).

It is unfortunate that there is no discussion of Pufendorf's emphasis of self-love or self-interest and sociability as a foundation of society in Forces' study. Nor does he mention Pufendorf as a direct predecessor of Locke, Montesquieu, Rousseau, Hutcheson and finally Smith. The fact that these scholars used Pufendorf's natural law work when they developed their own theories is not recognized by Force.

Donald Rutherford in his book, *In the Shadow of Adam Smith: Founders of Scottish Economics 1700–1900* (2012), mainly investigates Scottish and a few English predecessors of Smith, although he admits that some of their ideas were imported. However, there are no investigations into what kinds of ideas. Only a few continental authors are mentioned and not one is seriously discussed as a predecessor of Smith. Rutherford claims that one of the reasons for Smith's lasting appeal and interest is his great motive for exchange, self-interest. This is famously connected with his, much quoted, opinion that by pursuing their self-interest participants in markets promoted the public good. In his discussion, Rutherford does not seem to know that Pufendorf emphasized self-interest as the primary driving force in human behaviour.

In his discussion of value, Rutherford claims that lengthy debates seem to skirt the simple and obvious truth that value is merely a price determined by demand and supply and that this idea had a long ancestry. Carmichael provides a crucial link between Aristotle, Grotius, Pufendorf, and Hutcheson. He claims that Hutcheson followed Carmichael's notes on Pufendorf. However, Rutherford has missed the fact that Hutcheson in his writings on moral philosophy, which included political economy, built very strongly on Pufendorf's natural law works and in many cases just copied him.

Rutherford claims that the division of labour is central to Smith's account of economic growth. Social life made the division of labour into a cooperative form of production based on free labour. Here Rutherford mentions that Pufendorf, in his *De Officio*, pointed out that we have great comfort through the aid of others.

Rutherford concludes that Smith's basic principles – that self-interest is the primary force in the actions of man, that a natural order exists, and that every individual struggle for his own best, will also give the best result for society – does not come from Hutcheson. However, he does not consider that it might have come from Pufendorf.

This investigation has found only one book that have looked seriously into parts of Pufendorf's writings on political economy, as a fundamental source for Smith's works. That is the previously mentioned book by Terence Hutchison, *Before Adam Smith: The Emergence of Political Economy 1662–1776* (1988). The literature Smith had to study, as a student both at Glasgow and at Oxford, seems for many to have no relevance in understanding the provenance of his lectures and the books he wrote.

The Wood Collections

There are literally thousands of articles discussing different features of Smith's economic though. It is also reasonable to assume that many of these also discuss Smith's predecessors and the major sources of his writings. To shed some light on this issue, all articles concerned with Smith's writing in the so-called Wood collections from respectively 1984 and 1994 have been investigated.[1]

This examination demonstrates that in 50 out of the 225 articles, the authors discuss to some extent both Smith's predecessors and their influence on his work. However, out of these 50, there are amazingly 36 where Pufendorf's name is not mentioned at all. Of the remaining fourteen articles, there are six who mention Pufendorf's work only in passing, and five who only treat his contribution as superficial. There are only three articles, Jeffrey Young (1985), Enzo Pesciarelli (1986), and Jeffry Young and Barry Gordon (1992) that seriously discusses Pufendorf's contribution to some aspects of political economy, together with his influence on Smith. Jeffrey Young (1985) begins with a discussion of Smith's theory of human behaviour and the relation between *The Theory of Moral Sentiments* and *The Wealth of Nations.* There is no discussion of how Smith's theory of human behaviour was influenced by his predecessors in general and Pufendorf in particular. Last, this re-interpreted 'Smithian' theory is viewed, relative to other theories of value in the history of thought, as a unique, humanistic version of the just price.

Young argues against the popular view that Smith inherited a subjective theory of value and largely substituted for it a 'cost of production' theory of value. His interpretation 'leads to the conclusion that the natural price may be viewed as a general rule of justice, making the natural price a standard of justice in exchange and in distribution. This suggests a strong comparability with the just price … That there is such a strong correlation should come as no surprise when one considers the concept of natural price Smith inherited from Pufendorf'.

Enzo Pesciarelli (1986) first compares the jurisprudence section of Hutcheson's *System of Moral Philosophy* with Smith's corresponding treatment in his *Lectures on Jurisprudence.* Pesciarelli concludes that there is 'a remarkable similarity [between Smith's Lectures and] the corresponding order followed by Hutcheson'. Thereafter, he compares it with Pufendorf's treatment in *De Officio* and *De Jure Naturae et Gentium* and concludes, 'the order of treatment in Hutcheson's System strictly follows Pufendorf'. Pesciarelli emphasizes this by pointing to two elements in Pufendorf's works that had a deep influence on the Scottish thinkers: 'the subordination of jurisprudence to ethics, and the attempt to ground human laws in the observation and analysis of the observed characteristics of human nature'. Pesciarelli also stresses that there is direct evidence that Hutcheson's students, of whom Smith was one, were trained to use the main sources directly. Those sources included both Grotius' *De Jure Belli ac Pacis* and Pufendorf's main natural law work *De Jure Naturae et Gentium*, works they could find in the Glasgow University Library.

In their 1992 article, 'Economic justice in the natural law tradition: Thomas Aquinas to Francis Hutcheson', Jeffrey Young and Barry Gordon start by claiming that 'there was a decided movement following the bicentennial of the publication of *The Wealth of Nations* to broaden the agenda of Smithian studies'. Historians have begun to pay attention to Smith's concern with justice. This has 'evoked renewed interest in certain of Smith's intellectual antecedents who may have played a part in shaping his ideas. But whose influence has remained a matter of relative neglect in modern scholarship'. The purpose of their paper is to begin to examine the evolution of ideas on just price and market value from St Thomas Aquinas to Francis Hutcheson.

These authors believe that Scholastic economic analysis, which might have influenced Smith, 'was almost certainly derived chiefly from that which was taken up in the Protestant natural law tradition'. Pufendorf has much more to offer than Grotius 'by the way of economic analysis'. There were elements in Pufendorf's analysis of just price which 'might be accounted novel and which look forward to Smith's treatment of price'. The authors thereafter analyse Hutcheson's writings on the same issues. They begin by stating that Hutcheson explicitly acknowledges his debt to Pufendorf, 'thus showing the filiations of ideas from the Protestant natural lawyers to Smith'. However, they claim that an examination of Hutcheson's indebtedness to Pufendorf reveals the important role of Carmichael in transmitting the natural jurisprudence tradition to the Scottish universities. 'Probably because of Carmichael's elaboration of Pufendorf, Hutcheson is no mere reporter of his celebrated predecessor, and there are distinctive features in his economic issues'. They mention that Hutcheson explicitly uses the term 'demand' but do not mention that it was Carmichael who introduced the word, in brackets, in his *Comments*, which otherwise were written in Latin. Then they turn to Smith and the issue of a linkage between his thoughts and the Scholastic/natural law tradition. In their conclusion, they put him into the lineage of the Scholastic position and that of Hutcheson.

The authors of these three articles recognize that Pufendorf was a predecessor of Adam Smith. In particular, they point to his theory of value. Although Pesciarelli stresses that there is direct evidence that Smith was trained to use the main sources directly, there is no thorough discussion of how he used Pufendorf in his writings.

From this investigation, it can be concluded that most authors of articles in the Wood collections concerned with Smith's predecessors apparently had not, at the time of their writing, read Pufendorf, and they did not know or did not believe that he could be considered an important predecessor of Smith. Only a few recognize his general importance and noted that his theory of value might have influenced Smith. However, no one discusses how Pufendorf's theory of human behaviour or other writings on political economy might have influenced Smith.

Since the time of the publication of the second Wood collection in 1994, numerous articles have been published that also touch on Smith's predecessors. However, it does not look probable that many of them have discovered Pufendorf as one of Smith's major sources. One example illustrates this, in 2006 Leonidas Montes and Erik Schliesser edited a book entitled *New Voices on Smith*. The book contains 15 articles on Smith. The authors were supposed to discuss his sources and influence, moral theory, economics and knowledge. Not one single reference to Pufendorf is found in any of these articles.

From these inquiries into a few books and articles that have explored Adam Smith's sources the conclusions can be drawn that there are only a very few that seriously have looked at Samuel Pufendorf as a source for Adam Smith. The content of these articles unfortunately has not yet been discovered by the authors of textbooks on the history of economic thought.

Note

1 John Cunningham Wood edited two series entitled *Adam Smith: Critical Assessments*. The first series, published in 4 volumes in 1984, contained 150 articles. The second, published in 3 volumes in 1994, contained 75 articles, making 225 articles in all. Conferring with the editor's preface, these articles presented a detailed overview of analytical writings on Adam Smith from contemporary sources through to the present day, which was 1994. These volumes do not set out to reproduce all articles

written on Adam Smith. However, the editor claims that the articles have been carefully selected to reproduce: (i) all the articles considered seminal to the profession; (ii) articles most useful to the historians of thought, contemporary economists and policy-makers; (iii) those articles which, in total, yield a comprehensive account of Adam Smith's life, thoughts and economics; and (iv) only those articles from professional journals published in English.

23 Pufendorf the Grandfather of Political Economy

It has been the purpose of this book to first to give an account of Samuel Pufendorf's life and remarkable career. Second, to outline and explore in some detail his contribution to natural law and political economy. Third, to make an enquiry into the diffusion of his writings on political economy to the most recognized scholars of eighteenth-century Europe. The most important in this context is Adam Smith. Finally, to shed some light on the puzzling question of why he is almost forgotten.

Pufendorf's first nautral law work *Elementorum Jurisprudentiae Universalis* was published in 1660. This work started a remarkable career. From the University of Heidelberg he moved to Lund where he in 1672 published his major natural law work *De Jure Naturae et Gentium*, and the year after his student edition *De Officio Hominus et Civis*. In 1677 he moved to Stockholm and after twelve productive years he ended up in Berlin. Pufendorf died in 1694 and is buried in St Nikolaikirche.

In Hugo Grotius' work *De Jure Belli et Pacis* some elements of political economy can be found. However, it was not until his successor Pufendorf published his natural law works that political economy was established as a distinct an integral part of natural law. His doctrines of political economy that is his theory of human behaviour, the theory of property and the four stages, the theory of value, money and trade, the foundation of states and council decisions, and finally the division of state powers and principle of taxation, are in detail outlined in his major work. In his doctrines of political economy, Pufendorf as an eclectic, collected what the Greek, the Romans and the philosophers of the fourteenth, fifteenth and the sixteenth centuries had written about these subjects. In addition, he actively used the Bible, the Koran and Roman Law. He analysed and amalgamated all these ideas and thoughts with his own view on the nature of man into a comprehensive integrated system of natural law, with political economy as an important part.

Pufendorf's 'student edition' *De Officio* became an international bestseller and was translated into nine European languages and published in more than 150 editions. With its popularity natural law became a university subjects at almost all Protestant and even some Catholic universities across Europe. His doctrines of natural law and political economy were transmitted, not only across Europe, but also to North America. He had a huge impact on the European Enlightenment and earned himself a reputation as a one of the foremost European scholars of his time.

This representation demonstrates that his ideas of natural law, including political economy, were taken over and used extensively by the most important British and French philosophers. This can be established, although the eighteenth-century European writers very reluctantly gave their readers any information about the sources they used. This in sharp contrast to Pufendorf, who in his major natural law work had 400 names on the reference list, and an overwhelming amount of quotations.

John Locke was the first scholar of any importance who actively used Pufendorf's natural law works when he developed his own theories. With his writings, he had great influence across Europe and therefore also enhanced the Pufendorfian natural law.

In France, many philosophers used Pufendorf's works as a major source when they developed their own doctrines. It started with Pierre Nicole, Jean Domat, Pierre de Boisguilbert. The allusions to Pufendorf's self-interest and sociability are strong in their writings. His French translator Jean Barbeyrac had an important role in the diffusion of natural law and political economy. His French translations were also used to translate into other languages. Denis Diderot as the chief editor of the *Encyclopédie* also had an important role in transmitting natural law in France. Charles-Louis Montesquieu used Pufendorf's natural law works actively when he wrote his discourses and *De l'Esprit des lois.* Pufendorf's natural law works were Jean-Jaques Rousseau's primary source. The allusions are particularly strong when he discusses how private property develops in people's minds. The Physiocrats with their leader François Quesnay claimed that political economy was the science of natural law. Pufendorf's ideas was therefore appreciated and used in the milieu of the Physiocrats.

It is not known why Gershom Carmichael, at the University of Glasgow, selected Pufendorf's *De Officio* as a textbook in his moral philosophy class at the end of the 1690s, but Locke's recommendation of Pufendorf's natural law works might have been a decisive factor. When Francis Hutcheson took over the chair in moral philosophy in 1729, he continued Carmichael's practice and used *De Officio* as a textbook. It is clear from Hutcheson's works on moral philosophy that Pufendorf was his major source. Some parts of his writings were just copied from Pufendorf's natural law works. This is particularly the case when he writes on topics of political economy.

When Adam Smith matriculated at the University of Glasgow in 1737, he became one of Hutcheson's students in his introductory course in moral philosophy. Smith also benefited from Hutcheson's teaching of a private class in the lessons of the law of nature. Here he became acquainted with Pufendorf's writings on political economy. Hutcheson urged his students to investigate the sources of the works he referred to in his lectures. In his fourth year at Oxford Smith chose to follow the path of a student in civil law, where he possibly continued his study of the works of the natural law philosophers. From

Smith's library it is clear that he owned a copy of *De Jure Naturae et Gentium* and a French translation with Barbeyrac's comments. It is also clear that he used Pufendorf's doctrines of political economy extensively when he prepared his freelance lectures in Edinburgh. He continued using Pufendorf's natural law works in general and his writings on political economy in particular when he became professor at the University of Glasgow, and taught his ordinary courses in moral philosophy and jurisprudence.

Furthermore, this inquiry has established that Adam Smith had Pufendorf's natural law works ready at hand, and he used them when he wrote his first book *The Theory of Moral Sentiments* which was published in 1759, held his *Lectures on Jurisprudence* in the early 1760s, and wrote his second book *The Wealth of Nations*, published in 1776. It is clear that Pufendorf was, if not his major source, at least one of his major sources. Considering all these facts, it is difficult to understand how Smith's biographers and editors did not realize how important Pufendorf's natural law works was for him.

With so many famous scholars using Pufendorf's natural law works it is an enigma why he is almost forgotten. This inquiry points to the tremendous effect Immanuel Kant had on the development of philosophy. He and his followers eliminated the natural law philosophers, including Pufendorf, from the history of philosophy. A few books whose purpose has been to examine the origin of classical economics have been surveyed. It is hard to understand that not one of them has discovered Pufendorf as one of Smith's sources. An anonymous referee has claimed that everyone knew Pufendorf and his contribution to the history of economic thought. An investigation into forty-five textbooks on the history of economic thought proves that this is not true. The same result follows from an analysis of 225 articles in the so-called Wood collection.

It was the diffusion of Pufendorf's natural law, including his doctrines of political economy, through the popularization of his *De Officio*, which laid the foundation for the progress of political economy in the eighteenth century. This investigation claims that Pufendorf's contribution to political economy is of such importance that while Adam Smith unquestionably is considered the father of modern political economy, Samuel Pufendorf deserves to be remembered as the grandfather.

Mark Blaug (1997) has, in his book *Economic Theory in Retrospect*, quoted Glenn R. Morrow (1895–1973), who in a lecture, at the sesquicentennial commemoration of Smith's The *Wealth of Nations* at the University of Chicago, told of someone who actually read the whole volume: 'Once upon a time there was a man who read the Wealth of Nations; not a summary, not a volume of selected passages, the Wealth of Nations itself ... Now, of course I may have exaggerated somewhat. There probably never was any such man'. It is hoped that, as a result of this investigation, in the not-too-distant future, historians of economic thought will not only read Adam Smith's works but also Samuel Pufendorf's natural law works and in particular his doctrines of political economy.

References

Pufendorf: Books and bibliographies

Pufendorf, Samuel (1931 [1660, 1672]). *Elementorum Jurisprudentiæ Universalis Libri Duo* (The elements of universal jurisprudence in two books). (Facsimile of the 1672 Cambridge edition, with a list of errata which refers to the first edition of 1660 published in The Hague; translation of the 1672 edition by William Abbot Oldfather.) The Clarendon Press, Oxford.

Pufendorf, Samuel (2009 [1672, 1931]). *Two Books of the Elements of Universal Jurisprudence*. Edited with an introduction by Thomas Behme. Liberty Fund, Indianapolis. (Revised edition of the translation by William Abbot Oldfather, Oxford, 1931.)

Pufendorf, Samuel (2007 [1667]). *The Present State of Germany* (*De Statu Imperii Germanici*). Translated by Edmund Bohun in 1696, edited with an introduction by Michael J. Seidler. Liberty Fund, Indianapolis.

Pufendorf, Samuel (2005 [1672, 1729]). *Of the Law of Nature and Nations. Eight Books*. Done into English from the best edition by Basil Kennett. To which are added all the large notes of Mr. Barbeyrac. To which is also prefixed Mr. Barbeyrac's Prefatory Discourse, containing An Historical and Critical Account of the Sciences of Morality, and the Progress it has made in the World, from the earliest Times down to The Publication of this Work. Fourth edition, 1729 (First edition, 1703). The Lawbook Exchange, Clark, New Jersey.

Pufendorf, Samuel (1964 [1672, 1688]). *De Jure Naturae et Gentium Libri Octo* (On the law of nature and nations in eight books). Translation of the 1688 edition (with references to the first edition of 1672) by Charles Henry Oldfather and William Abbot Oldfather. Clarendon Press, Oxford, 1933; reprinted 1964.

Pufendorf, Samuel (1927 [1673, 1682]). *De Officio Hominis et Civis Juxta Legem Naturalem Libri Duo* (The duty of man and citizen according to the natural law in two books). (A facsimile of the edition of 1682 with a list of errata that refers to the first edition of 1673. A translation of the text by Frank Gardner Moore). Oxford University Press, New York.

Pufendorf, Samuel (1991 [1673]). *De Officio Hominis et Civis Juxta Legem Naturalem Libri Duo* (On the duty of man and citizen according to natural law). Edited by James Tully and translated by Michael Silverthorne. Cambridge University Press, Cambridge.

Pufendorf, Samuel (2003 [1673, 1735]). *The Whole Duty of Man, According to the Law the Nature*. Translated by Andrew Tooke, 1691. Edited and with an introduction by Ian Hunter and David Saunders (Two discourses and a commentary by Jean Barbeyrac, translated by David Saunders). Liberty Fund, Indianapolis.

Pufendorf, Samuel (1992 [1673, 1735]). *Les devoirs de l'homme et du citoyen, tells qu'ils lui Sont préscrits par la loi naturelle.* Translated by Jean Barbeyrac. Fifth edition. Amsterdam 1735; reprinted, Olms Verlag, Hildesheim.

Pufendorf, Samuel (2001 [1673]). *Om de mänskliga och medborgerliga plikterna enligt Naturrätten.* Translated into Swedish by Birger Bergh and edited with an introduction by Kjell Å. Modéer. City University Press, Stockholm.

Pufendorf, Samuel (1686). *Eris Scandica dia Adversus Libros de Jure Naturae et Gentium Objecta Diluuntur* (A collection of his polemic essays). Frankfurt ad Moenum 1686. Also published as *Eris Scandica und andere polemische Schriften über das Naturrecht* [see next entry].

Pufendorf, Samuel (2002 [1686]). *Eris Scandica und andere polemische Schriften über das Naturrecht.* Edited by Fiammetta Palladini. In *Gesammelte Werke,* edited by Wilhelm Schmidt-Biggemann, Band 5. Akademie Verlag GmbH, Berlin.

Pufendorf, Samuel (2002 [1687]). *Of the Nature and Qualification of Religion in References to Civil Society.* Translated from *De Habitu Religionis Christianae ad Vitam Civilem* by Joducus Cral. Edited and with an introduction by Simone Zurbuchen. Liberty Fund, Indianapolis.

Pufendorf, Samuel (2002 [1687]). *The Divine Feudal Law: Or, Covenants with Mankind, Represented.* Translated from *Jus Feciale Divinium Cive de Consensus et Dissensu Protestantium* by Theophilus Dorrington. Edited and with an introduction by Simone Zurbuchen. Liberty Fund, Indianapolis.

Pufendorf, Samuel (1894 [1690]). *Brief an Bruder Jeremias von 1690.* In Paul Meyer, *Samuel Pufendorf, Ein Beitrag zur Geschichte seines Lebens. Abhandlung zum Jahresbericth der Fürsten- und Landesschule zu Grimma über das Schuljahr1894–1895.* Druck von Julius Schiertz, Grimma.

Pufendorf, Samuel (1721). *Unvorgreiffliche Bedenken wegen Information eines Knaben von Condition.* Marienthal.

Pufendorf, Samuel (2009 [1749, 2005]). *Of the Law of Nature and Nations, Eight Books.* Translated by Basil Kennet, to which are added the large notes of Barbeyrac and also the prefixed Barbeyrac's Prefatory Discourse. Fourth printing. The Lawbook Exchange, Clark, New Jersey.

Carr, Craig L. (ed.) (1994 [1660]). *The Political Writings of Samuel Pufendorf.* Translation of Pufendorf's *Elementorum Jurisprudentiae Universalis* (1660) based on the 1672 edition. Editor's introduction and Translator's introduction. Oxford University Press, New York and Oxford.

Döring, Detlef (ed.) (1999). 'Samuel Pufendorf Briefwechsel'. In Wilhelm Schmidt-Biggemann (ed.), *Samuel Pufendorf Gesammelte Werke,* Band 1: *Esaias Pufendorf and Samuel Pufendorf, Copenhagen 31.3.1658*. Akademie Verlag GmbH, Berlin.

Luig, Klaus (ed.) (1994). *Samuel von Pufendorf über Die Plicht des Menschen und des Bürgers nach dem Gesetz der Natur.* Translated by Luig Klaus. Insel Verlag, Frankfurt am Main.

Palladini, Fiammetta (1999). *La Biblioteca di Samuelo Pufendorf. Catalogo dell'asta di Berlin del settembre 1697.* Harrassowitz Verlag, Wiesbaden.

Palladini, Fiammetta (ed.) (2002). *Einleitung. Samuel Pufendorf Eris Scandica und andere polemische Schriften über das Naturrecht.* In W. Schmidt-Biggemann (ed.), *Samuel Pufendorf Gesammelte Werke,* Band 5, Akademie Verlag GmbH, Berlin [Originally published in Frankfurt am Main 1686].

Schmidt-Biggemann, Wilhelm (ed.) (1996–2004). *Samuel Pufendorf Gesammelte Werke,* Band 1–6, und 9. Akademie Verlag GmbH, Berlin.

Seidler, Michael (ed.) (1990 [1678]). *Samuel Pufendorf's On the Natural State of Men (De Statu Hominum Naturali)*. (The 1678 Latin edition and English translation.) Translated, annotated and introduced by Michael Seidler. Studies in the History of Philosophy, Vol. 13. The Edwin Mellen Press, Lewiston/Queenston/Lampeter.

Seidler, Michael (ed.) (2014 [1695]). *Samuel von Pufendorf: An Introduction to the History of the Principal Kingdoms and States of Europe* [1695]. Liberty Fund, Indianapolis.

Secondary Sources

Arnaud, André-Jean (1969). *Les Origines doctrinales du Code Civil français* (Doctrinal Origins of the French Civil Code). R. Pichon & R. Durand-Auzias, Paris.

Aspromourgos, Tony and John Lodewijks (eds) (2004). *History and Political Economy: Essays in Honour of P.D. Groenewegen*. Routledge, New York.

Aure, Andreas Harald (2010). 'Samuel Pufendorfs avvisning av sedvaner og traktater som kilder for folkeretten' (Samuel Pufendorf's rejection of customs and treatises as sources for international law). In Sigbjørn Sødal (ed.), *Økonomi og Tid*. Fagbokforlaget, Bergen, pp. 133–142.

Aure, Andreas Harald (2014). 'Hugo Grotius – Individual Rights as the Core of Natural Law'. In Guttorm Fløistad (ed), *Philosophy of Justice*, Vol. 12. Springer, Dordrecht, Heidelberg, New York and London, pp. 75–94.

Axtell, J.L. (1968). *The Educational Writings of John Locke*. Cambridge University Press, Cambridge.

Bailyn, Bernard (1992). *The Ideological Origin of the American Revolution*. Belknap Press of Harvard University, Cambridge, Massachusetts.

Barbeyrac, Jean (1749). *An Historical and Critical Account of the Science of Morality: And the Progress it Made in the World from the Earliest Times down to the Publication of Pufendorf of the Law of Nature and Nations.* Translated by Mr. Carew. London.

Barton, J.L. (1986). 'Legal Studies'. In L.S. Sutherland and L.G. Mitchell (eds), *The History of the University of Oxford: The Eighteenth Century*. Clarendon Press, Oxford, pp. 593–605.

Baum, Alan (1979). *Montesquieu and Social Theory*. Pergamon Press, Oxford.

Bazzoli, Maurizio (1979). 'Giambattista Almici a la diffusione di Pufendorf nel Settecento italiano'. *Critica Storica* 16: 3–100.

Beck, Lewis White (1969). *Early German Philosophy: Kant and his Predecessors*. The Belknap Press of Harvard University Press, Cambridge, Massachusetts.

Behme, Thomas (ed.) (1999). *Samuel Pufendorf Elementa Jurisprudentiae Universalis* Akademie Verlag GmbH, Berlin.

Behme, Thomas (ed.) (2003). *Erhard Weigel Universi Corporis Pansophici. Caput Summum*, Jena 1673. *Werke*1. Friedrich Frommann Verlag-Günther Holzboog, Stuttgart-Bad Cannstatt.

Behme, Thomas (ed.) (2004). *Erhard Weigel Arithmetische Beschreibung der Moral-Weissheit von Personen und Sachen*. Jena 1674. *Werke* 2. Friedrich Frommann Verlag-Günther Holzboog, Stuttgart-Bad Cannstatt.

Behme, Thomas (ed.) (2008). *Erhard Weigel Analysis Aristotelica ex Euclide restituta*, Jena 1658. *Werke*3. Friedrich Frommann Verlag-Günther Holzboog, Stuttgart-Bad Cannstatt.

Behme, Thomas (ed.) (2009). 'Introduction'. In Samuel Pufendorf [1672, 1660], *Two Books of the Elements of Universal Jurisprudence*. Liberty Fund, Indianapolis.

Béraud, Alain and Gilbert Faccarello (eds) (1992). *Nouvelle histoire de la pensée économique.* Tome 1. Des scolastiques aux classiques. Éditions la Découverte, Paris.
Black, Duncan (1948). 'On the rationale of group decision making'. *Journal of Political Economy* 56(1): 23–34.
Blaug, Mark (1997). *Economic Theory in Retrospect.* Fifth edition. Cambridge University Press, Cambridge.
Boisguilbert, Pierre de (1851 [1707]). *Dissertation sur la nature des richesses, de l'argents et des tributs.* Économistes Financiers du XVIIIe Siècle. Deuxième Édition. Chez Guillaumin et Cie Libraries, Rue Richelieu 14, Paris. Library of University of Minnesota, Minneapolis.
Bonar, James (1932). *A Catalogue of the Library of Adam Smith.* Second edition. Macmillan, London.
Borda, J.C. de (1781). 'Mémoire sur les élections au scrutin'. *Histoire de l'Académie Royale Des Sciences*, Paris, pp. 657–665.
Bowley, Marian (1973). *Studies in the History of Economic Theory before 1870.* Macmillan, London.
Bresslau, H. (1888). '*Art.: Samuel Pufendorf*'. *Allgemeine Deutsche Biographie*, Band 26: *Durch die historische Kommission bei der Königlichen.* Akademie der Wissenschaften, Leipzig.
Brown, Maurice (1988). *Adam Smith's Economics: Its Place in the Development of Economic Thought.* Croom Helm, London.
Brown, Michael (2002). *Francis Hutcheson in Dublin 1719–30: The Crucible of his Thought*, Four Courts Press, Dublin.
Brucker, Iacob (1975 [1744]). *Historia Critica Philosophiae a Tempore Resuscitatarum in Occidente Litterarum ad Nostra Tempora.* Apud Bernhard Christoph Breitkopf. (Reprint of the 1744Leipzig edition.) Georg Olms Verlag, Hildesheim and New York. [English translation in William Enfield, *The History of Philosophy from the Earliest Periods.* London, 1837.]
Brühlmeier, Daniel (1995). 'Natural Law and Early Economic Thought in Barbeyrac, Burlamaqui, and Vattel'. In J.C. Laursen (ed.), *New Essays on the Political Thoughts of the Huguenots of the Refuge.* Brill, Leiden, pp. 53–71.
Buckle, Stephen (1991). *Natural Law and the Theory of Property: Grotius to Hume.* Clarendon Press, Oxford.
Buhle, Johann Gottlieb (1802 and 1803). *Geschichte der neuern Philosophie seit der Epoche Der Wiederherstellung der Wissenschaften.* Dritter und Vierter Band. Verlag Johann Friedrich Röwer, Göttingen.
Buhle, Johann Gottlieb (1804). *Lehrbuch der Geschichte der Philosophie und einer kritischen Literatur derselben*, 8 volumes. Lemgo.
Bull, Francis (1916). *Fra Holberg to Nordal Brun – Studier til norsk aandshistorie* (From Holberg to Nordal Brun – Studies in Norwegian intellectual history). Aschehough & Co., Kristiania.
Burlamaqui, Jean Jacques (2003 [1747]). *Principes du droit naturel* (The principles of natural law in which the true systems of morality and civil government are established; and the different sentiments of Grotius, Hobbes, Pufendorf, Barbeyrac, Locke, Clark and Hutcheson occasionally considered). Translated by Mr. Nugent. The Lawbook Exchange, Clark, New Jersey.
Burlamaqui, Jean Jacques (2006 [1763]). *The Principles of Natural and Political Law.* Translated by Mr. Nugent. Edited and with an Introduction by Petter Korkman. Liberty Fund, Indianapolis.

Burns, J.H. (ed.) (1991). *The Cambridge History of Political Thought 1450–1700*. Cambridge University Press, Cambridge.

Buroker, Jill Vance (ed.) (1996). *Antone Arnauld and Pierre Nicole: Logic and the Art of Thinking*. Cambridge University Press, Cambridge.

Campbell, R.H. and A.S. Skinner (1976). 'General Introduction'. In *The Glasgow Edition of The Works and Correspondence of Adam Smith*. Liberty Fund, Indianapolis.

Cannan, Edwin (ed.) (1896). *Lectures on Justice, Police, Revenue and Arms delivered in the University of Glasgow by Adam Smith*. Oxford University Press, Oxford.

Cannan, Edwin (1937 [1904]). *Editor's Introduction to Adam Smith's Wealth of Nations*. The Modern Library, Random House, New York.

Canterbery, E. Ray (1995). *The Literate Economist: A Brief History of Economics*. HarperCollins College Publishers, New York.

Carey, Daniel (ed.) (2000 [1755]). *'Introduction'*. In Francis Hutcheson, *A System of Moral Philosophy*, 2 vols. Thoemmes Press, Bristol.

Carmichael, Gershom (2002 [1718]). *Natural Rights on the Threshold of the Scottish Enlightenment: The Writings of Gershom Carmichael*. Edited by James Moore and Michael Silverthorne. Liberty Fund, Indianapolis.

Carr, Craig L. (ed.) (1994). *The Political Writings of Samuel Pufendorf*. Translated by Michael J. Seidler. (Includes the full translation of *Elementorum Jurisprudentiæ Universalis* and selections from *De Jure Naturae et Gentium*.) Oxford University Press, Oxford.

Catlin, Warren B. (1962). *The Progress of Economics: A History of Economic Thought*. Bookman Associates, New York.

Chappell, Vere (ed.) (1992). *Essays on Early Modern Philosophers: From Descartes and Hobbes to Newton and Leibniz*, Vol. 4: *Port-Royal to Bayle*. Garland Publishing, New York and London.

Chappell, Vere (ed.) (1994). *The Cambridge Companion to Locke*. Cambridge University Press, Cambridge.

Chipman, John (2012). 'Natural Law and the Existence and Optimality of Political Equilibrium'. In Christian Gehrke, Neri Salvadori, Ian Steedman and Richard Sturn (eds), *Classical Political Economy and Modern Theory: Essays in Honour of Heinz Kurz*. Routledge, London and New York.

Clapp, James Gordon (1967). *'John Locke'*. In *The Encyclopedia of Philosophy*. Macmillan, New York.

Clark, Charles M.A. (1992). *Economic Theory and Natural Philosophy: The Search for the Natural Laws of the Economy*. Edward Elgar Publishing, Brookfield, Wisconsin.

Clark, John M., Paul H. Douglas, Jacob H. Hollander, Glenn R. Morrow, Melchior Palyi and Jacob Viner (1928). *Adam Smith, 1776–1926: Lectures to Commemorate the Sesquicentennial of the Publication of 'The Wealth of Nations'*. The University of Chicago Press, Chicago.

Cohen, Alix (2014). *'31. Philosophy and History: The Paradoxes of History'*. In A. Garret (ed.), *The Routledge Companion to Eighteenth Century Philosophy*. Routledge, London and New York, pp. 754–772.

Cohler, Anne M. (ed.) (1748 [1989]). *'Introduction.' In Montesquieu, The Spirit of the Laws*. Cambridge University Press, Cambridge.

Condorcet, Marquis de (1785). *Essai sur l'application de l'analyse à la probabilité des Decisions rendues à la pluralité des voix*. Paris.

Cranston, Maurice (1967). 'Baron de Montesquieu'. In Paul Edwards (ed.) *The Encyclopedia of Philosophy*. Macmillan, New York.

Courtney, Cecil P. (1968). *Montesquieu*. In J. Cruickshank (ed.), *French Literature and its Background*, Vol. 3: *The Eighteenth Century*. Oxford University Press, Oxford, pp. 30–44.

Crowe, Michael B. (1977). *The Changing Profile of Natural Law*. Martinus Nijhoff, The Hague.

Cruickshank, John (ed.) (1968). *French Literature and its Background*, Vol. 3: *The Eighteenth Century*. Oxford University Press, Oxford.

Cumberland, Richard (2005 [1672]). *A Treatise of the Laws of Nature*. Edited with a foreword by Jon Parkin. (This is the first modern edition and it is based on John Maxwell's English translation from 1727 of the Latin *De Legibus Naturae*. It includes Maxwell's extensive notes and appendices, and material from Barbeyrac's 1744 French edition and John Tower's edition of 1750.) Liberty Fund, Indianapolis.

Darity, William A. (ed.) (2008). *International Encyclopedia of the Social Sciences*. Second edition. Macmillan Reference, Detroit.

Darwall, Stephen (1995). *The British Moralists and the Internal 'Ought', 1640–1740*. Cambridge University Press, Cambridge.

De Angelis, Simone (2004). *'Pufendorf und der Cartesianismus Medizin als Leitwissenschaft und die Rolle der Bibelhermeneutik in Pufendorfs Verteidigung des Naturrechts um 1680'*. *Internationales Archiv für Sozialgeschichte der deutschen Literatur* 29(1): 129–172.

Denzer, Horst (1972). *Moralphilosophie und Naturrecht bei Samuel Pufendorf*. Münchener Studien zur Politik, Band 22. C.H. Beck, Munich, pp. 364–365.

Denzer, Horst (1987). *Pufendorf (1632–94)*. In Hans Maier, Heiz Rausch and Horst Denzer (eds), *Klassiker des Politischen Denkens*, Zweiter Band: *von Locke bis Max Weber*. Fifth edition. Verlag C.H. Beck, Munich.

Derathé, Lois Robert (1970). *Jean-Jacques Rousseau et la Science politique de son temps*. Second edition. VRIN, Paris.

De Roover, Raymond (1974). *Business, Banking, and Economic Thought in Late Medieval and Early Modern Europe*. The University of Chicago Press, Chicago and London.

Dewey, Frank (1986). *Thomas Jefferson, Lawyer*. The University Press of Virginia, Charlottesville.

Dickel, Günther (1961). *Die Heidelberger Juristische Fakultät Stufen und Wandlungen ihrer Entwicklung. In Puperto – Carlola Sonderband aus der Geschichte der Univeristät Heidelberg und ihrer Facultäten*. Bausdrück GmbH, Heidelberg.

Diderot, Denis and Jean le Rond d'Alembert (eds) (1751–72). *Encyclopédie ou Dictionnaire raisonné des Sciences, des Arts et des Métiers*. Bibliothèque National, Paris.

Domat, Jean (1689–94). *Les Loix Civilies dans Leur Ordre Naturel*, Tomes 1–3. La Veuve de Jean Baptiste Coignard, Imprimeur & Librire ordinaire du Roy. À Paris. Bibliothèque Diderot de Lyons.

Domat, Jean (1701). *Le Droit Public suite Des Loix Civilies dans Leur Ordre Naturel*. Tome 1–5 (1689–1697). Second edition. Chez Guillaume Cavelier, dans la Grande Salle du Palis du costé de Cour des Aydes, à l'Ecu de France, & à la Palme. À Paris. Bibliothèque Diderot de Lyons.

Dreitzel, Horst (1995). 'Toleranz und Gewissenfreiheit im konfessionellen Zeitalter: Zur Diskussion im Reich Zwischen Augsburger Religionsfrieden und Aufklärung'. In Dieter Breuer (ed.), *Religion und Religiosität im Zeitalter des Barock*. Harrassowitz, Wiesbaden.

Drüll, Dagmar (1991). *Heidelberger Gelehrten lexikon 1652–1802*. Springer Verlag, Berlin.

Döring, Detlef (1994). 'Samuel Pufendorf als Student in Leipzig'. Eine Ausstellung. Universitätsbibliothek, Leipzig.

Döring, Ditlef (ed.) (1995). *Samuel Pufendorf Kleine Vorträge und Schriften: Texte zu Geschichte, Pädagogik, Philosophie, Kirche und Völkerrecht*. Vittorio Klostermann, Frankfurt am Main.

Döring, Detlef (1999). *Erhard Weigels Zeit an der Universität* Leipzig*(1647–1653)*. In Reinhard E. Schielicke, Klaus-Dieter Herbst and Stefan Kratochwil (eds), *Erhard Weigel –1625 bis 1699. Barocker Erzvater der deutchen Frühaufklärung. Beiträge des Kolloquiums anlässlich seines 300. Todestages am 20. März 1999 in Jena*. Acta Historica Astronomiae, Vol. 7. Verlag Harri Deutsch, Frankfurt am Main, pp. 73ff.

Döring, Detlef (2004). 'Das gelehrte Leipzig der Frühaufklärung am Rande und im Umfeld der Universität'. In H. Marti and D. Döring (eds), *Die Universität Leipzig und ihr gelehrtes Umfeld 1680–1780*. Schwabe AG, Basel, pp. 11–53.

Döring, Detlef (2006). 'Samuel Pufendorf und die Heidelberger Universität in der Mitte des 17. Jahrhunderts'. In C. Strohm, F.S Freedman and H.J. Selderhuis (eds), *Späthumanismus und reformierte Konfession*. Mohr Siebeck, Tübingen.

Dufour, Alfred (1986). 'Pufendorfs Ausstrahlung im französischen und im angloamerikanischen Kulturraum'. In Kjell Å. Modéer (ed.), *Samuel von Pufendorf 1632–1982. Ett rättshistorisk symposium in Lund 15–16 januari 1982*. A.-B. Nordiska Bokhandeln, Stockholm.

Dufour, Alfred (1991). 'Pufendorf'. In J.H. Burns (ed.), *The Cambridge History of Political Thought 1450–1700*. Cambridge University Press, Cambridge, pp. 561–588.

Dunning, William Archibald (1947). *A History of Political Theories: From Luther to Montesquieu*. Macmillan, New York.

Durant, Will and Ariel (1962–68). *The Story of Civilization*, Vols 1–11. Simon & Schuster, New York.

Eatwell, John, Murry Milgate and Peter Newman (eds) (1987). *The New Palgrave: A Dictionary of Economics*. Macmillan, London.

Edwards, Paul (ed.) (1967). *The Encyclopedia of Philosophy*. Macmillan and The Free Press, New York and London.

Ekelund, Jr., Robert, B. and Robert F. Hébert (1990). *A History of Economic Theory and Method*. McGraw-Hill, New York.

Enfield, William (1837). *The History of Philosophy from the Earliest Periods* (English Translation of Johann Jacob Brucker's *Historia Critica Philosophiæ*). London.

Englund, Peter (2000). *Den oövervinnerlige. Om den svenska stormaktstiden och en man i Dess mit*. (The Invincible. About the Swedish Time of Great Power and a Man in the Middle of it). Atlantis, Stockholm.

Eskildsen, Kasper Risbjerg (2008). 'Christian Thomasius, invisible philosophers and education for enlightenment'. *Intellectual History Review* 18(3): 319–336.

Evensky, Jerry (1987). 'The two voices of Adam Smith: Moral philosopher and social critic'. *History of Political Economy* 19(3): 447–468.

Eyffinger, Arthur (1982). *Inventory of the Poetry of Hugo Grotius*. Van Gorcum, Assen.

Faccarello, Gilbert (1999). *The Foundation of 'Laissez Faire': The Economics of Pierre de Boisguilbert*. Routledge, London.

Fehrman, Carl, Håkan Westling and Göran Blomquist (2004). *Lärdomens Lund. Lunds Universitets historia 1666–2004*. Lunds universitet, Lund.

Fetter, Frank W. (1965). 'The relation of the history of economic thought to economic history'. *American Economic Review* 55(1/2): 610–614.

Fiering, Norman (1981). *Moral Philosophy at Seventeenth-Century Harvard: A Discipline in Transition*. University of North Carolina Press, Chapel Hill.

Fiorillo, Vanda (1989). '*Von Grotius zu Pufendorf. Wissenschaftliche Revolution und Theoretische Grundlagen des Rechts*'. *Archiv für Rechts- und Sozialphilosophie* 75(4): 218–238.

Fløistad, Guttorm (ed.) (2014). *Philosophy of Justice* (International Institute of Philosophy. Contemporary Philosophy: A New Survey, Vol. 12). Springer, Dordrecht, Heidelberg, New York and London.

Force, Pierre (2003). *Self-Interest before Adam Smith: A Genealogy of Economics Science*. Cambridge University Press, Cambridge.

Foss, Kåre (1934). *Ludvig Holbergs Naturrett – På idehistorisk bakgrunn* (Ludvig Holberg's natural law – On the background of the history of ideas). Gyldendals Norske Forlag, Oslo.

Fox-Bourne, Henry Richard (1876). *The Life of John Locke*, 2 vols. Harper, New York.

Fox-Genovese, Elizabeth (1976). *The Origins of Physiocracy: Economic Revolution and Social Order in Eighteenth-Century France*. Cornell University Press, Ithaca and London.

Friederich, Carl J. (2002). 'Corruption Concepts in Historical Perspective'. In ArnoldJ. Heidenheimer and Michael Johnston (eds), *Political Corruption: Concepts and Context*. Transaction Publishers, New Brunswick, New Jersey, pp. 15–23.

Fukuyama, Francis (2011). *The Origins of Political Order: From Prehuman Times to the French Revolution*. Farrar, Strauss and Giroux, New York.

Gaertner, Wulf (2005). '*De Jure Naturae et Gentium*: Samuel Pufendorf's contribution to social choice theory and economics'. *Social Choice and Welfare* 25(2): 231–241.

Gaertner, Wulf (2006). *A Primer in Social Choice Theory*. Oxford University Press, Oxford.

Galiani, Ferdinando (1924 [1751]). *Della Moneta* (On Money). Translation of the substance of Book I, in Arthur E. Monroe, *Early Economic Thought*. Harvard University Press, Cambridge, Massachusetts, pp. 279–299 (The translation follows the reprint of the second edition (1780), published by Fausto Nicoli, Bari 1915.)

Garret, Aaron (ed.) (2014). *The Routledge Companion to Eighteenth Century Philosophy*. Routledge, London and New York.

Garve, Christian (1798). *Ubersicht der vornehmsten Principien der Sittenlehre*. Breslau.

Gehrke, Christian, Neri Salvadori, Ian Steedman and Richard Sturn (eds) (2012). *Classical Political Economy and Modern Theory: Essays in Honour of Heinz Kurz*. Routledge, London and New York.

Gelderen, M. van (1994). 'The challenges of colonialism: Grotius and Vitoria on natural and international relations'. *Grotiana* 14(1): 3–37.

Geyer, Bodo and Helmut Goerlich (ed.) (1996). *Samuel Pufendorf und seine Wirkungen bis auf die heutige Zeit*. Nomos Velagsgesellschaft, Baden-Baden.

Gihl, Torsten (1932). 'Samuel Pufendorf och Jus Naturae et Gentium'. *Nordisk Tidsskrift for Internasjonal Ret* 2: 37–64.

Gordon, Barry and Jeffrey T. Young (1992). 'Economic justice in the natural law tradition: Thomas Aquinas to Francis Hutcheson'. *Journal of the History of Economic Thought* 14(1): 1–17.

Gourevitch, Victor (ed. and trans.) (2007). 'Introduction'. In Rousseau, *The Social Contract and Other Later Political Writings*. Cambridge University Press, Cambridge.

Gourevitch, Victor (ed. and trans.) (2008). 'Introduction'. In Rousseau, *The Discourses and Other Early Political Writings*. Cambridge University Press, Cambridge.

Grice-Hutchinson, Marjorie (1952). *The School of Salamanca*. Oxford University Press, London.

Grimsley, Ronald (1967). 'Jean-Jacques Rousseau'. In Paul Edwards (ed.) *The Encyclopedia of Philosophy*. Macmillan, New York.

Grotius, Hugo (1964 [1625]). *De Jure Belli ac Pacis Libri Tres* (On the law of war and peace in three books), Vol. 2. Translated by Francis W. Kelsey (1925). Oceana Publications, New York and Wiley & Sons, London.

Groves, Harold M. (1974). *Tax Philosophers: Two Hundred Years of Thought in Great Britain and the United States*. University of Wisconsin Press, Madison, Wisconsin.

Haakonssen, Knud (1989). *The Science of a Legislator: The Natural Jurisprudence of David Hume and Adam Smith*. Cambridge University Press, Cambridge.

Haakonssen, Knud (1996). *Natural Law and Moral Philosophy: From Grotius to the Scottish Enlightenment*. Cambridge University Press, Cambridge.

Haakonssen, Knud (2006). 'The History of Eighteenth-Century Philosophy: History or Philosophy?'. In *The Cambridge History of Eighteenth-Century Philosophy*. Cambridge University Press, Cambridge, pp. 3–25.

Haakonssen, Knud (ed.) (2006). *The Cambridge History of Eighteenth-Century Philosophy*. Cambridge University Press, Cambridge.

Haakonssen, Knud (2012). *Naturretten, Pufendorf og Holberg – men hvilken naturrett? Hvilken Pufendorf?* (Natural law, Pufendorf and Holberg – but what kind of natural law? Which Pufendorf?) In Eiliv Vinje and Jørgen Magnus Sejersted (eds), *Ludvig Holbergs naturrett* (The Natural Law of Ludvig Holberg). Gyldendal Akademisk, Oslo.

Haft, Fritjof von (1997). *Einfürung in das juristische Lernen*. Verlag Erst und Werner Gieseking, Bielefeld.

Hammerstein, Nokter (1986). '*Zum Fortwirken von Pufendorfs Naturrechtslehre and den Universitäten des Heiligen Römisches Reiches Deutscher Nation während des 18. Jahrhunderts*'. In Kjell Å. Modéer (ed.), *Samuel von Pufendorf 1632–1982. Ett rättshistorisk symposium in Lund 15–16 januari 1982*. A.-B. Nordiska Bokhandeln, Stockholm.

Hartung, Gerald (ed.) (1997). 'Einleitung: Samuel Pufendorf und die Verbreitung der Naturrechtslehre in Europa'. Introduction to Samuel Pufendorf, *Gesammelte Werke*, edited by Wilhelm Schmidt-Biggemann, Band 2: *De officio hominis et civis*. Akademie Verlag, Berlin.

Hasbach, Wilhelm (1890). *Die allgemeinen philosophischen Grundlagen der von François Quesnay und Adam Smith begründeten politischen Ökonomie*. Duncker & Humblot, Leipzig.

Hecht, Jaqueline (1966). *Boisguilbert, Pierre Le Pesant de (1646–1714) ou la naissance de l'économie politique*. Institut national d'études démographiques, Paris.

Hegel, Georg WilhelmFriedrich (1971 [1833–36]). *Vorlesungen über die Geschichte der Philosophie. Auf der Grundlage der Werke von 1832–1845 neu edierte Ausgabe*. Redaktion Eva Moldenhauer und Karl Markus Michel. Suhrkamp taschenbuch wissenschaft. Suhrkamp Verlag, Frankfurt am Main.

Hegel, Georg Wilhelm Friederich. (1971). *Vorlesungen über die Geschichte der Philosophie*. Herausgeben von Gerd Irrlitz. Textredaktion von Karin Gurst. Verlag Philipp Reclam jun, Leipzig.

Heidenheimer, Arnold J. and Michael Johnston (eds) (2002). *Political Corruption: Concepts and Context*. Transaction Publishers, New Brunswick, New Jersey.

Heilbroner, Robert L. (1982). 'The socialization of the individual in Adam Smith'. *History of Political Economy*, 14(3): 427–439.

Heilbroner, Robert L. (ed.) (1986). *The Essential Adam Smith*. W.W. Norton & Co., New York.

Herdt, Jennifer A. (1997). *Religion and Faction in Hume's Moral Philosophy*. Cambridge University Press, Cambridge.

Hesse, Helge (2009). *Personlexikon der Wirtschaftsgeschichte. Denker, Unternehmer und Politiker in 900 Porträts. 2 Auflage*. Schäffer-Poeschel Verlag, Stuttgart.

Hobbes, Thomas (1961 [1640–60]). *English Works of Thomas Hobbes of Malmesbury*, 11 vols, *and Opera Philosophica (Latin Works)*, 5 vols, ed. William Molesworth, London1839–1845; reprinted Clarendon Press, Oxford.

Hobbes, Thomas (2002 [1642]). *De Cive* (The English version entitled in the first edition *Philosophical Rudiments Concerning Government and Society*). Edited by Howard Warrender. Clarendon Press, Oxford.

Hochstrasser, Tim J. (2000). *Natural Law Theories in the Early Enlightenment*. Cambridge University Press, Cambridge.

Holberg, Ludvig (1969–1971 [1716]). *Kunskab om Natur og Folkeretten*, Bind 2. In Ludvig Holberg (1711–1753), *Værker i tolv bind: Digteren-historikeren-juristen-vismanden*. Udgivet med Indledninger og kommentarer af F.J. Billeskov Jansen. Roskilde og Bagger, Copenhagen.

Hollander, Samuel (1973). *The Economics of Adam Smith*. Heinemann Educational Books, London.

Hollander, Samuel (1987). *Classical Economics*. Basil Blackwell, New York.

Hont, Istvan (1987). 'The Language of Sociability and Commerce: Samuel Pufendorf and the Theoretical Foundations of the "Four-Stages Theory"'. In A. Pagden (ed.), *The Languages of Political Economy in Early-Modern Europe*. Cambridge University Press, Cambridge.

Hont, Istvan (2005). *Jealousy of Trade: International Competition and the Nation-State in Historical Perspective*. The Belknap Press of Harvard University Press, Cambridge, Massachusetts, and London.

Hont, Istvan (2015). *Politics in Commercial Society: Jean-Jacques Rousseau and Adam Smith*. Edited by Béla Kapossy and Michael Sonenscher. Harvard University Press, Cambridge, Massachusetts, and London.

Hont, Istvan and Michael Ignatieff (eds) (1983). *Wealth and Virtue: The Shaping of Political Economy in the Scottish Enlightenment*. Cambridge University Press, Cambridge.

Hont, Istvan and Michael Ignatieff (eds) (1983). '*Needs and Justice in "The Wealth of Nations": An Introductory Essay*'. In *Wealth and Virtue: The Shaping of Political Economy in the Scottish Enlightenment*. Cambridge University Press, Cambridge.

Hope, Vincent (1984). *Philosophers of the Scottish Enlightenment*. Edinburgh University Press, Edinburgh.

Hueglin, Thomas D. (2008). *Classical Debates of the 21st Century: Rethinking Political Thought*. Broadview Press, Peterborough.

Hume, David (2011 [1739]). *A Treatise of Human Behaviour: A Critical Edition*. Edited by David Fate Norton and Mary J. Norton. Oxford University Press, Oxford.

Hunger, Wolfgang (1991). *Samuel von Pufendorf. Aus dem Leben und Werk eines deutschen Frühaufklärers*. Verlag Druck & Design, Flöha, Saxony.

Hunter, Ian (2001). *Rival Enlightenments: Civil and Metaphysical Philosophy in Early Modern Germany*. Cambridge University Press, Cambridge.

Hutcheson, Francis (1755). *A System of Moral Philosophy in Three Books.* Published from the original manuscript by his son FrancisHutchesonJr. Robert Foulis, Printer to the University, Glasgow.

Hutcheson, Francis (1969 [1747]). *A Short Introduction to Moral Philosophy, in Three Books; Containing the Elements of Ethicks and the Law of Nature.* Collected Works, Vol. 4. Georg Olms Verlagsbuchhandlung, Hildesheim.

Hutcheson, Francis (1969 [1747]). *A Short Introduction to Moral Philosophy, in Three Books; containing the Elements of Ethicks and the Law of Nature.* Translated from the Latin. Printed and sold by Robert Foulis, Printer to the University, Glasgow. Third edition. Scholars' Facsimiles & Reprints, Gainesville, Florida.

Hutcheson, Francis (1969 [1755]). *A System of Moral Philosophy.* Collected Works. Vols 5 and 6. Georg Olms Verlagsbuchhandlung, Hildesheim.

Hutcheson, Francis (1969 [1728, 1742]). *An Essay on the Nature and Conduct of the Passion and Affections with Illustration on the Moral Sense.* Scholars' Facsimiles & Reproductions, Gainesville, Florida.

Hutcheson, Francis (1973 [1725]). *An Inquiry Concerning Beaty, Order, Harmony Design.* Edited, with an Introduction, by Peter Kivy. Martinus Nijhoff, The Hague.

Hutcheson, Francis (1993 [1730, 1756]). *Two Texts on Human Nature: Reflections on Our Common Systems of Morality. On the Social Nature of Man.* Edited by Thomas Mautner. Cambridge University Press, Cambridge.

Hutchison, Terence (1988). *Before Adam Smith: The Emergence of Political Economy, 1662–1776.* Basil Blackwell, Oxford.

Hutchison, Terence (1990). '*Moral Philosophy and Political Economy in Scotland*' Chapter 3 in D. Mair (ed.), *The Scottish Contribution to Modern Economic Thought.* Aberdeen University Press, Aberdeen.

Israel, Jonathan I. (2001). *Radical Enlightenment: Philosophy and the Making of Modernity 1650–1750.* Oxford University Press, Oxford

Israel, Jonathan I. (2006). *Enlightenment Contested: Philosophy, Modernity, and the Emancipation of Man 1670–1752.* Oxford University Press, Oxford.

Jacobson, Gustav (1931). 'Peter Julius Coyet'. *Svensk Biografisk Lexikon.* Albert Bonniers Förlag, Stockholm.

James, Edward Donald (1981). *Pierre Nicole, Jansenist and Humanist: A Study of His Thought.* Martinus Nijhoff, Leiden.

Johnson, Edgar A.J. (1937). *Predecessors of Adam Smith: The Growth of British Economic Thought.* Prentice-Hall, New York.

Jolley, Nicolas (1999). *Locke: His Philosophical Thought.* Oxford University Press, Oxford.

Jones, John and Anne Sander (January 2009). 'Catalogue of an Exhibition arranged for a Conference of the International Adam Smith Society'.

Jourdain, Margaret (1916). *Diderot's Early Philosophical Works.* The Open Court Publishing Co., Chicago and London.

Jägerskiöld, Stig (1985). 'Samuel von Pufendorf in Schweden, 1668–1688: Einige Neue Beiträge'. In J.A. Ankum, J.E. Spruit, and F.B.J. Wubbe (eds), *Satura Roberto Feenstra.* University Press of Fribourg, Switzerland.

Kauder, Emil (1953). 'Genesis of the marginal utility theory. From Aristotle to the end of the eighteenth century'. *Economic Journal* 63: 638–650.

Kaye, F.B. (ed.) (1924 [1732]). 'Prefatory note on the method of this edition'. In Bernard Mandeville, *The Fable of the Bees: or, Private Vices, Publick Benefits.* Sixth edition. Clarendon Press, Oxford.

Keiren, Tim and Frank Meltion (1990). 'Thomas Manley and the rate of interest debate 1668–1673'. *Journal of British Studies* 29: 147–173.
Kennedy, Ellen and Susan Mendus (eds) (1987). *Women in Western Political Philosophy*. Wheatsheaf Press, Brighton.
Kevorkian, Tanya (2007). *Baroque Piety: Religion, Society, and Music in* Leipzig, *1650–1750*. Ashgate Publishing, Burlington, Vermont.
Khalil, Elias L. (1990). 'Beyond self-interest and altruism. A reconstruction of Adam Smith's theory of human conduct'. *Economics and Philosophy* 6(2): 255–273.
Kingston, Rebecca (1996). *Montesquieu and the Parliament of Bordeaux*. Librairie DROZ S.A, Geneva.
Korkman, Peter (ed.) (2006 [1763]). 'Introduction' *and notes*. In Jean-Jacques Burlamaqui, *The Principles of Natural and Politic Law. Translated by*Thomas Nugent. Liberty Fund, Indianapolis.
Korkman, Petter (2013). *Barlamaqui and Natural Law*. The Forum at the Online Library of Liberty. Liberty Fund, Indianapolis.
Kratochwil, Stefan (1999). 'Die Berufung Erhard Weigel and die Universität Jena'. In Reinhard E. Schielicke, Klaus-Dieter Herbst and Stefan Kratochwil (eds), *Erhard Weigel –1625 bis 1699. Barocker Erzvater der deutchen Frühaufklärung. Beiträge des Kolloquiums anlässlich seines 300. Todestages am 20. März 1999 in Jena*. Acta Historica Astronomiae, Vol. 7. Verlag Harri Deutsch, Frankfurt am Main.
Krause, Konrad (2003). *Alma mater Lipsiensis. Geschichte der Universität Leipzig von 1409 bis zur Gegenwart*. Leipziger Universitätsverlag, Leipzig.
Krieger, Leonard (1957). *The German Idea of Freedom*. Beacon Press, Boston.
Krieger, Leonard (1965). *The Politics of Discretion: Pufendorf and the Acceptance of Natural Law*. The University of Chicago Press, Chicago and London.
Kurz, Heinz D. (2008:267). 'Physiocracy'. In William A. Darity (ed.), *International Encyclopedia of the Social Sciences*. Second edition. Macmillan Reference, Detroit.
Lagerspetz, Erik (1986). 'Pufendorf on collective decisions '. *Public Choice* 49(2): 179–182.
Landreth, Harry and Colander, David C. (1994). *History of Economic Thought*. Third Edition. Houghton Mifflin, Boston.
Lapidus, Andre (1986). *Le Detour de Valeur*. Economica, Paris.
Laslett, Peter (ed.) (1964). 'Introduction and notes'. In *John Locke: Two Treatises of Government*. Cambridge University Press, Cambridge.
Laslett, Peter (1988). 'Introduction'. In *John Locke: Two Treatises of Government*. Revised edition. Cambridge University Press, Cambridge.
Laursen, John Cristian (ed.) (1995). *New Essays on the Political Thoughts of the Huguenots of the Refuge*. Brill, Leiden.
Leechman, W. (1754). *Preface to Hutcheson, Francis (1755)*.
Leidhold, Wolfgang (1986). 'Einleitung. Liebe, Moralsinn, Glück und Civil Gouvernment Anmerkungen zu einigen Zentralbegriffen bei Francis Hutcheson'. In Francis Hutcheson, *Eine Untersuchung über den Ursprung unserer Ideen von Schönheit und Tugend Über moralisch Gutes und Schlectes*. Felix Meiner Verlag, Hamburg.
Lenhart, N. (1985). Gershom Carmichael, On Samuel Pufendorf's *De officio hominis et civis*: Supplements and Appendix. Translated by C.H. Reeves. Privately published, Cleveland, Ohio.
Lerner, Max (1937). 'Introduction'. In Adam Smith, *The Wealth of Nations*. The Modern Library, New York. (Reprint of the 1904 Cannan edition.)

Lesaffer, Randall (2005). 'Argument from Roman law in current international law: Occupation and acquisitive prescription'. *European Journal of International Law* 16(1): 25–58.

Letwin, William (1963). *The Origins of Scientific Economics.* Methuen & Co., London.

Leyden, Wolfgang von (ed.) (1954). *Introduction to John Locke: Essays on the Law of Nature.* Clarendon Press, Oxford.

Leyden, Wolfgang von (ed.) (1954). 'Locke's Valedictory Speech as Censor of Moral Philosophy'. In John Locke [1664], *Essays on the Law of Nature.* (The Latin text with a translation, introduction and notes. Edited and first published by W. von Leyden.)

Lindberg, Bo (1976). *Naturrätten i Uppsala 1655–1720.* Liber Tryck, Stockholm.

Lindberg, Bo (1983). 'The doctrine of natural law in 17th century Sweden'. In Rättshistoriska Studier Tolfte Bandet (1986): *Samuel Pufendorf 1632–1982. Et rättshistorisk symposium in Lund 15–16 januari 1982.* Institutet för Rättshistorisk forskning. Serien II. A-B Nordiska Bokhandeln, Stockholm, pp. 71–80.

Lindberg, Bo (1997). 'Samuel von Pufendorf'. In *Svensk Biografisk Lexikon*, Band 29. Norstedts Tryckeri AB, Stockholm, pp. 512–522.

Lluch, Ernest and Luis Argemi (1994). 'Physiocracy in Spain'. *History of Political Economy* 26(4): 613–627.

Locke, John (1968 [1683–93]). *The Educational Writings of John Locke.* Edited by James Axtell. Cambridge University Press, Cambridge.

Locke, John (1690). *An Essay Concerning Human Understanding, in Four Books.* Second edition. Printed by Eliz. Holt, for Thomas Basset, at the George in Fleet Street, near St. Dunstan's Church. The Project Gutenberg Ebook.

Locke, John (1691). 'Some Consideration of the Consequences of the Lowering of Interest, and Raising the Value of Money'. In a letter sent to a Member of Parliament. Printed for Awnsham and John Churchill, at the Black Swan in Pater-Noster-Row, London. Available at http://socserv.socsci.mcmaster.ca/oldecon/ugcm/3113/locke/consid.txt.

Locke, John (1695). 'Short Observation on a Printed Paper Intituled, For Encouraging the Coining silver Money in England, and after for Keeping it here'. Printed in John Locke (1964 [1698]).

Locke, John (1968 [1696]). 'Further Consideration Concerning Raising the Value of Money'. Printed in Several Papers.

Locke, John (1964 [1698]). *Two Treatises of Government: In the Former, The False Principles and Foundation of Sir Robert Filmer, and his Followers are Detected and Overthrown. The Latter is an Essay Concerning The True Original, Extent, and End of Civil-Government.* Printed for Awnsham and John Churchill, at the Black Swan in Pater-Noster-Row, London. Also in Peter Laslett (ed.) (1964), *John Locke: Two Treatises of Government.* Cambridge University Press, Cambridge.

Locke, John (1954 [1662–1663]). *Essays on the Law of Nature.* (The Latin text with a translation, introduction and notes.) Edited and first published by W. von Leyden. Clarendon Press, Oxford.

Locke, John (1964 [1690]). *Two Treatises of Government.* Edited by Peter Laslett. (Reprinted 1989.) Cambridge University Press, Cambridge.

Locke, John (1965 [1668–1674]). *Locke's Early Manuscript on Interest.* Appendix 5 in William Letwin, *The Origins of Scientific Economics* Methuen & Co., London.

Locke, John (1968 [1696]). *Several Papers Relating to Money, Interest and Trade, & Co.* Printed for Awnsham and John Churchill, at the Black Swan in Pater-Noster-Row, London. Reprints of Economic Classics. Augustus M. Kelley, Publishers, Fairfield, New Jersey.

Luig, Klaus (1972). 'Zur Verbreitung des Naturrechts in Europa'. *Tijdschrift voor Rechtsgeschiedenis*, 40: 540–557.
Lütge, Friedrich (1960). *Deutsche Sozial und Wirtschaftsgeschichte.* Second edition. Springer Verlag, Heidelberg.
Lutz, Donald (1984). 'The relative influence of European writers on late eighteenth-century American political thought'. *The American Political Science Review* 78(1): 189–197.
McCosh, James (1875). *The Scottish Philosophy: Biographical, Expository, Critical, from Hutcheson to Hamilton.* Macmillan, London.
Macfie, Alec Lawrence (1952). 'Note on the Growth of Political Economy'. In *Fortuna Domus.* University of Glasgow, Glasgow.
Macfie, Alec Lawrence. (1967). *The Individual in Society.* Papers on Adam Smith. George Allen & Unwin, London.
MacPherson, Crawford Brough (1962). *The Political Theory of Possessive Individualism.* Oxford University Press, Oxford.
McReynolds, Paul (1969). *An Introduction to Francis Hutcheson* (1728, 1742).
Maier, Hans and Horst Denzer (eds) (2007). *Klassiker des politischen Denkens*, Band 1 und 2. Verlag C.H. Beck, Berlin.
Mair, Douglas (ed.) (1990). *The Scottish Contribution to Modern Economic Thought.* Aberdeen University Press, Aberdeen.
Mandeville, Bernard (1924 [1714]). *The Fable of the Bees: or, Private Vices, Publick Benefits* (Sixth edition, 1732), edited by F.B. Kaye. Clarendon Press, Oxford.
Maurseth, Anne Beate (2005). *Opplysningens sjonglør. Denis Diderot 1713–1784.* (A juggler of the Enlightenment. Diderot 1713–1784.) Humanist Forlag, Oslo.
Mautner, Thomas (1986). *'Pufendorf and 18th Century Scottish Philosophy'.* In Kjell Modéer (ed.), *Ett rättshistorisk symposium in Lund 15–16 januari 1982.* A.-B. Nordiska Bokhandeln, Stockholm, pp. 120–131.
Mautner, Thomas (ed.) (1993). *Francis Hutcheson: On Human Nature. Reflections on Our Common Systems of Morality. On the Social Nature of Man.* Cambridge University Press, Cambridge.
Mautner, Thomas (1996). '*Carmichael and Barbeyrac: The Lost Correspondence'.* In Fiammetta Palladini and Gerald Hartung (eds), *Samuel Pufendorf und die europäische Früaufklärung.* Akademie Verlag, Berlin, pp. 190–208.
Mautner, Thomas (ed.) (1999). *Dictionary of Philosophy.* Penguin Books, London.
Medick, Hans (1973). *Naturzustand und Naturgeschichte der bürgerlichen Gesellschaft.* Vandenhoeck & Ruprecht, Göttingen.
Meek, Ronald L. (1971). 'Smith, Turgot and the "Four Stages" Theory'. *History of Political Economy* 3(1): 9–27.
Meek, Ronald L. (1976). 'New light on Adam Smith's Glasgow lectures on jurisprudence'. *History of Political Economy* 8(4): 439–477.
Meek, Ronald L. (1976). *Social Sciences and the Ignoble Savage.* Cambridge University Press, Cambridge.
Meek, Ronald L. and Andrew S. Skinner (1973). 'The development of Adam Smith's ideas of the division of labour'. *Economic Journal* 83(332): 1094–1116.
Meek, Ronald L., D.D. Raphael and P.G. Stein (eds) (1978) *Adam Smith Lectures on Jurisprudence: An Introduction.* Clarendon Press, Oxford.
Meek, Ronald L., D.D. Raphael and P.G. Stein (1982). 'Introduction'. In Adam Smith, *Lectures on Jurisprudence.* Facsimile of the Oxford University Press edition of 1978. Liberty Fund, Indianapolis.

Meyer, Paul (1894). *Samuel Pufendorf, Ein Beitrag zur Geschichte seines Lebens. Abhandlung zum Jahresbericth der Fürsten- und Landesschule zu Grimma über das Schuljahr1894–1895*. Druck von Julius Schiertz, Grimma.

Milton L. Myers (1983). *The Soul of Modern Economic Man*. The University of Chicago Press, Chicago and London.

Mintz, Samuel (1962). *The Hunting of Leviathan*. Cambridge University Press, Cambridge.

Mirabeau, Victor Marquis de (1757). *L'ami des hommes, ou traité de la population* (Friend of Men, or a Treatise on Population). Bibliothèque National, Paris.

Mirabeau, Victor Marquis de (1760). *La theorie de l'impôt* (Theory of Taxation) Bibliothèque National, Paris.

Modéer, Kjell Å. (ed.) (1986). *Samuel von Pufendorf 1632–1982. Ett rättshistorisk symposium in Lund 15–16 januari 1982*. A.-B. Nordiska Bokhandeln, Stockholm.

Monroe, Arthur E. (1924). *Early Economic Thought*. Harvard University Press, Cambridge, Massachusetts.

Monroe, D.H. (1987). 'Self-interest'. In J. Eatwell, M. Milgate and P. Newman (eds), *The New Palgrave Dictionary of Economics*, Vol. 4. Macmillan, London.

Montes, Leonidas and Eric Schliesser (eds) (2006). *New Voices on Adam Smith*. Routledge, Abingdon, UK, and New York.

Montesquieu, Charles-Louis (1748 [1989]). *The Spirit of the Law*. Translated and edited by Anne M. Cohler, Basia Carolyn Miller and Harold Samuel Stone. Cambridge University Press, Cambridge.

Montesquieu, Charles-Louis (2003 [1748]). *The Spirit of the Law*. Translated into English by Thomas Nugent (1752). Revised by J.V. Prichard. The electronic edition. Copyright 2003, 2005. Lonang Institute.

Moore, James and Michael Silverthorne (1983). 'Gershom Carmichael and the natural jurisprudence tradition in eighteenth-century Scotland'. In Istvan Hont and Michael Ignatieff (eds), *Wealth and Virtue: The Shaping of Political Economy in the Scottish Enlightenment*. Cambridge University Press, Cambridge.

Moore, James and Michael Silverthorne (1984). 'Natural Sociability and Natural Rights in the Moral Philosophy of Gershom Carmichael'. In V. Hope (ed.), *Philosophers of the Scottish Enlightenment*. Edinburgh University Press, Edinburgh, pp. 1–12.

Moore, James and Michael Silverthorne (eds) (2002). *Natural Rights on the Threshold of the Scottish Enlightenment*. The Writings of Gershom Carmichael. Liberty Fund, Indianapolis.

Mossner, Ernest Campbell and Ian Simpson Ross (eds) (1987). *The Correspondence of Adam Smith*. Liberty Classics, Indianapolis.

Munro, John H. (2011). 'Usury, Calvinism, and Credit in Protestant England: From the Sixteenth Century to the Industrial Revolution'. Working Paper 439. Department of Economics, University of Toronto.

Murray, David (1927). *Memories of the Old College of Glasgow*. Jackson Wylie and Co., Publisher to the University, Glasgow.

Myers, Milton L. (1983). *The Soul of Modern Economic Man: Ideas of Self-Interest Thomas Hobbes to Adam Smith*. The University of Chicago Press, Chicago and London.

Naldi, Nerio (1993). *Gershom Carmichael on 'Demand' and 'Difficulty of Acquiring': Some Evidence from the First Edition of Carmichael's Commentary to Pufendorf's De Officio*. Scottish Economic Society. Blackwell, Oxford, and Cambridge, Massachusetts.

Nicole, Pierre (1671). *Essais de Morale contenus en divers Traittez syr plusieurs devoir Importans.* Volume Premier. Deuxième édition, reveuë, and corrigée. Chez la veuve Charles Savreux, Libraire juré `a Paris, au pied de la Tour de Notre-Dame, aux trois vertus. À Paris. Bibliothèque Diderot de Lyons.

Niléhn, Lars (1986). 'On the Use of Natural Law: Samuel Pufendorf as Royal Swedish State Historian'. In Rättshistoriska Studier Tolfte Bandet, *Samuel Pufendorf 1632–1982. Ett rättshistorisk symposium in Lund 15–16 januari 1982*. Institutet för Rättshistorisk forskning. Serien II. A-B Nordiska Bokhandeln, Stockholm.

Nilsén, Per (2012). *Holbergs natur- och folkrät i svensk översättning 1789* (The Natural and International Law of Holberg in a Swedish Translation 1789). In Eiliv Vinje and Jørgen Magnus Sejersted (eds), *Holbergs Naturrett*. Gyldendal Norsk Forlag, Oslo.

Norton, David Fate (1982). *Commonsense Moralist, Sceptical Metaphysician*. Princeton University Press, Princeton.

Norton, David Fate and Mary J. Norton (eds) (2011). *David Hume: A Treatise of Human Nature*, Vols 1 and 2. Clarendon Press, Oxford.

Nutkiewcez, Michael (1992). 'Samuel Pufendorf: Obligation as the Basis of the State'. In Vere Chappell (ed.), *Essays on Early Modern Philosophers: From Descartes and Hobbes to Newton and Leibniz*, Vol. 4: *Port-Royal to Bayle*. Garland Publishing, New York and London.

Othmer, Sieglinde C. (1970). Berlin *und die verbreitung des naturrechts in Europa*. Walter de Gruyter & Co., Berlin.

Pagden, Anthony (ed.) (1987). *The Languages of Political Theory in Early-Modern Europe*. Cambridge University Press, Cambridge.

Pagden, Anthony (1993). *European Encounters with the New World: From Renaissance to Romanticism*. Yale University Press, New Haven and London.

Palladini, Fiammetta (2008). 'Pufendorf disciple of Hobbes: The nature of man and the state of nature: The doctrine of socialitas'. *History of European Ideas* 34(1): 26–60.

Palladini, Fiammetta (2011). *Die Berliner Hugenotten und der Fall Barbeyrac. Orthodoxe und 'Sozinianer' im Refuge (1685–1720)*. Brill's Studies in Intellectual History. Brill, Leiden.

Palladini, Fiammetta and Gerald Hartung (eds) (1996). *Samuel Pufendorf und die europäische Früaufklärung*. Akademie Verlag, Berlin.

Pesciarelli, Enzo (1986). 'On Adam Smith's lectures on jurisprudence'. *Scottish Journal of Political Economy* 33(1): 74–85.

Pesciarelli, Enzo (1989). 'Aspects of the influence of Francis Hutcheson on Adam Smith'. *History of Political Economy* 31(3): 525–545.

Pownall, Thomas (1776). 'A Letter to Adam Smith'. In E.C. Mossner and I.S. Ross (eds), *The Correspondence of Adam Smith*. Liberty Classics, Indianapolis, Appendix A, pp. 337–376.

Pribram, Karl (1983). *A History of Economic Reasoning*. The Johns Hopkins University Press, Baltimore and London.

Puperto, Carlola (1961). *Sonderband aus der Geschichte der Univeristät Heidelberg und ihrer Facultäten*. Bausdrück GmbH, Heidelberg.

Quesnay, François (1759). *Tableau économique*. (Third edition, privately published at Versailles. First edition 1758 and second edition 1759 was not published.) Bibliothèque National, Paris.

Rabe, Horst (1958). *Naturrecht und Kirche bei Samuel von Pufendorf. Eine Untersuchung der Naturrechtlichen Einflüsse auf den Kirchenbegrieff Pufendorfs als Studie zur Entstehung des Modernes Denken*. University of Tübingen.

Rae, John (1965 [1895]). *Life of Adam Smith*. Macmillan, London. Reprinted with an Introduction by Jacob Viner. Augustus M. Kelley, Publishers. Fairfield, New Jersey.

Raphael, David D. (1991). *Introduction to Adam Smith the Wealth of Nations*. Everyman's Library, London.

Raphael, David D. and Alec L. Macfie (1976). *Introduction to Adam Smith's Theory of Moral Sentiments*. Liberty Classics, Indianapolis.

Rättshistoriska Studier Tolfte Bandet (1986). *Samuel Pufendorf 1632–1982. Ett rättshistorisk symposium in Lund 15–16 januari 1982*. Institutet för Rättshistorisk forskning. Serien II. A-B Nordiska Bokhandeln, Stockholm.

Rectenwald, Horst Claus (1978). 'An Adam Smith renaissance anno 1776? The bicentenary output – A reappraisal of his scholarship'. *Journal of Economic Literature* 16(1): 56–83.

Rendall, Jane (1987). 'Virtue and Commerce: Women in the Making of Adam Smith's Political Economy'. In Ellen Kennedy and Susan Mendus (eds), *Women in Western Political Philosophy*. Wheatsheaf Press, Brighton.

Ridderikhoff, C.M. (1995). *Een Hollands staatsman in buitenlands dienst. Hugo de Groot als ambassadeur van Zweden in Parijs, 1634–1645*. In Jaarboeknr. 87. Genootschap Amstelodanum, Amsterdam, pp. 165–178.

Rima, Ingrid Hahne (1991). *Development of Economic Analysis*. Fifth Edition. Richard D. Irwin, Inc., Homewood, Illinois.

Roberts, Hazel van Dyke (1935). *Boisguilbert: Economist of the Reign of Louis XIV*. Columbia University Press, New York.

Robertson, H.M. and W.L. Taylor (1957). 'Adam Smith's approach to the theory of value'. *The Economic Journal* 67(266): 181–198.

Rosenberg, Nathan (1987). 'Bernard Mandeville'. In John Eatwell, Milgate Murry and Peter Newman (eds), *The New Palgrave Dictionary of Economics*, Vol. 4. Macmillan, London.

Rosicka, Janina (ed.) (1996). *Physiocracy Yesterday and Today: Economy – Philosophy – Politics*. Cracow Academy of Economics, Cracow.

Ross, Ian Simpson (2010). *The Life of Adam Smith*. Second edition. Oxford University Press, Oxford.

Rotwein, Eugene (ed.) (1955). *David Hume*. Writings on Economics. Nelson & Sons, Edinburgh.

Rousseau, Jean-Jacques (1959). *Oeuvres Complètes de Rousseau*. Gallimard-Pléiade, Paris.

Rousseau, Jean-Jacques (1968 [1762]). *The Social Contract*. Edited with an introduction by Maurice Cranston. Penguin Books, London.

Rousseau, Jean-Jacques (2007 [1762]). *The Social Contract and Other Later Political Writings*. Edited and translated by Victor Gourevitch. Cambridge University Press, Cambridge.

Rousseau, Jean-Jacques (2008 [1750]). *The Discourses and Other Early Political Writings*. Edited and translated by Victor Gourevitch. Cambridge University Press, Cambridge.

Rousseau, Jean-Jacques (2014 [1762]). *Émile or Education*. Translated by Barbara Foxley. J.M. Dent, London and Toronto. Online Library of Liberty. Liberty Fund, Indianapolis.

Rutherford, Donald (2012). *In the Shadow of Adam Smith: Founders of Scottish Economics 1700–1900*. Palgrave Macmillan, Basingstoke and New York.

Sandelin, Bo (1987). *Samuel von Pufendorf*. Ekonomisk Debatt, Stockholm.

Sandelin, Bo (ed.) (1991). *The History of Swedish Economic Thought*. Routledge, London and New York.

Saastamoinen, Kari (1995). *The Morality of the Fallen Man: Samuel Pufendorf on Natural Law.* Studia Historica 52. SHS, Helsinki.

Sandelin, Bo, Hans-Michael Trautwein and Richard Wundrak (2008). *A Short History of Economic Thought*. Routledge, New York.

Saunders, David (2003). 'The natural jurisprudence of Jean Barbeyrac: Translation as an art of political adjustment'. *Eighteenth-Century Studies* 36(4): 473–490.

Schabas, Margaret (2014). 30. 'Philosophy of the Human Sciences'. In Aaron Garret (ed.), *The Routledge Companion to Eighteenth Century Philosophy.* Routledge, London and New York, pp. 731–752.

Schielicke, Reinhard E., Klaus-Dieter Herbst and Stefan Kratochwil (eds) (1999). *Erhard Weigel –1625 bis 1699. Barocker Erzvater der deutschen Frühaufklärung. Beiträge des Kolloquiums anlässlich seines 300. Todestages am 20. März 1999 in Jena*. Acta Historica Astronomiae, Vol. 7. Verlag Harri Deutsch, Jena, pp. 69–90.

Schneewind, Jerome B. (1987). 'Pufendorf's place in the history of ethics'. *Synthese* 72(1): 123–155.

Schroeder, Klaus-Peter (2001). 'Der Dreissigjährige Krieg, das Alte Reich und Samuel von Pufendorf (1632–1694)'. In *Vom Sachsenspiegel zum Grundgesetz. Eine deutsche Rechtsgeschichte in Lebensbildern*. Verlag C.H. Beck, Munich.

Schroeder, Klaus-Peter (2008). *Vom Sachsenspiegel zum Grundgesetz. Eine deutsche Rechtsgeschickte in Lebensbildern*. Verlag C.H. Beck, Berlin.

Schumpeter, Joseph A. (1954). *History of Economic Analysis*. Oxford University Press, New York.

Schwartzberg, Melissa (2008). 'Voting the general will: Rousseau on decision rules'. *Political Theory* 36(3):403–423.

Schüling, Herman (1970). *Erhard Wiegel (1625–1699). Materialen zur Erforschung seines Wirkens*. Universitetsbibliotek, Giessen.

Scott, John T. (ed.) (2006). *Jean-Jacques Rousseau: Critical Assessments of Leading Political Philosopher*. Routledge, New York.

Scott, William Robert (1900). *Francis Hutcheson: His Life, Teaching and Position in the History of Philosophy.* Cambridge University Press, Cambridge.

Scott, William Robert (1937). *Adam Smith as a Student and Professor*. Jackson, Son & Co., Glasgow.

Seidler, Michael (ed.) (2007). 'Introduction'. In *Samuel Pufendorf: The Present State of Germany.* Liberty Fund, Indianapolis, pp. ix–xxvii.

Seidler, Michael (2013). 'Pufendorf's Moral and Political Philosophy'. In Edward N. Zalta (ed.), *The Stanford Encyclopedia of Philosophy.* Available athttp://plato.stanford.edu/archives/spr2013/entries/pufendorf-moral/.

Selden, John (1640). *De Jure naturali et gentium Juxta disciplinam Ebraeoram.* London.

Shackleton, Robert (1961) *Montesquieu: A Critical Bibliography.* Oxford University Press, Oxford.

Shorto, Russell (2005). *The Island at the Centre of the World: The Untold Story of the Founding of* New York. Black Swan edition. Cox & Wyman, Reading.

Simons, Walter (1934). *'Introduction'* to Samuel Pufendorf's *De Jure Naturae et Gentium Libri Octo* (On the law of nature and nations), Vol. 2. The translation of the edition of 1688 (with references to the first edition of 1672). Oceana Publications, New York, and Wiley & Sons, London.

Skinner, Andrew (ed.) (1974). *Adam Smith: The Wealth of Nations.* Penguin Books, London.

Skinner, Andrew, (1995). 'Pufendorf, Hutcheson and Adam Smith: Some principles of political economy'. *Scottish Journal of Political Economy* 42(2): 165–182.

Smidt, Jacobus Th. de (1986). 'Pufendorf und Leiden'. In Kjell Å. Modéer (ed.), *Samuel von Pufendorf 1632–1982. Ett rättshistorisk symposium in Lund 15–16 januari 1982*. A.-B. Nordiska Bokhandeln, Stockholm.

Smith, Adam (1759). *The Theory of Moral Sentiments* (Sixth edition, Glasgow, 1790). Edited by D.D. Raphael and A.L. Macfie. Oxford University Press, Oxford, 1976. (Reprinted 1991; and in 1982 by Liberty Press / Liberty Classics, Indianapolis.)

Smith, Adam (1789 [1776]). *An Inquiry into the Nature and Causes of the Wealth of Nations.* Fifth edition. Edinburgh.

Smith, Adam (1904 [1776]). *An Inquiry into the Nature and Causes of the Wealth of Nations.* Edited by Edwin Cannan. Methuen& Co., London.

Smith, Adam (1937 [1776]). *An Inquiry into the Nature and Causes of the Wealth of Nations.* Introduction by Max Lerner (reprint of the 1904 edition). The Modern Library, New York.

Smith, Adam (1965 [1937/1763]). 'An Early Draft of Part of the Wealth of Nations'. In W.R. Scott (1965 [1937]), *Adam Smith as Student and Professor.* Jackson, Son & Co., Glasgow, pp. 317–356.

Smith, Adam (1976). *The Glasgow Edition of the Works and Correspondence of Adam Smith*, Vol. 2. Edited by R.H. Campbell, A.S. Skinner, and W.B. Todd. Clarendon Press, Oxford.

Smith, Adam (1977 [1776]). *The Wealth of Nations.* Preface by George J. Stigler (reprint of the 1904 edition). The University of Chicago Press, Chicago.

Smith, Adam (1982 [1762–1763]). *Lectures on Jurisprudence, Report of 1762–3 and Report Dated 1766 Together with an Appendix Containing the 'Early Draft' of the Wealth of Nations from the 1760s.* (Edited by R.L. Meek, D.D. Raphael and P.G. Stein, Clarendon Press, Oxford, 1978; facsimile published by Liberty Classics, Indianapolis, 1982.)

Smith, Adam (1991 [1776]). *The Wealth of Nations.* Edited with an Introduction by D. D. Raphael. Everyman's Library, New York.

Soper, Philip (1992). 'Some natural confusions about natural law'. *Michigan Law Review* 90(8): 2343–2423.

Spengler, Joseph J. (1948). 'The problem of order in economic affairs'. *Southern Economic Journal* 15: 1–29; reprinted in J.J. Spengler and W.R. Allen (eds), *Essays in Economic Thought: Aristotle to Marshall.* Rand McNally & Co., Chicago.

Spengler, Joseph J. and W.R. Allen (eds) (1960). *Essays in Economic Thought: Aristotle to Marshall.* Rand McNally & Co., Chicago 1960.

Spiegel, Henry William (1983). *The Growth of Economic Thought.* Revised and expanded edition. Duke University Press, Durham, North Carolina.

Spiess, Edmund (1881). *Erhard Weigel, weiland Professor der Mathematik und Astronomie zu Jena, der Lehrer von Leibniz und Pufendorf.* Verlag von Julius Klinkhardt, Jena.

Sprague, Elmer (1967). 'Francis Hutcheson'. In Paul Edwards (ed.), *The Encyclopedia of Philosophy.* Macmillan, New York, pp. 99–101.

Spurlin, Paul Merrill (1940). *Montesquieu in America 1760–1801.* Louisiana State University Press, Baton Rouge.

Stein, Peter G. (1982). 'From Pufendorf to Adam Smith: The Natural Law Tradition in Scotland'. In Norbert Horn (ed.), *Europäisches Rechtsdenken in Geschichte und Gegenwart. Festschrift für Helmut Coing*, Band 1. C.H. Beck'sche Verlagsbuchhandlung, Munich, pp. 667–679.

Stein, Peter. G. (1987). 'Samuel von Pufendorf'. In J. Eatwell, M. Milgate and P. Newman (eds), *The New Palgrave Dictionary of Economics*, Vol. 4. Macmillan, London.

Stewart, Dugald (1982 [1793]). 'Account of the Life and Writings of Adam Smith, LL. D.' From the Transactions of the Royal Society of Edinburgh. Edited by I.S. Ross. In W.P.D. Wightman and J.C. Bryce (eds), *Adam Smith Essays on Philosophical Subjects*. Liberty Classics, Indianapolis.

Stigler, George (1971). 'Smith's travels on the ship of state'. *History of Political Economy* 3(2): 265–277.

Strohm, C., F.S. Freedman and H.J. Selderhuis (eds) (2006). *Späthumanismus und reformierte Konfession*. Mohr Siebeck, Tübingen.

Sæther, Arild (1996). 'Pufendorf – Grandfather of Modern Economics'. In Fiammetta Palladini and Gerald Hartung (eds), *Samuel Pufendorf und die europäische Früaufklärung*. Akademie Verlag, Berlin.

Sæther, Arild (1996). 'Samuel Pufendorf's Natural Law and Physiocracy'. In Janina Rosicka (ed.), *Physiocracy Yesterday and Today: Economy – Philosophy – Politics*. Cracow Academy of Economics, Cracow, pp. 25–34.

Sæther, Arild (2000). 'Self-Interest as an Acceptable Mode of Human Behaviour'. In Michalis Psalidopoulos (ed.), *The Canon in the History of Economics: Critical Essays*. Routledge, London and New York.

Sæther, Arild (2017). *Samuel Pufendorf – The Grandfather of Modern Political Economy*. The Norwegian School of Economics, Bergen.

Tamm, Ditlev (1986). 'Pufendorf and Dänemark'. In Kjell Å. Modéer (ed.), *Samuel von Pufendorf 1632–1982. Ett rättshistorisk symposium in Lund 15–16 januari 1982*. A.-B. Nordiska Bokhandeln, Stockholm, pp. 81–89.

Taylor, Overton, H. (1930). 'Economics and the Jus Naturale'. *Quarterly Journal of Economics* 44(2): 205–241.

Taylor, William Leslie (1955). 'Gershom Carmichael: A neglected figure in British political economy'. *South African Journal of Economics* 23: 251–255.

Taylor, William L. (1965). *Francis Hutcheson and David Hume as Predecessors of Adam Smith*. Duke University Press, Durham, North Carolina.

Teachout, Zephyr (2014). *Corruption in America: From Benjamin Franklin's Snuff Box to Citizens United*. Harvard University Press, Boston.

Teichgraeber III, Richard F. (1986). *'Free Trade' and Moral Philosophy: Rethinking the Sources of Adam Smith's 'Wealth of Nations'*. Duke University Press, Durham, North Carolina.

Tennemann, Wilhelm Gottlieb (1798–1819). *Geschichte der Philosophie*, 11 vols. Leipzig.

Thiel, Udo (1999). 'Locke'. In Thomas Mautner (ed.), *Dictionary of Philosophy*. Penguin Books, London.

Treitschke, Heinrich von (1897). *Historische und politische Aufsätze*. G. Hirzel, Leipzig.

Tuck, Richard (1979). *Natural Rights Theories: Their Origin and Development*. Cambridge University Press, Cambridge.

Tuck, Richard (1987). 'The "Modern" Theory of Natural Law'. In Anthony Pagden (ed.), *The Languages of Political Theory in Early-Modern Europe*. Cambridge University Press, Cambridge.

Tuck, Richard (1993). *Philosophy and Government 1572–1651*. Cambridge University Press, Cambridge.

Tully, James (1980). *A Discourse on Property: John Locke and His Adversaries*. Cambridge University Press, Cambridge.

Tully, James (1991). 'Editor's Introduction'. In Samuel Pufendorf (1991).

Tully, James (1991). *Locke*. In J.H. Burns (ed.), *The Cambridge History of Political Thought 1450–1700*. Cambridge University Press, Cambridge.

Ueberweg, Friedrich (1868). *Grundriss der geschichte der philosophie von Thales bis auf die Gegenwart* (Outline of the history of philosophy from Thales to the present) [microform]. Dritter theil: *Die neuzeit*. Mittler, Berlin.

Vaggi, Gianni (1987). 'Physiocracy'. In J. Eatwell, M. Milgate and P. Newman (eds), *The New Palgrave Dictionary of Economics*, Vol. 4. Macmillan, London.

Vaggi, Gianni (2004). 'Adam Smith's Socio-Economic Man – and the Macrofoundation of Microeconomics'. In Tony Aspromourgos and John Lodewijks (eds), *History and Political Economy: Essays in Honour of P. D. Groenewegen*. Routledge, New York.

Vaggi, Gianni and Peter Groenewegen (2003). *A Concise History of Economic Thought: From Mercantilism to Monetarism*. Palgrave Macmillan, Basingstoke.

Vardi, Liana (2012). *The Physiocrats and the World of Enlightenment*. Cambridge University Press, Cambridge.

Vaughn, Karen Iversen (1980). *John Locke Economist and Social Scientist*. The University of Chicago Press, Chicago and London.

Vet, de, J.J.V.M. (1996). 'Some Periodicals of the United Provinces on Pufendorf: Reconnoitring the Reception of his Ideas in the Seventeenth and Eighteenth Centuries'. In Fiammetta Palladini and Gerald Hartung (eds), *Samuel Pufendorf und die europäische Früaufklärung*. Akademie Verlag, Berlin.

Viner, Jacob (1927). 'Adam Smith and laissez faire'. *Journal of Political Economy* 35(2): 198–232. Reprinted in John M. Clark, Paul H. Douglas, Jacob H. Hollander, Glenn R. Morrow, Melchior Palyi and Jacob Viner (eds), *Adam Smith, 1776–1926: Lectures to Commemorate the Sesquicentennial of the Publication of 'The Wealth of Nations'*. The University of Chicago Press, Chicago.

Viner, Jacob (1960). 'The intellectual history of laissez faire'. *Journal of Law and Economics* 3: 45–69.

Viner, Jacob (1965). 'Introduction'. In *John Rae, Life of Adam Smith*. Augustus M. Kelly, Publishers, New York.

Vinje, Eiliv and Jørgen Magnus Sejersted (eds) (2012). *Holbergs Naturrett*. Gyldendal Norsk Forlag, Oslo.

Vivenza, Gloria (2001). *Adam Smith and the Classics: The Classical Heritage in Adam Smith's Thought*. Oxford University Press, Oxford.

Waddicor, Mark H. (1970). *Montesquieu and the Philosophy of Natural Law*. Martinus Nijhoff, The Hague.

Walde, Otto (1920). *Storhetstidens litterära krigsbyten. En kulturhistorisk studie*. (A literary spoils of war: A cultural historical study). Almqvist & Wiksell, Uppsala and Stockholm.

Walras, Léon (1977 [1874]). *Elements of Pure Economics or the Theory of Social Wealth*. Augustus M. Kelley, Publishers, Fairfield, New Jersey. (A translation of the Édition Définitive (1926) of the *Éléments d'économie politique pure*. First published 1874.)

Wehberg, Hans (1931). *Introduction to Pufendorf* (1660).

Weigel, Erhard (2003 [1673]). 'Universi Corporis Pansophici'. In *Caput Summum*, Jena. In Thomas Behme (ed.), *Werke* 1. Friedrich Frommann Verlag-Günther Holzboog, Stuttgart-Bad Cannstatt.

Weigel, Erhard (2004 [1674]). *Arithmetische Beschreibung der Moral-Weissheit von Personen und Sachen*, Jena. In Thomas Behme (ed.), *Werke* 2. Friederich Frommann Verlag-Günther Holzboog, Stuttgart-Bad Cannstatt.

Weigel, Erhard (2008 [1658]). *Analysis Aristotelica ex Euclide restituta*, Jena. In Thomas Behme (ed.), *Werke* 3, Friedrich Frommann Verlag-Günther Holzboog, Stuttgart-Bad Cannstatt.

Welzel, Hans (1958). *Die Naturrechtslehre Samuel Pufendorfs. Ein Beitrag zur Ideen-Geschichte des 17. und 18. Jahrhunderts.* Verlag de Gruyter, Berlin.

Welzel, Hans (1986). *Die Naturrechtslehre Samuel Pufendorfs ein Beitrag zur Ideengeschichte des 17. und 18. Jahrhunderts.* Neuaufgabe. Verlag de Gruyter, Berlin.

Weppler, Albert Paul (1928). *Samuel Pufendorf ein Bahnbrecher auf dem Gebiet der Wissen schaftlichen Urteilsfreiheit 1632–1694.* Albert Paul, Giessen.

Werhane, Patricia H. (1991). *Adam Smith and His Legacy for Modern Capitalism.* Oxford University Press, New York.

Wesel, von Uwe (2008). '*Unantastbar*'. *Die Zeit*, no. 49, 27 November 2008. Frankfurt.

West, Edwin George (1976). *Adam Smith: The Man and His Works.* Liberty Press, Indianapolis.

Westerman, Pauline C. (1998). *The Disintegration of Natural Law Theory: Aquinas to Finnis.* Brill, Leiden and New York.

Wightman, W.P.D. and J.C. Bryce (eds) (1981). *Adam Smith Essays on Philosophical Subjects.* Liberty Classics, Indianapolis.

Wills, Gary (1978). *Inventing America: Jefferson's Declaration of Independence.* Vintage Books. The University of Michigan Press, Ann Arbor.

Winch, Donald (1978). *Adam Smith's Politics: An Essay in Historiographic Revision.* Cambridge University Press, Cambridge.

Winter, Eduard (1971). 'Erhard Weigels Ausstrahlungskraft. Die Bedeutung der Weigel-Forschung'. *Studia Leibnitiana* 3(1): 1–5.

Wodrow, Robert (1842–1843). *Analecta.* Printed for the Maitland Club. Glasgow.

Wokler, Robert (1994). 'Rousseau's Pufendorf: Natural law and the foundations of commercial society'. *History of Political Thought* 15(3): 373–402.

Wokler, Robert (2006). 'Rousseau on Rameau and Revolution'. In John T. Scott (ed.), *Jean-Jacques Rousseau Critical Assessments of Leading Political Philosopher.* Routledge, New York.

Wolf, Erik (1963). *Pufendorf. Grosse Rechtsdenker der deutschen Geistesgeschichte.* Fourth edition. Mohr Siebeck, Tübingen.

Wood, John Cunningham (ed.) (1984). *Adam Smith: Critical Assessments.* Croom Helm, New York. (Reprinted 1993 and 1996 by Routledge, London.)

Wood, John Cunningham (ed.) (1994). *Adam Smith: Critical Assessments.* Second Series. Routledge, London and New York.

Woolhouse, Roger (2007). *Locke: A Biography.* Cambridge University Press, Cambridge.

Wynne, Richard (1995 [1761]). *Essays on Education by Milton, Locke, and the Authors of the Spectator.* Thoemmes Press, Bristol, and Unifacmanu, Taipei.

Young, Hobart Peyton (1988). 'Condorcet's theory of voting'. *The American Political Science Review* 82(4): 1231–1244.

Young, Jeffrey T. (1985). 'Natural price and the impartial spectator: A new perspective on Adam Smith as a social economist'. *International Journal of Social Economics* 12(6/7): 118–133.

Young, Jeffrey T. (2008). 'Law and economics in the Protestant natural law tradition: Samuel Pufendorf, Francis Hutcheson, and Adam Smith'. *Journal of the History of Economic Thought* 30(3): 283–296.

Young, Jeffrey T. and Barry Gordon (1992). 'Economic justice in the natural law tradition: Thomas Aquinas to Francis Hutcheson'. *Journal of the History of Economic Thought* 14(1): 1–17.

Zagorin, Perez (2009). *Hobbes and the Law of Nature.* Princeton University Press, Princeton, New Jersey.

Zuckert, Michael P. (1994). *Natural Rights and the New Republicanism.* Princeton University Press, Princeton, New Jersey.

Zurbuchen, Simone (1998). 'Samuel Pufendorf and the foundation of modern natural law: An account of the state of research and editions'. *Central European History* 31(4): 413–428.

Index

advance of civilization *see* four-stages theory
agreements 4; association and subjection 4, 110–11; Boisguilbert 172; Hutcheson 222; Locke 156, 160–1; private property 78; Rousseau 196; Smith 239, 246
Agriculture *see* four-stages theory
all men are equal 73
aristocracy *see* forms of states

Baccalaureus 17
Balliol College 6, 228
Barbeyrac, Jean 173–4
bedevilled historians: of economic thought 259; of philosophy 255–9
Berlin 34–6
Boisguilbert, Pierre Le Pesant de 171–3, 269
Brandenburg-Prussia 2, 15
budget discipline *see* taxation
Burlamaqui, Jean-Jacques 174–9

Carmichael, Gershom 6, 211–14, 269
Caroline Academy of the Goths 29
Catholic League 11
certainty of moral science 58
Collegium Anthologicum 16
commercial society *see* four-stages theory
comparative advantages *see* foundation of states
Copenhagen 2, 20
corruption 128, 129; Locke 162; Montesquieu 184; Rousseau 198
cost of production *see* price and value
council decisions and voting procedures 112; equality of votes 4, 114; Hutcheson 222–3; insoluble problem 116; paradox of voting 4, 115; qualified majority 4, 114; Rousseau 197; simple majority 4, 113; Smith 246–7; unanimity 4, 113; veto rights 4, 112; voting manipulation 4, 116; weighted voting 4, 113

democracy *see* forms of states
De Jure Belli et Pacis 40, 41, 45, 49, 52, 265, 268
De Jure Naturae et Gentium 2, 3, 22, 30, 32, 33, 37, 43, 45, 55, 136, 137, 141, 143–4, 149, 163, 175, 219, 232–3, 255, 268
De Officio Hominis et Civis 2, 4, 31, 32, 37, 45, 137, 175, 211–12, 217–20, 228, 231–2, 263, 268–70; editions and translations 140–3; international bestseller 138–40
depleted natural resources *see* private property
De Statu Imperii Germanici 28, 30, 137
Diderot, Denis 179–80, 269
dignity of man's nature 63
discounted value 73
distinct light of intelligence 60
division of state powers 4, 52, 119–27; Burlamaque 177; constituent power 4, 121; Hutcheson 223; judicial power 4, 121; legislative power 4, 120; levy taxes 4, 122; Locke 155; Montesquieu 188; prerogatives 123; punitive power 4, 121; Rousseau 197–8; Smith 247–8; war and peace 4, 121
Domat, Jean 5, 170, 269
Dorfchemnitz 11
duties of the Sovereign 4

economic development *see* four-stages theory
Edict of Nantes 34, 36
Edict of Potsdam 34
education 72
elastic and inelastic demand 92
Elementorum Jurisprudentiae Universalis 2, 3, 22, 24, 29, 31, 37, 45, 54, 137, 151, 268; Enlightenment 5, 37, 49
Euclidean Aristotelian geometrical 3, 54
European Union 29
Evangelic Union 11
externalities 73

Flöha 12
forms of states: aristocracy 4, 124; democracy 4, 123; monarchy 4, 125
foundation of states 2, 52, 107; Burlamaqui 177; Carmichael 213; comparative advantages 121; contractual nature 109; establishment 107; Hutcheson 222; internal structure 108; Locke 160; Montesquieu 187; necessary agreements 110–12; physiocrats 206; Rousseau 196; Smith 245–7; the will of the state 112
four-stages theory 3, 5, 52, 82; agriculture 3, 84; commercial society 3, 84–5; gathering and hunting 3, 83; Hutcheson 221; Montesquieu 187; shepherding 3, 83; Smith 243
freedom of the will 62

gathering and hunting *see* four-stages theory
German Enlightenment 15
Grimma 12

human attributes *see* self-interest and sociability
human behaviour 3, 52, 60–75; dignity of man's nature 63; Hutcheson 220–1; internal director 62; Locke 154; Rousseau 193; self-interest and sociability 3, 68, 69; Smith 234–7
human motives: conspicuous consumption 92; consumer surplus 92; snob and bandwagon effects 92
Hutcheson, Francis 6, 215–27, 269

impartial spectator 231
imprisonment in Copenhagen 20
Index of Authors 55, 56
Index Librorum Prohibitorum 22
innate ideas 5, 6, 67; Burlamaqui 176; Locke 154; Hutcheson 221; Montesquieu 185; Rousseau 194; Smith 235
internal director 62, 74
internal mediator 74

Jena 17, 18

Kant, Immanuel 173, 270
Kastelle fortress 20

labour theory of property: Carmichael 213; Hutcheson 221; Locke 155; Quesnay 204; Rousseau 195; Smith 240
labour theory of value: Locke 158; Smith 244
law of nature 67
Lectures on Jurisprudence 7, 230–3, 236, 270
legal price 3
Leiden 21
Leipzig 14, 15, 17
Locke, John 4, 148–65, 269

Magister 17, 18
man's distinct light of intelligence 60–1
man's duties 71–2
market *see* price and value
method of analysis 52, 53; resolutive-compositive 53
monarchy *see* forms of states
money 3, 52; to aid commerce 3, 98, 172; debasement 3, 62, 99, 187, 222, 242–5; Hutcheson 121–2; origin 3, 97, 98; Locke 158–9; Montesquieu 187; and price level 100; quantity theory of money 100, 159, 186; rate of interest 104–5, 187; Smith 242–5; can states change the value 99
monopolies 103–4
Montesquieu, Charles-Louis 5, 182–90, 269
moral philosophy 211, 218

natural law 45–8; Cumberland 44; dissemination of 146; Grotius on 40–3; Hobbes on 43–4; Locke on 152; Selden on 43; university subject 144–5
natural price *see* price and value
natural state of man 65; is peace 66
Nicole, Pierre 5, 169–70
Nobel Peace Prize 29

pacts *see* agreements
paradox of value 90; Hutcheson 221; Locke 158; Smith 243
Peace of Augsburg 14, 38
physiocrats 5, 201–8
power of man's soul 63–5
price and value 3, 52, 87–97; aptitude 88; Burlamaqui 176; changes in market price 95; cost of production 92; foundation of price 88; how is the price determined 94; human motives 90–2; Hutcheson 221; legal and natural price 93–6; legitimate price 93; Locke 157–8; Montesquieu 186; paradox of value 90; physiocrats 205; question of information 96–7; rise and fall 90; Rousseau 194; scarcity 90; Smith 240–5; some goods lack a price 89; subjective theory 87
Prince's School of St Augustin 12
private property 52, 76–86; agreement 78, 81; Burlamaqui 176; common 77, 80; depleted natural resources 82; growing population 82; historical process 79; Hutcheson 221; limitation of 78; Locke 154–7; origin 77; Rousseau 194; secure peace 80; Smith 237–9; tacit or express agreements 82; use of labour 79, 81

Restitution Edict 11
Rhineland Palatinate 22, 27
Roman-German Empire 11, 22, 27–30
Rousseau, Jean-Jaques 5, 191–200, 269

St Nikolaikirche 36, 268
Scania 23, 29
scarcity and vent *see* human behaviour
Scholastic method 56
self-interest and sociability 3, 5, 68; Boisguilbert 172–3: Burlamaqui 176; Hutcheson 220–1; Locke 154; Montesquieu 185; Nicole 169; Smith 234–7
shepherding *see* four-stages theory
A Short Introduction to Moral Philosophy 218–20, 229
Smith, Adam 6, 7, 228–51, 269–70
social contract 5, 196
social life of man 45, 56
Stockholm 31–5
supreme sovereignty 115
sustainable harvest 76
Sweden 23, 40
A System of Moral Philosophy 217, 219–20

taxation 2; Boisguilbert 171; budget disciplines 129; Burlamaqui 178; collection 129–30; consumption 131; the duties 128; equal and just 130–1; exports and imports 132; Hutcheson 224; indirect taxation 131; Locke 162; Montesquieu 189; physiocrats 206; the power 127; proportional 131; responsibilities of a sovereign 129; Rousseau 199; Smith 248–50
The Theory of Moral Sentiments 7, 229–37, 264, 270
Thirty Years War 11, 12, 14–16, 27, 28, 30
Treaty of Westphalia 12, 28

University of Glasgow 6, 211, 216, 228–9, 269–70
University of Halle 15, 19, 32
University of Heidelberg 22, 27–30, 45, 268
University of Jena 2, 14, 15, 17
University of Kiel 49
University of Leiden 21, 22
University of Leipzig 2, 14–17
University of Lund 29–32, 48
University of Oxford 6, 149, 269
Uppsala 21

voting rules *see* council decisions and voting procedures

Wood collection 7, 264
The Wealth of Nations 7, 229, 231, 236, 261, 264–5, 270

Zeeland 21